The Spanish Caribbean
& the Atlantic World in the
Long Sixteenth Century

The Spanish Caribbean
& the Atlantic World in the
Long Sixteenth Century

Edited and with an introduction by
Ida Altman *and* David Wheat

University of Nebraska Press | Lincoln

© 2019 by the Board of Regents of the University of Nebraska. All rights reserved. ∞

Library of Congress Cataloging-in-Publication Data
Names: Altman, Ida, editor. | Wheat, David, 1977– editor.
Title: The Spanish Caribbean and the Atlantic world in the long sixteenth century / edited and with an introduction by Ida Altman and David Wheat.
Description: Lincoln: University of Nebraska Press, [2019] | Includes bibliographical references and index.
Identifiers: LCCN 2018039746
ISBN 9780803299573 (pbk.: alk. paper)
ISBN 9781496214355 (epub)
ISBN 9781496214362 (mobi)
ISBN 9781496214379 (pdf)
Subjects: LCSH: Caribbean Area—History—16th century.
Classification: LCC F2161 .S653 2019
| DDC 972.9/02—dc23 LC record available at https://lccn.loc.gov/2018039746

Set in Arno Pro by E. Cuddy.

In memory of Richmond F. Brown, teacher,
colleague, friend, and beloved husband

Contents

List of Maps	ix
List of Tables	x
Acknowledgments	xi
Introduction	xiii
IDA ALTMAN AND DAVID WHEAT	

Part 1. *Indians in the Early Spanish Caribbean*

1. The Cemí and the Cross: Hispaniola Indians and the Regular Clergy, 1494–1517 LAUREN MACDONALD	3
2. The Revolt of Agüeybaná II: Puerto Rico's Interisland Connections CACEY FARNSWORTH	25
3. War and Rescate: The Sixteenth-Century Circum-Caribbean Indigenous Slave Trade ERIN STONE	47

Part 2. *Europeans in the Islands*

4. Vasco Porcallo de Figueroa: Ambition, Fear, and Politics in Early Cuba IDA ALTMAN	71
5. Two Doñas: Aristocratic Women and Power in Colonial Cuba SHANNON LALOR	91

6. Between Acceptance and Exclusion: Spanish
   Responses to Portuguese Immigrants
   in the Sixteenth-Century Spanish Caribbean   113
   BRIAN HAMM

Part 3. *Africans and the Spanish Caribbean*

7. The Early Slave Trade to Spanish America:
   Caribbean Pathways, 1530–1580   139
   MARC EAGLE

8. Biafadas in Havana: West African Antecedents
   for Caribbean Social Interactions   163
   DAVID WHEAT

Part 4. *Environment and Health*

9. Environment and the Politics of Relocation
   in the Caribbean Port of Veracruz, 1519–1599   189
   J. M. H. CLARK

10. Hospitals and Public Health in the
    Sixteenth-Century Spanish Caribbean   211
    PABLO F. GÓMEZ

Part 5. *International Commercial Networks*

11. The Hispano-German Caribbean: South German
    Merchants and the Realities of European
    Consolidation, 1500–1540   235
    SPENCER TYCE

12. The Azorean Connection: Trajectories of Slaving,
    Piracy, and Trade in the Early Atlantic   257
    GABRIEL DE AVILEZ ROCHA

Glossary   279
Contributors   283
Index   287

Maps

1. The Spanish Caribbean — xviii
2. The Greater Antilles: Selected Sites — 46
3. The Southern Caribbean: Selected Sites — 112
4. West Africa and the Atlantic Islands — 162

Tables

1. Slaves taken from Santiesteban in 1528–1529 — 53
2. Biafadas as godparents for other Africans in Havana, 1590–1600 — 171
3. Regional origins of selected conquest and settlement campaigns — 247

Acknowledgments

We are grateful to the University of Florida History Department, Center for Latin American Studies, College of Liberal Arts and Sciences, and Office of Research for the generous support that made it possible for the contributors to this volume to meet in Gainesville in October 2016. The workshop provided a splendid opportunity to exchange thoughts about initial drafts of our papers and to benefit from the questions and comments of other scholars who attended. We thank Alisa Plant, editor in chief at the University of Nebraska Press, for her interest in and encouragement of the project from the very outset. We are also grateful to Michael Waylen, who produced the maps, and we would like to extend a special word of thanks to external reviewers Kris Lane and Ernesto Bassi, who provided a number of very helpful suggestions for improving the volume. Above all the editors are grateful to the colleagues whose work is presented here. Their innovative research and commitment to the project have made our idea for this book a reality.

Introduction

IDA ALTMAN AND DAVID WHEAT

This volume brings together recent original research on the Spanish Caribbean in the sixteenth century. Historians often have treated the Caribbean during the century or so following the arrival of Europeans as important chiefly as a launching ground for expansion into the mainland areas that would become the principal sites for Spanish American society and institutional and economic development. In this perspective it is relegated to the position of a backwater, significant mainly for its strategic value and as a facilitator of the Indies trade. Although there certainly have been notable exceptions to this view, until fairly recently the Caribbean has not attracted anything like the scholarly interest that has fueled an enormous expansion of our knowledge of socioeconomic and cultural formation and change in what are usually considered the "core" mainland areas of early Spanish America—Mesoamerica and the Andean region.[1] Yet in the sixteenth century no other part of the Americas was more diverse and international or as closely tied to Spain, the islands of the Atlantic, western Africa, and the Spanish American mainland. The Caribbean experienced rapid growth, encompassed considerable ethnic, religious, and national diversity, mixing and interaction, and developed extensive networks of exchange both within and beyond the region while continuing to play an important role in the larger Spanish American colonization project.

Although interest in the Atlantic world has risen steadily in the past two or three decades, perhaps surprisingly that interest for the most part has not—at least until fairly recently—encouraged a closer look at the early Spanish Caribbean. Not only was the region in many senses a microcosm of the larger Atlantic world; arguably it was also the first full-fledged incarnation of that world, rapidly becoming the setting for imperial and national rivalries and geopolitics, interethnic conflict and accommodation, the mixing, movement, and displacement of peoples, new economic ambitions and opportunities, social experimentation, the testing and pursuit of new ideological and religious aspirations, and social and cultural interaction and hybridity.

How do we account for the scholarly neglect of the Caribbean in the years following the arrival of Europeans, particularly after Spaniards began to turn their sights toward the adjoining mainland? For several decades following their publication in the 1910s and 1920s, a series of journal articles by Irene A. Wright was perhaps the best available English-language scholarship on the early Spanish Caribbean.[2] Historical geographer Carl O. Sauer's *The Early Spanish Main*, published in 1969, was a signal contribution to the Anglophone literature on the early Spanish Caribbean. Based mostly on the work of early chroniclers and historians (Peter Martyr, Bartolomé de Las Casas, Gonzalo Fernández de Oviedo) and published documentary sources, Sauer's book provided a detailed look at the region's places and peoples and the impact of Spanish activity on both, and vice versa. In doing so he demonstrated the connections that tied one locality to another and laid the groundwork for understanding the greater Caribbean as both a coherent and a disparate and volatile region. Instead of inspiring other scholars to take a closer look at this early history, however, Sauer's book for many years was widely accepted as definitive rather than seminal and did not inspire much further exploration in the Anglophone scholarship of the topics and themes that it suggested.[3]

During the years that interest in the sixteenth-century Caribbean languished among Anglophone historians, however, scholars from the Spanish-speaking Caribbean and Spain were pursuing archivally based research, mainly in the holdings of the Archive of the Indies in Seville. One result was the publication of a growing number of important compilations of transcribed documents, an effort that has continued to the present and been of enormous benefit to students and scholars.[4] That undertaking has been matched by the publication of work based on close and extended research in the archives that has gone beyond most of the existing Anglophone scholarship in elucidating not only the weight and complexity of the early history but also the necessity of placing local or country-specific studies in a larger regional and even Atlantic context, demonstrating their interconnectedness.[5]

The nature of the surviving historical records from the first century of European activity in the Caribbean may account in part for the reluctance of scholars to undertake serious research on the region. Although the documentation in the Archive of the Indies for the period is very—even dauntingly—substantial, it mainly consists of official reports, ordinances, and letters that focus principally on economic, fiscal, and administrative matters that were of greatest interest to the Spanish crown. The kinds of records on which historians in recent years have relied to address issues such as social and cultural change, the role and structure of family, kinship and households, the formation of ethnically diverse societies, or the process and impact of Christianization can be difficult to find in Seville.[6] Pre-eighteenth-century notarial, city council, and parish records in the Caribbean itself are available only for certain locales, usually beginning in the second half or final third of the sixteenth century.[7] Whereas Inquisition proceedings and trial records were generated in Lima and Mexico City as early as 1579, the Inquisition tribunal with the most direct jurisdiction over residents of Spain's Caribbean settlements was only established (in Cartagena de Indias) in 1610. It is not surprising, then, that much of the most important recent work on the early Spanish Caribbean focuses on the last part of the sixteenth century, extending into the seventeenth.[8] Archives in Spain and the Caribbean fortunately are not the only sources of information on which historians can draw. Relevant documentation can also be found in centralized national repositories located far from Caribbean shores, including the national archives in Bogotá, Mexico City, and Lima.[9] Archaeological work in the region, traditionally focused principally on periods well before European contact, increasingly is addressing both contact and postcontact periods and revealing significant new dimensions of the process and implications of cultural and racial/ethnic mixing—or lack of such.[10]

The work presented in this book demonstrates that, notwithstanding the apparent limitations of existing documentation, it is possible to use sources that are both well and lesser known to examine a range of topics that until recently have scarcely been addressed. This volume's chapters address such topics as the process and significance of religious conversion and the role of religious orders, the development of commercial systems that encompassed transatlantic trade and local and regional exchange, the dynamics of insular and regional politics and their articulation in relation to imperial objectives, the formation of colonial societies comprising diverse communities, and the importation and incorporation of large numbers of indigenous captives and enslaved Africans. Consideration of topics such as indigenous resistance to European occupation and exploitation, the presence and perception of foreigners in the region, the role and influence of elite Spanish women, official responses to the challenges of dealing with disease and public health, and the impact of the region's environment on settlement patterns and colonial ambitions reflect the breadth of the Spanish colonial project in its first overseas empire. Far from being simply a transitional and ultimately insignificant staging grounds for what is often understood as the evolution of Spanish American society toward a stage of maturity achieved most fully in the mainland centers of Mexico and Peru, almost from the outset—as these topics suggest—the Spanish Caribbean was a multidimensional milieu characterized by many of the features we associate with Spanish America at later stages of development. Those characteristics include mixed economies based on mining, agriculture, and trade; the formation of elites who combined office holding with varied economic enterprises and frequently intermarried; extensive transatlantic as well as local and regional mobility, both voluntary and forced, on the part of all socioeconomic and ethnic groups; both friction and cooperation between the personnel representing institutions of church and state; networks of collusion and trade that crossed imperial boundaries despite metropolitan designs and legislation; and rapid environmental and demographic change.

The sixteenth-century Spanish Caribbean has long been of interest to historians of northern Europe as a site of early English, French, and Dutch incursions and encounters that preceded the formal establishment of non-Iberian European colonies in the Americas.[11] A principal drawback of analytical frameworks that portray the Spanish Caribbean as merely a backdrop for the rise of other western European empires, however, is that they typically emphasize the dynamism of the latter, offering at best limited insight into the development and vitality of Spanish Caribbean societies in their own right. Such scholarship also tends to overlook the chronological depth and geographical breadth of the early Spanish Caribbean. In the colonial histories of areas subsequently claimed by other European powers (e.g. Jamaica, Saint-Domingue, Curaçao, Trinidad), the century or so of prior intense activity in the region generally has received little attention.[12] Unlike the Guianas, Suriname, and Belize, which usually are treated as integral parts of the British West Indies and the French and Dutch Antilles, coastal Spanish settlements from eastern Venezuela to the Gulf of Mexico are much less frequently considered to belong to the Spanish Caribbean.

If the sixteenth- and seventeenth-century Spanish Caribbean is understood to include both the islands and closely connected parts of the surrounding mainland, the region can be seen as being roughly divided into four overlapping geographical quadrants: (I) the major islands or Greater Antilles: Hispaniola, Puerto Rico, Cuba, and Jamaica; (II) the southeastern Caribbean, consisting of Venezuela and neighboring islands such as Curaçao, Cubagua, La Margarita, and Trinidad; (III) the southwestern mainland including Panama and the provinces of Cartagena de Indias, Santa Marta, and Riohacha; and (IV) the Gulf region, comprising western Cuba, Yucatán, Veracruz, and Florida. Such a division does not, of course, negate the vital links that tied these subregions to one another as well; Hispaniola and Puerto Rico, for example, had significant ties to Venezuela and the islands of the Lesser Antilles. The contributors to this volume collectively portray the early Spanish Caribbean as a distinct and interconnected region, a diverse set of societies loosely united under Spanish rule, with chapters addressing both the islands, especially Hispaniola, Cuba, and Puerto Rico, and mainland locations, including Venezuela, Cartagena de Indias, Santa Marta, Nombre de Dios, Portobelo, and Veracruz.

While this volume is organized topically, it also points to significant change over the course of the "long" sixteenth century. Chapters by Cacey Farnsworth on indigenous resistance in early Puerto Rico and Lauren MacDonald on early attempts to Christianize the native inhabi-

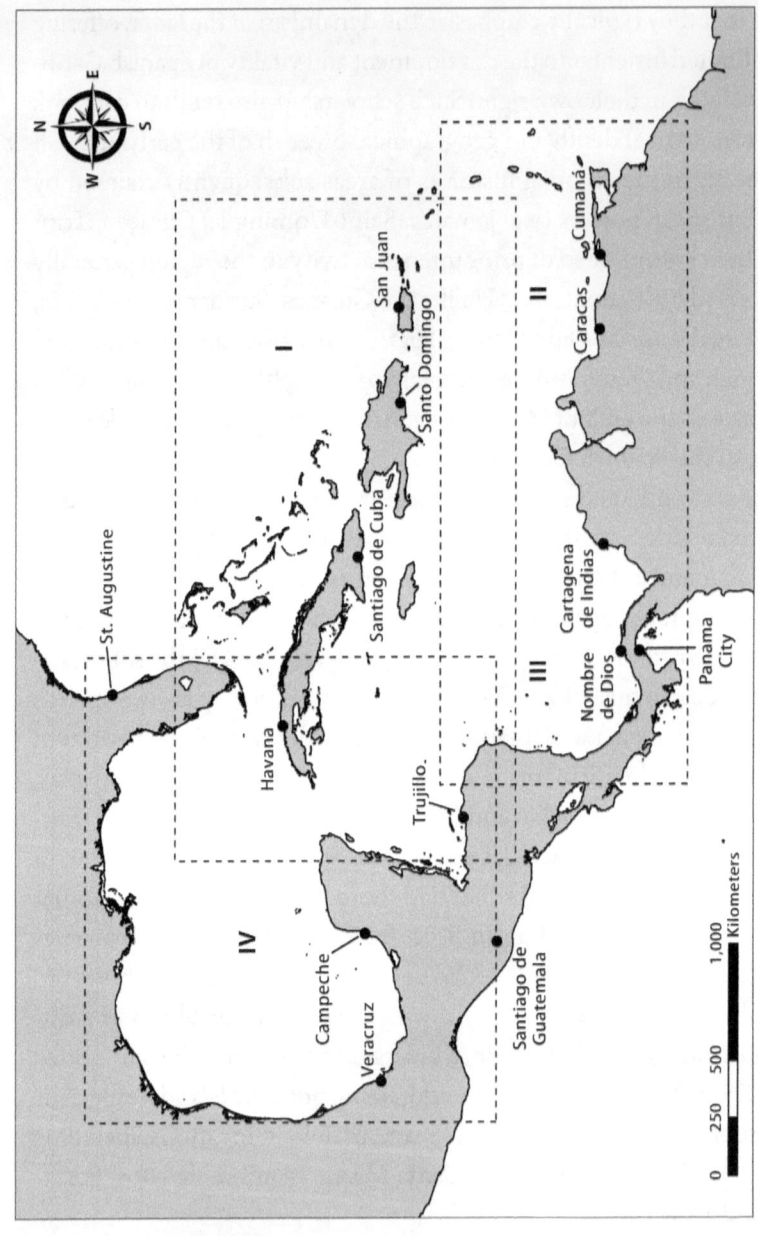

Map 1. The Spanish Caribbean, in four overlapping quadrants: (I) the Greater Antilles, (II) the southeastern mainland and Lesser Antilles, (III) the southwestern mainland, and (IV) the Gulf of Mexico.

tants of Hispaniola shed light on the contested beginnings of Spaniards' efforts to establish themselves in the islands and impose their institutions, while the contributions from Shannon Lalor, Ida Altman, and Spencer Tyce point to the complex ramifications of European political and economic ambitions in the region. Chapters by Erin Stone, Marc Eagle, and Gabriel Rocha detail the development and long-term impact of significant forms of transatlantic and regional commerce, including slave trafficking. Joe Clark examines the interplay of environmental factors and political and economic aspirations in the key port city of Veracruz over time, while Pablo Gómez shows how environment, demography, and epidemiology fostered innovation in imperial approaches to public health needs. Contributions from David Wheat and Brian Hamm suggest how free and enslaved Africans in Cuba and Portuguese merchants and settlers adapted to and helped to shape life in the Caribbean with its ever-changing ethnic, religious, and national mix.

The scholarship presented here not only underscores the complexity and dynamism of an understudied region that made vital contributions to Spanish overseas expansion. It also makes a strong argument for revising our interpretation of the longer-term development of the Caribbean.[13] Historical understanding of the Caribbean above all has hinged on the centrality and long-term impact of the sugar-and-slavery complex that developed in the islands of the Lesser Antilles under British and French control and that in the seventeenth and eighteenth centuries came to dominate much of the region, including not only the large islands of the northern Caribbean that were strongholds of Spanish rule but adjoining parts of the mainland as well. This view of the region's history not only emphasizes national rivalries and conflicts but also overwhelmingly privileges the sugar plantation as the defining institution that shaped and constrained the situation of Africans and African-descended peoples in the Caribbean. The scholarship presented in this volume (see chapters by Eagle and Wheat), however, suggests a much fuller and more nuanced history of the experiences and contributions of blacks in the Caribbean than the focus on sugar and slavery allows.[14] Likewise the complex roles and impact of non-Spanish Europeans in the region (see chapters by Hamm, Tyce, and Rocha) suggest that the interpenetration of European communities overseas was as important as were European rivalries, a development borne out by other recent research.[15]

In addition to highlighting the region's global importance as a nexus of cross-cultural exchange, overlapping diasporas, and trans-imperial maritime networks, this volume's chapters collectively portray the sixteenth-century Caribbean as a discrete region of colonial Latin America marked by vibrant, internal dynamics that cannot be accurately reduced to the mute funneling of royal *cédulas* or precious metals in one direction or another. Long before the establishment of northern European plantation colonies, Old World migrants of diverse origins and competing blocs of merchants struggled to balance imperial priorities in the Caribbean with their own economic self-interest and survival in a rapidly changing physical and biological environment (chapters by Gómez, Clark). While ostensibly answering to distant centers of power in Europe, Mesoamerica, or the Andes, in practice Spanish Caribbean ports and settlements frequently exercised considerable autonomy. The large swaths of territory that came under the jurisdiction of the Audiencia of Santo Domingo in Hispaniola stand in striking contrast to the region's political fragmentation during later eras. Yet even within this seemingly coherent royal domain, powerful individuals could be decisive actors in establishing colonial rule and family patronage networks in specific Caribbean locales (chapters by Altman and Lalor), particularly during the first half of the sixteenth century. Although Spanish objectives often contrast dramatically with indigenous Caribbean peoples' responses to Iberian colonization, which ranged from areitos to pan-Caribbean (if mostly localized) resistance (chapters by MacDonald, Farnsworth, Stone), both Spanish and Amerindian experiences in the sixteenth-century Caribbean take on new importance in light of broader regional contexts and transatlantic perspectives.

We see here, then, a world that barely has figured in the scholarly work on British activities and aspirations that has dominated Atlantic historiography. The early Atlantic world depicted here, centered on the Caribbean and the site of varied and constantly changing interactions among peoples of indigenous, European and African origins on both a collective and individual basis, arguably was the crucible in which the modern world was forged. Viewing this first Atlantic world as foundational and central rather than preliminary or marginal affords a far more complete understanding of the origins, nature, timing and implications of a host of processes and developments that we associate strongly with Atlantic history—voluntary and forced migration, labor exploitation, environmental and health challenges, religious conversion and its limitations, gendered responses to new opportunities, extension and proliferation of trade networks, and the complexities of resistance to European control—than focus on a later period can provide.

Notes

1. For ideas about core and periphery and arguments regarding a hierarchy of places and their respective importance within colonial Spanish America, see, for example, articles in Daniels and Kennedy, *Negotiated Empires* and Lockhart and Schwartz, *Early Latin America*. Notwithstanding their emphasis on cores and fringes in this synthesizing work, Lockhart and Schwartz are among a relatively small number of historians who have emphasized the foundational importance of the Spanish Caribbean.
2. Among others, see Wright, "Commencement" and "Rescates." By contrast, her *Early History of Cuba* was based on extensive archival research but provided no source citations other than a brief note in the introduction.
3. Important exceptions in the 1970s and 1980s were Floyd, *The Columbus Dynasty*; Andrews, *The Spanish Caribbean*; and Hoffman, *The Spanish Crown*.
4. See, for example, Murga Sanz, *Historia documental*; Rodríguez Demorizi, *Relaciones históricas*; Rodríguez Morel, *Cartas de la Real Audiencia*; Otte, *Cédulas de la monarquía*. More recent works include Jopling, *Indios y negros*; Alegría, *Documentos históricos*.
5. Important examples include Otte, *Las perlas del Caribe*; Arcila Farias, *Hacienda y comercio*; Borrego Plá, *Cartagena de Indias*; Mena García, *La sociedad*; Mira Caballos, *El indio antillano*; and Sued Badillo, *El Dorado borincano*.
6. For evidence that such records can be found, however, see *First Blacks in the Americas: The African Presence in the Dominican Republic*, www.firstblacks.org (accessed March 1, 2018).
7. For examples of notarial and cabildo records, see de Rojas, *Índice y extractos*; Briceño Iragorry, *Actas del Cabildo de Caracas*; and Vidal Ortega, *De las Indias remotas*. Parish records for late sixteenth-century Havana and St. Augustine, Florida, may be viewed at the *Slave Societies Digital Archive*, www.vanderbilt.edu/esss/ (accessed March 1, 2018).

8. See Gelpí Baíz, *Siglo en blanco*; Vidal Ortega, *Cartagena de Indias*; de la Fuente, *Havana*; Castillero Calvo, *Sociedad, economía y cultura material*; Tardieu, *Cimarrones*; Wheat, *Atlantic Africa*; Gómez, *Experiential Caribbean*. For earlier in the sixteenth century, see Warsh, "A Political Ecology," and Altman, "Key to the Indies."
9. For relevant studies that make use of these centralized national repositories, see Vidal Ortega, *Cartagena de Indias*; Newson and Minchin, *From Capture to Sale*; García de León, *Tierra adentro, mar en fuera*.
10. See, for example, Deagan and Cruxent, *Columbus's Outpost*; Valcarcel Rojas, *Archaeology of Early Colonial Interaction*; Anderson-Córdova, *Surviving Spanish Conquest*; Keegan, *Taíno Indian Myth and Practice*.
11. Classic works include Wright, *Spanish Documents* and *Further English Voyages*; Andrews, *The Spanish Caribbean*.
12. Even the magisterial work of historian J. H. Elliott, *Empires of the Atlantic World*, devotes little space to the sixteenth-century Spanish Caribbean.
13. For work that has begun to do this, see de la Fuente, *Havana*; Schwartz, ed., *Tropical Babylons*; Wheat, *Atlantic Africa*.
14. See also Ireton, "They Are Blacks"; Stark, *Slave Families*.
15. See Rupert, *Creolization and Contraband*.

Bibliography

Alegría, Ricardo E., ed. *Documentos históricos de Puerto Rico*. 5 vols. San Juan, PR: Centro de Estudios Avanzados de Puerto Rico y el Caribe, 2009.

Altman, Ida. "Key to the Indies: Port Towns in the Spanish Caribbean, 1493–1550." *Americas* 74, no. 1 (January 2017): 5–26.

Anderson-Córdova, Karen F. *Surviving Spanish Conquest: Indian Fight, Flight, and Cultural Transformation in Hispaniola and Puerto Rico*. Tuscaloosa: University of Alabama Press, 2017.

Andrews, Kenneth R. *The Spanish Caribbean: Trade and Plunder, 1530–1630*. New Haven: Yale University Press, 1978.

Arcila Farias, Eduardo, dir. *Hacienda y comercio de Venezuela en el siglo XVI*. Serie Proyecto Hacienda Pública Colonial Venezuela, vol. 2. Caracas: Banco Central de Venezuela, 1983.

Borrego Plá, María del Carmen. *Cartagena de Indias en el siglo XVI*. Seville: Escuela de Estudios Hispano-Americanos, Consejo Superior de Investigaciones Científicas, 1983.

Briceño Iragorry, Mario, comp. *Actas del Cabildo de Caracas*. 6 vols. Caracas: Editorial Elite, 1943–1956.

Castillero Calvo, Alfredo. *Sociedad, economía y cultura material: Historia urbana de Panamá la vieja*. Panamá: Imprenta Alloni, 2006.

Daniels, Christine, and Michael V. Kennedy, eds. *Negotiated Empires: Centers and Peripheries in the Americas, 1500–1820*. New York: Routledge, 2002.

Deagan, Kathleen A., and José María Cruxent. *Columbus's Outpost among the Taínos: Spain and America at La Isabela, 1493–1498*. New Haven: Yale University Press, 2002.

Deive, Carlos Esteban. *Tangomangos: Contrabando y piratería en Santo Domingo, 1522–1606*. Santo Domingo: Fundación Cultural Dominicana, 1996.

de la Fuente, Alejandro, with the collaboration of César García del Pino and Bernardo Iglesias Delgado. *Havana and the Atlantic in the Sixteenth Century*. Chapel Hill: University of North Carolina Press, 2008.

de Rojas, María Teresa, ed. *Índice y Extractos del Archivo de Protocolos de la Habana, 1578–1588*. 3 vols. Havana: [s.n.], 1947–1950; Ediciones C. R., 1957.

Elliott, John H. *Empires of the Atlantic World*. New Haven: Yale University Press, 2006.

First Blacks in the Americas: The African Presence in the Dominican Republic, www.firstblacks.org, accessed March 1, 2018.

Floyd, Troy S. *The Columbus Dynasty in the Caribbean, 1492–1526*. Albuquerque: University of New Mexico Press, 1973.

García de León, Antonio. *Tierra adentro, mar en fuera. El puerto de Veracruz y su litoral a Sotavento, 1519–1821*. México DF: Fondo de Cultura Económica; Xalapa: Gobierno del Estado de Veracruz, Universidad Veracruzana, 2011.

Gelpí Baíz, Elsa. *Siglo en blanco: estudio de la economía azucarera en el Puerto Rico del siglo XVI (1540–1612)*. San Juan: Editorial de la Universidad de Puerto Rico, 2000.

Gómez, Pablo F. *The Experiential Caribbean: Creating Knowledge and Healing in the Early Modern Atlantic*. Chapel Hill: University of North Carolina Press, 2017.

Hoffman, Paul E. *The Spanish Crown and the Defense of the Caribbean, 1535–1585: Precedent, Patrimonialism, and Royal Parsimony*. Baton Rouge: Louisiana State University Press, 1980.

Ireton, Chloe. "'They Are Blacks of the Caste of Black Christians': Old Christian Black Blood in the Sixteenth- and Early Seventeenth-Century Iberian Atlantic." *Hispanic American Historical Review* 97, no. 4 (November 2017): 579–612.

Jopling, Carol F., comp. *Indios y negros en Panamá en los siglos XVI y XVII: selecciones de los documentos del Archivo General de Indias*. Antigua: Centro de Investigaciones Regionales de Mesoamérica, 1994.

Keegan, William F. *Taíno Indian Myth and Practice: The Arrival of the Stranger King*. Gainesville: University Press of Florida, 2007.

Lockhart, James, and Stuart B. Schwartz. *Early Latin America: A History of Colonial Spanish America and Brazil*. New York: Cambridge University Press, 1983.

Mena García, María del Carmen. *La sociedad de Panamá en el siglo XVI*. Seville: Diputación Provincial de Sevilla, 1984.

Mira Caballos, Esteban. *El indio antillano: repartimiento, encomienda y esclavitud (1492–1542)*. Seville: Muñoz Moya, 1997.

Murga Sanz, Vicente. *Historia documental de Puerto Rico*. Vols. 1–3. Río Piedras, PR: Editorial Plus Ultra, 1948 [vol. 1]; Santander: Aldus, 1956 [vol. 2]; Río Piedras: Universidad de Puerto Rico, 1961 [vol. 3, t.1].

Newson, Linda A., and Susie Minchin. *From Capture to Sale: The Portuguese Slave Trade to Spanish South America in the Early Seventeenth Century*. Leiden: Brill, 2007.

Otte, Enrique, comp. *Cédulas de la monarquía española relativas a la parte oriental de Venezuela, 1520–1561*. Caracas: Fundación John Boulton, Fundación Eugenio Mendoza y Fundación Shell, 1965.

Otte, Enrique. *Las perlas del Caribe: Nueva Cádiz de Cubagua*. Caracas: Fundación John Boulton, 1977.

Rodríguez Demorizi, Emilio, comp. *Relaciones históricas de Santo Domingo*, vols. 2 and 3. Ciudad Trujillo [Santo Domingo]: Editorial Montalvo, 1945–57.

Rodríguez Morel, Genaro. *Cartas de la Real Audiencia de Santo Domingo (1530–1546)*. Santo Domingo: Archivo General de la Nación, Academia Dominicana de la Historia, 2007.

Rupert, Linda M. *Creolization and Contraband: Curaçao in the Early Modern Atlantic World*. Athens: University of Georgia Press, 2012.

Schwartz, Stuart B., ed. *Tropical Babylons: Sugar and the Making of the Atlantic World, 1450–1680*. Chapel Hill: University of North Carolina Press, 2004.

Slave Societies Digital Archive, www.vanderbilt.edu/esss/, accessed March 1, 2018.

Stark, David M. *Slave Families and the Hato Economy in Puerto Rico*. Gainesville: University Press of Florida, 2015.

Sued Badillo, Jalil. *El Dorado borincano: la economía de la conquista, 1510–1550*. San Juan, PR: Ediciones Puerto, 2001.

Tardieu, Jean-Pierre. *Cimarrones de Panamá: la forja de una identidad afroamericano en el siglo XVI*. Madrid: Iberoamericana, 2009.

Valcarcel Rojas, Roberto. *Archaeology of Early Colonial Interaction at El Chorro de Maíta, Cuba*. Gainesville: University Press of Florida, 2016.

Vidal Ortega, Antonino. *Cartagena de Indias y la región histórica del Caribe, 1580–1640*. Sevilla: Consejo Superior de Investigaciones Científicas, Escuela de Estudios Hispanoamericanos, Universidad de Sevilla, Diputación de Sevilla, 2002.

———. *De las Indias remotas: cartas del cabildo de Santa Marta (1529–1640)*. Barranquilla: Ediciones Uninorte, 2007.

Warsh, Molly A. "A Political Ecology in the Early Spanish Caribbean." *William and Mary Quarterly* 71, no. 4 (October 2014): 517–48.
Wheat, David. *Atlantic Africa and the Spanish Caribbean, 1570–1640*. Chapel Hill: University of North Carolina Press, 2016.
Wright, Irene A. "The Commencement of the Cane Sugar Industry in America, 1519–1538." *American Historical Review* 21, no. 4 (July 1916): 755–80.
———. *The Early History of Cuba, 1492–1586*. New York: Macmillan, 1916.
———, trans. and ed. *Further English Voyages to Spanish America, 1583–1594: Documents from the Archives of the Indies at Seville Illustrating English Voyages to the Caribbean, the Spanish Main, Florida, and Virginia*. London: Hakluyt Society, 1951.
———. "Rescates: With Special Reference to Cuba, 1599–1610." *Hispanic American Historical Review* 3, no. 3 (August 1920): 333–61.
———, trans. and ed. *Spanish Documents Concerning English Voyages to the Caribbean, 1527–1568: Selected from the Archive of the Indies at Seville*. London: Hakluyt Society, 1929.

PART 1

Indians in the Early Spanish Caribbean

The arrival of Europeans in the Caribbean in the late fifteenth century had multiple and devastating consequences for the native peoples of the region. Spaniards' ambitions to bring them into the Roman Catholic Church meant that conversion efforts got under way very early. Their campaigns to occupy the islands and surrounding mainland led to violent confrontations and stubborn indigenous resistance. These conflicts in turn provided a pretext for Spaniards to conduct "just war" and take captives who were enslaved and often sent elsewhere to meet the constant and escalating labor needs of gold mines, pearl fisheries, and sugar estates. These three chapters shed light on these processes and the resulting interactions between Europeans and the peoples of the Caribbean with particular focus on the early postcontact period.

1

The Cemí and the Cross

Hispaniola Indians and the Regular Clergy, 1494–1517

LAUREN MACDONALD

Three years after the arrival of cross-bearing Europeans into his lands, one of the most powerful local leaders on the island of Hispaniola began each day by reciting Christian prayers. Guarionex made an elaborate performance of this practice and obliged his entire household to perform their prayers twice every morning. Guarionex's prayers were witnessed by two outsiders: Ramón Pané, a "humble friar" from the Order of Saint Jerome, and Guatícabanú, a Christian Indian from the northern coast of Hispaniola. Both men had been sent by Christopher Columbus to the island's interior, in part to learn about the area and in part to monitor Guarionex, whose loyalty to Columbus was uncertain. Their time among Guarionex's people was not always easy—among other things, it meant proximity to Guarionex's mother, whom Pané described as "the worst woman I have known in these parts"—but, as Pané wrote later, Guarionex himself "gave us hope that he would do whatever we wished and that he wanted to be a Christian."[1]

Pané's satisfaction was to be short-lived. By 1498 Guarionex had abandoned Christian practices and, suspected of supporting rebellion against Columbus, fled his domains.[2] Meanwhile, Guatícabanú, who had been baptized by Pané under the name "Juan Mateo," was murdered by men associated with Guarionex. Mourning his lost companion, Pané wrote, "I am certain he died a martyr." While writing an account of his experiences for Columbus in 1498, Pané predicted two future paths for Christian evangelization on the island. There was the possibility, Pané wrote, of converting some Indians through simple religious instruction, for he had seen Guatícabanú become a Christian easily. For others, such as the inconstant Guarionex, "there is need for force and ingenuity ... there is need for force and punishment."[3]

Ramón Pané's diverging paths foreshadowed a repeated motif in colonial American history. Subsequent missionaries and colonial officials oscillated between the open palm and the closed fist, from the tentative embrace of indigenous concepts and practices to the violent punishment of heterodox beliefs. Yet while historians have studied these religious dynamics elsewhere in the Americas, little attention has been paid to the islands where the Spanish conquest began, possibly due to the paucity of archival sources for religion in the early Spanish Caribbean.

Much of the existing scholarship on religiosity in the early Spanish Caribbean falls into two categories: studies that use Spanish-authored sources to reconstruct precontact beliefs, or works cataloging the inexorable accretion of papal bulls and the growing numbers of priests, friars, churches, and parishes that signaled the establishment of the Church as a Caribbean institution. In both approaches, conquest-era "religion," whether indigenous or imported, is treated as a static, monolithic entity that could recede or advance but never change.[4] In contrast, recent scholarship on other regions in the colonial Americas has investigated religious identities as dynamic, responsive, overlapping, and entangled.[5] In that vein, this chapter argues that in the first three decades of Spanish settlement on Hispaniola, missionary figures and American Indians tried to understand foreign religiosity within familiar frameworks.

Writing to the Catholic Monarchs in 1493, Columbus claimed that the men and women of the Caribbean were people without any religion of their own.[6] He saw no buildings of worship, no robed priests, no sacred texts. Yet the stories told by the people of central Hispaniola, translated by Guatícabanú and recorded by Pané, attested to creation myths, gods, and the marvelous. Pané's account contained stories of mankind issuing from turtles and birds, divine *cemís* of stone and wood, and shamans who made the dead speak. While scholars have analyzed Pané's account in order to reconstruct indigenous worldviews prior to the arrival of Europeans, little attention has been paid to the immediate environment surrounding the composition of the account, which was drawn from stories told, sung, or danced to the accompaniment of wooden drums in Hispaniola during the 1490s. The orality and choreography of each evanescent *areito* potentially allowed its performer to reproduce the stories of her or his community selectively and strategically. Pané described the areito as both a form of memory and a source of political legitimacy: "Just as the Moors, they have their laws gathered in ancient songs, by which they govern themselves."[7] Long after the arrival of the Europeans, the areito continued to be a significant act of memory, negotiation, and resistance for Caribbean Indians. In subsequent decades, Spanish settlers repeatedly described the persistence of the areito on the islands.

The volatility and violence of Spanish Hispaniola shaped the stories that the people of the island's interior chose to tell Guatícabanú and Pané, as well as the stories that the two outsiders chose to record.[8] During the first decade of the Spanish conquest, Hispaniola's indigenous inhabitants experienced violence, social upheaval, coerced labor, and political destabilization. Native leaders revolted against Columbus's tributary demands in 1494, 1495, and 1497; hunger assailed their communities during periods of famine in 1495 and 1496; and in 1497 a group of disaffected Spaniards revolted against Columbus's authority, further destabilizing political organization on the island.[9] The stories recorded by Pané between 1495 and 1498—full of death, exile, transformations, and frustrated desires—mirrored this disordered world.

Women, an early point of contention between Europeans and indigenous Caribbean communities, were elusive and slippery figures in Pané's stories. In the early years of Spanish Hispaniola, colonial kitchens were operated by indigenous women, and some European men married high-ranking women in hopes of acquiring the land and labor of their households. The dramatically declining population of Hispaniola was partly due to the fall of births within endogamous relationships (and a concomitant rise in births within European-Caribbean unions).[10] Tellingly, many of Pané's stories depended on the absence or alienation of women. Women appeared in animal forms; women were exiled to inaccessible islands; and bachelors were forced to build their own women using the bodies of birds and turtles.[11]

In other stories, at a time when they were encountering influenza and other alien pathogens, the native peoples of Hispaniola grappled with the decline of perceived power held by their religious leaders.[12] Pané recounted the retributive murder of a Hispaniola *behique* [shaman] by a grieving family when the man's cures proved ineffective for their loved one. "They take out his eyes and smash his testicles because they say that none of these physicians can die, however much they may beat him, if they do not remove his testicles," he wrote.[13] The violent dismemberment of an impotent behique mirrored, in miniature, the ways in which traditional forms of indigenous power and authority were threatened, altered, or undone by the first years of Spanish colonization.

By and large, Pané did not explicitly identify parallels between Caribbean beliefs and Christian orthodoxy, with one significant exception: the cemís of stone, wood, and cotton, who acted as intermediaries between indigenous leaders and the divine. The cemís were conscious and mobile, and to be accompanied by a cemí, especially one that had elected to remain with successive members of the same lineage, was a prestigious sign of a leader's power and rectitude.[14] Pané perceived them as demonic. "Those simple, ignorant people believe that those idols—or, more properly speaking, demons—make such things happen because they have no knowledge of our holy faith," Pané wrote. He reported that the cemís were capable of digesting food, escaping captivity, and engaging in sexual intercourse; the cemís had names, origins, and gender. "And so may God help them if the cemí eats any of those things because the cemí is a dead thing, shaped from stone or made of wood," Pané wrote.[15]

Several years later, he was still repeating the idea that the cemís were comprehensible religious objects, and when the Indians converted, "they will burn their cemís and idols."[16] For their part, at least some Caribbean Indians agreed on the commensurability of cemís and Christian iconography; José R. Oliver has identified two cases of Cuban Indians treating Marian icons as if they were cemís in 1511.[17]

After Columbus's first voyage, the pope recognized Castile's claim to the Americas with the understanding that Castile would have governance over non-Christian peoples in exchange for instructing them about Christianity.[18] Despite Castile's ostensible need to evangelize its new possessions, ecclesiastical figures were scarce in the early years of the Spanish Caribbean. In late medieval Europe, the clergy of Rome were divided between the secular clergy, who belonged to individual cathedrals or parishes, and the regular clergy, who belonged to monastic or mendicant communities and lived according to the "rules" and various objectives of their orders. In their internal histories, the regular clergy cultivated a self-image of frequent and heroic evangelical outreach among non-Christian peoples in frontier missions, but many of these missions were either small in scale or mythic.[19] Most Dominicans, Franciscans, and other mendicant friars had little firsthand experience with mission work and were slow to participate in American evangelization. There is no clear evidence that any friar accompanied Columbus on his first voyage, and while the regular clergy joined Columbus's second expedition in 1493, many of them returned to Castile less than a year later to complain to the Catholic Monarchs about Columbus's mismanagement of the islands.

The small handful of regular clergy remaining in Hispaniola in 1494 included Ramón Pané, although it remains unclear why he had left Catalonia and joined Columbus's second voyage. The religious order to which he belonged, the Order of St. Jerome, was monastic, contemplative, and had no explicit commitment to frontier missions.[20] When Hieronymites engaged with non-Christian peoples in the fifteenth and sixteenth centuries, they did not follow a standard script. For example, the Hieronymite Hernando de Talavera, who served as the first bishop of conquered Granada and its Muslim inhabitants from 1493 to 1507, created an Arabic dictionary, grammar, and prayer book for the non-Christian inhabitants of his diocese.[21] In contrast, on the other side of the Atlantic, Pané resisted learning Indian languages, and there is no evidence that he emulated Talavera's methods of conversion.

By early 1495 Pané was living at the Spanish fort of Magdalena and proselytizing among the indigenous people who lived near the fort. His first Christian convert was Guatícabanú, the Macorix-speaking man who would become his companion and collaborator in religious instruction.[22] Pané later wrote that Guatícabanú was "the best of the Indians," and Pané "considered him a good son and brother."[23] When Columbus asked Pané to move to Guarionex's provinces, Pané asked Columbus for permission to bring along Guatícabanú as someone who could translate for him.

Among Pané's fellow ecclesiastics on the island were two Franciscan friars, Juan de la Duele and Juan Tisin. If Pané—bereft of obvious models for conversion from his own order—was developing his missionary program on the spot, the two Franciscans had recourse to a long (if somewhat embellished) institutional history of frontier missionary work. From their thirteenth-century founding, the Franciscan Order had promoted apostolic poverty, mendicant preaching, and missionary work to the edges of the Christian world, including the Islamic kingdoms ringing the Mediterranean.[24]

At times, Pané was accompanied by Duele, and Pané likely patterned his missionary efforts after the Franciscan model. Echoing a practice associated with the Franciscans, Pané performed at least one baptism of a large group, the household of the Hispaniola leader Guanáoboconel.[25] While the Dominicans would later criticize mass baptisms as lacking meaning for their uncomprehending participants, the Franciscans would develop a reputation for mass baptisms in New Spain as they sought to maximize the reach of the sacrament.[26] Many Franciscans believed that the end of the world was fast approaching, which contributed to the emotional urgency of their conversion efforts.[27] In contrast, Pané testified in 1500 that Christopher Columbus had deliberately limited baptisms so that he could continue to legally enslave men and women who remained non-Christian.[28]

Guarionex, who was briefly the most powerful leader on Hispaniola, was never baptized. Despite his demonstration of Christian prayer, Guarionex avoided other Christian practices and, with time, even his prayer schedule slackened. While initial conversion efforts seemed propitious, the political and social tensions between indigenous leaders and Spanish authorities soured the relationship between Guarionex and his missionaries. According to Pané, "other leaders of that land . . . reproached" Guarionex "because he wanted to obey the law of the Christians, because the Christians were wicked and had taken possession of their lands by force."[29]

Guarionex was adept at Caribbean forms of political legitimization and, given the uncertain political atmosphere of Hispaniola, he may have briefly chosen dramatic expressions of Christianity to reassure the hostile forces surrounding his territory. He was skilled at negotiating with other indigenous leaders, and he benefited politically from the performance of areitos, the ceremonial song-dances that were used for the transmission of history and myth in the Greater Antilles. The areito included both vocal and bodily expressions, and Guarionex may have found a familiar echo of its physicality within the Christian prayers that Pané taught him. Guarionex's skill in the areito allowed him to leverage favors from another native leader when he ultimately fled the Europeans. In exchange for an areito performance, he successfully gained refuge for a short time.[30] He was finally apprehended by Columbus and incarcerated, then in 1502 he perished aboard a ship bound for Castile during a storm. Guarionex's encounter with Christianity—strategic and selective—would be echoed by many Christian converts in the later missions of Spanish America.

Before Guarionex distanced himself from Christianity, Pané erected a shrine in his lands and installed icons, likely of the Virgin Mary, within. After Pané left Guarionex, a group of men associated with Guarionex broke into the chapel, stole the images, buried them in a cultivated field, and urinated on them. Some scholars have interpreted this episode as an early episode of cultural synthesis, in which Christian materials were pointedly subordinated to a Caribbean agricultural ritual. Given that the men broke into the chapel over the objections of its keepers, it seems likely that the act was intended, at least in part, as a deliberate repudiation of Christianity and the departed Pané. The Europeans understood the act in this way, and Pané reported with some satisfaction that the perpetrators were eventually burned alive by Bartolomé Columbus.[31]

The aftermath of the icon burial revealed another merger of Christian and Caribbean meanings. To mark the spot where the icons had been buried, yams sprouted in the shape of a cross, according to Pané. This cross was discovered by the mother of Guarionex, a woman much loathed by Pané. But it was this woman who saw the cross and "took it to be a great miracle." To the Castilian authorities, she said, "This miracle has been wrought by God where the images were found. God knows why."[32] Pané interpreted this event as a sign of the strength of Christianity: God could persuade even the "worst woman" in the Caribbean. Pané did not emphasize the fact that she was talking to "the commander of the fortress of Concepción" in the aftermath of local unrest and violence. By seizing upon this "miracle" of a Christian icon bursting forth from the Caribbean ground, she was demonstrating her diplomatic understanding of the complicated religiosity of the island's invaders.

Damp icons and green crosses were not the only potential moments of cultural synthesis in Pané's account. Guatícabanú died at the hands of unknown men while crying out his allegiance to Christianity, using both Castilian and Caribbean words: "Dios naboría daca." The indigenous word *naboría* was used to describe a servile class of people on the island of Hispaniola.[33] In describing himself as the naboría of God, at least in the version of events reported to the absent Pané, Guatícabanú was bending Christianity into a Caribbean frame.

The rebellion among Spanish settlers against Columbus in 1497 and 1498 intensified violence on the island. Hispaniola's unstable politics, however, may have also created opportunities for indigenous people to make strategic alliances with the alien invaders or to evade interference with their daily life. In 1500 Pané testified that Columbus had knowingly permitted non-Christian practices to persist on the island.[34] Under Columbus's governance in the first decade of the Spanish Caribbean, the scarcity of Spanish settlers and selective indifference of the administrators may have created opportunities for Hispaniola's native peoples to maintain their own traditional practices and to resist Christian and Spanish cultural intrusions.[35]

The political landscape of Hispaniola shifted in 1499, when Christopher Columbus made peace with the rebellious Spaniards by giving them *repartimientos* (grants of indigenous labor) in what would later come to be known as the *encomienda* system.[36] Under the new system, the indigenous people of Hispaniola no longer paid tribute to Columbus but instead contributed their labor to individual Europeans "entrusted" with their care. That system was formally recognized and institutionalized by Castile when a new governor, Nicolás de Ovando, arrived in 1502 with more Spanish settlers. Ovando began to systematically destroy any perceived threat of native resistance, and many people responded to the mounting violence by fleeing their communities, as Guarionex had, or even escaping to other Caribbean islands.

Other men and women on Hispaniola responded by cooperating or negotiating with the Spanish settlers. The Franciscans, who had been arriving in increasing numbers, participated in this interaction, and in 1500 they claimed to have performed a mass baptism involving three thousand people.[37] In 1512 the Laws of Burgos mandated that at least one son from each indigenous leader must be educated by the Franciscan friars when the boy reached thirteen years of age. While the Franciscans were not known for the scholastic zeal and *studia* that characterized the Dominican Order, they had a long-established system of grammar schools in Europe, as well as some institutional experience with educating non-Christian children in fourteenth-century China and the Mediterranean.[38] In 1513 the Franciscans on Hispaniola received twenty grammar books, twenty inkstands, a ream of paper, and ten volumes of the gospels and homilies designated for the instruction of the children of the island's Indian elite.[39]

The benefit of teaching elite indigenous boys how to read, write, and understand religious matters, according to the Laws of Burgos, was that they could, in turn, more effectively teach other people, as their neighbors were more likely to be persuaded by their fellows than by Spanish settlers.[40] The degree to which the young men within Franciscan schools embodied this infectious ideal varied. One of these boys was Enriquillo, who would later successfully resist Spanish domination and whose ability to negotiate with Spanish leaders was often ascribed to his tutelage under the Franciscans.[41]

In 1510 Dominican friars belatedly arrived on Hispaniola. As latecomers, they were inclined to resent the established relationships between the Castilian administrators and the Franciscan friars on the island; as Dominicans, they were inclined to criticize the Franciscan order and its reputation for prizing affective religiosity over rigorous arguments about the finer points of Christian doctrine. In the Iberian peninsula the Dominican order had experience with frontier missions during the medieval Reconquista, but they were primarily focused on rooting out heresy in Christian communities; they were closely associated with the Spanish Inquisition and urban preaching.[42] Their behavior on Hispaniola—which included castigating Spanish settlers and sending proposed reforms to

Spanish administrators—echoed their institutional orientation toward the Christian faithful. However, the Dominicans were also the "Order of Preachers," and persuasive discourse was highly prized by its members. Preaching provided one type of contact between Dominicans and other peoples.

In early 1511 Pedro de Córdoba, leader of the Hispaniola Dominicans, laboriously traveled from Santo Domingo to Concepción de la Vega—sleeping on the ground in the fields and mountains with only his cape for a pillow—in order to meet the island's governor and to preach a sermon before the leading Spanish settlers. Afterward, using interpreters, he preached to their Indian servants, beginning "from the creation of the world and going until Christ, the Son of God, was put on the cross."[43] According to Las Casas, it was the first time that many people in his audience had ever heard Christian preaching.

Several months later, the Dominicans performed a much more incendiary sermon. On December 21, 1511, the Sunday before Christmas, the Dominican friar Antonio de Montesinos castigated a church of wide-eyed Spanish settlers for the "cruel and horrible servitude" of Caribbean peoples. Montesinos's sermon upheld a traditional Dominican rhetorical tactic by upbraiding the lay audience for their Christian lapses. He held the Spanish to be violent, oppressive, and cruel, concerned solely with finding gold, in contrast to peaceful Caribbean peoples who mutely suffered and died from hunger, illness, and overwork. Montesinos accused the settlers not only of injuring Caribbean peoples but also of preventing their laborers from enacting Christian practices, such as being baptized, receiving instructed in religion, hearing regular mass, and observing holy days and Sundays. If the Spanish settlers refused to recognize their own cruelty, they were as distant from salvation as the "Moors or Turks," Montesinos said.[44]

Preaching was not the only point of contact between Dominican friars and Caribbean peoples. Despite their criticisms of Hispaniola's labor regime, in 1514 the Dominican monastery in Santo Domingo was allotted the labor of fourteen Indians. Meanwhile, the Franciscan monasteries of Concepción de la Vega and Santo Domingo were each assigned the labor of "six naborías." In addition, the Santo Domingo monastery belonging to a third set of regular clergy—the Mercedarians, who labored to redeem Christian captives from the Muslim kingdoms of the Mediterranean and had recently arrived in the Caribbean to raise money for their work in North Africa—was allotted the labor of three naborías.[45]

Castilian administrators sluggishly enacted laws to protect the island's labor force in response to the Dominican criticism, but the spread of the Spanish conquest through the islands and the nearby mainland was accelerating in scope and violence. Juan de la Duele, Pané's erstwhile companion, participated in the conquest and settlement of Jamaica, where he died between 1508 and 1511.[46] His fellow Franciscan Juan de Tisin went to Cuba in 1512 as part of Diego Velázquez y Cuéllar's invasion of the island, and may have played a supporting role in the story of Hatuey, one of the prototypical figures of American Indian resistance to colonization and Christian conversion. According to Las Casas's highly polemical version of events, Hatuey had been a leader in Hispaniola, but in 1503 he and his people fled to Cuba, where they attempted to organize resistance to the Spanish among the people there. In 1512 Hatuey was defeated and captured by Velázquez's forces, who prepared to burn him alive. When Hatuey was bound to the stake, a Franciscan friar—who may have been Tisin—gave him a rapid introduction to Christianity and said that Hatuey would go to heaven if he would only embrace the friar's faith. Hatuey asked if Christian Spaniards went to heaven and was told that, yes, the virtuous ones did. Hatuey did not respond to this good news with the enthusiasm that the Franciscan friar may have expected: "[Hatuey] said without thinking on it any more, that he did not desire to go to the sky, but rather down to hell, so that he would not be where [the Spanish] were and would not see such cruel people."[47]

According to Las Casas, this defiant speech was not Hatuey's first criticism of Christianity and the Spanish conquest. In his attempt to rally Cuba's indigenous peoples, Hatuey had called them together to show them the god that the Spanish worshipped: a basket of gold and gems. The group danced an areito in a vain attempt to please this foreign god, Las Casas claimed, before throwing Hatuey in the river. In his account, which was likely exaggerated or fictitious, Las Casas imagined how indigenous Caribbean peoples viewed European religion, based on what he dimly knew about Caribbean beliefs. Hispaniola's Indians venerated material objects of wood, cloth, and stone; Las Casas chose to portray Hatuey as "understanding" the Christian god as a tactile bundle of valuables that upended traditional expectations of reverence. On Hispaniola, indigenous people performed song-dances with recognizable religious and political meaning; Las Casas created a parable in which they sought to incorporate a misunderstood deity into a performance that was anchored in the beliefs and practices of the islands' native inhabitants. Las Casas's portrayal of Hatuey's death resembled the satirical punch line of a contemporary joke told in both Europe and the Americas: one should fear ending up in an afterlife that included a Castilian.[48]

In writing his accounts of the Spanish conquest, Las Casas could draw upon many years spent living in the Caribbean. He arrived on Hispaniola in 1502 and participated, as a secular priest, in the 1512 conquest of Cuba. On Cuba, he later claimed, his efforts at peaceful conversion among the bloody violence of the conquest led his Cuban converts to start calling him "behique" in an indigenous Caribbean approximation of his clerical identity.[49] Although he was initially unmoved by the Dominican efforts at reform, he gave up the Indians who labored for him in 1514 and began delivering sermons in Cuba against the current labor system. While Las Casas would not formally enter the Dominican order until 1522, he worked and studied with the Dominicans of Hispaniola. The support of the order enabled Las Casas and Montesinos to go to Spain together in 1515 and advocate for the reform of the Spanish Caribbean and the end of the encomienda.[50] The proposal Las Casas drew up in 1516 took into account the hardships of the Caribbean environment, such as mosquitoes and hurricanes, and also demonstrated the influence of the Dominicans on his thinking. He called for increased regulation of labor conditions, as well as the formal introduction of the Spanish Inquisition to the Caribbean, in order to prevent the "simple" Indians from coming into contact with "diabolical" heretics.[51]

In response to the Dominican calls for reform, the reigning regent of Castile, Franciscan cardinal Francisco Jiménez de Cisneros, named three Hieronymite monks as joint governors of the Caribbean in 1516. The choice of the Hieronymites at this juncture owed nothing to the order's ideological bent toward evangelization; the happily contemplative Hieronymites had not developed any newfound interest in frontier missions in the decades since Ramón Pané arrived on Columbus's second voyage. Nor was the choice related to Pané himself; there is no evidence that the order had any particular awareness of Pané or his life in the Caribbean.[52] Instead, Cisneros chose the three men to be neutral observers and evenhanded reformers due to the perceived indifference of the Hieronymites. They were aloof from the long tradition of squabbles between Dominicans and Franciscans, and they were known for their great loyalty to the ruling powers of Castile.

The Dominicans were disappointed in the Hieronymites. Las Casas complained later that the three monks had fallen into the clutches of the Spanish settlers who vigorously opposed the Caribbean Dominican efforts to end the encomienda. These Spaniards "spoke of nothing but ill of the Cleric [Las Casas] and of the miserable Indians, vilifying them as beasts and saying that they were dogs."[53] On Hispaniola, Las Casas was enraged by the Hieronymite friars' slowness in enacting reforms, and he indignantly returned to Spain to register his complaints.

As governors, the Hieronymites pursued a series of programs to "reform" the Caribbean. They recommended the pursuit of agricultural ventures and increased sugar production, loaned money to prospective planters, and recommended to Cisneros that more enslaved African men and women should be brought to the Caribbean. Responding to settlers' repeated demands to move Indians closer to spaces under Spanish control, the Hieronymites wrote that they had rearranged the scattered Hispaniola Indians into thirty new settlements. Far from easing the problems of a declining indigenous population, this action accidentally exacerbated the demographic collapse when smallpox broke out on the island for the first time at the end of 1518.[54]

The Hieronymites based their policies on the information they received from Spanish settlers, and they began their administration of the islands by collecting testimonies from Hispaniola's principal Spanish householders. Contrary to Dominican accusations of negligence, these initial actions were in accordance with their original instructions from Cisneros. While the Hieronymite governors had been sent to ensure the continuation of the Caribbean colonies and the religious instruction of the indigenous people, they were also instructed to approach these tasks using the guidance and input of the Spanish settlers.[55] In other respects the Hieronymites were less attentive to Cisneros's instructions. For example, they were instructed to cooperate with both the Franciscans and the Dominicans in their plans for religious reform, but that cooperation proved elusive, and there is no evidence that the friars ever talked to the Indian leaders on Hispaniola, despite Cisneros's explicit directive to seek their goodwill and information. However, the testimonies of the fourteen men they interviewed, some of whom had memories of the island stretching back to the first years of conquest and evangelization, reveal changing views of Spain's legacy after three decades of expansion in the Caribbean.

Two of the men interviewed by the Hieronymites were friars from the regular orders. Franciscan friar Pedro Mexia had arrived in the Caribbean around 1506. Mexia reported that he had experienced extensive contact with the people of the island and that his conversations with them suggested that they only desired "to be free and idle and move around at their pleasure." Mexia did not approve of this idleness. Despite his low opinion of the Indians, Mexia opposed the continuation of the encomienda.[56] The other friar interviewed was a Dominican, Bernardo de Santo Domingo, one of the first Dominican friars to come to the Caribbean in 1510. He also opposed the encomienda and recommended stricter regulations to protect people against overwork, abuse, and violence.

Some Spaniards had lived on Hispaniola long enough to remember the earliest schemes of Spanish control, starting with Christopher Columbus's command that each Indian "vassal" was required to bring him enough gold to fill a hawksbell every month. As some recalled, the early days of harmony on the island were soon overtaken by the threat of violence. According to one Spaniard, it was not long before Indians stopped bringing gold in favor of dancing areitos and taking hallucinogenic snuff and "pondering how they would kill all of the Spanish."[57]

Yet, although the violence and disorder of the early Spanish Caribbean had predisposed some Spaniards to view Indians with suspicion or disgust, others had experienced different types of contact with them. Pedro Romero, who had married an Indian woman, filled his testimony with frequent insider knowledge of indigenous culture and noted that he acquired his knowledge by "asking my wife as well as the other *caciques* and *cacicas* [male and female chiefs]." As Romero's marriage indicates, cultural exchanges between indigenous and Spanish people occurred at many levels and in many different registers. One Spaniard said that, in the past, the Indians had been known as enthusiasts for ball games and areitos and hallucinogenic snuff and "drinking herbs so that they could expel from their bodies everything that they had eaten," a reference to ritual vomiting. Now, he continued, they were also known for their enthusiasm for Spanish wine, which they said was better than snuff or ball games.[58]

As in Pané's collection of Hispaniola stories from 1498, the testimonies collected in 1517 allowed the fourteen men who testified to be selectively emphatic about the stories they told the Hieronymite friars. Their accounts drew upon both their own personal memories and experiences as well as their shared history with the island's Native American inhabitants. According to one Spaniard, in 1517 the indigenous people of Puerto Rico still celebrated their revolt against Spanish forces in 1511.[59] Caribbean Indians undoubtedly had multiple approaches to the preservation of storytelling, history, and religious expressions, but the 1517 testimonies suggest that the Spanish were intensely conscious of two channels in particular: areito song-dances and social relationships.

The 1512 Laws of Burgos specifically permitted and protected the areitos, although the reasoning behind their protection was not explained in the laws.[60] These provisions may have reflected a wider Castilian practice of concessions granted to conquered peoples, as similar legal protections were initially granted to the *moriscos* (people of Muslim origin or antecedents) of Granada. The areito was not the only element of indigenous Caribbean culture that the laws sought to preserve. Oddly enough, the hammock was strongly endorsed by the laws, and it is possible that, by preserving these fragments of precontact Hispaniola, the legislators of Burgos sought to re-create the population that had lived on the island before Columbus arrived. By 1517 Spanish residents of Hispaniola were still using the word *areito* to describe the apparently flamboyant combination of song and movement that potentially expressed a memory of the past, an interpretation of the divine, or an affirmation of social relationships. In Puerto Rico, memories of anti-Spanish defiance were likely reproduced, at least in part, through areitos. By protecting areitos, the Laws of Burgos were inadvertently protecting a potential medium for cultural transmission for Caribbean Indians.

The other indigenous medium for religious expression that troubled the Spanish was the non-Spanish social networks that persisted on Hispaniola. According to one Spaniard, Indian elders would mock other people if they discussed Christian beliefs among themselves, which inhibited conversion efforts. Another noted that most religious instruction only penetrated so far as the laboring Taíno, who were adults, and thus missed the opportunity to convert presumably malleable children, who instead were reared in the "vices and bad customs" of their mothers. Similarly, one settler said that because people did not begin to serve (and, implicitly, mingle with) the Spanish until they were at least twelve or thirteen years old, they absorbed the customs of their parents and never were able to embrace Christianity. Yet another Spaniard testified that, if released from their labor obligations, the indigenous people of the island "would return to their rites and ceremonies and empty superstitions ... and go about naked and live bestially as they are the enemies of intercourse with the Christians."[61]

The long-dead Guarionex might have recognized these indigenous methods of cultural preservation and resistance; they echoed his own skill at areitos and participation in political negotiations in the 1490s. Yet many expressions of religiosity on Hispaniola would have seemed alien to him, because an increasingly diverse group of people were coming to the island. By 1517 the first generation of children born from Spanish men and indigenous Caribbean women were reaching adulthood and having children of their own. Meanwhile, many Native American communities on the island were in the midst of an accelerating population collapse, due to alien pathogens and a declining birthrate. In response Spaniards imported unfree laborers. Enslaved men and women from elsewhere in the Americas and Africa were brought to Hispaniola, and these people brought with them their own practices and religious beliefs.[62] These new cultural configurations appeared in the creation of traditional religious objects with unprecedented attributes and materials. At some point in the early sixteenth century, craftsmen created a beaded cemí incorporating Caribbean shell beads, Venetian mirrors, and an African rhinoceros horn.[63] The figure's human face, carved out of the dark brown horn, was topped with curly black fibers representing hair.

As a historical category, "religion" is expansive; it potentially includes a belief in the supernatural, a set of practices in relation to the sacred, a moral guide to daily life, the codified recognition of community relationships, the founding of institutions, the maintenance of congregations, and a physiological flush of euphoria or terror or satisfaction. In the early Spanish Caribbean as elsewhere, religious practices and rituals were inextricably tied to expressions of identity, community, and memory. The early years of Spanish rule in Hispaniola were marked by indigenous Caribbean people's persistence in maintaining their traditional religious practices and in deliberately approaching Christianity through their own intellectual frameworks, despite the violence and coercion of the Spanish conquest. Expressions of Caribbean religiosity shifted in response to changing colonial conditions and missionary efforts, just as the regular clergy on the island adapted their mission efforts to local circumstances and frustrations—in part because the friars, mostly inexperienced with frontier missions, few in number, and adapting to local exigencies, were forced to improvise with the Caribbean materials at hand.

Notes

ABBREVIATIONS

AGI		Archivo General de Indias
	-IG	Gobierno: Indiferente General
	-Patr	Patronato Real

1. Pané, *An Account*, 3, 34–35, 37.
2. Las Casas, *Historia de las Indias* 1:459–60; Wilson, *Hispaniola*, 107.
3. Pané, *An Account*, 32–33, 38.
4. One exception is the treatment of early Caribbean syncretism in Oliver, *Caciques and Cemí Idols*, 233–44.
5. See Griffiths and Cervantes, *Spiritual Encounters*; Greer and Bilinkoff, *Colonial Saints*; Kirk and Rivett, *Religious Transformations*.

6. Varela, *Cristóbal Colon: Textos*, 37.
7. Pané, *An Account*, 20. For more on the areito as a memorial or political act, see Wilson, *Hispaniola*, 100. In contrast, Paul Scolieri has argued that the early chroniclers projected their own interpretations and scholarly preoccupations upon the areito. Scolieri, *Dancing the New World*, 42–43.
8. López-Baralt, *El mito taíno*, 133.
9. Wilson, *Hispaniola*, 74; Floyd, *Columbus Dynasty*, 36.
10. Deagan, "Colonial Transformations," 135–60; Livi-Bacci, "Return to Hispaniola," 3–51; Altman, "Marriage, Family, and Ethnicity," 225–50.
11. Pané, *An Account*, 8–9, 12, 16.
12. Cook, *Born to Die*, 44.
13. Pané, *An Account*, 25.
14. Oliver, *Caciques and Cemí Idols*, 73–76.
15. Pané, *An Account*, 21, 23, 27–30.
16. Varela and Aguirre, *La caída*, 203.
17. Oliver, *Caciques and Cemí Idols*, 221–31.
18. Muldoon, *Popes, Lawyers, and Infidels*, 137–40.
19. Roest, "From *Reconquista* to Mission," 331–62.
20. Highfield, "The Jeronimites in Spain," 523–26; Rice, *Saint Jerome*, 74.
21. Harvey, *Muslims in Spain*, 28.
22. Pané, *An Account*, 32; Stevens-Arroyo, "Juan Mateo Guaticabanu," 614–36.
23. Pané, *An Account*, 34.
24. Burns, "Christian-Islamic Confrontation," 1386–1434.
25. Pané, *An Account*, 32.
26. Pardo, *The Origins of Mexican Catholicism*, 20–48.
27. Phelan, *Millennial Kingdom*.
28. Varela and Aguirre, *La caída*, 200, 203.
29. Pané, *An Account*, 35.
30. Wilson, *Hispaniola*, 102–8.
31. Pané, *An Account*, 36, 36n155; Stevens-Arroyo, "Juan Mateo Guaticabanú," 635.
32. Pané, *An Account*, 37.
33. Pané, *An Account*, 33n141.
34. Varela and Aguirre, *La caída*, 203.
35. Deagan, "Reconsidering Taíno Social Dynamics," 597–626.
36. Simpson, *Encomienda in New Spain*.
37. Tibesar, "Franciscan Province," 379–81; Oliger, "Earliest Record," 64.
38. Roest, *A History of Franciscan Education*, 242–43.
39. AGI-IG 419, L.4, fol. 124v.
40. Altamira, "El texto," 35.

41. Altman, "Revolt of Enriquillo," 589; Tibesar, "Franciscan Province," 381n26.
42. Vose, *Dominicans, Muslims, and Jews*, 58.
43. Las Casas, *Historia de las Indias* 2:384.
44. Las Casas, *Historia de las Indias* 2:441–42.
45. Rodríguez Demorizi, *Los domínicos*, 102, 157, 167. For more on the haphazard role of the first Mercedarians in the Americas, see Taylor, *Structures of Reform*, 82–85, 87–88.
46. Tibesar, "Franciscan Province," 384.
47. Las Casas, *An Account*, 19.
48. For variations on this joke-type in sixteenth-century Cuba and seventeenth-century Aragon, see "The Account by a Gentleman from Elvas," in Clayton, Knight, and Moore, *The De Soto Chronicles*, 53–54, and Kamen, *Inquisition and Society*, 205.
49. Las Casas, *Historia de las Indias* 2:532.
50. Wagner and Parish, *Life and Writings*, 13.
51. Las Casas, "Memorial de remedios," 34, 36.
52. For a history of the order dating from 1605 that does not mention Pané, see Sigüenza, *Historia de la orden de San Jerónimo*.
53. Las Casas, *Historia de las Indias* 3:119.
54. Simpson, *Encomienda in New Spain*, 39–55; Cook, *Born to Die*, 60–63; Rodríguez Morel, "Sugar Economy," 88.
55. AGI-Patr 172, R.7.
56. Rodríguez Demorizi, *Los domínicos*, 328–30.
57. Rodríguez Demorizi, *Los domínicos*, 295.
58. Rodríguez Demorizi, *Los domínicos*, 292, 334.
59. Rodríguez Demorizi, *Los domínicos*, 346.
60. Altamira, "El texto," 33.
61. Rodríguez Demorizi, *Los domínicos*, 284, 307, 340.
62. Guitar, "Cultural Genesis," 407–10.
63. Taylor, Biscione, and Roe, "Epilogue: The Beaded Zemi," 162–64; Ostapkowicz et al, "Integrating the Old World."

Bibliography

ARCHIVES

Archivo General de Indias (Seville, Spain).

PUBLISHED WORKS

Altamira, Rafael. "El texto de las Leyes de Burgos de 1512." *Revista de Historia de América* 4 (1938): 5–79.

Altman, Ida. "Marriage, Family, and Ethnicity in the Early Spanish Caribbean." *William and Mary Quarterly*, 3rd series, 70, no. 2 (April 2003): 225–50.

———. "The Revolt of Enriquillo and the Historiography of Early Spanish America." *The Americas* 63, no. 4 (April 2007): 587–614.

Burns, Robert I. "Christian-Islamic Confrontation in the West: The Thirteenth-Century Dream of Conversion." *American Historical Review* 76, no. 5 (December 1971): 1386–1434.

Clayton, Lawrence A., Vernon James Knight Jr., and Edward C. Moore, eds. *The De Soto Chronicles: The Expedition of Hernando de Soto to North America in 1539–1543*. Tuscaloosa: University of Alabama Press, 1993.

Cook, Noble David. *Born to Die: Disease and New World Conquest, 1492–1650*. Cambridge: Cambridge University Press, 1998.

Deagan, Kathleen A. "Colonial Transformations: Euro-American Cultural Genesis in the Early Spanish American Colonies." *Journal of Anthropological Research* 52, no. 2 (Summer 1996): 135–60.

———. "Reconsidering Taíno Social Dynamics after Spanish Conquest: Gender and Class in Culture Contact Studies." *American Antiquity* 69, no. 4 (2004): 597–626.

Floyd, Troy S. *The Columbus Dynasty in the Caribbean, 1492–1526*. Albuquerque: University of New Mexico Press, 1973.

Greer, Allan, and Jodi Bilinkoff, eds. *Colonial Saints: Discovering the Holy in the Americas, 1500–1800*. New York: Routledge, 2003.

Griffiths, Nicholas, and Fernando Cervantes, eds. *Spiritual Encounters: Interactions between Christianity and Native Religions in Colonial America*. Birmingham, UK: University of Birmingham Press, 1999.

Guitar, Lynne A. "Cultural Genesis: Relationships among Indians, Africans, and Spaniards in Rural Hispaniola, First Half of the Sixteenth Century." PhD diss., Vanderbilt University, 1998.

Harvey, L. P. *Muslims in Spain, 1500–1614*. Chicago: University of Chicago Press, 2005.

Highfield, J. R. L. "The Jeronimites in Spain, Their Patrons, and Success, 1373–1516." *Journal of Ecclesiastical History* 34, no. 4 (October 1983): 513–33.

Kamen, Henry. *Inquisition and Society in Spain in the Sixteenth and Seventeenth Centuries*. Bloomington: Indiana University Press, 1985.

Kirk, Stephanie, and Sarah Rivett, eds. *Religious Transformations in the Early Modern Americas*. Philadelphia: University of Pennsylvania Press, 2014.

Las Casas, Bartolomé de. *An Account, Much Abbreviated, of the Destruction of the Indies*. Edited by Franklin W. Knight. Translated by Andrew Hurley. Indianapolis: Hackett, 2003.

———. *Historia de Las Indias*. Edited by Agustín Millares Carlo. 3 vols. México DF: Fondo de Cultura Económica, 1951.

———. "Memorial de remedios para las Indias (1516)." In *Obras Completas, Vol. 13: Cartas y Memoriales*, edited by Paulino Castañeda, Carlos de Rueda, Carmen Gordínez, and Inmaculada de La Corte, 23–48. Madrid: Alianza Editorial, 1995.

Livi-Bacci, Massimo. "Return to Hispaniola: Reassessing a Demographic Catastrophe." *Hispanic American Historical Review* 83, no. 1 (February 2003): 3–51.

López-Baralt, Mercedes. *El mito taíno: Levi-Strauss en las Antillas*. 2nd ed. Río Piedras, PR: Ediciones Huracán, 1985.

Muldoon, James. *Popes, Lawyers, and Infidels: The Church and the Non-Christian World, 1250–1550*. Philadelphia: University of Pennsylvania Press, 1979.

Oliger, Livarius. "The Earliest Record on the Franciscan Missions in America." *Catholic Historical Review* 6, no. 1 (April 1920): 59–65.

Oliver, José R. *Caciques and Cemí Idols: The Web Spun by Taíno Rulers between Hispaniola and Puerto Rico*. Tuscaloosa: University of Alabama Press, 2009.

Ostapkowicz, Joanna, Fiona Brock, Alex C. Wiedenhoeft, Rick Schulting, and Donatella Saviola. "Integrating the Old World into the New: An 'Idol from the West Indies,'" *Antiquity* 91, no. 359 (2017): 1314–29.

Pané, Ramón. *An Account of the Antiquities of the Indians*. Edited by José Juan Arrom. Translated by Susan C. Griswold. Durham: Duke University Press, 1999.

Pardo, Osvaldo F. *The Origins of Mexican Catholicism: Nahua Rituals and Christian Sacraments in Sixteenth-Century Mexico*. Ann Arbor: University of Michigan Press, 2004.

Phelan, John L. *The Millennial Kingdom of the Franciscans in the New World*. Berkeley: University of California Press, 1970.

Rice, Eugene F. *Saint Jerome in the Renaissance*. Baltimore: Johns Hopkins University Press, 1985.

Rodríguez Demorizi, Emilio, ed. *Los domínicos y las encomiendas de indios de la Isla Española*. Santo Domingo: Editora del Caribe, 1971.

Rodríguez Morel, Genaro. "The Sugar Economy of Española in the Sixteenth Century." In *Tropical Babylons: Sugar and the Making of the Atlantic World, 1450–1680*, edited by Stuart B. Schwartz, 85–114. Chapel Hill: University of North Carolina Press, 2004.

Roest, Bert. "From *Reconquista* to Mission in the Early Modern World." In *A Companion to Observant Reform in the Late Middle Ages and Beyond*, edited by James D. Mixson and Bert Roest, 331–62. Leiden: Brill, 2015.

———. *A History of Franciscan Education (c. 1210–1517)*. Leiden: Brill, 2000.

Scolieri, Paul A. *Dancing the New World: Aztecs, Spaniards, and the Choreography of Conquest*. Austin: University of Texas Press, 2013.

Sigüenza, José de. *Historia de la orden de San Jerónimo*. Madrid: Bailly/Bailliere e Hijos, 1909.

Simpson, Lesley Byrd. *The Encomienda in New Spain: The Beginning of Spanish Mexico*. Berkeley: University of California Press, 1950.

Stevens-Arroyo, Anthony M. "Juan Mateo Guaticabanu, September 21, 1496: Evangelization and Martyrdom in the Time of Columbus." *Catholic Historical Review* 82, no. 4 (October 1996): 614–36.

Taylor, Bruce. *Structures of Reform: The Mercedarian Order in the Spanish Golden Age*. Leiden: Brill, 2000.

Taylor, Dicey, Marco Biscione, and Peter G. Roe. "Epilogue: The Beaded Zemi in the Pigorini Museum." In *Taíno: Pre-Columbian Art and Culture from the Caribbean*, edited by Fatima Bercht, Estrellita Brodsky, John Alan Farmer, and Dicey Taylor, 158–69. New York: Monacelli Press, 1997.

Tibesar, Antonine S. "The Franciscan Province of the Holy Cross of Española, 1505–1559." *Americas* 13, no. 4 (April 1957): 377–89.

Varela, Consuelo, ed. *Cristóbal Colón: Textos y documentos completos: relaciones de viajes, cartas y memoriales*. 2nd ed. Madrid: Alianza, 1989.

Varela, Consuelo, and Isabel Aguirre, eds. *La caída de Cristóbal Colón*. Madrid: Marcial Pons, 2006.

Vose, Robin. *Dominicans, Muslims, and Jews in the Medieval Crown of Aragon*. Cambridge: Cambridge University Press, 2009.

Wagner, Henry Raup, and Helen Rand Parish. *Life and Writings of Bartolomé de las Casas*. Albuquerque: University of New Mexico Press, 1967.

Wilson, Samuel M. *Hispaniola: Caribbean Chiefdoms in the Age of Columbus*. Tuscaloosa: University of Alabama Press, 1990.

2

The Revolt of Agüeybaná II

Puerto Rico's Interisland Connections

CACEY FARNSWORTH

As the smallest of the Greater Antilles, Puerto Rico played a surprisingly important part in the history of the early Spanish Caribbean. Thwarted by significant indigenous resistance, Spanish colonization of the island was slow in comparison to later theaters of interest in the Caribbean. The resistance varied in intensity and was a product of factors dividing the native population along political, rather than ethnic, lines. The native groups did not respond uniformly to the Spanish presence; some benefited from alliance with the Spanish while most chose resistance. The first Spaniards on the island soon recognized that its inhabitants were grouped into distinct sociopolitical units that responded differently to the challenges and opportunities presented by the Spanish attempt to occupy the island. Busy with their own political struggles and a burgeoning gold economy, the Spaniards failed to fully comprehend the extent of the division.

Matters were further complicated by an ongoing dispute between the king, don Fernando, and the viceroy of the Indies, don Diego Colón, over the right to name individuals to offices in the newly opened lands. This in turn led to constant changes of personnel and labor assignments, which combined to create considerable frustration and violence on the part of both Spanish and Indians. Such squabbles undermined Spanish understandings of the severe animosity between warring native factions on the island. As a result, roughly half of the Spanish population was wiped out in the first widespread revolt that swept across much of the island beginning in 1510. Initial hostilities were quelled only to return more strongly with the participation of indigenous groups from the neighboring islands of the Lesser Antilles. Conflict continued to deter

Spanish settlement in Puerto Rico until the 1515 armada of Juan Ponce de León, after which internal resistance on the island among native groups began to diminish. In the meantime, the revolt, along with other factors, sparked an uprising by the relatively small African slave population on the island in 1514.

Documentation detailing the exact events of the revolt in 1510 is sparse and dominated by Spanish voices. When read with a critical eye, however, the material allows indigenous perspectives to emerge and reveals considerable detail about Spanish-Indian relations in the early years on Puerto Rico. The historiography of the revolt spans several generations of scholarship from the early Spanish chroniclers to present-day ethnohistorians and archaeologists. Among these, one stands out for impact and controversy. Aurelio Tió, a self-trained historian, published *Nuevas fuentes para la historia de Puerto Rico* in 1961. The first document in the volume is of particular interest and has created controversy among scholars who question its utility in writing the early history of the conquest. The document, a deposition that Juan González Ponce de León (hereafter referred to as Juan González) executed in 1532 in Mexico City, alleges that he played a vital role in the conquest of Puerto Rico by virtue of his mastery of native languages. Historians have pointed to its biases and inaccuracies, although it appears to contain some elements of truth and perhaps warrants consideration.[1]

My discussion will contextualize the revolt by emphasizing its influence on the evolution of Spanish-indigenous relations and the lasting challenges for Spanish occupation of the island that it created. Examination of the available Spanish accounts sheds light on the revolt's intra- as well as interisland nature and the various alliances that formed during the period. While some of the events followed a pattern seen previously on Hispaniola, the evidence will highlight Puerto Rico's unique role in the early history of the Caribbean. The evolving role and identity of native groups, as existing conflicts were amplified by the arrival of the Spaniards, suggest connections with the themes of the "new conquest history" that principally have been studied in relation to New Spain. Puerto Rico offered perhaps the most difficult challenge to conquest for the Spanish in the early Caribbean.[2]

Contact

Upon returning to the Indies in 1502 with the royal governor, frey Nicolás de Ovando, Juan Ponce de León (also known as Juan Ponce) no doubt remembered the island of Puerto Rico from his previous experience there during Columbus's second voyage. Puerto Rico continued to figure in his plans as he played a crucial role in the final pacification of Hispaniola in the easternmost province of Higüey. After suppressing local resistance, Ponce was appointed captain over the newly founded village of Salvaleón.[3] Hearing rumors of large gold deposits on Puerto Rico from the natives of Higüey, he began sending reconnaissance missions to survey the island with his own ship.[4] Pleased with the captain's military service, Ovando sent a special recommendation to the king suggesting that he award an *asiento*, or right of conquest, to Juan Ponce. The previous holders of the license, Vicente Yáñez Pinzón and García de Salazar, had done nothing. Already busy preparing his ships, Ponce set sail almost immediately when royal approval for the expedition finally arrived in 1508.[5]

The royal license granted to Juan Ponce provided strict instructions. The Spaniard was to contact the head cacique of the island, begin planting *conucos* (cultivated fields) for future colonization, and establish mines, then return to Hispaniola with samples of gold.[6] The expedition set out from Hispaniola in August 1508 with two Indians from Higüey acting as guides and translators. After a brief stop on the small island of Mona, the ships landed somewhere on the southern coast of Puerto Rico. Ponce learned from his interpreter that he had landed precisely where he desired, in the lands of the head cacique, Agüeybaná I.[7]

Disembarking, Ponce met the head cacique, who received him warmly. The events of the exchange demonstrate cultural misunderstanding on both sides. In line with custom, Agüeybaná I welcomed Ponce as a great lord, inviting him to exchange names in the ceremony of *guatiao* and giving him his sister as wife.[8] Both actions were intended in native culture to unite kinship groups. These acts, understood by Agüeybaná I as agreement to an alliance, were perceived by Ponce as submission. Gonzalo Fernández de Oviedo, writing years later, reflected the same distorted view of the exchange: "[Agüeybaná I] was a good person and very obedient to his mother; and she was a good woman, and she was mature, she had news of what happened in the conquest and pacification of the island of Hispaniola, and like a prudent person continually told and counseled her son and the other Indians to be good friends of Christians, if they did not wish to all die at their hands. And so, because of this advice, the son went with Captain Juan Ponce and gave him a sister of his as a mistress."[9]

Oviedo's account inadvertently points to the native interconnectedness of the early Caribbean; Agüeybaná I and his mother were clearly aware of events on Hispaniola and sought alliance with the arriving Spaniards. Altogether the meeting lasted a few days, after which Ponce set sail in search of a more suitable harbor and gold-rich rivers. His search led him to the northeast coast. It was there in 1508, at the site later known as Caparra, that he would establish the first Spanish settlement on the island.[10]

Upon returning to Santo Domingo with samples of the gold recovered near Caparra, Ponce related his account of the meeting between himself and people in Puerto Rico, noting in particular that he had conversed with many caciques and also "Caribs."[11] This reference to Caribs is noteworthy. The term, first heard by Columbus during his initial expedition to the Indies and seemingly repeated by other groups with whom the Spaniards later came into contact, was misunderstood by the Spaniards, who quickly became convinced that Caribs were the enemy of all peaceful Indians. Ostensibly they lived in the east, practiced cannibalism, and possibly held vast quantities of gold.[12] Yet, in this instance, Ponce appears to have conversed amicably with these supposed savages. Further complicating questions about the presence of Caribs in Puerto Rico and their relations with the other native groups on the island is the testimony of Juan González, who claimed that he acted as interpreter on an expedition in 1506 in which Spaniards contacted a friendly cacique named Mabo somewhere on the west coast of Puerto Rico. Mabo was reported to have greatly desired to have the "Christians be their friends so they would be favored and defended from the Caribs who do them much harm, kill them, and eat them."[13] If true, González's account supports Dr. Chanca's report that during

Columbus's second voyage, natives of Puerto Rico fled from the Spaniards thinking that they were Caribs.[14]

Considering these testimonies, it is clear that at this stage Spanish usage and understanding of the term *Carib* remained widely ambiguous. The use of the term could signify a recognition by Spaniards of cultural or political differences among native groups on the island, contributing to the confusion as to what groups were present in Puerto Rico in this period. Archaeological and ethnohistorical evidence has established the existence of a distinct ethnic group known today as Island Caribs who were confined largely to the Windward Islands in the Lesser Antilles and who interacted through trade and warfare with the natives of Puerto Rico and the Virgin Islands.[15] There is further evidence that the natives of Puerto Rico and the Virgin Islands shared cultural and political ties. It is therefore likely that Juan Ponce de León and other Spaniards mislabeled some of the native groups on early sixteenth-century Puerto Rico as Caribs when in reality they were probably people from the neighboring Virgin Islands.[16]

Spanish settlement in Caparra brought sustained contact with the local caciques of the northeast, most of whom quickly saw the advantage of cooperation with the Spaniards as a means of solidifying an alliance against their enemies in the south. As in the other large islands of the Caribbean, indigenous Puerto Rican society was based upon chiefdoms ruled by single caciques who themselves were allied in a hierarchical relationship under the rule of a paramount cacique in units known as *cacicazgos*.[17] Unbeknownst to the Spaniards, at the time of contact Puerto Rico was divided between two competing cacicazgos, one in the northeast ruled by Caguax, and another ruled by Agüeybaná I, who dominated the western, central, and southern regions, along with the eastern islands of Vieques and Santa Cruz.[18]

The Spaniards found native inhabitants in the northeast to be very cooperative. In Caparra they exchanged names with the local caciques and received native women who were baptized and christened before being handed over to the men. This practice continued among the loyal natives on the north coast long after the end of the revolt. Despite being used sexually to strengthen alliances, women in native Puerto Rican society were by no means the simple instruments of men. Many fought in battle, and some ruled individual chiefdoms.[19] It also appears, as the encounter with Agüeybaná I highlighted, that older women exercised significant social and political influence even when they were not cacicas. Along with their male counterparts, cacicas in many instances became valued Spanish allies.[20]

With Caparra established and strong alliances made, Ponce turned his attention to the original goal of the expedition: gold. For the native peoples of the Caribbean, gold held great value. As a symbol of power, it was predominantly worn by caciques and nobles.[21] Viewing Ponce as a great cacique, the region's indigenous inhabitants initially helped him to find gold, thus further solidifying the alliance between the two groups. It soon became apparent that the rivers of the northeast were full of gold. The earliest figures for the exact amount extracted are from 1510, when the Spaniards refined 12,625 *pesos de oro de 450 maravedís;* roughly equivalent to around $2 million at today's rate![22] No wonder that as soon as rumors of such wealth spread to Hispaniola, Puerto Rico began to attract other would-be settlers.[23]

Beginnings of an Uprising

The king had long taken an interest in Puerto Rico, awarding the first asiento (monopoly contract) for the colonization of the island to Vicente Yáñez Pinzón in 1505, and another—which was much more effectively exploited—to Juan Ponce de León in 1508. The right to award titles to conquest and offices in the Indies was one of many demands that don Diego Colón brought before the royal court in a series of legal proceedings known as the *Pleitos colombinos*, which aimed to untangle the complicated rights and privileges awarded to Christopher Columbus and his heirs in the New World from the claims of the monarchy.[24] The court eventually ruled in Colón's favor in 1509, and Fernando named him viceroy of the Indies.[25] Before the final verdict, however, the king had granted various appointments in Puerto Rico, including Ponce's 1508 asiento and another awarded to a certain don Cristóbal de Sotomayor.[26] Both asientos were included in the king's instructions to his new viceroy at the time of his departure for the Indies. Comparison of the two asientos provides a basis for understanding the pattern of Spanish settlement on Puerto Rico and its effects on the native populations. Ponce's asiento, as iterated in the instructions provided to Colón, stipulated that "Concerning the populating of the island of San Juan, Juan Ponce de León has accepted an asiento of my command, and it is my favor and will in this that no changes be made unless I command. Furthermore, I command that in all things he requires, you favor him with resources from the island of Hispaniola for the supplying of San Juan as well as any other thing necessary for the growth and populating of the said island." The license awarded to Sotomayor read: "Having been obedient in our service, we award you license and faculty, along with those whom you wish to take, to populate and inhabit any place or part that best pleases you on the island of San Juan . . . and that you may take for yourself a cacique on the said island of San Juan with the Indians that pertain to him."[27]

As viceroy, Colón honored both asientos but undermined Ponce's political power by appointing one of his own loyal supporters, Juan Cerón, lieutenant-governor and *alcalde mayor* (district administrator) of Puerto Rico. Cerón immediately began modifying the *repartimientos* of native labor on the island previously issued by Ponce.[28] At the same time, however, Colón sought to avoid unnecessary contention over native labor. Since Ponce had already established himself in the northeast, Sotomayor would be directed toward the subjugation of the southern part of the island.[29] Thus Sotomayor's previously ambiguous asiento was now concretely defined as including the labor of three hundred Indians under the cacique Agüeybaná II, brother to the head cacique Agüeybaná I in the southwest.[30] Sotomayor arrived with a company of men and founded the village of Távora near Agüeybaná I's village of Guánica on October 28, 1509. Sometime after their arrival in Guánica, Agüeybaná I died, passing his authority to his brother.[31]

Sotomayor immediately began searching for gold in the surrounding rivers and establishing a village. With a permanent settlement now within their half of the island, Agüeybaná II and his allied chiefs became increasingly resentful. The situation deteriorated daily with constant demands for food and labor from the interlopers.[32] Sotomayor was frustrated. Far from the prosperous gold fields of the northeast, and hoping to make his repartimiento profitable despite difficulties motivating the native inhabitants to work, he protested that some of the people awarded to Ponce belonged to his cacique. The king ordered Colón, the viceroy, to arbitrate any possible disputes that could arise between the two men.[33] In a letter to the king, Colón lauded his own efforts in both settling the matter and effectively colonizing the island. He wrote:

> To [Ponce] I gave the same share he already possessed, providing him with as many Indians as he needed to develop the said portion, and this was because don Cristóbal [Sotomayor] was determined to take from him these Indians, claiming they were better and were under [the rule of] his cacique ... and the island would not be settled, because in it there are only two [caciques], and if one by himself takes one [of them] with the Indians that are attached there would not be an Indian left for the settlers, and for that reason I assigned him three hundred Indians.[34]

The dispute between Ponce and Sotomayor over rights to native labor effectively divided Spanish society on the island.

Unhappy with the viceroy's modification of his original asiento, Sotomayor continued to plead with the crown to provide him more Indians.[35] In response, King Fernando gave him license to outfit two ships to take captives from nearby islands.[36] In this document the inhabitants of the surrounding islands were not referred to as Caribs but rather as *indios*. Sotomayor also hired Spaniards to enforce the compliance of caciques who had refused to provide labor and fled.[37] The enslavement and importation of other Indians and the use of violence to enforce labor requirements led some caciques to retaliate. Sotomayor soon realized that tensions had reached a boiling point and decided to relocate his settlement northward along the western coast in 1510, near the river Guaorabo, in order to be closer to the productive mining regions of the northeast.[38] He named the new site Sotomayor.[39]

As a result of contention among the Spaniards over the new labor allotments, the king issued a royal decree dated March 2, 1510, officially naming Juan Ponce de León captain-governor of Puerto Rico, contravening Colón's viceregal authority.[40] Seizing the opportunity Ponce immediately sent Cerón (Colón's lieutenant-governor) back to Spain in chains.[41] The existence of Sotomayor's new settlement continued to divide Spanish forces, weakening their ability to respond effectively to the impending indigenous revolt. Quite unintentionally the Spaniards had succeeded in dividing themselves along the traditional lines of the warring *cacicazgos*.[42]

Indigenous resistance in the southwest grew as small acts gave way to planned attacks. Not long after the Spaniards moved to the town of Sotomayor, Agüeybaná II convened a council of allied caciques who ultimately agreed to make war on all Spaniards, beginning with don Cristóbal Sotomayor.[43] Oviedo made the possibly apocryphal claim that Sotomayor himself learned of the designs on his life from his indigenous concubine, Guanina, kinswoman of Agüeybaná II.[44] Juan González later testified that Sotomayor, fearing the reports to be true, had immediately sent for him. Making his way across the island, González ostensibly stripped off his clothes, adorned himself in traditional war paint, and set off to discover the subversive designs of the rebellious caciques.[45] It is difficult to accept the authenticity of Juan González's account of his actions. Regardless of linguistic ability and body paint, it seems unlikely that any Spaniard would enter hostile indigenous communities unnoticed. No matter how they were acquired, Sotomayor decided to follow the warnings and leave for Caparra, yet foolishly he demanded that Agüeybaná II provide native porters to carry supplies for his journey. Shortly after setting out, Sotomayor was overtaken and killed by Agüeybaná II and his men in September 1510.[46] News of the uprising, however, never reached the village of Sotomayor, and the men there were caught completely unawares when Guarionex, the cacique of Otuao, attacked shortly thereafter. Guarionex's forces burned the village and surrounding estates. Most of the Spaniards were killed, with only a few escaping to Caparra.[47]

Civil War

Realizing the gravity of the situation, Ponce organized a force to quell the rebellion.[48] The Spaniards were not the only ones to declare war on the forces of Agüeybaná II.[49] Allied caciques provided warriors who played a vital role in ensuring the Spaniards' survival, considering that roughly half of the Spanish population had been massacred at the town of Sotomayor.[50] While the historiography consistently overlooks the integral part played by indigenous allies, Ponce testified to their importance in 1514, stating that "the Christians and Indians who were with [me] went to war."[51]

The forces under Agüeybaná II clashed with the Spaniards and their native allies on three separate occasions. Both the first and second skirmishes resulted in casualties for the insurgents. In the third and last battle of this opening phase of the rebellion, Gonzalo Fernández de Oviedo claims the native forces numbered 11,000.[52] Apparently fourteen canoes of warriors from the nearby islands joined in the fight against the Spaniards and their indigenous allies.[53] It also appears that, as a result of slaving expeditions such as the one outfitted by Sotomayor, the natives of these islands were quite willing to come to Agüeybaná's aid.[54]

The term *Carib* does not appear in any of the documents from the period connected with the revolt. Very likely the Spaniards, although gradually coming to understand the interisland nature of the rebellion but still unaware of the political makeup of the early Caribbean, misrepresented the composition of the revolt and included Caribs among the rebels in order to justify future expeditions of enslavement against neighboring islands.[55] This explanation makes more sense if the previously mentioned examples of native peoples on Puerto Rico expressing fear of Carib attacks are taken into account. If Agüeybaná II did convince Caribs to join him, it would have been an unprecedented example of previously hostile indigenous ethnic groups uniting in the face of a new threat.

The final skirmish took place in the valley of Yagueca near the river Guaorabo. The encounter did not last long, ending abruptly when a musket ball killed the indigenous leader. While historians have assumed that this leader was Agüeybaná II, Oviedo (the most nearly contemporary writer) provides no evidence that such was the case.[56] Nevertheless, following this loss, the insurgents retreated out of musket range, effectively allowing Ponce and his men (who saw the large number of Indians gathered there) to slip away at nightfall. Thus Agüeybaná II's revolt survived.[57]

Disturbed and shocked by these events, and aware of native involvement from neighboring islands, the king issued a royal decree allowing the Spaniards of Puerto Rico to wage war on the people now labeled as Caribs. The document clearly highlights the emerging realization by the Spanish of the interisland context of the rebellion. It served as further justification for attacking and enslaving Indians who resisted throughout the rest of the Caribbean phase of conquest. It reads:

> There are certain Indians known as Caribs who have never listened, or want to listen to, or welcome our captains and clerics, having resisted various times so that these cannot enter or inhabit their islands, and in their said resistance they have killed many Christians, and in this hardness the said Caribs from the said islands have continued, and many others have joined them, making war against the Indians in our service, capturing them in order to eat them, as they have done and do still, and thus they influence other Indians to commit many horrible acts and excesses such as that occurred recently, on the island of San Juan, some of the Indians from there cunningly and in diabolic form betrayed and killed don Cristóbal de Sotomayor... and burned one of the only two villages on the said island, and they killed many Christians there, and rebelled against our service, in all of which they were incited, aided, and favored by many of the said Caribs who came in canoes. And seeing similar excesses and scandals that until now have occurred, and those that could occur, and the danger to the said islands of San Juan, Hispaniola, the others, and Tierra firme, I have issued a general decree, in which license and faculty is given to all... so that they may make war on the Caribs.[58]

The declaration includes the islands of Trinidad, San Bernardo, Isla Fuerte, Barbuda, Dominica, Matanino, Santa Lucia, San Vicente, La Ascensión, Tobago, Mayo, Baru, and the ports of Cartagena as lands occupied by the Caribs. In previous instructions of a nature similar to those issued to viceroy Diego Colón, King Fernando specifically mentioned only the Caribs from the island of Santa Cruz. He suggested that the enslavement of its people would be "one of the principal remedies that can be accomplished for the pacification of the island of San Juan."[59] Although these documents were not the first decrees to allow the enslavement of Caribs, they represent a significant shift in the Spaniards' definition and treatment of Caribs from the time of Ponce's initial encounter with them in 1508 on Puerto Rico. Besides suggesting an emerging Spanish realization of the interisland connections that existed in the Caribbean, the increasingly common inclusion of the term *Carib* during the period is directly connected with the economic development of Puerto Rico and Hispaniola. As more Spaniards flooded these islands, eager to profit from mining bonanzas, demand for native labor skyrocketed. Thus, as Jalil Sued Badillo has argued, the increasing use of the term allowed the Spaniards to justify the enslavement of other native groups in the nearby Lesser Antilles by labeling them as participants in the rebellion on Puerto Rico.[60]

Despite his services to the crown in defeating the initial revolt, Ponce once again found himself in the middle of the reignited dispute between King Fernando and viceroy Colón over rights to jurisdiction in Puerto Rico.[61] With the high court again ruling in favor of Colón, the king was forced to politely oust Ponce as captain-governor of Puerto Rico.[62] In recompense to the conquistador, the king provided him an asiento for the conquest and settlement of Biminí, an island of rumored wealth, in 1512.[63] Reinstated as alcalde mayor by royal command, Juan Cerón rebuilt the village of Távora near its original site in the same year, renaming it San Germán in honor of Fernando's new bride, Germaine de Foix.[64] Subsequent officials chose to reside at the new site, creating further problems for the Spanish as early as 1513. As one witness reported:

> All of the citizens and others of the said island went to the said pueblo of San Germán, where the said *comendador* resided, to negotiate their suits and other concerns, and thus the said pueblo of Puerto Rico [Caparra], and her estates and *conucos* of the island were depopulated.... The caciques and Indians of the island, as well as the Caribs of the surrounding islands, seeing that all of the Christians had left the said pueblo of Puerto Rico and her estates, rose up and rebelled, and even worse they killed two citizens of the

said island, Garci Fernández and [Francisco] Mexía, who we, the officials of Your Highness, sent to retrieve the cacica doña Luysa, whom Your Highness had in encomienda... not to mention the other Christians that were killed seeking to recover Indians and particular people on the said island, and together with the said two Christians [Garci Fernández and Mexía] they killed the said cacica Luysa... and after all of this, the Caribs and Indians seeing that everyone had left [Caparra]... burned it.[65]

In addition to burning Caparra, indigenous people and their ostensible Carib allies roamed the surrounding countryside attacking Spanish estates.[66] Various punitive expeditions were organized not only against the caciques of Puerto Rico but also against neighboring islands in an effort to cut off the lifeline that sustained the insurgents.[67] The destruction of Caparra was a heavy blow to the already weakened Spanish presence on the island. In a matter of roughly two years, a second major Spanish settlement had been destroyed by native forces.

In addition to having to rebuild and fortify Caparra, the Spanish faced hunger as a result of the destruction of their cultivated plots. With no time to replant and harvest due to the constant threat of attack, hunger was widespread. In 1512 King Fernando, quickly recognizing the pressing nature of the problem, commanded his officials at the Casa de la Contratación to order ships going to the Indies to stop and sell food to the embattled men on Puerto Rico.[68] In 1514 a large hurricane struck the island, further damaging vital food stores.[69]

Broader Effects

With their full attention on the indigenous rebellion, the Spaniards in Puerto Rico were taken by surprise when around one hundred enslaved Africans on the island rose up in 1514. This rebellion is the first African uprising known to have taken place anywhere in the Indies.[70] The movement appears to have responded to the same factors that pushed the island's native inhabitants to violence: hunger and an abusive labor regime enforced by a limited number of Spaniards. The reasons for both the indigenous and African movements of resistance can be explained briefly. In 1514 the new *juez de residencia* Velásquez arrived.[71] Despite the ongoing native rebellion, Velásquez, following royal orders, reassigned the natives in yet another *repartimiento*. Fearful of losing their indigenous laborers to new assignments, Spanish proprietors worked the natives mercilessly. This action led to a severe decrease in the prescribed rest time of three months as stipulated in the 1512 Laws of Burgos. With a boom in gold mining and increased labor demands, the rest time allowed in 1514 barely reached a single month, with major implications for the daily lives of Indians who worked in the mines and the growing number of African slaves who worked alongside them.[72] Hungry, abused, and exhausted, it is of little wonder that both indigenous and African workers began to flee the gold mines en masse.

Juan Ponce de León returned from his expedition in 1514. In his absence viceroy Colón had pushed to have Caparra abandoned altogether and had commanded one of his own relatives to found a new village on the eastern coast. The new settlement was to serve as a buffer against potential attacks from the nearby islands.[73] Known as Santiago del Daguao, the site was soon abandoned by royal decree due to high costs. Colón further worked to undercut Ponce by proposing to make San Germán the island's new capital.[74] To make matters worse, Ponce discovered that some of the previously allied caciques had revolted in his absence.[75] With the state of Spanish settlement threatened once again, Fernando decided that the most effective means of ending the turbulence on Puerto Rico would be to outfit an armada against Caribs on the neighboring islands and, by so doing, cut off the lifeline that kept the revolt alive once and for all.[76] Fernando appointed Ponce as captain of the punitive armada. Bound for the Lesser Antilles, the fleet set sail from Spain on May 14, 1515.[77]

Although resistance against Spanish settlement continued, Ponce's armada marked the beginning of the end of indigenous resistance on the island itself as native lands were increasingly occupied by Spanish colonizers, noncompliant caciques enslaved or exiled, and native populations ravaged by hunger and disease.[78] Some left Puerto Rico for the neighboring Lesser Antilles to continue their resistance.[79] Thus Juan Ponce's armada represents a watershed moment in the revolt, signifying the Spaniards' success in gaining the upper hand in Puerto Rico and their consequent ability to move to and from the neighboring islands.

Conclusion

Agüeybaná II's revolt of 1510 in Puerto Rico was a critical moment in the evolution of Spanish policy regarding natives in the Caribbean. Spanish misunderstandings of the complex political and ethnic makeup of the early Caribbean and their need for indigenous labor, together with the actions of dissenting native groups in and around Puerto Rico, led the Spaniards to designate some Indians as Caribs, a term that came to signify any native who rebelled against Spanish efforts to establish dominion. This relabeling of certain groups in turn facilitated further conquest in Puerto Rico and the larger Caribbean.

Scholarship on the revolt scarcely mentions the integral part played by indigenous allies on both sides. The Spaniards' indigenous allies participated in many of the physical confrontations that would result in pacification of the rebel forces. The existence of groups willing to ally with the Spaniards was the result of a centuries-long interisland conflict on and around Puerto Rico, something the Spaniards barely understood yet unintentionally exacerbated. Rebels on the island drew allies from surrounding islands; the latter may have included distinct yet related cultural groups. The insurgents put up such formidable resistance that Spanish colonization of the island was limited for quite some time to only two major settlements, underscoring Puerto Rico's unique place in early Caribbean history as perhaps the most challenging efforts of conquest in the Greater Antilles. The documents demonstrate that the involvement of these extra island allies might have made the Spaniards aware, if only to a small degree, that the revolt was linked to a larger Caribbean context.

Notes

I would like to thank Efraín Barradas, Jeffrey D. Needell, and Ida Altman for their useful comments on the piece. While I recognize their input, I would stress that if there remain any imperfections, they are wholly mine. All translations from Spanish to English are mine other than citations of the English translation of Oviedo's work.

1. Critiques of the document focus on Juan González's claim that the initial expedition to the island under Juan Ponce de León was in 1506 and not 1508. In addition, the deposition was executed more than twenty years after the initial events on Puerto Rico. It is therefore likely that the account is either false, or much embellished. See TePaske, "Nuevas fuentes," 283–85.
2. Sued Badillo, *Agüeybaná el bravo*, 38. Also see Siegel, *Ancient Borinquen*, 345. On the importance of Spanish-indigenous alliances in New Spain, see Matthew and Oudijk, eds., *Indian Conquistadors*. On Spanish-indigenous alliances during the conquest of Hispaniola, see Wilson, *Hispaniola*. The end of the revolt by around 1517 did signal the end of indigenous resistance in Puerto Rico, whereas resistance continued much longer in Cuba and Hispaniola.
3. Murga Sanz, *Juan Ponce de León*, 25, 27.
4. Murga Sanz, *Historia documental*, 1:14. For a discussion on the natives of Higüey confirming rumors of gold on Puerto Rico see the work of the seventeenth-century Spanish chronicler Herrera y Tordesillas, *Historia general*, 3:113.
5. Murga Sanz, *Juan Ponce de León*, 34–35. Despite the original document outlining the agreement between Juan Ponce de León and Nicolás de Ovando being lost, mention of the transaction appears in Hernández, *Colección de documentos inéditos*, 34:358.
6. Conucos were agricultural fields that consisted of raised mounds known as *montones* planted with tubers and other root crops. See Rouse, *The Taínos*, 12.
7. Sued Badillo, *El Dorado borincano*, 41.
8. Sued Badillo, *La mujer indígena*, 14. Spaniards eventually generalized the term to denote all friendly natives, see Whitehead, *Of Cannibals and Kings*, 14. Also see Mira Caballos, *El indio antillano*, 263. On the ceremony of Guatiao see Herrera y Tordesillas, *Historia general*, 3:114.
9. Oviedo y Valdés, *The Conquest and Settlement*, 14.
10. Murga Sanz, *Juan Ponce de León*, 36.
11. Murga Sanz, *Historia documental*, Vol. 2, 520.
12. Sued Badillo, *Los caribes*, 38. For deeper discussion the mislabeling of Caribs, see Keegan, *Taíno Indian Myth*, 20.
13. Tió, *Nuevas fuentes*, 46. Also see Sued Badillo, *Los caribes*, 148.
14. Alvaro Huerga, *Ataques de los caribes*, 50.
15. Rouse, *The Taínos*, 6, 23. While Carib pottery has been discovered on St. Croix, it is believed that the island represented a raiding outpost for Carib attacks on Puerto Rico rather than one of the Carib-dominated islands. See Paquette and Engerman, *The Lesser Antilles*, 43, 45. The assertion that a distinctive ethnic group labeled as Caribs largely inhabited the Windward Islands is upheld generally by Keegan and Hofman, although they argue

that the Taíno versus Carib dichotomy greatly oversimplifies the Caribbean's ethnic diversity and interconnectedness. See Keegan and Hofman, *The Caribbean before Columbus*, 237–38.

16. Rouse, *The Taínos*, 155. Sued Badillo, *Los caribes*, 149.
17. Sued Badillo, *El Dorado borincano*, 61. Recent archaeological evidence upholds the historical accounts describing Puerto Rico as being split between competing native polities. Evidence also points to a greater number of caciques on the island compared to the larger island of Hispaniola. While politically splintered among various caciques, archaeologists do not yet know for certain whether the island lacked a higher level of political alignment in the form of cacicazgos despite the increased number of caciques. With a lack of conclusive evidence, I have relied upon the historical record, which clearly points to a high level of political integration based upon cacicazgos. For more information, see Keegan and Hofman, *The Caribbean before Columbus*, 112–13.
18. Sued Badillo, *Agüeybaná el bravo*, 37–38. Sued Badillo, *Los caribes*, 148. Archaeological evidence concerning the distribution, size, and uses of ceremonial ball courts on the island upholds the ethno-historical accounts of various indigenous polities on the island. See Rouse, *The Taínos*, 15, 115; Keegan and Hofman, *The Caribbean before Columbus*, 112.
19. Sued Badillo, *La mujer indígena*, 7–8. The existence of female rulers prior to the arrival of Europeans is disputed; see Moscoso, *Caguas*, 88–89, 101, 143–44.
20. Murga Sanz, *Juan Ponce de León*, 132.
21. José R. Oliver, *Caciques and Cemí Idols*, 78, 211.
22. Sued Badillo, *El Dorado borincano*, 144, 348, 477. Gold from the Antilles was often measured in peso units of 450 *maravedís* of 22½ karat purity which contained roughly 4.6009 grams of gold. For conversion rates, see Hoffman, *The Spanish Crown*, 254.
23. Sued Badillo, *El Dorado borincano*, 45, and Sued Badillo, *Agüeybaná el bravo*, 136. Gold recovered by Ponce and others sparked imperial interest and set off a mining boom on the island that would last for decades. Labor-intensive by nature, gold mining depended on a continual supply of indigenous laborers in the early period through the Spanish system of *repartimiento*. Spanish brutality and increasing labor demands accelerated the already rapid population decline from exposure to unfamiliar disease among the native groups on the island. See Giménez Fernández, *Bartolomé de Las Casas*, Vol. I, 126.
24. Murga Sanz, *Historia documental*, 1:xv.
25. Fernández Méndez, *Las encomiendas y esclavitud*, 6.
26. Murga Sanz, *Historia documental*, 1:xiv.

27. Alegría, ed., *Documentos históricos*, 1:71, 107.
28. Fernández Méndez, *Las encomiendas y esclavitud*, 6.
29. Oliver, *Caciques and Cemí Idols*, 201.
30. Sued Badillo, *El Dorado borincano*, 57.
31. Sued Badillo, *Agüeybaná el bravo*, 68.
32. Sued Badillo, *El Dorado borincano*, 58.
33. Sued Badillo, *El Dorado borincano*, 57.
34. Colón and Falcó y Osorio Alba, *Autógrafos de Cristóbal Colón*, 87.
35. Sued Badillo, *El Dorado borincano*, 62.
36. Alegría, ed., *Documentos históricos*, 1:149.
37. Murga Sanz, *Juan Ponce de León*, 63.
38. Sued Badillo, *El Dorado borincano*, 58.
39. Fernández Méndez, *Las encomiendas y esclavitud*, 16.
40. Alegría, *Documentos históricos*, 1:173; Murga Sanz, *Juan Ponce de León*, 48.
41. Fernández Méndez, *Las encomiendas y esclavitud*, 7.
42. Sued Badillo, *Los caribes*, 148.
43. Sued Badillo, *El Dorado borincano*, 62.
44. Oviedo y Valdés, *The Conquest and Settlement*, 23.
45. Oviedo y Valdés, *The Conquest and Settlement*, 23–24, Tió, *Nuevas fuentes*, 34.
46. Sued Badillo, *Agüeybaná el bravo*, 71–72n75, which details the date of Sotomayor's death from the probanza of his heir, Pedro de Sotomayor.
47. Oviedo y Valdés, *The Conquest and Settlement*, 19.
48. Fernández Méndez, *Las encomiendas y esclavitud*, 16.
49. Sued Badillo, *Los caribes*, 148.
50. Oviedo y Valdés, *The Conquest and Settlement*, 27.
51. Murga Sanz, *Historia documental*, 1:xxxiii–xxxiv. Although the use of the term *cristiano* during this early period generally referred to Spaniards, it more than likely included mestizos and Christianized Indians.
52. Oviedo y Valdés, *The Conquest and Settlement*, 42.
53. Huerga, *Ataques de los caribes*, 56.
54. Sued Badillo, *Los caribes*, 148.
55. Oliver, *Caciques and Cemí Idols*, 212.
56. Sued Badillo, *Agüeybaná el bravo*, 95.
57. Oviedo y Valdés, *The Conquest and Settlement*, 42.
58. Huerga, *Ataques de los caribes*, 167–69.
59. Alegría, ed., *Documentos históricos*, 1:251.
60. Sued Badillo, *Agüeybaná el bravo*, 136–37. This claim is further supported by the fact that when he returned to Hispaniola from his initial voyage to Puerto Rico in 1508, Ponce stopped on the island of Santa Cruz and enslaved some of the natives who he claimed were Caribs, only to be

forced by king Fernando (despite believing them to be cannibals) to return these natives to the island. After doing so, Ponce held the Indians in *repartimiento* between 1509 and 1510 with no instances of rebellion.

61. Murga Sanz, *Historia documental*, 1:xxxvii.
62. Murga Sanz, *Historia documental*, 1:xlii.
63. Alegría, ed., *Documentos históricos*, 1:405.
64. Fernández Méndez, *Las encomiendas y esclavitud*, 24.
65. Huerga, *Ataques de los caribes*, 60, 173–74.
66. Huerga, *Ataques de los caribes*, 58.
67. Sued Badillo, *Los caribes*, 152–53.
68. Vicente Murga Sanz, *Historia documental*, 3:143.
69. Sued Badillo and López Cantos, *Puerto Rico negro*, 175.
70. Sued Badillo and López Cantos, *Puerto Rico negro*, 175.
71. *Juez de residencia* was a royally appointed official who conducted the judicial review of a governing official at the conclusion of his term.
72. For details concerning the Laws of Burgos, see Fernández Méndez, *Las encomiendas y esclavitud*, 29. For the reduction of the allotted rest period in 1514 under Velásquez, see Sued Badillo and López Cantos, *Puerto Rico negro*, 176–78.
73. Huerga, *Ataques de los caribes*, 64–65. Oviedo y Valdés, *The Conquest and Settlement*, 52.
74. Huerga, *Ataques de los caribes*, 65.
75. Alegría, *Documentos históricos*, 1:607.
76. Huerga, *Ataques de los caribes*, 65–66.
77. Murga Sanz, *Juan Ponce de León*, 143, 148. Although some of the allied caciques had rebelled, others remained loyal and were thus continual targets for the rebel forces.
78. Sued Badillo, *Los caribes*, 154.
79. Sued Badillo, *Agüeybaná el bravo*, 137.

Bibliography

Alegría, Ricardo E., ed. *Documentos históricos de Puerto Rico*. 5 vols. San Juan: Centro de Estudios Avanzados de Puerto Rico y el Caribe, 2009.

Colón, Cristóbal, and María del Rosario Falcó y Osorio Alba. *Autógrafos de Cristóbal Colón y papeles de América: los publica la duquesa de Berwick y de Alba, condesa de Siruela*. Madrid: Estab. tip. "Sucesores de Rivandaneyra," 1892.

Fernández Méndez, Eugenio. *Las encomiendas y esclavitud de los indios de Puerto Rico, 1508–1550*. Sevilla: Escuela de Estudios Hispano-Americanos, 1966.

Giménez Fernández, Manuel. *Bartolomé de Las Casas*, vol. 1, *Delegado de Cisneros para la reformación de las Indias, 1516–1517*, no. 70. Seville: Escuela de Estudios Hispano-Americanos, 1953.

Hernández, Manuel G. *Colección de documentos inéditos, relativos al descubrimiento, conquista y organización de las antiguas posesiones españolas de América y Oceanía, sacados de los archivos del reino, y muy especialmente del de Indias.* Vol. 34. Madrid: Manuel G. Hernández, 1875.

Herrera y Tordesillas, Antonio de. *Historia general de los hechos de los castellanos en las islas y tierra firme del mar océano.* Vol. 3. Madrid: Academia de la Historia, 1935.

Hoffman, Paul E. *The Spanish Crown and the Defense of the Caribbean, 1535–1585: Precedent, Patrimonialism, and Royal Parsimony.* Baton Rouge: Louisiana State University Press, 1980.

Huerga, Alvaro. *Ataques de los caribes a Puerto Rico en el siglo XVI.* San Juan, PR: Academia Puertorriqueña de la Historia, 2006.

Keegan, William F. *Taíno Indian Myth and Practice: The Arrival of the Stranger King.* Gainesville: University Press of Florida, 2007.

Keegan, William F., and Corinne L. Hofman. *The Caribbean before Columbus.* New York: Oxford University Press, 2017.

Matthew, Laura E., and Michel R. Oudijk, eds. *Indian Conquistadors: Indigenous Allies in the Conquest of Mesoamerica.* Norman: University of Oklahoma Press, 2007.

Mira Caballos, Esteban. *El indio antillano: repartimiento, encomienda y esclavitud (1492–1542).* Seville: Muñoz Moya, 1997.

Moscoso, Francisco. *Caguas en la conquista española del siglo 16.* Río Piedras, PR: Publicaciones Gaviota, 2016 (rev. ed.).

Murga Sanz, Vicente. *Historia documental de Puerto Rico.* Vol. 1, *El concejo o cabildo de la ciudad de San Juan de Puerto Rico (1527–1550).* Río Piedras, PR: Editorial Plus Ultra, 1948.

———. *Historia documental de Puerto Rico.* Vol. 2, *El juicio de residencia, moderador democrático: juicio de residencia del licenciado Sancho Velázquez, juez de residencia y justicia mayor de la isla de San Juan (Puerto Rico), por el licenciado Antonio de la Gama (1519–1520).* Santander: Aldus, 1956.

———. *Historia documental de Puerto Rico.* Vol. 3, *Cedulario puertorriqueño, Tomo I (1505–1517).* Río Piedras: Universidad de Puerto Rico, 1961.

———. *Juan Ponce de León: fundador y primer gobernador del pueblo puertorriqueño, descubridor de la Florida y del estrecho de las Bahamas.* San Juan: Ediciones de la Universidad de Puerto Rico, 1959.

Oliver, José R. *Caciques and Cemí Idols: The Web Spun by Taíno Rulers between Hispaniola and Puerto Rico.* Tuscaloosa: University of Alabama Press, 2009.

Oviedo y Valdés, Gonzalo Fernández de. *The Conquest and Settlement of the Island of Boriquen or Puerto Rico.* Edited and translated by Daymond Turner. Avon CT: Printed for the members of the Limited Editions Club, 1975.

Paquette, Robert L., and Stanley L. Engerman, eds. *The Lesser Antilles in the Age of European Expansion*. Gainesville: University Press of Florida, 1996.
Rouse, Irving. *The Taínos: Rise and Decline of the People Who Greeted Columbus*. New Haven: Yale University Press, 1992.
Siegel, Peter E. *Ancient Borinquen: Archaeology and Ethnohistory of Native Puerto Rico*. Tuscaloosa: University of Alabama Press, 2005.
Sued Badillo, Jalil. *Agüeybaná el bravo: la recuperación de un símbolo*. San Juan, PR: Ediciones Puerto, 2008.
———. *Los caribes, realidad o fábula: ensayo de rectificación histórica*. Río Piedras, PR: Editorial Antillana, 1978.
———. *El Dorado borincano: la economía de la conquista, 1510–1550*. San Juan, PR: Ediciones Puerto, 2001.
———. *La mujer indígena y su sociedad*. Río Piedras, PR: Editorial El Gazir, 1975.
Sued Badillo, Jalil, and Angel López Cantos. *Puerto Rico negro*. Río Piedras, PR: Editorial Cultural, 1986.
TePaske, John J. "Nuevas fuentes para la historia de Puerto Rico: Book Review." *Hispanic American Historical Review* 43, no. 2 (May 1963): 283–85.
Tió, Aurelio. *Nuevas fuentes para la historia de Puerto Rico: documentos inéditos o poco conocidos cuyos originales se encuentran en el Archivo General de Indias en la ciudad de Sevilla, España*. San Germán: Ediciones de la Universidad Interamericana de Puerto Rico, 1961.
Whitehead, Neil, L. *Of Cannibals and Kings: Primal Anthropology in the Americas*. University Park: Pennsylvania State University Press, 2011.
Wilson, Samuel M. *Hispaniola: Caribbean Chiefdoms in the Age of Columbus*. Tuscaloosa: University of Alabama Press, 1990.

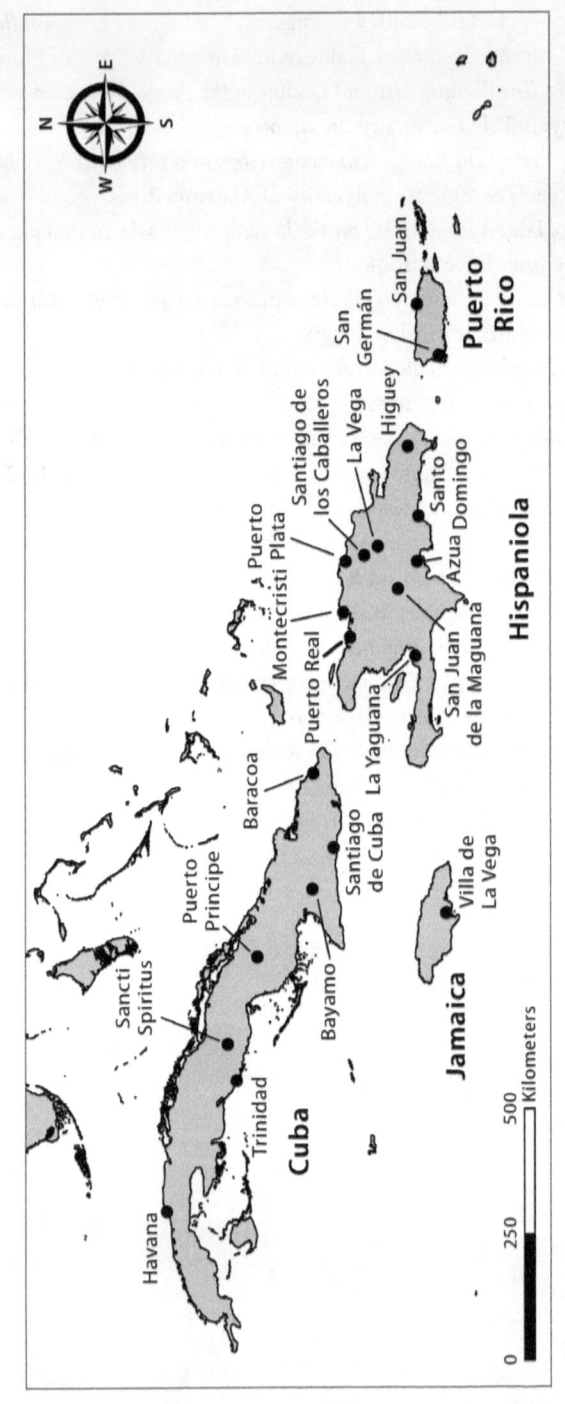

Map 2. The Greater Antilles: Selected Sites.

3

War and Rescate

The Sixteenth-Century Circum-Caribbean Indigenous Slave Trade

ERIN STONE

From the 1490s onward Spanish colonists, conquistadors, and merchants relied upon a circum-Caribbean Indian slave trade to supply them with laborers. Although the high mortality rate of indigenous Caribbean peoples over the subsequent decades is well known, the common assumption that Indian slavery was a limited and short-lived practice in colonial Spanish America, with African slavery replacing it in a matter of years, overlooks a key aspect of the first half of the sixteenth century. The early transatlantic slave trade from Africa to the Caribbean coincided with the explosive growth of the Indian slave trade, not its conclusion. The two trades coexisted for several decades, with indigenous slaves outnumbering enslaved Africans in some areas as late as the mid-sixteenth century. Indians did not simply die of disease; many thousands were first enslaved and displaced across the Spanish Empire.

From 1503 until 1542 the circum-Caribbean indigenous slave trade fluctuated as Europeans captured and removed thousands of Indians from their homelands. These slave trafficking surges were responses to local conditions and to the shifting frontiers of the growing empire. As initial conquest enterprises, from the pearl fisheries of Cubagua to the gold mines of Hispaniola, began to decrease in profitability, colonists looked for new opportunities, one of them being the capture and sale of indigenous slaves. While the profits made from Indian slaves were often minimal, the capturing of these slaves was usually connected to other endeavors such as the exploration of new territories. As Spanish expeditions searched the islands and mainland of the New World, many of the lands they encountered, including locations like central Mexico,

Yucatan, and present-day Nicaragua and Honduras, served as temporary centers of the Indian slave trade. In many instances Spanish attempts to conquer nonsubmissive indigenous populations provided the legal rationale to take Indian captives.

This essay outlines and examines the indigenous slave trade both as a unique system and as an important institution within the developing Spanish Empire. From Christopher Columbus in the 1490s to the German conquistadors of the 1530s and beyond, European explorers, raiders, and colonizers enslaved thousands of Indians. Within early Spanish American economies, the Indian slave trade rapidly became a business that generated profits for both slavers and officials. The crown even paid some administrators, including religious officials, with slave licenses, or authorizations to capture Indians.[1] The victims of the circum-Caribbean slave trade were often relocated to sites quite distant from their places of origin. Enslaved Indians would help Spanish colonists exploit the pearl beds of Cubagua and establish new settlements in Peru. Others were sent to the islands of Hispaniola, Cuba, and Puerto Rico or as far away as Spain. Enslaved and displaced, indigenous peoples became plantation workers, military auxiliaries, guides, miners, pearl divers, servants, and, in the case of women, unwilling sexual partners. In short, an extensive traffic in Indian slaves played a key role in helping to propel and shape the early Spanish Atlantic.

A Sketch of the Legal Indigenous Slave Trade to 1542

Beginning with Columbus's second voyage to Hispaniola and the ensuing enslavement of Taínos there in 1493, the Indian slave trade evolved in tandem with legal justifications for taking Indians as slaves.[2] The Spanish initially justified this through the doctrine of "just war."[3] Then in 1503 the crown made it legal to enslave "Caribs"—meaning resistant Indians—and designated the coastline of Colombia and Panama as "Carib" territories.[4] In 1508 it became legal to enslave Indians living in "useless" islands, essentially meaning those lacking gold.[5] Additionally, Indians who resisted relocation or *encomenderos'* demands could be declared slaves and legally sold.[6] Following a major indigenous rebellion on Puerto Rico in 1511, in which Indians from the Lesser Antilles were also implicated, the crown issued a decree that associated "Caribs" with cannibalism and expanded the definition of "Carib" lands to include most of the Lesser Antilles.[7] In addition to the mechanisms of "just war" and the designation of targeted groups as "Caribs," the Spanish obtained indigenous slaves through *rescate*, which meant purchasing or bartering for Indian captives previously held in bondage by an indigenous group. In addition to voluntary trade, *rescate* could also involve coercion or the threat of violence.[8] Loopholes in Spanish law, the American territories' distance from the crown, and Spanish officials' general ambivalence ensured that unauthorized and legally ambiguous slaving raids, accompanied by contraband slave trafficking, existed alongside these legally sanctioned means of capturing and selling indigenous slaves.[9]

At times the taking and enslaving of indigenous peoples yielded financial benefits for both the crown and for slave merchants. As with other slaves, and as with most types of merchandise that exchanged hands in the Spanish Americas, royal taxes were typically levied on the sale of Indian captives. Exceptions to this general rule—for example, after the 1511 revolt in Puerto Rico, when profits made from the sale of slaves were not subject to the royal fifth—were relatively rare.[10] In this particular instance, the crown's decree may have also served as recognition of the limited gains made by most slave traders, since Indian slaves usually sold for low prices. Very few Indian slaves sold for more than 10 or 12 gold pesos, an exception being Lucayos (Bahamas) Indians in the pearl fisheries. The value of Lucayos Indians soared to between 50 and 150 pesos as the Spanish recognized their ability to dive for pearls.[11]

In general, though, most slavers used the meager profit made from the selling of Indian slaves to supplement their other incomes. One such trader was Lucas Vázquez de Ayllón, one of the most prolific slavers in the early Caribbean. Of the slaves taken on the multiple expeditions that he supported, many were put to work on his properties in Hispaniola: a large sugar mill near Puerto Plata, a smaller mill near Azua, and some mines close to Concepción de la Vega.[12] He sold other captives but at such low rates (most for four pesos or less) that his profits came from the minimal investment he put into their capture and sale.[13] On one slaving venture Ayllón and his cohorts, Pedro de Quejo and Francisco Gordillo, captured at least nine hundred Indians, half of whom died in pens in the Lucayos Islands while awaiting an additional ship for their voyage to Hispaniola, where they would be sold.[14] During the 1510s the Spaniards viewed the supply of Indians in the Caribbean islands as practically inexhaustible. Although the decreasing availability of enslaved Indians would eventually cause their sale prices to rise, they never approached the prices of African slaves.

While African and Indian slaves often worked and lived together in the Caribbean, Spanish colonists viewed them distinctly. In 1532 the residents of Cuba threatened to stop mining gold if they were required to continue paying the *quinto* on gold mined by Indians. They agreed to pay the royal fifth, however, on all gold mined by their African slaves.[15] Colonists also were probably willing to pay more for the return of their runaway African slaves than for their indigenous slaves. As early as 1518 the royal treasurer of Hispaniola, Gil González Dávila, wrote to the crown of the need for a *recogedor*, or slave catcher.[16] If rewards for apprehending maroons in Hispaniola resembled those of New Spain during the sixteenth century, prices paid for the recapture of enslaved Africans would have been considerably more substantial than those for indigenous slaves. In 1527 Mexico City recogedores were reimbursed all costs incurred in finding the slaves, plus five gold pesos for each African slave, half a peso for each Indian slave, and one gold peso for each head of livestock.[17] Spanish colonists appear to have viewed Indian slaves not only as less valuable than enslaved Africans but as even less valuable than livestock.

Trading Indians for Livestock in Pánuco

The circum-Caribbean indigenous slave trade existed in one form or another starting in 1493, but Spanish encounters with previously unknown Indian populations frequently brought upsurges in the slave trade to and within the region. From January 1521 until May 1522, a few months before and immediately after the fall of Tenochtitlan, the seat of the Mexica Empire, Hernando Cortés and his fellow conquistadors registered and paid taxes on nearly eight thousand indigenous slaves.[18] While some of these captives would serve colonists in New Spain, many others were shipped to the Caribbean Islands. As Spanish expeditions of attempted conquest spread to areas south and west of Tenochtitlan, thousands of additional captives would be shipped from present-day Guatemala, Honduras, Nicaragua, and Mexico.[19]

The controversial shipping of thousands of indigenous slaves from Pánuco, a region northeast of Mexico City, to the islands responded to conditions in both New Spain and the Caribbean. Some captives were exchanged for livestock, especially cattle and mares, which had proliferated in Hispaniola, underscoring the close connections between the islands and the neighboring mainland.[20] Nuño de Guzmán arrived in New Spain to take up the governorship of Pánuco in May 1527 after an illness that had detained him in Hispaniola for several months. Although some slaves had been taken in Pánuco and sent to central Mexico before he arrived, the volume, pace, and direction of the trade accelerated considerably during his governorship, notwithstanding a royal prohibition on the export of captives outside of Mexico.[21]

In 1529 the bishop of Mexico, fray Juan de Zumárraga, sued Guzmán, who by then was president of the first audiencia of New Spain as well as governor of Pánuco, and another audiencia judge for continuing to grant licenses to enslave captives in Pánuco after the royal prohibition of 1526.[22] Guzmán had begun to issue slaving licenses to the residents of Pánuco's only Spanish town, Santisteban, soon after his arrival in Mexico the following year. These licenses provided authorization to participate in an *entrada* into the interior of the province and take between twenty and thirty Chichimec Indians as slaves; higher-ranking members of Pánuco society received licenses to take much larger numbers of captives. The ostensible rationale for the entrada—which lasted four to five months, and resulted in the capture of hundreds of Indian slaves—was to retaliate against previous Chichimecs raids that had resulted in the death of several Spaniards. Although the entrada had been legitimized through the doctrine of "just war," observers later claimed that most of the captives taken during the expedition had in fact been acquired through rescate. Witnesses testified that Nuño de Guzmán took any slaves held or offered by caciques that he encountered during the entrada. While these individuals could be legally traded according to Spanish law if they were slaves, per indigenous social structures, the Spanish criteria for determining when an Indian was a legal slave were ambiguous. This meant that various Spanish factions often disagreed over individual cases. For example, many Spaniards opposed the taking of Indians who had just been enslaved by indigenous leaders hoping to take advantage of the Spanish presence. In the case of Guzmán's entrada, some witnesses claimed that many caciques presented free Indians belonging to enemy groups as slaves to the Spanish. One young female Indian captive acquired through rescate in such fashion had only accepted the mark of a slave under the threat of death. Although the Spaniard Lope de Saavedra told Guzmán that he had known the girl as a free person, this testimony did not help her. Despite her former status, she was sent to the Caribbean islands alongside other indigenous slaves.[23]

Public inspections and interviews prior to the branding of slaves should have revealed any Indians who had been wrongly (or at least questionably) enslaved. However, the inspection and branding were largely handled by Guzmán or his mayordomo Pérez de Gijón, both of whom were accused of accepting bribes and ignoring testimony that contradicted enslavement.[24] Once captives were declared to have been legally enslaved, Indians would be branded on the left side of their faces with either the letter R (standing for either *real marca* [royal mark] or *rescate*) or G (for *guerra*, or war).[25]

In the wake of the entradas at least fifteen ships (the witness Saavedra put the number as high as twenty-one) sailed from Santisteban to Hispaniola, Cuba, or Puerto Rico with indigenous slaves.[26] Two merchants who transported captives on these vessels were allegedly authorized by Guzmán to embark as many as 1,000 captives each.[27] Others carried between 100 and 400 slaves. But the shipping of indigenous slaves did not end in 1528. As late as April 1529, only a few months prior to the start of the investigation into Guzmán's activities, several more ships laden with indigenous slaves departed Santisteban for Santo Domingo. Among them, Juan de Urrutia's craft sailed with 800 souls aboard. One witness, Juan Pardo, was surprised to see that nearly half the slaves on Urrutia's vessel survived the journey to Santo Domingo.[28]

Table 1. Slaves taken from Santiesteban in 1528–1529

DATE	SLAVERS	ESTIMATED NUMBER OF INDIANS TRANSPORTED
1528	Guzmán removes slaves from Pánuco encomiendas	At least 70 Indian slaves exchanged for livestock in Hispaniola
	Guzmán ships Chichimecs captured in "just war"	300 Indian slaves to Cuba
	Miguel de Ibarra	1,000 Indian slaves
	Juan de Urrutia	1,000 Indian slaves
	Alonso Valiente	400 Indian slaves
	Juan de Cordero	120 Indian slaves
	Licenciado Zuazo	200 Indian slaves
	Cristóbal de Bezos	400 Indian slaves
	Quintero	250 Indian slaves
	Duero	200 Indian slaves
	Comacho	350 Indian slaves
		4,290 total (1528)
April 1529	Alonso Valiente	150 Indian slaves
	Pedro de Mina	300 Indian slaves
	Miguel de Ibarra	300 Indian slaves
	Juan Pérez de Gijón	330 Indian slaves to Santo Domingo
	Juan de Urrutia	800 Indian slaves
		1,880 total (April 1529)
		6,170 total (combined)

Source: AGI-Patr 231, N.4, R.1 and R.2; Chipman, "The Traffic in Indian Slaves," 150. These numbers are higher than those provided by Chipman for reasons discussed in the text.

By the end of his term in Pánuco Guzmán was accused of facilitating the enslavement and transportation of up to 12,000 Indians, many of whom were at the very least questionably enslaved. Bishop Juan de

Zumárraga estimated that by 1529, and the start of Guzmán's trial, nearly 9,000 Indians had been enslaved and removed from his jurisdiction.[29] In fact, only 300 were taken in actual combat or "just war," according to witness Lope de Saavedra. Some witnesses stated that as a result of the entradas carried out by Guzmán, there were no longer any indigenous people left to enslave in the province; any remaining Indians were fleeing to the mountains in fear.[30] Meanwhile, if all of the Indian captives had been exchanged for livestock, this would have resulted in an enormous influx of cattle and horses to the region.

One of the central problems with the study of the early indigenous slave trade is determining accurate numbers. First, incomplete documentation presents a significant obstacle. In this instance, there is an eight-month gap in the registries of ships departing from Santisteban, for which we can only estimate the number of slaves and vessels that may have set sail for the Caribbean islands.[31] Second, the witnesses who accused Guzmán of transporting enslaved Indians from New Spain to the Caribbean provided a variety of estimates for the total number of captives exported, ranging from as low as 3,441 to as high as 12,000. One should consider why different witnesses and royal officials would minimize or exaggerate Guzmán's actions. Clearly many, including the vocal witness Saavedra, had personal reasons to attack Guzmán. Guzmán's appointment as governor of Pánuco took power from Cortés and his associates in Mexico City. Pánuco was a stronghold for pro-Cortés sentiment, and the arrival of a new, crown-appointed governor threatened the region's elite, many of whom depended on personal favors from Cortés.[32] This group included the official Lope de Saavedra, who was arrested for mismanaging the estates of deceased persons and lost his encomienda (granted to him by Cortés) only days after Guzmán took power in Pánuco.[33] Possibly some witnesses inflated the numbers of slaves taken in order to hurt and delegitimize Guzmán. In any case it is clear that the indigenous slave trade thrived for a brief period in Pánuco and that the trade produced an influx of livestock into the area including mules, horses, cattle, sheep, goats, and swine.[34] It also produced a surge of indigenous slaves for Cuba in particular, as governor Manuel de Rojas mentioned the arrangement five years later, in 1534.[35] This experience also may have inspired Guzmán's later slave raiding during his conquest and exploration of Nueva Galicia.[36]

The Search for El Dorado or an Excuse to Capture Indian Slaves?

By the 1530s, as European expeditions moved beyond the coastline and into the interior of the South American continent, different Spanish factions competed for access to indigenous slaves. During this period, a series of jurisdictional disputes erupted between colonists residing in the Pearl Islands and slavers from Hispaniola and Cuba, largely over the question of who had the right to take Indians from the southern Caribbean mainland, known to contemporaries as Tierra Firme. In addition to intracolonial disputes over the circum-Caribbean slave trade, these episodes reveal the crown's efforts to control and at times limit the trade. Most notably, a royal provision passed in August 1530 abolished all forms of indigenous enslavement in the islands and coast of Tierra Firme, including "just war."[37]

The new legislation ended an earlier policy that had permitted the capture and enslavement of Carib Indians in the region for nearly three decades beginning in 1503. While the policy had attempted to regulate and limit the slave trade in Tierra Firme, the ambiguous nature of the term *Carib* provided the legal basis for an explosion of slave raiding along the coast in the 1510s and 1520s.[38] For European colonists in Tierra Firme, the change in 1530 was unwelcome. Just a few weeks before the crown's decree, Antonio de Alfinger, the German governor of Venezuela, had described the province as poor and possessing only one resource: indigenous slaves. (This observation was offered as an explanation for his recent capture of 107 Indians whom he then sold in Hispaniola without paying the *quinto* to the crown; he promised to send the royal fifth at the first chance he got in the form of either slaves or gold.)[39] Spanish colonists immediately protested the new law and solicited its abolishment. López de Archuleta, a judge in Nueva Cádiz (Cubagua), went so far as to refuse to publish the new legislation.[40] And Archuleta was not the only official to ignore it. Many of Cubagua's elite continued to grant licenses for rescate and to attack recalcitrant Indians for the purpose of capturing slaves. Pedro Ortiz de Matienzo, alcalde mayor of Cubagua, issued a license permitting Andrés de Villacorta and Hernández Riberos to pacify the Indians of Cumaná in March 1531. The conquistadors would receive payment for their efforts in the form of Indian slaves acquired during the expedition. Villacorta captured at least 500 Indians and branded them as slaves, and sold 300 in Hispaniola and Puerto Rico.[41] While most illegal slaving voyages probably went unpunished or even unquestioned by Spanish authorities in the Caribbean, some of the most prolific slave traders did face legal repercussions.

One such group were the German conquistadors of Venezuela, who launched several expeditions of exploration into the interior. Upon first arriving in Venezuela, they sought the indigenous population's support and refrained from engaging in slave raiding.[42] The crown contributed to this endeavor by passing legislation in 1528 that attempted to curtail the transport of enslaved Indians away from the province of Venezuela; furthermore, all Indians captured by the Germans were to be employed within the province of Venezuela.[43] Conquistador Nicolás Féderman was harshly censured for his notorious abuse of indigenous people during his 1530 entrada. From each settlement he encountered during his seven-month expedition, Féderman took nearly 100 Indians to serve as porters and guides. When principal Indians or caciques failed to supply guides willingly, or fled and hid from his approaching force, he captured as many Indians as he could. He especially favored the detention of caciques' female relatives.[44] Féderman considered them to be permanent slaves and divided them up among his men to serve them during their journey. If they survived the expedition, their sale would supplement the soldiers' salaries.[45]

Toward the end of Féderman's entrada, which failed to discover any indigenous civilization of great wealth, his actions became even more violent. Following an altercation and battle with the Indians of the towns Paraguana and Tocayo (located southwest of Coro on Lake Maracaibo), all of the "rebel" Indians fled to a series of small islands located in the center of the lake. These Indians were described by the Spanish of Coro as "rancheados," meaning they were isolated in these small camps or "ranchos" away from their homes and villages. They could not leave the islands or they would be enslaved. With the Indians isolated on the islands, Féderman's expedition freely looted their villages and settlements, taking all the gold and other trade goods they could locate. These actions destabilized the entire province, spurring many indigenous groups to rebel against the Spanish.[46]

Immediately following his return to Coro, Féderman's cruelties were publicly denounced, and he was exiled from the province for four years. At the same time the crown issued a new royal order again prohibiting the removal of any Indians from Venezuela, even on exploratory missions into the interior of the continent.[47] Additionally, a new policy made it illegal to take the Indians from the town of Paraguana as slaves. These Indians, known as Caquetíos in contrast to their "Carib" neighbors, received this special consideration as *indios amigos*, Spanish allies and friends. The Caquetíos then participated in Spanish, and later German, slave raids against other Indians designated as Caribs.[48] Thus, while the Spanish crown tried to protect at least some of the Indians of Tierra Firme, Spanish and German colonists in Venezuela continued to argue that they depended upon the servitude of these Indians, especially when undertaking entradas into the interior. A local slave trade remained in effect.[49]

Within a matter of years, the German conquistadors began to turn to slaving as one of their only means of making a profit. As entrada after entrada failed to locate the fabled wealth of another Inca Empire, the explorers and would-be conquistadors of Nueva Granada (Colombia), Venezuela, and Trinidad found themselves desperate to make even a small profit out of their ventures. But they did find consolation prizes in the indigenous slave trade. Although their entradas failed, they could still sell the guides and porters they had acquired or captured along the way. To compensate for small numbers of Indian slaves who typically remained at the conclusion of lengthy entradas due to the very high death rates suffered by Indians and Spaniards alike, they often captured as many Indians as possible as they approached Spanish settlements like Coro or Santa Marta.[50]

After Féderman's first entrada, the governor, Antonio de Alfinger, embarked on his second expedition into the interior of the province, a journey that would last two and a half years (from June 1531 to November 1533) and end in the conquistador's death. It is also in this particular venture that the practice of taking Indian slaves to supplement soldiers' meager salaries or to turn a profit from an otherwise unsuccessful expedition appeared. Upon reaching Maracaibo, Alfinger captured and branded Indian slaves, arranging for 222 captives to be transported to Santo Domingo for sale. Over the course of the expedition, despite crown policy prohibiting the removal of Indian slaves from Venezuela, Alfinger's men continued to take captives, later branding and selling them in Santo Domingo and Jamaica. In 1533 González de Leiva, the same man who shipped 222 slaves to Hispaniola on Alfinger's behalf, sold an additional 65 Indians in Jamaica. Leiva was ultimately punished for failing to pay royal taxes on the sale of these illegally acquired slaves.[51]

Other larger shipments of Indian slaves taken during Alfinger's entrada began arriving in Santo Domingo by April 1534, only a few months after its conclusion. The Protector of the Indians himself, Bishop Bastidas, wrote to the crown from Santo Domingo reporting the arrival of many Indian slaves from the "government of the Belzares" (Welsers).[52] Alfinger had assaulted and sequestered Indian villages in order to acquire both slaves and gold.[53] For example, after attacking a group called the Pacabueyes, Alfinger constructed a corral in the town of Tamara where he imprisoned up to 200 local Indians, depriving them of all water and food until their relatives ransomed their release at a hefty price of slaves and gold.[54]

The first entradas of Alfinger and Féderman destabilized the interior of Venezuela and extended into Nueva Granada; a series of entradas in the mid-1530s placed even greater pressure on indigenous populations. Among these expeditions were the double-pronged entrada conducted by Nicolás Féderman and Georg Hohermuth von Speyer (Jorge Espira) from 1535 until 1539, the venture of Gonzalo Jiménez de Quesada from April 1536 to early 1539 deep into Muisca territory, and the rival missions of Antonio Sedeño and Gerónimo de Ortal in 1535–36 into Paria and Meta. Although these entradas met with varying degrees of success, all of them covered vast amounts of territory, encountered diverse indigenous groups, and enslaved hundreds of indigenous peoples.[55] Even Quesada, whose lucrative expedition encountered stores of emeralds in the

Muisca capital of Tunja, briefly engaged in the enslavement of Indians to serve as payment for his soldiers.[56] The competing claims of participants in these various expeditions and legal challenges against them mounted by other colonists and the crown filled colonial courts with litigation regarding the capture of indigenous slaves. An excellent example is the case brought against conquistador Gerónimo Ortal by a group of Cubaguan officials from 1535 to 1537. At the center of the dispute was the taking and enslaving of hundreds of Indians in the province and gulf of Paria.[57] Central to the debate was the question of who possessed legal jurisdiction over the region's indigenous population.

In February 1536 the *factor* (royal agent) of Nueva Cádiz, Alonso Díaz de Gibraleón, wrote to the crown reporting the seizure of Ortal's vessel and its cargo of indigenous slaves.[58] Here the factor reminded the king of the ordinances forbidding any person from taking Indians from the Pearl Islands or the adjacent coastline without license from the city of Nueva Cádiz. These laws ensured that the residents of Cubagua controlled the trade of Indian slaves along the coast of Tierra Firme. They also limited the capture of Indians to those taken during "just war" or to hostile (Carib) Indians. Among the Indians who were *not* considered to be hostile, and therefore could not legally be enslaved, were those inhabiting the coast of Tierra Firme from Maracapana to Enmanagoia.

Yet Ortal had engaged in slave raiding in the interior of this territory. Ortal and his men had entered the province of Cumanagoto via the territory of Paria, supposedly in search of El Dorado. However, it seems that their real purpose was to capture indigenous slaves, which Ortal did not possess a license to do.[59] Therefore, when a ship laden with slaves belonging to Ortal anchored in the Cubaguan port of Nueva Cádiz, local officials took control of the 100 Indians onboard and began a lengthy process to determine if any had been legally enslaved.

Ortal's testimony reveals that he was not the only Spaniard executing slave raids in Paria at the time. In the province of Meta (100 leagues into the interior of Venezuela), his men encountered a competing entrada led by Antonio Sedeño, the governor of Trinidad. With financial and legal backing from the Audiencia of Santo Domingo, Sedeño led up to 600 men, making his expedition much larger than that of Ortal (who only possessed 200 soldiers). Sedeño's entrada succeeded in capturing close to 400 Indians in the provinces of Cumanagoto and Neveri, whom he then transported to Puerto Rico. After several weeks, both slaving parties left the formerly peaceful province barren and largely depopulated, or so it was reported by the Cubaguans.[60] They also claimed that Sedeño and Ortal burned entire villages to the ground and turned the province into a war zone.[61]

Regardless of the atrocities supposedly committed by Ortal and Sedeño, the court decided that the slaves taken by Ortal were legal. This ruling ignored testimony presented at the trial that described the Indians of Cumanagoto, Paria, and the River Huyaporia as allies of the Spanish. Despite the discourse censoring the capture of Indians, especially those allied with the Spanish, the allure of profit from their sale superseded both political strategy and any moral impulses. After the verdict, the surviving 34 Indians were sold in public on November 14, 1536, for anywhere between 5 and 12 pesos, depending upon their sex and age. Males and mature slaves fetched the highest prices, from 8 to 15 pesos. Resident Francisco de Milan paid the most for an adult male slave, 15 pesos.[62] At least half of the Indian slaves were referred to as "piezas" (pieces or units), further demonstrating their commodification.[63]

The entradas of Ortal and Sedeño were only the tip of the iceberg; dozens of other Spaniards (and some Germans) engaged in legal and illegal slaving raids. By late 1538 multiple officials reported to the Spanish crown that there were no Indians from which to create repartimientos in the entire province of Venezuela.[64] While precise numbers remain elusive, the amount of illegal slaving documented by Spanish officials provides some idea of the extent of this circum-Caribbean slave trade and the untold suffering, chaos, and violence that resulted in the depopulation of huge swaths of territory.

Indian Slavery Moves to the Edges of Empire

After years of debate, pressure from religious leaders, and a visible decline in the indigenous population of the Americas, Charles V promulgated legislation known as the "New Laws" in November 1542.[65] The laws reduced the prerogatives of powerful encomenderos and outlawed Indian slavery. Although it would take decades, and even centuries in some isolated areas along the frontiers of the Spanish Empire, the New Laws marked the end of the widespread and legal Indian slave trade in the Caribbean.

By this point African slaves outnumbered Indian slaves in some colonies. The expansion of the African slave trade had been facilitated, in part, by opposition to the Indian slave trade just a quarter century earlier. In an attempt to reform the relationship between the indigenous inhabitants and colonists of the New World, Cardinal Cisneros had sent a group of three Hieronymite friars to investigate and govern the growing Spanish Empire in 1517.[66] After interviewing many residents and observing the conditions of the indigenous peoples in the Americas, they made several policy changes. First, they outlawed the Indian slave trade to the coast of Tierra Firme.[67] Next, they began to advocate the importation of thousands of African slaves to take the place of Indian workers. The Hieronymites preferred African slaves for several reasons, including their immunity to many of the diseases that struck down the indigenous populations and their ostensible suitability for sugar cultivation.[68] Following the petitions and directives of the Hieronymite friars in 1518, the crown issued the first large licenses to transport African slaves to the Americas.[69]

As more African slaves arrived in the Caribbean, they worked and lived with indigenous residents, both enslaved and free. For example, in 1522 the judge Alonso de Zuazo reported that 120 African slaves and 10 Indian slaves worked on his various properties.[70] A 1530 census of Hispaniola's nineteen sugar ingenios identified nearly 2,000 African slaves and 200 Indian slaves. It also recorded 700 "other" laborers who might have been Indian slaves, perhaps acquired through less scrupulous ways, or individuals of mixed ancestry. Either way, colonists may have underreported the number of Indian slaves they possessed. Although it contrasts dramatically with other Hispaniola population estimates for that period, one assessment of the island's population in 1545 mentioned 5,000 Indian slaves and fewer than 4,000 African slaves.[71]

By the late sixteenth century, as the availability of African slaves increased, the risks involved in the now illegal indigenous slave trade proved to be too high, especially since profits from sales were often very low. Spanish colonists and merchants did not give up the Indian slave trade without a fight, however. The 5,000 Indian slaves that may have been working on the island of Hispaniola in 1545 could have still been considered legally enslaved if they had been identified as Caribs.[72] Indeed, complaining about enslaved Africans' high prices—which reached 350 gold pesos by the 1560s—residents of the island occasionally sought permission to buy enslaved "Caribs" from the Portuguese territory of Brazil, who were priced at 12 gold pesos each.[73]

Regardless of a few officials' efforts to prolong the circum-Caribbean Indian slave trade, by the early seventeenth century Indian slavery was in decline.[74] Yet as African slavery increased and Spanish enslavement of Indians waned, Indian slavery in the Americas did not disappear altogether; rather it moved to the edges of the Spanish Empire and to newer colonies established by northern Europeans, where it continued to flourish.[75] Viewed in this pan-American context, the Indian slave trade was not a short-lived or unsuccessful practice quickly replaced by African slavery. Instead, Iberian colonists' enslavement of Indians in the sixteenth-century Caribbean set a precedent that for long afterward continued to shape the evolving Atlantic World.

Notes

ABBREVIATIONS

AGI	Archivo General de Indias
	-Caracas Gobierno: Audiencia de Caracas
	-IG Gobierno: Indiferente General
	-Just Justicia
	-Patr Patronato Real
	-SD Gobierno: Audiencia de Santo Domingo

1. Otte, *Las perlas*, 216–17.
2. The first shipment of slaves arrived in Spain in February 1494. "Memorial que para los Reyes Católicos dio el Almirante Don Cristóbal Colón" (30 January 1494), transcribed in Varela, *Cristóbal Colón*, 259–61. See also Keegan, *Taíno Indian Myth*; Sauer, *The Early Spanish Main*; Deagan and Cruxent, *Archaeology at La Isabela*; Guitar, "What Really Happened."
3. van Deusen, *Global Indios*, 3–4; Rushforth, *Bonds of Alliance*, 92.
4. AGI-IG 418, L.1, fols. 116r–116v, Cedula Real (1503); Deive, *La Española y la esclavitud*, 72.

5. Guitar, "Cultural Genesis," 127; Otte, *Las perlas*, 103.
6. Deive, *La Española y la esclavitud*, 92; "El Rey al Almirante" (14 August 1509), transcribed in Marte, *Santo Domingo en los manuscritos*, 45.
7. AGI-IG 418, L.3, fol. 91r, "Licencia para hacer guerra a los caribes" (24 December 1511); Whitehead, *Of Cannibals*, 12. On the 1511 revolt and its repercussions, see Cacey Farnsworth's chapter in this volume.
8. Sauer, *The Early Spanish Main*, 85.
9. Van Deusen, *Global Indios*, 5.
10. "Carta de Don Fernando" (22 February 1512), in Marte, *Santo Domingo en los manuscritos*, 102.
11. Otte, *Las perlas*, 116. See also Warsh, "Enslaved Pearl Divers"; Perri, "Ruined and Lost." Likewise in 1530 the crown gave residents of Hispaniola a reprieve from paying the royal *diezmo* on indigenous slaves purchased from New Spain or Santa Marta; see AGI-SD 118, R.1, N.17, Carta de los oficiales reales de Cuba (23 November 1530), fol. 1r.
12. Quattlebaum, *The Land Called Chicora*, 7; Hoffman, *A New Andalucía*, 15, 40.
13. Keegan, *The People Who Discovered Columbus*, 221.
14. Hoffman, *A New Andalucía*, 5, 44.
15. AGI-SD 118, R.1, N.22, Carta de los oficiales reales de Cuba (9 July 1532), fol. 2v.
16. "Relación de Gil González Dávila" (1518), in *Colección de documentos inéditos*, 1: 342–44.
17. Zavala, *Los esclavos indios*, 9.
18. Reséndez, *The Other Slavery*, 62.
19. Sherman, *Forced Native Labor*, 22–32; Altman, *War for Mexico's West*, 20–56; Restall and Asselbergs, *Invading Guatemala*, 10–12; Newson, *The Cost of Conquest*, 97–110; Radell, "The Indian Slave Trade," 68–75.
20. AGI-Patr 231, N.4, R.1, fols. 3r–3v and R.2, fol. 9r.
21. Chipman, *Nuno de Guzman*, 200; Chipman, "The Traffic in Indian Slaves," 144.
22. AGI-Patr 231, N.4, R.1 (5 July 1529), fol. 1r.
23. Chipman, *Nuno de Guzman*, 157; AGI-Patr 231, N.4, R.1, fol. 10v.
24. Chipman, "The Traffic in Indian Slaves," 149.
25. Chipman, *Nuno de Guzman*, 208; Sherman, *Forced Native Labor*, 66.
26. AGI-Patr 231, N.4, R.1, fols. 6v, 9v; Chipman, "The Traffic in Indian Slaves," 150.
27. AGI-Patr 231, N.4, R.1, fol. 3v.
28. AGI-Patr 231, N.4, R.1, fols. 13r, 14r–14v.
29. Chipman, "The Traffic in Indian Slaves," 144, 150.
30. AGI-Patr 231, N.4, R.1, fols. 4r, 6v–7r, 10v.
31. Chipman, "The Traffic in Indian Slaves," 150.
32. Adorno and Pautz, *The Narrative of Cabeza de Vaca*, 9; Chipman, *Nuno de Guzman*, 144–45.

33. Chipman, *Nuno de Guzman*, 165.
34. Chipman, "The Traffic in Indian Slaves," 151.
35. AGI-SD 77, R.4, N.50, Carta de Manuel de Rojas (10 November 1534), fol. 579r.
36. Altman, *The War for Mexico's West*, 42–52.
37. "Real Provisión que no se pueda cautivar, ni hacer esclavo a ningún indio" (2 August 1530), in Konetzke, *Colección*, 134–36; Jiménez, *La esclavitud indígena*, 180–81.
38. Stone, "Slavers vs. Raiders," 154–68. For a discussion of the use of the term *Carib*, see also Cacey Farnsworth's chapter in this volume.
39. AGI-SD 203 (19 June 1530), fols. 1r–2v. For more on German expeditions to New Granada, see Avellaneda Navas, *The Conquerors*, 23–55. On German participation in the Iberian colonization of Venezuela, see Spencer Tyce's chapter in this volume.
40. Jiménez, *La esclavitud indígena*, 182.
41. Jiménez, *La esclavitud indígena*, 181–82.
42. Friede, *Vida y viajes*, 13–18.
43. 27 March 1528, transcribed in Otte, *Cédulas reales*, 250.
44. AGI-SD 206, R.1, N.4, Carta de los oficiales de Venezuela de Coro (6 October 1533), fol. 14v.
45. Friede, *Vida y viajes*, 58–67.
46. AGI-SD 206, R.1, N.4, fol. 20r.
47. Jiménez, *La esclavitud indígena*, 223–24.
48. AGI-Caracas I, Orden al gobernador de Venezuela sobre el cacique Marcos (1535), fols. 13r–13v.
49. Jiménez, *La esclavitud indígena*, 223–24.
50. AGI-Just 56, N.2 (1538).
51. AGI-Just 56, N.2, fols. 34r–34v, 55v, 57v–59r; see also Jiménez, *La esclavitud indígena*, 232. The Indians transported to Jamaica were sold for seven and a half pesos each.
52. AGI-SD 218, N.5 (16 April 1534), fol. 1r.
53. AGI-SD 206, N.4, fols. 33r–33v (18 August 1534).
54. Jiménez, *La esclavitud indígena*, 232.
55. For an overview, see Avellaneda Navas, *The Conquerors*.
56. Francis, *Invading Colombia*, 83–85.
57. AGI-Just 974, N.2, R.2 (1536), fol. 2r.
58. AGI-Just 974, N.2, R.2, fol. 6r.
59. AGI-Just 974, N.2a (1535), fol. 1r.
60. AGI-SD 183, R.4, N.147 (27 February 1537), fol. 1r.
61. Saco, *Historia de la Esclavitud*, 1:255; Perri, "Ruined and Lost," 145.
62. AGI-Just 974, N.2a, fols. 8v–9r.

63. AGI-Just 974, N.2a, fols. 10r, 16v–17r.
64. AGI-SD 218, N.12 (2 April 1538), fol. 2r.
65. In 1537 Pope Paul III issued a papal decree against the enslavement of America's indigenous peoples.
66. Cisneros appointed the group of Hieronymites to serve as an impartial religious government in Hispaniola. Fernández de Retana, *Cisneros y su siglo*, 311–13; Mena, *Iglesia, espacio y poder*, 294.
67. "Los Jerónimos enviados a la Española por el Cardinal Cisneros" (1516), in Marte, *Santo Domingo en los manuscritos*, 208–10.
68. Guitar, "Boiling It Down," 46.
69. AGI-IG 420, L.8, fols. 37v–38r, Licencias para llevar esclavos (1519). On the early transatlantic slave trade, see Marc Eagle's chapter in this volume.
70. Deive, *La esclavitud del negro*, 443.
71. Guitar, "Boiling It Down," 48–49, 64–65.
72. In 1547 the crown exempted male Caribs from the New Laws, making their enslavement legal. Arens, *The Man-Eating Myth*, 49.
73. Rodríguez Morel, "The Sugar Economy," 104–7; AGI-SD 71, L.2, fol. 452r, Carta de Arzobispo Fray Andrés de Carvajal (25 August 1569). See also AGI-SD 74, R.1, N.35, Carta de los oficiales reales de la isla Española (12 September 1536), fol. 2v.
74. Slave expeditions into the interior of Brazil increased in the 1580s as relations between the Portuguese and indigenous groups deteriorated. Monteiro, *Negros da Terra*, 51–52.
75. Arena, "Indian Slaves from Guiana."

Bibliography

ARCHIVES

Archivo General de Indias (Seville, Spain).

PUBLISHED WORKS

Adorno, Rolena, and Patrick Charles Pautz, eds. *Álvar Núñez Cabeza de Vaca: His Account, His Life, and the Expedition of Pánfilo de Narváez*. 3 vols. Lincoln: University of Nebraska Press, 1999.

Altman, Ida. *The War for Mexico's West: Indians and Spaniards in New Galicia, 1524–1550*. Albuquerque: University of New Mexico Press, 2010.

Arena, Carolyn. "Indian Slaves from Guiana in Seventeenth-Century Barbados." *Ethnohistory* 64, no. 1 (2017): 65–90.

Arens, William F. *The Man-Eating Myth: Anthropology and Anthropophagy*. Oxford: Oxford University Press, 1980.

Avellaneda Navas, José Ignacio. *The Conquerors of the New Kingdom of Granada*. Albuquerque: University of New Mexico Press, 1995.

Chipman, Donald E. "The Traffic in Indian Slaves in the Province of Pánuco, New Spain, 1523–1533." *The Americas* 23, no. 2 (October 1966): 142–55.

———. *Nuno de Guzman and the Province of Panuco in New Spain, 1518–1533*. Glendale CA: Arthur H. Clark, 1967.

Colección de documentos inéditos para la historia de Ibero-America/Hispano-America. 15 vols. Madrid: Compañía Ibero-Americana de Publicaciones, 1925–37.

Deagan, Kathleen A., and José María Cruxent. *Archaeology at La Isabela: America's First European Town*. New Haven: Yale University Press, 2002.

Deive, Carlos Esteban. *La esclavitud del negro en Santo Domingo (1492–1844)*. Santo Domingo, DR: Editora Taller, 1980.

Deive, Carlos Esteban. *La Española y la esclavitud del indio*. Santo Domingo, DR: Fundación García Arévalo, 1995.

Fernández de Retana, Luis. *Cisneros y su siglo: estudio histórico de la vida y actuación pública del Cardenal D. Fr. Francisco Ximénez de Cisneros*. Vol. 2. Madrid: Administración de "El Perpetuo Socorro," 1930.

Francis, J. Michael. *Invading Colombia: Spanish Accounts of the Gonzalo Jiménez de Quesada Expedition of Conquest*. University Park: Pennsylvania State University Press, 2007.

Friede, Juan. *Vida y viajes de Nicolás Féderman, conquistador, poblador y cofundador de Bogotá, 1506–1542*. Bogotá: Ediciones Librería Buchholz, 1960.

Guitar, Lynne A. "Boiling It Down: Slavery on the First Commercial Sugarcane Ingenios in the Americas (Hispaniola, 1530–45)." In *Slaves, Subjects, and Subversives: Blacks in Colonial Latin America*, edited by Jane G. Landers and Barry M. Robinson, 39–82. Albuquerque: University of New Mexico Press, 2006.

———. "Cultural Genesis: Relationships among Indians, Africans, and Spaniards in Rural Hispaniola, First Half of the Sixteenth Century." PhD diss., Vanderbilt University, 1998.

———. "What Really Happened at Santo Cerro? Origin of the Legend of the Virgin of Las Mercedes." *Issues in Indigenous Caribbean Studies* 3 (February 2001): 1–5.

Hoffman, Paul E. *A New Andalucía and a Way to the Orient: The American Southeast during the Sixteenth Century*. Baton Rouge: Louisiana State University Press, 1990.

Jiménez, Morella A. *La esclavitud indígena en Venezuela (Siglo XVI)*. Caracas: Fuentes para la Historia Colonial de Venezuela, 1986.

Keegan, William F. *The People Who Discovered Columbus: The Prehistory of the Bahamas*. Gainesville: University Press of Florida, 1992.

———. *Taíno Indian Myth and Practice: The Arrival of the Stranger King*. Gainesville: University Press of Florida, 2007.

Konetzke, Richard. *Colección de documentos para la historia de la formación social de Hispanoamérica, 1493–1810*. Vol. 1. Madrid: Consejo Superior de Investigaciones Científicas, 1953.

Marte, Roberto, ed. *Santo Domingo en los manuscritos de Juan Bautista Muñoz*. Vol. 1. Santo Domingo, DR: Ediciones Fundación García Arévalo, 1981.

Mena, Miguel D. *Iglesia, espacio y poder: Santo Domingo (1498–1521), experiencia fundacional del Nuevo Mundo*. Santo Domingo, DR: Archivo General de la Nación, 2007.

Monteiro, John Manuel. *Negros da Terra: Indios e Bandeirantes nas origens de São Paulo*. São Paulo: Companhia das Letras, 1994.

Newson, Linda A. *The Cost of Conquest: Indian Decline in Honduras under Spanish Rule*. Boulder: Westview Press, 1986.

Otte, Enrique. *Cédulas reales relativas a Venezuela (1500–1550)*. Caracas: Edición de la Fundación John Boulton y la Fundación Eugenio Mendoza, 1963.

———. *Las perlas del Caribe: Nueva Cádiz de Cubagua*. Caracas: Fundación John Boulton, 1977.

Perri, Michael. "Ruined and Lost: Spanish Destruction of the Pearl Coast in the Early Sixteenth Century." *Environment and History* 15 (2009): 129–61.

Quattlebaum, Paul. *The Land Called Chicora: The Carolinas under Spanish Rule with French Intrusions, 1520–1670*. Gainesville: University of Florida Press, 1956.

Radell, David R. "The Indian Slave Trade and Population of Nicaragua during the Sixteenth Century." In *The Native Population of the Americas in 1492*, edited by William M. Denevan, 67–76. Madison: University of Wisconsin Press, 1976.

Reséndez, Andrés. *The Other Slavery: The Uncovered Story of Indian Enslavement in America*. Boston: Houghton Mifflin Harcourt, 2016.

Restall, Matthew, and Florine Asselbergs, eds. *Invading Guatemala: Spanish, Nahua, and Maya Accounts of the Conquest Wars*. University Park: Pennsylvania State University Press, 2007.

Rodríguez Morel, Genaro. "The Sugar Economy of Espanola in the Sixteenth Century." In *Tropical Babylons: Sugar and the Making of the Atlantic World, 1450–1680*, edited by Stuart B. Schwartz, 85–114. Chapel Hill: University of North Carolina Press, 2004.

Rushforth, Brett. *Bonds of Alliance: Indigenous and Atlantic Slaveries in New France*. Chapel Hill: University of North Carolina Press, 2012.

Saco, J. A. *Historia de la esclavitud de los indios en el Nuevo Mundo*. 2 vols. Havana: Librería Cervantes, 1932.

Sauer, Carl Ortwin. *The Early Spanish Main*. Berkeley: University of California Press, 1966.

Sherman, William L. *Forced Native Labor in Sixteenth-Century Central America.* Lincoln: University of Nebraska Press, 1979.

Stone, Erin. "Slave Raiders vs. Friars: Tierra Firme, 1513–1522." *Americas* 74, no. 2 (April 2017): 139–70.

Sued Badillo, Jalil. "The Island Caribs: New Approaches to the Question of Ethnicity in the Early Colonial Caribbean." In *Wolves from the Sea: Readings in the Anthropology of the Native Caribbean*, edited by Neil L. Whitehead, 61–89. Leiden: KITLV Press, 1995.

van Deusen, Nancy E. *Global Indios: The Indigenous Struggle for Justice in Sixteenth-Century Spain.* Durham: Duke University Press, 2015.

Varela, Consuelo, ed. *Cristóbal Colón: Textos y documentos completos: relaciones de viajes, cartas y memoriales.* 2nd ed. Madrid: Alianza Editorial, 1992.

Warsh, Molly A. "Enslaved Pearl Divers in the Sixteenth-Century Caribbean." *Slavery & Abolition* 31, no. 3 (September 2010): 345–62.

Whitehead, Neil L. *Of Cannibals and Kings: Primal Anthropology in the Americas.* University Park: Pennsylvania State University Press, 2011.

Zavala, Silvio. *Los esclavos indios en Nueva España.* México DF: Colegio Nacional Luis González Obregón, 1967.

PART 2

Europeans in the Islands

When word got out that gold had been discovered, Europeans began to pour into the Caribbean, beginning with Hispaniola, the first focus of Spanish colonizing efforts. The great majority of immigrants were men, but Spanish women joined them almost from the beginning. They often played important roles in managing households filled with Indian and African slaves and servants and sometimes in more public capacities as well. Officials and high-ranking men dominated the private and public sectors, maintaining close connections through marital ties and economic interests but also engaging in bitter rivalries. The Spanish crown encouraged migration to the islands while simultaneously trying to control who could settle there. The surprisingly robust presence of the Portuguese in the region resulted from the need to recruit more settlers and to take advantage of their maritime and commercial expertise.

4

Vasco Porcallo de Figueroa

Ambition, Fear, and Politics in Early Cuba

IDA ALTMAN

In August 1539 the bishop of Cuba, don fray Diego Sarmiento, and the island's former lieutenant governor, Gonzalo de Guzmán, separately wrote to Charles V complaining in very similar terms about the harm that Hernando de Soto had done to the island by organizing and equipping his ambitious expedition to Florida. The bishop wrote that Soto had commandeered extensive supplies and horses, both to support his expeditionary force as they waited in Cuba for a year to depart and to equip them for the expedition; in addition, "he has taken with him the men of the island who are of use in war. This will cause the Indians to revolt."[1] Guzmán condemned Soto's actions during the year he spent on the island in the strongest terms and criticized him in particular for having recruited a man whom he considered essential to the island's well-being:

> In the province of the town of Trinidad which is in the middle of this island there lived an honored citizen named Vasco Porcallo disposed to pursue these rebellious Indians, and he was better equipped for it than the four towns together that lie from Puerto del Príncipe to Havana. And the Indians of that province *had such fear of him* that it was sufficient to secure those Spanish towns that are in that region of Sancti Espíritus and Trinidad. The *adelantado* [Soto] took Vasco Porcallo as his lieutenant [so] that I fear that with his not being in that province they are sure to burn two or three towns of Spaniards that are in it in misery. Please God my opinion should be mistaken, but he did us great harm in taking him from this island along with other Spaniards.[2]

Who was Vasco Porcallo? He was an early arrival to the island who was part of the occupying force organized by Diego Velázquez in Hispaniola in 1510–11 in which men like Pánfilo de Narváez and Juan de Grijalva participated as well. Outlasting several other men who played important roles in Cuba's early history, Vasco Porcallo de Figueroa established a large estate with hundreds of Indian and African slaves and servants that continued to thrive when many other enterprises were failing. Although according to some sources he was Governor Diego Velázquez's choice to lead the expedition to Mexico instead of Hernando Cortés,[3] Porcallo seemingly preferred to amass socioeconomic rather than political power. He held local offices and sway over his personal domain in Cuba, but never occupied higher positions of authority.[4] Brutal, shrewd, status conscious, and an adept survivor, his long and varied career took him to Mexico with Narváez, possibly to Spain with Cortés in 1530 and again to Mexico in the 1530s, and briefly to Florida as Hernando de Soto's second-in-command. In all instances he returned to Cuba, quite soon in the case of Soto's expedition, leaving behind his mestizo son Gómez Suárez de Figueroa, who figured among the survivors of the ill-fated expedition and eventually rejoined his father in Cuba.[5] He had helped to provide supplies for Narváez's earlier, also ill-fated expedition to La Florida in 1527. Porcallo did not participate in that one, although according to Cabeza de Vaca's account, his brother Alonso de Sotomayor did.[6]

Porcallo's biography is confusing and contradictory, notwithstanding a fairly extensive documentary record and references to him in sixteenth-century chronicles. All concur that he was a native of Cáceres in Extremadura. There is a good deal of disagreement regarding other aspects of his life, however, including his date of birth and how long and under what circumstances he lived in Mexico after participating in the conquest (he is said to have been awarded an *encomienda* or part of one that he subsequently either lost or retained and passed on to a son,[7] and also to have killed two men there).[8] He was also said to have married a high-born Spaniard or the daughter of a powerful Cuban cacique, yet no documentary evidence has been found that he ever married at all. The failure to marry was an unusual choice for a man of his times and stature, although he apparently had numerous children with indigenous women. From a family related to the high-ranking duques de Feria, in Cuba he clearly was highly regarded, and for much of his career he was probably the highest-ranking man on the island in terms of social status and family origin. Ostensibly he had military experience in Spain and Italy before he arrived in the Caribbean, which, if true, is incompatible with a birth date of 1494. Yet while Spaniards often offered fairly vague estimates of their ages—the phrase "poco mas o menos" (more or less) frequently appears with personal statements regarding age—his own claim to be twenty-eight years old in 1522 and the contention of some scholars that he was as much as ten years older are difficult to reconcile. A birth date in the mid-1490s would have meant he was in his late teens when Spaniards invaded Cuba, an age at which many young men were arriving in the islands. Most sources agree that he died around 1550, so his life and career spanned the formative decades of Spanish Cuba. Outside of Cuba, other than his truncated participation in Soto's expedition, Vasco Porcallo figures very little in the history of early Spanish America or even of the Spanish Caribbean.[9]

The many uncertainties about his life and career suggest that possibly there were two men who have been conflated, one Vasco Porcallo de Figueroa and another de la Cerda. Some scholars even refer to Vasco Porcallo de Figueroa y de la Cerda, although I have yet to find a contemporary document that combines the two surnames.[10] The existence of a second Vasco Porcallo could explain the discrepancies in accounts of his activities in Mexico and especially the arrival in Seville from Mexico in 1540 of a five-year-old girl named doña Maria de la Cerda accompanied by her indigenous nanny, a slave named Elena, and in the care of her grandfather Luis de la Serna, who stated that the little girl was the daughter of Vasco Porcallo and doña Leonor de Zúñiga.[11] Her age would place Porcallo de Figueroa in Mexico in the mid-1530s, which is conceivable, although the documentary record definitely shows that he was in Cuba in 1533–34 and, of course, in the late 1530s when Soto was organizing his expedition.

The focus here is on some lesser-known, mostly violent episodes in early Cuba in which Porcallo played a decisive role, following his return from Mexico in the early 1520s. These episodes highlight both the unrest on the island a decade after Velázquez's expedition of conquest and the ways in which Porcallo used these incidents as opportunities to bolster his position in a turbulent frontier society. The events of the early 1520s may have been at least indirectly related to Hernando Cortés's expedition to Mexico, which, like Soto's twenty years later, entailed the departure of hundreds of men—Spanish, indigenous, and African—together with livestock and supplies. This large-scale enterprise may well have raised concerns about security on the part of the Spaniards who remained and, for the island's indigenous people, fostered the illusion of a weakening Spanish commitment to retaining control in Cuba.

Comuneros in the Caribbean

Ironically, perhaps, what likely was the first of these incidents pitted Spaniard against Spaniard and town against town. Porcallo held the office of *teniente de justicia* (lieutenant justice of the peace) in the towns of Trinidad, Sancti Spíritus, and San Cristóbal de la Havana. Soon after Porcallo assumed that office in the spring of 1521, a *vecino* (citizen) of Sancti Spíritus named Juan Rodríguez de Córdoba went to Trinidad to inform him of a disturbance in Sancti Spíritus in which some of his fellow townsmen had declared themselves a *comunidad* or commune. The vecinos explicitly evoked the more or less contemporary rebellion of the comunidades of Castile, which they assumed had been successful, as their model.[12] They had chosen new officials and threatened serious injury or even death to one of their fellow vecinos and erstwhile *alcalde ordinario* (magistrate of the first instance), Juan de Ribera, should he attempt to return to the town with orders regarding changes to *encomienda* grants.[13]

Ribera had been sent to Cuba's capital, Santiago, as the town's *procurador* (representative) and apparently failed in the expectation of at least some of the townspeople that he would oppose and refuse to accept the revised encomienda assignments, which many residents claimed would cause them considerable harm. In these early years Spaniards in Cuba were almost entirely dependent on Indian labor, whether encomienda workers or slaves or permanent servants (*naborías*) brought from elsewhere. Swearing allegiance to the comunidad, a handful of activists—mainly members of the town council, including the town's notary—urged and perhaps partly coerced others into participating, dispatching the town's *alguacil* (constable) to the countryside to collect people from their rural holdings and ringing the town's bell to summon the townspeople so vigorously that the clapper broke. Once a crowd had gathered in the town's church, Diego Mendes, who had been chosen for (or perhaps claimed for himself) the position of procurador for the comunidad, "took from all their faith and word . . . and they proclaimed all for one and one for all."[14]

An official response came swiftly from near at hand. In his role as teniente de justicia Porcallo mustered some twenty or twenty-five men in the town of Trinidad, arriving in Sancti Spíritus at night. Among the group were Juan Rodríguez de Quiñones, a notary, Juan de Grijalva, who led one of the early expeditions to New Spain, and Dr. Cristóbal de Hojeda, who subsequently became an encomendero and regidor of Mexico City before returning to Spain in 1531. The leaders of the comunidad had been meeting in the church at night, which perhaps accounted for Porcallo's timing, or he might have hoped to take advantage of an element of surprise. The alguacil Sebastián de la Fuente testified that Diego Mendes and the other principals had armed themselves and that other people in the town "had their mares and horses saddled and their lances and arms ready" by the time that Porcallo with a few of his men "entered the said cabildo . . . and demanded that . . . they obey [and said] that he had come to bring them to peace and justice."[15] Following this declaration Porcallo left the aspiring *comuneros* to discuss what they would do, but he soon returned to demand that the officials turn over their staffs of office (*varas*) to him. One of the alcaldes did so, but the other resisted. With everyone carrying arms, not surprisingly a violent confrontation took place in which several men were injured, including Vasco Porcallo, who was wounded in the left hand and took a blow to his ribs. The alguacil succeeded in turning away others who were arriving with their arms. No doubt as a result of his intervention and the presence of Porcallo's heavily armed posse, the violence did not escalate further. The ringleaders were arrested and sent to Santiago, including the town notary who some witnesses believed was most culpable because he was an educated man. Jorge Velázquez, the alcalde who had handed over his staff, had been so seriously wounded that Porcallo feared that he would not survive the journey. He allowed Velázquez to remain in Sancti Spíritus under house arrest.

Only one woman is mentioned in the lengthy testimony about the episode, the wife of one of the ringleaders, Pedro de Salazar. If not an active participant, she surely witnessed the events, asking the alguacil why Indians (presumably slaves or servants) were being taken out of their houses. This also was the only instance in which Indians were mentioned; they were summoned in order to construct a gallows and *picota* (pillory), traditional Spanish symbols of justice and municipal autonomy.

Officials in Santiago and Santo Domingo probably condoned Porcallo's actions. Although almost certainly he acted without the prior approval of any higher authority and indeed ended up under house arrest, Porcallo succeeded in cutting short the revolt, which surely was in the interest of the crown's officials. Although the comunidad had gained the support of many men in the town, it apparently did not spread beyond Sancti Spíritus. Trinidad was its nearest neighbor, and its repudiation of the idea of the comunidad possibly was a reflection of the considerable rivalry and resentment that had developed between it and Trinidad over rights to encomiendas and which town was more favorably situated, a dispute that continued through the 1520s and early 1530s when official efforts were made to merge the shrinking towns into one municipality at the site of one or the other.[16] Initially Sancti Spíritus seemed to have an advantage over Trinidad because of its proximity to gold mines, and some of Trinidad's vecinos relocated there in the 1520s—to the considerable resentment of those who stayed behind. But in the end the two survived as separate entities into modern times.

While he may have been upholding royal authority, Porcallo's intervention in events was hardly disinterested. He benefited from the redistribution of encomiendas, having been assigned two caciques and a total of 175 Indians and 30 naborías in Trinidad, one of the larger grants on the island and the largest in Trinidad.[17] In 1534, a little over ten years after the comunidad episode in Sancti Spíritus, Vasco Porcallo was the only encomendero of any substance in either of the two towns, holding 150 Indians in encomienda along with 50 Indian and 15 or 16 African slaves.

Alonso Sánchez del Corral, who held the second largest encomienda in Sancti Spiritus, had only 22 Indians (although he also owned 20 Indian slaves); Pedro de Carmona held an encomienda of 30 Indians with an additional 10 Indian slaves in Trinidad.[18]

The fate of Porcallo's encomienda in face of the continuing loss of indigenous population is not known, but a report by the bishop Sarmiento in 1544 that described Porcallo's estate of Sabana (later San Juan de los Remedios) referred to "twenty houses and huts, lodging for Indians and Spaniards" and noted that "there are 80 and 120 [sic] black slaves. He has ten Spaniards apart from another ten who personally serve Porcallo."[19] Given that in 1534 virtually all the men who testified in Sancti Spíritus and Trinidad before lieutenant governor Manuel de Rojas stated that not only had their numbers of Indian workers dwindled, sometimes to nothing, but that the Spaniards they formerly had employed also for the most part were gone, the dimensions of Porcallo's domain are all the more impressive.[20] Porcallo's success in maintaining his wealth, labor force, and social influence must be set in the context of the general economic contraction that affected many other residents of the islands.

Instilling Fear

Another episode that may have occurred fairly soon after this confrontation between Spaniards involved Porcallo's participation in a campaign to suppress indigenous groups that continued to resist Spanish authority. In response to ongoing disorder, especially along Cuba's southern coast and nearby islands, that had resulted in the deaths of Spaniards and some allied Indians, Porcallo traveled to a focal point of the conflict with fifteen of his cousins (*quince hombres primos hermanos suyos*) and an additional force, some forty-five men in total. Earlier fighting on some small islands (*cayos*) off the coast had not gone well for the Spaniards, but in this instance Porcallo's men were able to seize the indigenous leader, known to them as "el Piloto," along with forty or fifty others who were taken to Sancti Spíritus. Witnesses testified that a number of other Indians agreed to cease their hostilities and return to their pueblos. Here again, then, Porcallo seems to have relied as much on his personal relationships (another witness described his entourage as consisting of *hasta quince personas de su posada de sus hermanos y otros hidalgos desta villa [de la Trinidad]*) as on the authority conferred by office to muster an effective fighting force and to deal a decisive blow to a group in rebellion, this time native Cubans as opposed to other Spaniards.[21]

In the two episodes discussed so far Vasco Porcallo successfully combined his personal resources and political clout to accomplish ends desired by royal authorities (if not necessarily explicitly articulated) and advantageous to himself and his circle of relatives, friends and retainers. A third episode in which Porcallo again took the lead, noted by scholars as an example of the extreme brutality used by Spaniards in the islands, apparently shocked even some contemporaries, although it is not clear that any measures were taken to censure his behavior other than placing him under house arrest for some time in February and March 1522. While he was there, two judges from the *audiencia* (high court) in Hispaniola, Licenciados Marcelo de Villalobos and Juan Ortiz de Matienzo, solicited testimony from him regarding the confrontation in Sancti Spíritus as well as his treatment of Indians who he claimed were eating earth, which he (and others) thought was a means of committing suicide.[22] Testimony subsequently compiled at Porcallo's instigation makes it clear that Spaniards' concern about this practice hinged on the loss of labor threatened by widespread suicide and that they were grateful that Porcallo's extreme measures seemed to put a stop to the practice.[23]

When questioned about allegations that he had cut off the genitals and "other body parts" of Indians whom he accused of eating earth, Porcallo admitted that he had done so, burning the severed parts and forcing three Indians "who were almost dead from eating earth" to eat their genitals covered in mud, only sparing a boy who survived the ghastly punishment from this last horror. Porcallo also acknowledged that he had burned to death another dozen people and apparently burned or scalded the mouths of others who would not desist from the practice. Porcallo claimed that "in all the provinces of Camagüey and Guamohaya they kill themselves, and more than three quarters or half have died just from eating earth, and to avoid that so they don't kill themselves he inflicted that punishment, and first he had many masses said and processions conducted so that they would stop doing that harm but they never would stop nor abandon doing it until he inflicted that punishment." The masses and processions suggest the presence of someone from the clergy, although whether a priest actually witnessed the horrific punishments that Vasco meted out is not known.[24]

Porcallo's neighbors in Trinidad had no misgivings about his methods of dealing with the Indians. One close associate, Francisco de Agüero, stated that during the time that Porcallo was punishing Indians "who ate earth and charcoal and other disgusting things" Agüero "threatened his [own] Indians with the said *teniente* and with his punishment and for that reason many of them desisted from" eating those things. He and other men in Trinidad reported that they had participated in the processions that Porcallo had organized in that connection. The witnesses emphasized that the state of affairs in the town had improved greatly under Porcallo's authority—one man claimed that the residents of Trinidad were "*contentos y alegres*"—and that many indigenous lives had been saved owing to Porcallo's extreme measures.

In these three episodes Porcallo readily used force as he saw fit, even against other Spaniards, and he commanded the manpower and arms to enforce his will and that of the crown according to his understanding of it. Levi Marrero writes about the events that led to Porcallo's arrest and the subsequent inquiry, but says little about their unusual nature, although the first and third episodes described here were sufficiently outside the norm to attract the attention of the audiencia officials in Santo Domingo. One of them entailed violence by Spaniards against Spaniards, and the other featured extreme cruelty against Cuba's indigenous inhabitants that most likely fell beneath even the abysmally low standards of contemporary practice.[25] Yet Porcallo's responses to these apparent threats to the barely decade-old Spanish regime in Cuba served the interests of the crown and its officials, on the one hand undercutting local aspirations for autonomy and self-assertion and on the other terrorizing the native inhabitants into submission to Spanish demands. It comes as no surprise, then, that Vasco Porcallo suffered no lasting repercussions from his actions and continued to be regarded as a key and respected figure in Cuban society. When the crown solicited loans in 1529 to support Spain's struggle against the Turks in the Mediterranean, Porcallo was one of a handful of wealthy men in Cuba to whom the request was made personally.[26]

Vasco Porcallo was not unique in the early Spanish Caribbean. Other men—although admittedly not many—were able to use their personal and political connections and positions to secure sizeable encomiendas and build up substantial estates, often engaging in a mix of enterprises that included gold mining, sugar production, and investment or participation in commerce (including, increasingly, the trade in African slaves) or slave raiding. Yet the trajectory of his career is striking. He moved around a good deal but always returned to his seigneurial base in Cuba. Also rather unusual was his failure to secure his position in Cuban society by making a favorable marriage, either in Castile or the Caribbean, and establish a legitimate family. Instead he apparently focused his familial ambitions on his mestizo children, both sons and daughters, whom Levi Marrero has characterized as "incredibly numerous."[27]

We also see in Porcallo's life and career in Cuba indications of how this new Spanish Caribbean society struggled to define itself in the face of both tenacious indigenous resistance and the aspiration to preserve familiar traditions in a strikingly new context. Notwithstanding the abrupt and violent end that Sancti Spíritus's comunidad met, less than a decade later the crown upheld the right of Cuba's towns to conduct annual elections of procuradores who would hold general powers of attorney to act on their behalf. Lieutenant Governor Guzmán had continued to sabotage the process, in Santiago holding the election in his house even though at least twice he received explicit instructions from the crown that town councils should be allowed to conduct their elections independently.[28] While Spaniards in the islands might have been loath to give up their traditional corporate privileges, Porcallo followed his own course, using his status and resources to meet the challenge of balancing the need to enforce Spanish control over Cuba's native inhabitants while maintaining order within Spanish society itself. In doing so he consolidated his wealth and social power, operating with relative impunity both inside and outside the law and accepted norms.

Maintaining that balance clearly had much to do with his high social status and reputation as one of the island's most powerful residents. In an *información* (deposition) prepared at his own behest soon after the inquiry by the audiencia judges into his conduct in relation to the punishment of the Indians accused of eating dirt and the mini-comunero revolt in Sancti Spíritus, Porcallo's witnesses testified to his chaste and honest character and the improvement in civic order that resulted from his tenure as teniente de justicia for Trinidad, Sancti Spíritus, and San Cristóbal de la Havana. The witnesses referred to the disorder that had existed under the authority of *alcaldes ordinarios* who, because of the towns' distance from the administrative center of Santiago, exercised their offices corruptly and virtually without restraint or supervision from outside authorities. Not surprisingly the witnesses from Trinidad seemed far more enthusiastic in their praise than did those from Sancti Spíritus, where less than a year previously Vasco had so forcefully asserted his authority.

Negotiating Authority

The combination of respect and fear that Porcallo inspired in his fellow Spaniards affected even the island's most powerful. Gonzalo de Guzmán, who in 1539 expressed his concern about the impact of Vasco Porcallo's departure for Florida with Hernando de Soto, was a longtime associate of Cuba's conqueror and first governor, Diego Velázquez. One of the island's strongest and most enduring political figures, he held a series of offices in Cuba, including two terms as lieutenant governor.[29] His deference to Porcallo is evident in a 1527 episode in which Porcallo tried to balance his loyalties to his fellow vecinos of Trinidad with his need to maintain workable relations with Guzmán—on his own terms, as usual.

By 1527 a man named Alonso Sánchez del Corral had succeeded Porcallo as teniente de justicia for Trinidad and Sancti Spíritus, while Porcallo was serving as *regidor* (town councilman) in Trinidad.[30] Sánchez apparently made himself unpopular among the residents of both towns, whose councils drew up a set of grievances that they empowered Hernando Gutiérrez Calderón, a notary and vecino of Sancti Spíritus, to convey to the audiencia judges in Santo Domingo. They hoped to bypass Lieutenant Governor Guzmán because Sánchez was Guzmán's relative and close friend.[31] When Calderón traveled to Santiago in order to depart from there for Hispaniola, Guzmán got wind of his intentions. He insisted that it was within his purview to address the complaints that had been raised against his teniente Sánchez and that it was inappropriate for Calderón to bypass his authority by going directly to the audiencia. Calderón insisted that the two town councils only empowered him to present their complaints before the audiencia, not Guzmán.

Although exactly what happened is somewhat murky, Guzmán managed to confiscate the documents that detailed the towns' complaints against Sánchez del Corral and refused to release them. He also was accused of intimidating Calderón verbally and publicly with "certain arrogant and abusive words" (*palabras soberbias y de maltratmiento*) and demanding that Calderón hand over the documents. The thoroughly rattled representative of the towns was uncertain how to proceed and turned to a powerful ally, Vasco Porcallo, who testified that he was one of the aggrieved parties to the petition. Porcallo, along with his longtime *criado* (retainer) Juan Álvarez Pantoja, had accompanied Calderón to Santiago, where the three men lodged in the home of Andrés de Parada. Calderón discussed the state of affairs with Parada and Porcallo, who advised him to go to one of the city's notaries to have a copy of the powers of attorney made before returning the next day to hand over the originals to Guzmán as the governor demanded. Calderón's intention, according to Parada, was to travel "secretly" to bring the towns' complaints before the audiencia, using the copies. Calderón was unable to retrieve the originals; indeed, when he went to Guzmán's home accompanied by a notary to demand their return, Guzmán ostensibly refused to answer the door or to listen to what he had to say. Calderón also alleged that Guzmán had ordered the shipmasters in the harbor at the time not to take him to Hispaniola under threat of a fine.

Stymied by this obstacle to his departure, Calderón again consulted Porcallo and Parada. The three decided to send Porcallo's retainer, Juan Álvarez, to appear before the audiencia with the copies of the powers of attorney. He would embark for Hispaniola on the pretext that he had other business to attend to there. At that point, in addition to presenting the towns' complaints against Alonso Sánchez, Álvarez also was to lodge a complaint about the "force and affront" that Guzmán had deployed against Calderón. According to Andrés de Parada, he, Porcallo, and another leading citizen of Santiago, Andrés de Duero, discussed the situation at length. The upshot was that Vasco Porcallo, "wanting to help citizens of those towns in their [pursuit of] justice," volunteered to finance Álvarez's trip. He provided more than two hundred pesos for the purpose, a sum substantial enough to suggest he had a fair degree of self-interest in the outcome of the dispute. Calderón remained in Santiago in Parada's house for quite a few days awaiting Álvarez's return but finally decided to return home, having failed to accomplish his charge. Álvarez eventually returned to Cuba with decrees from the audiencia, one of them fining Guzmán and ordering him to allow Calderón to appear freely before the audiencia and another directed at Alonso Sánchez del Corral regarding certain items that Parada could not recall. According to Parada, nothing more was done about the affair.

Not long after that, Guzmán traveled to Trinidad and Sancti Spíritus because of conflict with Indians in that area. While there he was able to reconcile Sánchez with the parties who had grievances against him, and the matter was considered settled. In April 1534 Vasco Porcallo himself testified before Manuel de Rojas in Sancti Spíritus that by the time the orders from the audiencia arrived, they no longer were relevant "because they already were all friends." What happened to the orders thereafter was uncertain. Calderón assumed that they had ended up in Porcallo's possession. Porcallo's response to Rojas's query about them was vague. He said he had given them to Alonso Guillén and some other people "who asked for them because he had need of them" and that possibly a few might have ended up in his possession.[32] When Rojas ordered him to produce them, Porcallo said that most of the time he lived at his estate of La Sabana twenty leagues from there and when he went back there he would look for them.

Perhaps the most interesting testimony came from Juan Álvarez Pantoja, Porcallo's retainer and relative. He saw events in a rather different light than did the other parties involved and, perhaps surprisingly, portrayed Guzmán's actions much more sympathetically than had the other witnesses. According to Álvarez, Guzmán was not trying to protect Alonso Sánchez so much as he was concerned that *"pasión"* between

Sánchez and Calderón was at the heart of the accusations against the former. Álvarez apparently acted as Porcallo's go-between, going to speak with Guzmán whom he claimed "showed complete willingness to punish the said Alonso Sánchez for whatever he had done and to do entire justice and he offered to send for that [purpose] *whatever judge Vasco Porcallo wanted even if it were Sotomayor his brother.*"[33] Álvarez claimed that on hearing this, Porcallo was ready to settle things with Guzmán and Sánchez, but because Calderón continued to push him to take action, he did not desist. Álvarez went on to say that even though he "is a longtime criado of Vasco Porcallo and his relative it seemed to him that Gonzalo de Guzmán had done everything he should have done as a good judge" and that when his efforts to resolve the matter got nowhere "he had reason to become angry"; it was in this angry state that he took the powers of attorney from Calderón. Álvarez said he went to Hispaniola at Porcallo's behest and cost and returned with the decrees from the audiencia, which he handed over to Porcallo. At that time he realized that "they weren't necessary because the vecinos and Alonso Sánchez were all at peace." Hernán Gutiérrez Calderón then admitted that Guzmán indeed had offered to send a judge to settle matters and possibly to punish Alonso Sánchez but that he was determined not to go before Guzmán to lodge the complaints of the townspeople—of whom he was one—because of the kinship between Guzmán and Sánchez.

In the end the dispute was settled to the apparent satisfaction of most if perhaps not all of the principals. The details of what occurred, however, not only reflect the position that Vasco Porcallo had attained as a key player in early Cuban politics and society but also shed light on how political authority was negotiated among royal and local officeholders and prominent local men. In this episode Porcallo emerged even more clearly than in the earlier ones as both political insider and outsider, able to manipulate events and intimidate Guzmán without directly challenging his authority while defending and placating local grievances to the extent that such action accorded with his interests. As seen in the excerpt from Guzmán's 1539 letter to the king quoted at the beginning of this piece, Guzmán continued to admire and defer to Porcallo and was convinced that his power to instill fear in the hearts of Cuba's diminished indigenous population was essential to the island's well-being. Many of Porcallo's neighbors and associates shared Guzmán's conviction that only brutal force could protect Spanish society from danger at the hands of resentful Indians, and they were willing to support him regardless of the means he used.

Vasco Porcallo's ambitions did not lie in the political arena. Unlike Gonzalo de Guzmán and Manuel de Rojas, who alternated as lieutenant governors of Cuba from the time of Diego Velázquez's death in 1524 until 1537, Porcallo had little interest in dedicating his career—and wealth—to the king's service. Guzmán's service to the crown could hardly be described as disinterested, and he was much more successful than Rojas in ensuring his own financial well-being.[34] Yet notwithstanding the very different reputations of the two men, both contemporary and historical, their shared dedication to upholding the legacy of Velázquez and maintaining royal authority on the island provided early Cuba with a fair degree of stability. Their service allowed Porcallo to concentrate his own efforts on building up his rural estates, holding local office, maintaining a substantial entourage of relatives and retainers as well as a large, mixed labor force, and keeping fellow Spaniards and Indians in line with a strong hand when they threatened to disturb the conditions that allowed his personal fortunes to flourish.

Notwithstanding the high social status conferred by his aristocratic origins in Spain, Porcallo perhaps reflected more closely than did many other prominent Spaniards the nature of the new society that was taking root in Cuba and elsewhere in the islands. Eschewing the usual aspiration of ambitious men to marry a wealthy or at least well-born Spanish woman, Porcallo placed his lineage's future in the hands of his mestizo children, who took their place among the island's increasingly mixed residents. He was not alone in finding opportunities in the early Spanish Caribbean to forge a life that deviated a good deal from the conservative Iberian society he left behind.[35] Cuba in the 1530s in many ways remained a frontier society relatively lacking in the social and political constraints that Porcallo might have faced had he stayed in Mexico. Yet as human and other resources on the island contracted, Porcallo flourished where many others failed, a reminder that of the thousands of

Europeans who flocked to the islands in the early years, very few became wealthy. Fewer yet passed their wealth along to their heirs, even if they married an appropriate partner, suggesting that Porcallo's choice not to establish a legitimate family might have reflected his understanding of both the potential and the limitations of this new society.

Notes

ABBREVIATIONS

AGI   Archivo General de Indias
    -IG   Gobierno: Indiferente General
    -Patr   Patronato Real
    -SD   Gobierno: Audiencia de Santo Domingo

1. Quoted in Clayton, Knight, and Moore, *De Soto Chronicles*, 1:184n37. I have not found the original of Sarmiento's letter. See also Wright, *Early History of Cuba*, 175.
2. Emphasis is mine. Gonzalo de Guzmán's letter to the king from Santiago, August 28, 1539 (in AGI-SD 118, R.1, N.71), specifically mentioned that during the previous two years more than twenty-five Spaniards had died in the province of Santiago due to conflict with the Indians. Guzmán, who had served in one office or another in Cuba for nearly three decades, was overseer of smelting on the island at the time he wrote. He was a controversial figure at times, but few men knew the island better than Guzmán. Soto, in contrast, was an outsider interested in Cuba mainly as a source of men, horses, and supplies for his expedition to La Florida. My thanks to Shannon Lalor for a copy of the letter.
3. See Marrero, *Cuba*, 1:203, who writes of Porcallo that "su riqueza, hidalguía y experiencia militar lo hicieron uno de los candidatos entre los cuales seleccionó Velázquez al jefe de la expedición que enviaría a la conquista de México en 1519."
4. Porcallo doubtless was well aware that the cost of holding office could be steep. Another longtime important figure in early Cuba, Manuel de Rojas, who served twice as lieutenant governor in the 1520s and 1530s, stated that he received no compensation for his term in office and spent a good deal of his own money in connection with his service, particularly in conducting a visit of inspection of the island's towns and mines and suppressing indigenous revolts. He was so financially strapped that in response to a royal order that men who had been living in Cuba without their wives for five years must bring or return for them or provide an explanation of why

they could not, Rojas had to include himself among the number, explaining that he could not afford to bring his wife and family to the island; see AGI-SD 10, N.8 (1534). In 1543, by then in his sixties, Rojas traveled to Peru to visit a brother whom he hoped could help him out financially and ended up stranded there, unable to leave because of the turmoil caused by Gonzalo Pizarro's revolt; see AGI-Patr 94, N.2, R.1.
5. Both Gonzalo Fernández de Oviedo and Inca Garcilaso de la Vega mention Porcallo's *hijo natural* Gómez Suárez de Figueroa; see Marrero, *Cuba*, 1:209. His son's name is a traditional one in the family of the Duques de Feria, with whom Porcallo was said to be related.
6. See Adorno and Pautz, *Cabeza de Vaca*, 2:48–51.
7. The entry on Vasco Porcallo in Himmerich y Valencia, *Encomenderos*, 271, reads in part: "Porcallo was a *vecino* of Mexico City by 1525—at least he was there in jail, suspected of having had a hand in the death of Hernando Cabrera. His innocence must have been established, for in the early 1530s the second Audiencia reassigned him half of the *encomienda* of Tlalcozautitlan.... Porcallo was married, and ca. 1550 a son, Lorenzo Porcallo de Figueroa, succeeded him." These dates are difficult to reconcile with the times that Porcallo is known to have been in Cuba, nor does any of the documentation on Porcallo in Cuba refer to a marriage or a son in Mexico, although that is not conclusive evidence that such a son did not exist.
8. Adorno and Pautz, *Cabeza de Vaca*, 2:49–50.
9. The most extensive scholarly treatment of Vasco Porcallo is that of Marrero, who devotes several pages to a biographical profile in *Cuba*, 1:203–10.
10. An *información de méritos y servicios de Lorenzo de Godoy* (AGI-Patr 70, R.7) from 1570 mentions a captain Vasco Porcallo de la Cerda, who participated in the suppression of the rebellion of the Yopelcingos in New Spain. See also Marrero, *Cuba*, 1:206.
11. AGI-IG 1963, L.7, fol. 217v.
12. On the comuneros revolt in Spain, see Haliczer, *Comuneros of Castile*, among others. The información that Porcallo had prepared in November 1521 stated that he had been appointed teniente de justicia around seven months earlier; AGI-SD 77, N.6 for testimony of Juan Rodríguez Córdoba as well. My thanks to David Wheat for a copy of this and other documents from AGI-SD 77.
13. *Repartimientos*, or *encomiendas* as they were starting to be called by officials, were grants that provided their holders with the use of indigenous labor from a specified community on a rotating basis. This form of access to labor was hotly contested, although within two decades of Spanish occupation of Cuba, the numbers of available indigenous workers already

had decreased to the point that most of the grants were nearly useless. Many vecinos turned instead to Indian slaves captured during campaigns in Cuba or elsewhere in the circum-Caribbean; see Erin Stone's article in this volume.

14. The testimony regarding this episode appears in AGI-Patr 295, N.107. The alguacil, Sebastián de la Fuente, testified that the principal instigators, including an alcalde and two regidores, had agreed that "one would die for all and all for one" (*tenian concertado que muriese uno por todos y todos por uno*). A much abbreviated version of the testimony appears in *Colección de documentos inéditos de Ultramar*.
15. Sebastián de la Fuente offered the most detailed testimony on what took place after Porcallo arrived in Sancti Spíritus with his men.
16. On this dispute and bad feeling between the towns, see the report of Lieutenant Governor Manuel de Rojas (AGI-Patr 177, N.1, R.18) and his 1534 letter to the king (AGI-SD 77, N.50). A recommendation to merge the towns at the site of Sancti Spíritus never was implemented.
17. See AGI-Patr 177, N.1, R.13 and Mira Caballos, *El indio antillano*, 164 (cuadro 16). By comparison, Gonzalo de Guzmán received four caciques with 180 Indians in Santiago and Juan de Grijalva received two caciques with 134 Indians in Trinidad.
18. AGI-Patr 177, N.1, R.18. See also Mira Caballos, *El indio antillano*, 186 (cuadro 14). Porcallo's ownership of a group of African slaves when there were still relatively few Africans in Cuba is another indication of his wealth. Cuba lagged behind Puerto Rico and Hispaniola in obtaining African slaves; see the article by Marc Eagle in this volume.
19. Quoted in Marrero, *Cuba*, 1:210.
20. AGI-Patr 177, N.1, R.18. A prestigious establishment, a so-called *casa poblada*, would have had Spanish retainers (relatives, servants) as well as servants and slaves. The lack of such was an indication of falling far below the ideal.
21. AGI-SD 77, R.2, N.35, probanza que hizo en la villa de la Trinidad (Isla Fernandina) a pedimiento del señor Vasco Porcallo de Figueroa teniente de justicia (December 1522). Mira Caballos, *El Indio Antillano*, 331, writes that the Indians led by el Piloto had killed a large number of Spaniards who arrived along in the coast in a small fleet dispatched by Juan López de Aguirre from Trinidad in 1522.
22. The version of the testimony used here is in *Colección de documentos inéditos*, 1:124–25. I have not located the original *información*. The version consulted suggests that the testimony about the *comunidad* in Sancti Espíritus and Porcallo's testimony about his punishment of Indians eating dirt are

part of the same deposition. The audiencia in Santo Domingo was the highest governing authority in the islands.

23. See AGI-SD 77, N.6. There is an extensive literature about geophagy or geophagia. It has been described in numerous parts of the world, not necessarily associated with suicidal behavior. Some scientists suggest that dirt, especially clay, may provide humans or other animals with essential minerals or have a detoxifying effect. For a brief discussion of the possible functions of geophagia, see Stark and Slabach, "The Scoop on Eating Dirt."

24. On this episode see also Floyd, *Columbus Dynasty*, 212. He suggests that Spaniards believed that the Indians were committing suicide because of their fear of being uprooted and sent to New Spain. Francisco Ponce, who identified himself as the priest in Trinidad, testified in the información that Vasco Porcallo had prepared there in December 1522. Although some of the witnesses referred to the punishment of the Indians who were eating earth, Ponce did not say if he had been present or if he conducted the processions; see AGI-SD 77, N.6. This document consists of two informaciones prepared at Porcallo's behest, the first in Sancti Spíritus in November 1521 and the second in Trinidad almost a year later.

25. It was not until 1534, by which time Cuba's indigenous population already was sharply reduced, that lieutenant governor Manuel de Rojas attempted to enforce a ban on encomenderos' practice of hiring men to hunt down fugitive Indians. AGI-Patr 177, N.1, R.15.

26. AGI-SD 1121, L.1.

27. Marrero, *Cuba*, 1:210.

28. AGI-SD 1121, L.1.

29. Manuel de Rojas became lieutenant governor of Cuba after Diego Velázquez died in 1524. Guzmán assumed the office in 1526 and held it until late 1531 when one of the oidores of the audiencia, Lic. Juan Vadillo, arrived to initiate the *residencia* (judicial review) of his term in office. In March 1532 Vadillo once again appointed Rojas, who served two more years as lieutenant governor before Guzmán returned to office and served another two years. See Wright, *Early History of Cuba*, 101–2, 115.

30. Unless otherwise noted, all the information on this incident is found in AGI-SD 9, N.53. In 1533 Manuel de Rojas as lieutenant governor was instructed by the crown to look into this episode, which had resulted in one of the charges brought against Guzmán as part of the residencia of his term in office.

31. Witness Andrés de Parada, who was vecino and regidor of Santiago, referred to "el deudo y amistad que [Guzmán] tenia con el dicho Alonso Sanchez." AGI-SD 9, N.53.

32. This testimony is confusing because earlier witnesses referred to two decrees from the audiencia whereas subsequent statements from Porcallo referred to a number of orders. Conceivably Rojas was looking for multiple documents from the audiencia that at some time were sent to Trinidad, not just the ones pertaining to the dispute with Guzmán.
33. In 1527 Alonso de Sotomayor, Porcallo's brother, was alcalde in Trinidad and Porcallo and Alonso Guillén were regidores. Emphasis in the quote is mine.
34. For an example, see Gabriel de Avilez Rocha's chapter in this volume.
35. For a discussion of the limited socioeconomic opportunities of Extremadura, where Porcallo originated, see Altman, *Emigrants and Society*, especially 280–83.

Bibliography

ARCHIVES

Archivo General de Indias (Seville, Spain).

PUBLISHED WORKS

Adorno, Rolena, and Patrick Charles Pautz, eds. *Álvar Núñez Cabeza de Vaca: His Account, His Life, and the Expedition of Pánfilo de Narváez*. 3 vols. Lincoln: University of Nebraska Press, 1999.

Altman, Ida. *Emigrants and Society: Extremadura and Spanish America in the Sixteenth Century*. Berkeley: University of California Press, 1989.

Clayton, Lawrence A., Vernon James Knight Jr., and Edward C. Moore, eds. *The De Soto Chronicles: The Expedition of Hernando de Soto to North America in 1539–1543*. Tuscaloosa: University of Alabama Press, 1993.

Colección de documentos inéditos de Ultramar. Vol. 1, Cuba. Madrid, 1886–1932.

Floyd, Troy S. *The Columbus Dynasty in the Caribbean, 1492–1526*. Albuquerque: University of New Mexico Press, 1973.

Haliczer, Stephen. *The Comuneros of Castile: The Forging of a Revolution, 1475–1521*. Madison: University of Wisconsin Press, 1981.

Himmerich y Valencia, Robert. *The Encomenderos of New Spain, 1521–1555*. Austin: University of Texas Press, 1991.

Marrero, Levi. *Cuba: Economía y Sociedad*. Vol. 1. Río Piedras, PR: Editorial San Juan, 1972.

Mira Caballos, Esteban. *El indio antillano: repartimiento, encomienda y esclavitud (1492–1542)*. Seville: Muñoz Moya, 1997.

Stark, Philip T. B., and Brittany L. Slabach. "The Scoop on Eating Dirt." *Scientific American*, June 1, 2012.

Wright, Irene A. *The Early History of Cuba, 1492–1586*. New York: Macmillan, 1916, 2012.

5

Two Doñas

Aristocratic Women and Power in Colonial Cuba

SHANNON LALOR

In his will signed in Seville on October 13, 1537, Pedro de Paz, *contador* for the island of Cuba, requested that his minor son, Pedro de Paz de Guzmán, replace him in that position as remuneration for his thirty years of service to the crown in the Caribbean and in consideration for services rendered in the New World by young Pedro's uncles, Pero Núñez de Guzmán and Antonio de Quiñones.[1] He charged his wife, doña Guiomar de Guzmán, with the task of returning to Cuba from Seville after his death to oversee their properties, mining operations, Indians, and slaves. She would prove to be a formidable defender of her children and of her family's Caribbean properties. Doña Isabel de Bobadilla, who served as acting governor of Cuba from 1539 until 1542, arrived on the island with the ill-fated expeditionary force of her husband, Hernando de Soto. In his absence, she would work to maintain control of the colonial government, supply Soto's forces in La Florida, and defend their wealth and position. Unlike doña Guiomar, however, doña Isabel found that her efforts would bear little fruit.

This chapter examines these two aristocratic women's strategies to maintain and when possible enhance the position of their families and, by extension, their patronage networks in the early circum-Caribbean. Their attempts, both successful and unsuccessful, to further familial ambitions for control of territory and wealth can shed light on social hierarchies and expectations and their transfer from Spain to the colonial Caribbean as well as the roles played by elite women and men in shaping early Caribbean society. Although this study ostensibly begins in the late 1530s, these aristocratic widows' experiences in the colonial Caribbean stretched back to the first two or three decades of the conquest period. During this time men strove to carve out concessions from the crown that they hoped would serve as foundations for family wealth and power. For the vast majority of families that participated in the early stages of conquest, the Caribbean represented an opportunity to expand Old World wealth by acquiring property and power in the New World. The uncertainty of conquest and colonization and the evolving objectives of the crown, however, tended to force families to focus most of their attention on either Spain or Spanish America. The efforts of doña Isabel and doña Guiomar reflect this reality and demonstrate the ways in which the improvisational nature of many pursuits in the early Caribbean rewarded some and penalized others. Both women conducted transactions and with varying degrees of success established households, integrated themselves into local patronage networks, and utilized litigation as a means to maintain wealth and property. Their experiences illuminate the nature of early civil society in the Caribbean and transatlantic continuities and discontinuities that were foundational to the development of the Spanish Empire.

Due to their comparatively small numbers and infrequent appearance in official records and memoirs, Spanish women have remained relatively obscure in historical treatments of the first four or five decades following the arrival of Columbus in the New World. Primarily relying on accounts of Spanish chroniclers of the conquest, historians have tended to describe women of the early period in overly romanticized terms that reflect the idealized cultural constructions of the era instead of the lives of real women. More recent scholarship based upon customary forms of documentary evidence such as wills, transactions, and correspondence acknowledges the essential roles women played in the development and consolidation of the Spanish Empire in the Caribbean as well as the ways in which women of all ethnicities and social classes influenced societal norms.[2]

By the late 1530s the elite Bobadilla and Guzmán families boasted at least semipermanent residence in the circum-Caribbean region. Doña Isabel de Bobadilla's father, the conquistador Pedrárias de Ávila, arrived in Darién (present-day Panama) in 1514 and remained in Central America until his death in 1531. Her husband, Hernando de Soto, arrived in

Panama in the armada of Pedrárias in 1514 and eventually found his way to Peru with Francisco Pizarro in 1531. There is ample documentation of Pedro de Paz's activities on the island of Hispaniola, where as early as 1514 where he held an *encomienda* in partnership with his wife's brother, Pero Núñez de Guzmán, and later in Cuba, where in 1520 he became the new *contador* or royal accountant. Paz claimed to have been in the Caribbean as early as 1507, establishing himself on the island of Hispaniola in the company of men such as Diego Velázquez, Hernando Cortés, and Juan Ponce de León.

Befitting their aristocratic status and familial connections in the emerging colonial empire, both doña Isabel and doña Guiomar received substantial dowries based on property ownership in the Caribbean and Tierra Firme. Doña Isabel received an estate in Panama that included cattle, horses, slaves, land, and a *"cabaña redonda"* (round hut or structure) that had belonged to her father and had been administered by her mother since his death.[3] In effect she inherited her father's encomienda in Tierra Firme even though legally he could not pass it on to her in his will.[4] Signifying only the right to the use of Indian labor and not a grant of land, encomiendas typically were granted in areas where Spaniards already owned land, allowing them access to a nearby labor force to tend fields and livestock.[5] The language used in Isabel de Bobadilla's dowry deftly skirts the legal issues associated with inheriting encomiendas, a point of contention between conquistadors and the crown.[6] Doña Guiomar's dowry was based upon the Caribbean holdings of her brother, Pero Núñez de Guzmán, a longtime resident and royal treasurer of the island of Cuba and an encomendero of Hispaniola, Puerto Rico, and Cuba. Both women brought to their marriages grants of encomienda or monies resulting from the activities of their encomendero relatives in the Caribbean and high-ranking positions within the patronage networks that were the legacy of their elite peninsular origins. While encomenderos "felt themselves to be an aristocracy whatever their origins," the undisputed aristocracy of the Bobadilla family and the hidalgo status of Guiomar's branch of the Guzmán family were simply underscored by their control of encomiendas on the island and on the mainland.[7]

Doña Isabel de Bobadilla y Peñalosa

Doña Isabel belonged to the Castilian nobility and had direct connections to the crown through her family's service in the royal household, their leadership in the crown's military enterprises, and their positions as royal officials administering the earliest colonial enterprises. After her father, Pedrárias de Ávila, died in 1531 in Panama, it fell to doña Isabel's mother to consolidate and, insofar as possible, expand the influence and power that she and her husband spent more than twenty years ruthlessly pursuing in the Indies. Both Isabel de Bobadilla and her sister María de Peñalosa married conquistadors in the Indies while the youngest sister, Elvira, remained in Spain where she married Urban de Arellano. María, the eldest, married the conquistador and future governor of Nicaragua, Rodrigo de Contreras, in 1523. Contreras, a fellow Segovian, had been a close associate of Pedrárias since at least the early 1520s if not earlier and was his handpicked successor in Nicaragua. Contreras was appointed governor in 1534 and served in that capacity until 1544.[8]

In 1536 Isabel Arias de Bobadilla y Peñalosa married Hernando de Soto, who had begun his career in the Indies in the 1514 armada of her father. In partnership with Hernán Ponce de León and Francisco Compañón since around 1517 or 1518, Soto controlled extensive holdings in Central America. In late 1523 Soto and Compañón were appointed captains of Francisco Hernández de Córdoba's conquest of Nicaragua, spending the better part of 1524 engaged in that task.[9] Nicaragua proved to be far more lucrative for the *compañeros* than Castilla del Oro because they were the principal founders of the city of Santiago de León de los Caballeros and received encomiendas in an area of heavy salt deposits that were integral to Spanish survival. They also began trafficking in slaves. By 1529 the *compañía* was reduced to just two partners, Ponce and Soto, who expanded into shipping with the construction of the vessel *San Gerónimo*. Ponce and Soto used this ship to help Pizarro and Almagro's agents move recruits and slaves from shore to ship for the expedition to Peru, thereby thwarting attempts by Pedrárias to usurp control of the expedition. While Soto fought alongside the Pizarros in Peru, Ponce provided supplies and men from their base in Panama. Soto returned to Spain in

1536 with his fortune greatly enhanced by Incan treasure, looking for concessions from the crown and a noble wife.[10]

Sometime in 1536 or 1537, Soto petitioned unsuccessfully for governorship in perpetuity of the area north of Pizarro's holdings in South America and south of the town of Panama or, if not there, then in Guatemala.[11] On April 20, 1537, the king offered him instead the governorship of Cuba, the conquest of the area from the Rio de Las Palmas to La Florida, and the title of adelantado. While Soto's appointment as adelantado of La Florida and governor of Cuba appears to run counter to the goal of consolidating power in Central America, at the time of the wedding in 1536 the family most likely assumed Soto would have the governorship he requested, thereby further strengthening Bobadilla-Arias interests in the region. In any event the granting of another region for conquest did not necessarily spell disaster for their original goal; Spaniards of the early colonial period were opportunistic and flexible in their pursuit of titles and wealth. Soto's acquiescence, however, proved to be more than a miscalculation. It left the door open for his business partner, Hernán Ponce, who disagreed with Soto over the potential value of Florida and refused to support him in the expedition, to press his advantage in Central America and Peru. Meanwhile Soto and Isabel landed on an island where they found themselves in a social context that neither of them fully understood nor had the uncommitted capital or connections to navigate adequately.

Cuba, it seems, served as the stage for the final conflict between Soto and Ponce. The contentious interactions between the two men in 1539 were the culmination of at least three years of growing distrust and a general divergence of goals and personal interests. The tensions between the two likely began when Ponce learned that the king had granted Soto a license to conquer and settle Florida. These tensions were exacerbated by Ponce's public attempts to avoid Soto's *mayordomo* (steward) in Panama and his unwillingness to make port in Cuba until forced to do so by a storm. These signs of growing discord between them over the distribution of their accumulated wealth paled in comparison to their confrontation on the island in the spring of 1539.

Even before his arrival in Havana, Ponce de León had clearly begun to sour on his partnership with Soto. Alonso de Ayala, Soto and Isabel's mayordomo, offered damning testimony that he attempted over the course of three months to see Ponce in Panama to present letters from Soto. Ponce, however, had managed to avoid him.[12] Soto and Isabel had dispatched Ayala to Panama to sell the encomienda that constituted the bulk of her dowry, as Soto was now in desperate need of cash to purchase supplies and outfit his expeditionary force. Ayala also carried letters from Soto requesting money from Ponce, who was in Panama liquidating assets in preparation for his return to Spain and should have been in a position to meet Soto's demands.

In early 1539 Ponce began the journey back to Spain from Panama, intending to bypass Cuba altogether in what appears to have been a consistent strategy of avoiding Soto and his agents. Isabel presented witnesses on the island of Cuba during this period who watched Ponce's ship flounder off the coast for several days before making port due to a storm.[13] Ponce produced only one witness of his own, Alonso Martín, who testified that the ship made port voluntarily. Once in Cuba, those attached to the household of Soto and Isabel watched Ponce carefully, gathering information on his belongings and their value. Isabel presented witnesses who testified to the movable luxury goods Ponce carried with him and to the existence of at least one trunk reportedly containing gold and silver.[14] According to Juan Ruiz Lobillo, Soto seized but never opened the chest, returning it to Ponce within an hour of taking it. Lobillo testified that Ponce promptly returned the chest to Soto of his own will to pay for the expedition.[15] If true, the mysterious trunk proved to be the only monies Soto would receive from the liquidation of his vast holdings in Central and South America.

Ponce left Cuba for Spain almost four months after Soto departed for Florida. Upon Soto's departure, Ponce appeared before an *escribano* (notary) of the island to nullify the new partnership agreement he claimed Soto forced him to sign. He testified that Soto had threatened to drag him to Florida in chains and leave him there to die. Through Isabel's interventions and those of her brother fray Francisco de Bobadilla, Ponce recanted and accepted the agreement.[16]

The failed conquest of Florida dealt a staggering blow to Bobadilla ambitions in the New World. The alienation of Soto's property in Peru, Nicaragua, and Panama placed his patrimony in a precarious position. When combined with the 1539 sale of Isabel's Panamanian estate, the losses effectively negated the efforts of almost twenty-five years of manipulation, violence, and exploitation in the service of familial legacy and estate building. Although her sister María de Peñalosa remained in Nicaragua until 1550, she and her husband left ignominiously for Peru after their sons Hernando and Pedro unsuccessfully rebelled against the new governor.[17] The couple were stripped of their encomiendas and most of their accumulated wealth.

During Soto's absence from Cuba and perhaps even more so after his death, Isabel remained outside the island oligarchy; she lacked island-specific financial resources, and her household included no one with useful connections to the island's patronage networks. In spite of, or perhaps because of, her position as acting governor of the island from 1539 until 1543, doña Isabel appears to have made few lasting connections or to have received much help from the two men assigned to assist her. With their decade-long experience in Cuba, Licenciado Bartolomé Ortiz and Juan de Rojas brought much needed expertise to the Soto/Bobadilla government, though it is unclear how much, if any, assistance they provided to the governor's wife during her tenure. It also remains unclear how much the factionalism resulting from her husband's exchanges with Hernán Ponce de León in 1539 undermined her ability to govern and command resources.

According to a real cédula dated 1539, Soto designated Ortiz as *teniente de gobernador* of Cuba, making him responsible for military issues in Soto's absence. Later that same year, on November 8, 1539, Ortiz sent a letter to the king claiming to suffer from an illness that left him bedridden for three months after Soto's departure and unable to complete the fortifications begun by Soto at Havana. In response to an earlier command from the king he also claimed he could not persuade the city's leaders to provide the necessary funds to finish the bastion or continue to prosecute the war against unsubmissive Indians; it is unlikely that they had the funds.[18] It appears that after Soto's departure, doña Isabel was on her own with little support from Ortiz, who perhaps took the opportunity to assess Isabel's resolve and that of her supporters. The fact that Soto commandeered both people and materials for his expedition, much to the general dismay of the island's vecinos, would not have made Isabel de Bobadilla particularly popular either.

The other primary participant in the Soto/Bobadilla government, Juan de Rojas, was a vecino of Havana at least as early as 1529 and *alcalde ordinario* (magistrate) in 1538.[19] While it is not clear whether Rojas was politically useful for doña Isabel, he did accept carved silver pieces in pawn for 470 pesos so that she could pay ordinary household expenses.[20] Without ties to the patronage networks of the island, her position as the ranking Spanish lady seems to have been of little use in governing Cuba or even in maintaining her own household. Again, it would appear that doña Isabel lacked the necessary resources to thrive on the island. The men who were in the best position to help her did so in ways that underscored her status as an outsider.

The composition of Isabel de Bobadilla's household, together with its location in Havana, may have contributed to her inability to integrate effectively into Cuba's social milieu. The ladies who were part of doña Isabel's entourage in Havana were doña María de Guzmán[21] and doña Leonor de Bobadilla, both married to high-ranking lieutenants in Soto's expeditionary force. Doña María, apparently not a close relative of the island's Guzmáns, was married to Baltasar de Gallegos, one of the leaders of the Florida expedition and a personal confidant of Soto. The other aristocrat accompanying doña Isabel was the granddaughter of her second cousin, Leonor de Bobadilla. Leonor joined Isabel when the ships stopped in the Canary Islands to take on additional supplies for the Atlantic voyage. When the expedition arrived in Cuba, it was discovered that Leonor was pregnant with the child of Soto's lieutenant general and fellow Extremeño, Nuño de Tobar.[22] The ill-fated Tobar was stripped of his title as lieutenant-general, marrying Leonor over Soto's objections.

After the ladies, Isabel's household included male attendants, maids, and indigenous and African slaves. Of her six male attendants, the only adults were Alonso de Ayala, her mayordomo, and Pedro Gamez, an octogenarian and vecino of Jaén, although her brother fray Francisco de

Bobadilla appears to have been present for at least some of her tenure. The rest were *pajes* (pages) under the age of eleven, including Pedro de Soto, the son of Soto's sister Catalina. Additionally, doña Isabel traveled to Cuba with six *criadas* (servants): María Arias, Catalina Ximenes, Isabel Mexía, an Arellano, a Carreño, and Isabel de Bolaños, who was the wife of Alonso Sánchez Mejía.[23] Of doña Isabel and Soto's slaves, eighteen were listed in the final inventory of their joint possessions and presumably resided within the household. Few details were provided for seven individuals, who were simply said to have originated *"fuera de la ysla"* or outside the island. Their remaining eleven slaves included Isabel, a *morisca* (woman of Muslim descent); a family group comprised of Joanillo, his wife, Francisca, and their daughter, Margarita; and others identified as Manuel, Domingo, Hernando, Jorge, and Julian. Doña Isabel and Soto also owned two boys (one unnamed and one listed as Francisco) who were Joanillo and Manuel's sons from unions with enslaved Indian women.[24] While the ladies, male attendants, and criadas appear to have had connections to each other and to other members of the expeditionary force brought from Spain, there is no indication that any of them had been to Cuba prior to this journey nor that they had relatives on the island. Several members of doña Isabel's household returned to Spain with her in 1544.[25]

Doña Guiomar de Guzmán

If Pedro de Paz is to be believed, he came to the Caribbean sometime around 1507, just prior to Juan Ponce de León's conquest of the island of Puerto Rico, then known as San Juan.[26] Paz noted that when he arrived in Hispaniola he carried with him 500 *ducados*, which were promptly stolen by some Frenchmen.[27] In spite of the setback, Paz became an encomendero and vecino of San Juan de la Maguana in the western part of Hispaniola and a business partner of Pero Núñez de Guzmán with whom he jointly controlled the Maguana encomienda. The Paz-Guzmán encomienda situated in the former seat of the cacique Caonabo boasted an abundance of Indians who could be exploited for their labor in the gold mining districts to the east. Of the 1,107 *indios de servicio* listed in the 1514 *repartimiento* (division of native peoples) of San Juan de la

Maguana, Paz and Guzmán together received 140, or about 12 percent of those assigned.[28] In 1516 Paz registered a complaint with the crown reporting that Diego Velázquez had unjustifiably seized an encomienda of 140 Indians held jointly by himself and Guzmán. The crown ordered that the Indians be restored to the two encomenderos.[29]

From professed humble beginnings—although 500 ducados seems scarcely humble—Pedro de Paz fashioned a place for himself in the Caribbean, working to develop a firm foundation for wealth and power in Spain's nascent empire that would continue beyond his own lifetime. Sometime before 1519 he married doña Guiomar de Guzmán, the sister of his business partner. Together they had four children between 1519 and 1526, the oldest born on Hispaniola while the other three presumably took their first breaths on the island of Cuba where Paz was appointed royal contador in 1520. In Cuba Paz joined Guzmán, who had been appointed Cuba's treasurer in 1518.[30] In addition to the position of contador, Paz received lucrative encomiendas in Baracoa and Santiago. His will places the total annual yield of these two encomienda holdings at 4,000 and 3,000 *montones* of yuca and aje, a kind of sweet potato. Paz also controlled mining interests, owned livestock, and possessed urban rental properties located in areas frequented by officials for royal business.

In December 1529 he requested permission to return to Seville on the basis of poor health. He received a license to travel to Spain for a period of sixteen months. Over the course of the next eight years Paz requested extensions every year and a half, the last being granted in December 1537, a scant two months after his death. In 1536 doña Guiomar and her daughters applied for licenses to travel to the Caribbean, each with three black slaves for their personal service, suggesting that they planned to return to Cuba to live or at the very least to convince the crown that their property and the position of contador would again be occupied.[31]

Shortly after her husband's death, doña Guiomar instigated official proceedings against Cuba's *factor*, Hernando de Castro, arguing that Castro intentionally mismanaged the family's holdings on the island in order to retain the bulk of the profits for himself and his associates.[32] In 1530 Pedro de Paz had officially left Castro in charge of his holdings and the office of contador, expecting that the proceeds from his various investments would be forwarded to him in Seville. One of the codicils of Paz's will explained that the *poder* or power of attorney given to Hernando de Castro required Castro to produce a full accounting of the profits from his various properties for official review as Paz believed the family was not receiving what was due to them. As part of the suit, Doña Guiomar alleged that her arrival in Cuba in 1540 was motivated in no small part by Castro's unwillingness to honor his obligations. She argued that he collected close to 20,000 gold pesos belonging to Pedro de Paz and his heirs but had remitted to them only 6,000 ducados. As the documentation attests, doña Guiomar continued to prosecute these claims against Castro to greater effect once she was in residence on the island.

In preparation for the family's return to Cuba, at least two of Paz's associates preceded them. Of the executors listed in Pedro de Paz's will, two were vecinos of long standing on the island of Cuba and thus in a position to support doña Guiomar and her children's inheritance claims. According to Paz's will, both men were *"amigos de mys haziendas"* and held in high esteem.[33] Juan Calvillo probably arrived on the island shortly after Pedro de Paz became contador of Cuba in 1520. Calvillo had a *mestiza* daughter by an Indian woman he described as single and free.[34] After taking his six-year-old child to Spain to be raised and instructed in the Catholic faith by his mother and sisters, Calvillo returned to Cuba in 1536. The other man, Rodrigo Romero, was a vecino of Asunción (Baracoa) who, like Calvillo, received a license to return to Cuba in 1536. Romero was married to a Spanish woman whom he refused to bring to the Indies. A real cédula of 1536 notes his assurances to the crown that he would be attentive to his house and patrimony and see that his wife was treated justly and with great care in his absence.[35] The granting of licenses for both men to return to the island and a 1537 license to travel to Cuba for Paz's criado Hernando de Orejón coincide neatly with doña Guiomar's own requests for licenses to return to Cuba, suggesting that Paz's death was understood to be imminent in early 1536.[36]

Doña Guiomar traveled to Cuba in 1540 with an entourage of at least fourteen people.[37] In his will Pedro de Paz had underscored the need for a member of his family to be on the island to protect the family's property and to see to the welfare of the Indians in his charge.[38] Upon her arrival, doña Guiomar testified that she found Castro and those around him cheerful, owing no doubt to their good fortune at having Paz's good fortune. Castro soon stopped calling on her, however, presumably because she demanded from him a full accounting of the proceeds of Paz's holdings on the island.[39]

The lawsuit is an interesting one that ranges from one side of the Atlantic to the other, unfolding in the proceedings and mandates of the Council of the Indies, the Casa de la Contratación, the Audiencia of Santo Domingo, and in the cabildo of Santiago de Cuba. There are two primary issues in the Castro suit that reflect strategies for commandeering property and the rights to tribute in the colonial world. The first issue centers on the fact that none of Pedro de Paz's heirs resided on the island. Both the crown in 1535 and Pedro de Paz in his 1537 will demanded that someone from the family be in Cuba actively managing Indians and property. Paz requested that in addition to assuming the roles of *tutora* (tutor) and *curadora* (guardian) for her four minor children, doña Guiomar also should travel to Cuba with or without their only son to oversee the property in the best interests of their children.[40] In his testimony Hernando de Castro seized upon this point to argue that the children were obligated by their father's will to reside on the island in order to oversee and collect what was due to them. He further pointed out that no bond had been provided for the money he was expected to remit to Seville and, therefore, he should not have to pay. He stated that he had sent 6,000 ducados and would pay the *quinto* (royal tax), which he had not done. Beyond that, he argued, his conscience was clear.

In her successful response to this challenge doña Guiomar pointed out that her husband had appointed her as his representative regardless of whether her children accompanied her to the Indies. As they were all still minors, she asserted her control of the goods and properties of her husband until such time as her children could assume their responsibilities. She noted that her daughter doña María de Paz was prohibited from traveling to the Indies until the case between her and her betrothed, Francisco Muñoz de Pamplona, could be settled, intimating that it was precisely because her family had not received what it was justly due that doña María was unable to wed honorably.[41] At the time, doña María resided in the monastery of San Clemente in Seville along with her younger sister, doña Leonor de Quiñones, waiting to join their mother in Cuba. Doña Guiomar's son, Pedro de Paz de Guzmán, was studying in Salamanca, which she explained in her testimony as being very necessary.[42] Her youngest child, doña Isabel de Paz, had died about the same time as her husband and, therefore, is not mentioned in any of the proceedings.[43] To better thwart Castro's focus on the children, doña Guiomar further requested that the guardianship of the children and the administration of property be separated and Castro be forced to pay everything that had been collected in the name of her husband.

The second issue hinged on doña Guiomar's rights as tutora and curadora of her four minor children, as stipulated in her husband's will. Sometime after the death of her husband in 1537 but before her departure for Cuba in 1540, doña Guiomar married Sebastián del Hoyo Villota.[44] This marriage proved to be detrimental, at least in the short term, to the roles designated for her by her husband. The guardianship of the couple's only son and eldest child, Pedro de Paz de Guzmán, was turned over to Luis de Orbaneja, while it appears doña Guiomar retained the tutoría and curaduría for her daughters.[45] In order to confirm doña Guiomar's continuing guardianship of her daughter María de Paz, Villota instigated a summons in March 1541 requesting testimony from María and from the abbess and nuns of the monastery of San Clemente in Seville.[46] The following year, doña Guiomar and her three surviving children participated in a lawsuit against Luis de Orbaneja, arguing for the reinstatement of her guardianship of all three children despite her remarriage.[47] In order to succeed in her suit against Hernando de Castro, she required uncontested control of her late husband's estate, which could not be obtained without unfettered access to her children. At the time of the petition doña Guiomar was not present in Spain, where all her children then resided, but instead was reestablishing her household in Cuba in order to better control the property and enslaved Indians that were ostensibly her children's legacy. Nonetheless, she regained her position as curadora for all three children, as a real cédula of 1541 addressed to the governor and officials of Cuba affirms, which certainly aided in her administration of the family's Cuban properties.

In the end, doña Guiomar emerged the victor in the lawsuit, though there are royal cedulas in the case file that suggest Hernando de Castro responded slowly to the mandates of the crown, audiencia, and cabildo. Her presence in Cuba undoubtedly served much the same purpose in the conclusion of the suit as it had in its prosecution. She was a highly visible reminder of Castro's obligations to her family and the patronage network on the island in which it was embedded. While her second husband, Villota, did receive a license to travel to the Indies in 1541 presumably to join her, it is unclear if he ever made it there. By 1545, she was married for a third time to the new governor of Cuba, Juanes de Ávila, who arrived in Santiago in late 1543 to replace the deceased conquistador Hernando de Soto. According to Irene Wright, contemporary accounts, which placed Ávila at near thirty years of age and doña Guiomar at more than fifty, suggested that they lived as man and wife in her house in Santiago before officially marrying.[48] The match was a fortuitous one for doña Guiomar, as Hernando de Castro noted, "He [Ávila] was as blind in his own business as he has been in the interests of everybody except Doña Guiomar."[49]

Conclusion

While there certainly are similarities in the experiences of doña Isabel de Bobadilla and doña Guiomar de Guzmán—the colonial base of their wealth, their noble status, and their families' long-term association with the Caribbean—the differences between them provide some intimation of the structure of early colonial Caribbean society and the improvisational nature of the early Spanish Caribbean more generally. Doña Guiomar was at her weakest in defending her Caribbean property and wealth as long as she remained in Spain. Upon her arrival in Cuba, however, she quickly reestablished her household in Santiago and affirmed control over her varied interests on the island. By asserting her role in Cuban society through her place in patronage networks and among her kinship group, she was able to undermine Hernando de Castro's support and prevail in her quest to have her husband's money and property restored to her control.

If an explanation can be determined, it appears to lie in the deep connections that doña Guiomar and her family cultivated in the Caribbean.

The Paz-Guzmán family clearly viewed the Caribbean and Cuba specifically as integral to their familial ambitions and therefore an arena in which they were best served when ascendant. Once doña Guiomar arrived on the island, the defense launched by Castro seemed to simply fall apart. One can only assume that her presence reset patronage networks that had been cultivated for more than thirty years or at least motivated members of that network to get in line behind her claims against Castro. Her physical presence supplied the reassurance that her family's retainers had been lacking during the Paz-Guzmán family's long absence from the island.

Doña Isabel de Bobadilla, on the other hand, did not fare so well. One would assume that, given Isabel's position in peninsular society and her direct connections to the crown, she would have been the more likely of the two women to capitalize on class and status consciousness among Spaniards in Cuba. The opposite, however, proved true. Unlike Guiomar, doña Isabel had no networks to activate on the island and no way to access any residual patronage or obligatory relationships that her husband or her parents may have maintained in Panama or Nicaragua. It is unclear who in the Bobadilla family remained in Central America to oversee the family's properties beyond María de Peñalosa and her husband, Rodrigo de Contreras, which may offer some insights as to Isabel's apparent lack of connection to Central American patronage networks.

With the liquidation of assets in Central America, including doña Isabel's encomienda, any connections Soto may have had there were effectively severed, leaving Isabel in Cuba with no network of support other than her own household and no source of income other than the encomiendas assigned to the Cuban governor, which she was sure to lose in light of Soto's extended absence. The fact that no one in her household had any direct or strong connections to well-established Cuban elites, coupled with her residence in Havana at the far end of the island from the capital of Santiago, ensured that she would have great difficulty integrating herself into the island's oligarchy. Her failure to receive any assistance for at least the first three months after Soto's departure suggests that she was being apprised circuitously of her place in the social and political hierarchy.

These roughly contemporaneous episodes in Cuban history argue for a deeper look at the construction of early civil society in the Caribbean as well as its relationship to the structure of transatlantic networks. Doña Isabel's experience reflects a peninsula-focused transatlantic patronage network in which the family relied upon their personal connections at the Spanish court to enhance peninsular wealth through the integration of Spanish and Spanish American holdings. Much of the progress made by the Bobadilla-Arias family in Panama and Nicaragua was directly attributable to strategic appearances at court by Isabel de Bobadilla's mother, who traveled frequently between Panama and Spain during the 1510s and 1520s.[50]

Without her interventions, it is doubtful Pedrárias would have survived two *residencias* (judicial reviews of royal officials) and the negative campaigns launched by Gonzalo Fernández de Oviedo and the supporters of Vasco Núñez de Balboa. Bobadilla's designs for a transatlantic empire faltered within the first twenty-five years; Pedrárias's diminishing influence at the Spanish court and his loss of property and positions of power in Central America resulted from bad luck, mismanagement, and the Spanish crown's efforts to curtail the ambitions of elite families. The Bobadilla network in the Americas failed due to its dependence upon patronage networks that remained fixed in Spain and to weak connections in the circum-Caribbean region that are perhaps best evidenced by Ponce's ability to avoid doña Isabel's mayordomo in Panama for more than three months.

Doña Guiomar's experience illustrates how economic diversification, facilitated by long-term residence and royal administrative appointments and grants, supported the development of an extensive network of family members and clients. Caribbean familial networks in turn allowed for both the expansion and defense of colonial privileges and properties. Interactions between doña Guiomar and others in Cuba during the first half of the sixteenth century suggest that an established and recognizable oligarchy had emerged on the island by the late 1520s, with possible connections to broader Caribbean patronage networks. A small number of interconnected families in early Cuba dominated royal offices, encomiendas, and economic enterprises; these included the two branches of the Guzmán family represented by Pero Núñez and Gonzalo as well as the Paz, Cuellar, and Rojas families. When Pedro de Paz moved his family from Cuba to Seville in 1530, he faced the harsh reality that the transatlantic context complicated management of their Cuban assets. His absence encouraged graft among those on the island charged with seeing to his family's interests. Only with Doña Guiomar's arrival in Cuba in 1540 was the family able to protect and expand their colonial holdings.

Comparison of the divergent outcomes for doña Isabel and doña Guiomar in Cuba indicates that households played a significant role in structuring colonial society, especially at the level of the elite, as they were both constituted by and constituent of local conditions. In structure and composition, the Caribbean household acted as a microcosm of civil society and thus merits greater attention, particularly in light of the differences between members of the households of doña Isabel and doña Guiomar and the potential impact of those differences upon their experiences in Cuba. Because the household served as the primary locus of activity for women in the colonial period, more sustained examination is needed of the Caribbean household as a primary site of interaction across social and ethnic boundaries and as a key to the formation of Caribbean patronage networks. Doña Isabel de Bobadilla's and doña Guiomar de Guzmán's experiences in Cuba tell us much more than that aristocratic women were present in the Caribbean in the first half of the sixteenth century. The intersections between their lives and colonial social and administrative structures provide insights into the nature of early colonial society, the role of familial patronage networks in the development of a transoceanic empire, and the value of the Caribbean as a proving ground for strategies of colonization and settlement with far-reaching implications for the expansion of the nascent Spanish Empire. The interactions that characterized the doñas' lives in colonial Spanish America are a reminder not only that women of all classes participated in the colonization of Spanish America but also that they fought, won, and lost as active and integral participants in the construction of the colonial world.

Notes

Research for this essay was conducted in Seville with the assistance of a University of Florida Graduate School Dissertation Research Grant. I would like to thank Ida Altman, David Wheat, Matt Childs, and the contributors to this volume for their thoughtful feedback.

ABBREVIATIONS

AGI	Archivo General de Indias
-Cttn	Casa de la Contratación
-IG	Gobierno: Indiferente General
-Just	Justicia
-Patr	Patronato Real
-SD	Gobierno: Audiencia de Santo Domingo
AVP	Ignacio Avellaneda Papers

1. AGI-Just 726, N.5.
2. See Altman, "Spanish Women," in which the author examines the role of women in the formation of civil society in the Caribbean until 1540. See also David Wheat, *Atlantic Africa and the Spanish Caribbean*, for a detailed examination of the varied roles of African-descended women in early colonial Cartagena.
3. AGI-Just 750A, N.1, fols. 117r–127v. See also Antonio del Solar's transcription of the same document in *El Adelantado*.
4. Doña Isabel was no stranger to the colonial milieu, having spent a portion of her childhood in Darien or modern-day Panama with her father, the conquistador Pedro Arias Dávila.
5. For further discussion of the nature and significance of encomienda grants, see Haring, *The Spanish Empire* and Góngora, *Studies*. James Lockhart discusses the connections between repartimiento, encomienda, and hacienda in *Of Things of the Indies*, chap. 1. See also Sauer's discussion of repartimiento in *The Early Spanish Main*.
6. The precipitous demographic decline of indigenous populations in the Caribbean through the first few decades of the sixteenth century undermined the value of encomiendas as a foundation for sustainable wealth.
7. Lockhart, *Of Things of the Indies*, 11.
8. For a discussion of Contreras's governorship and his subsequent issues with the crown, see Herrera, *Historia general*, 123–30. See also Aram, *Leyenda negra*, for more on Segovians in the conquest of Nicaragua.
9. Paul Hoffman, "A Brief Biography," in Clayton, Knight, and Moore, *De Soto Chronicles*, 1:427.

10. Lockhart, *Men of Cajamarca*, 197–98.
11. Solar, *El adelantado*, 91–117.
12. AVP, box 8/folder 188, 9.
13. AVP, box 8/folder 188, 2.
14. AVP, box 8/folder 188, 29.
15. AVP, box 8/folder 188, 7.
16. AVP, box 8/folder 188, 4.
17. Herrera, *Historia general*, 130. In 1548 Contreras traveled to Spain to petition for the retention of his encomienda and to retrieve goods and monies confiscated during his residencia. While he was in Spain, his sons fomented rebellion and apparently were killed near Panama City, although their bodies were never identified.
18. AGI-SD 1121, L.2, fol. 129v. The cédula dated February 1539 and received prior to Soto's departure ordered him to "make war on the Indians of the heights and the *cimarrones* [escaped African slaves] and to repulse French corsairs."
19. AGI-SD 868, L.1, fols. 114r–15r.
20. Solar, *El Adelantado Hernando*, 239.
21. Not to be confused with doña María de Paz, also sometimes referred to as doña María de Guzmán.
22. Vega, "Relation," in Clayton, Knight, and Moore, *De Soto Chronicles*, 1:56.
23. Solar, *El Adelantado*, 207–21.
24. Vega, "Relation," in Clayton, Knight, and Moore, *De Soto Chronicles*, 1:227. The slaves Domingo, Hernando, Jorje, and Julian are indicated by names only.
25. The failure of Soto's expedition had an important effect on the fortunes and subsequent movement of the members of doña Isabel's entourage. In the early spring of 1544, Isabel de Bobadilla left Cuba for Spain never to return to the Indies. Accompanying her were doña María de Guzmán and her husband, Baltasar Gallegos, and Catalina Jiménez and her husband, Rodrigo Rangel. See also Scott Cave's discussion of a woman believed to be one of doña Isabel's indigenous servants in "Madalena."
26. Sauer, *Early Spanish Main*, 158.
27. AGI-Just 725, N.5. Paz did not elaborate on the incident, which presumably occurred during a corsair raid.
28. Sauer, *Early Spanish Main*, 151, 201. Sauer notes that at the time of the 1514 repartimiento conducted by Miguel de Pasamonte, San Juan de la Maguana reported twenty-seven vecinos, only one of whom had a Castilian wife.
29. AGI-IG 419, L.6, fol. 560r.

30. AGI-IG 421, L.11, fols. 83v–84r. The business partnership between Paz and Guzmán continued to flourish until Guzmán died in 1527.
31. AGI-SD-1121, L.2, fol. 56r. A real cédula of January 1536 describes Pedro Paz as dying, though he managed to hang on through that year and into 1537. This may explain why licenses for travel were granted in 1536 but travel was not undertaken until 1540.
32. AGI-Just 726, N.5.
33. AGI-Just 726, N.5.
34. AGI-SD 1121, L.2, fol. 57v (11 January 1536).
35. AGI-SD 1121, L.2, fol. 55r (11 January 1536).
36. AGI-SD 1121, L.2, fol. 65r; AGI-IG 422, L.16, fol. 253r(4) (11 January 1536).
37. AGI-Cttn 5536, L.5, fol. 231v(1) (31 January 1540).
38. AGI-Just 726, N.5.
39. AGI-Just 726, N.5. Doña Guiomar testified that she made certain concessions to Hernando de Castro because she wished to protect the goods that remained as now she was alone.
40. AGI-Just 726, N.5.
41. AGI-IG 1962, L.6.
42. AGI-Just 726, N.5. "E que Pedro de Paz su hijo quedo en la ciudad de Salamanca estudiando lo qual le convenia y era muy necesario."
43. AGI-IG 1962, L.5, fols. 263r–263v.
44. The only references I have been able to locate for Sebastian del Hoyo Villota are AGI-IG 1963, L.7, fols. 226v–227v (16 November 1540), AGI-IG 423, L.20, fol. 533v, and AGI-Patr 279, N.1, R.63. All are related to doña Guiomar and Pedro de Paz.
45. AGI-Just 726 (1540). Doña Guiomar is the curadora "de las damas hijas despues ella se ha casado segunda vez."
46. AGI-Patr 279, N.1, R.63.
47. AGI-Just 976, N.6.
48. AGI-Just 992, R.3 (1543), concerns an illicit relationship between Juanes de Ávila, newly arrived, and a lady of Cuba, presumably doña Guiomar.
49. Wright, *Early History*, 178.
50. Aram, *Leyenda negra*, 160–67.

Bibliography

ARCHIVES

Archivo General de Indias (Seville, Spain).
Ignacio Avellaneda Papers. Latin American and Caribbean Collection. George A. Smathers Libraries, University of Florida (Gainesville).

PUBLISHED WORKS

Altman, Ida. "Spanish Women in the Early Caribbean, 1493–1540." In *Women of the Iberian Atlantic*, edited by Sarah E. Owens and Jane E. Mangan, 57–81. Baton Rouge: Louisiana State University Press, 2012.

Aram, Bethany. *Leyenda negra y leyendas doradas en la conquista de América*. Madrid: Marcial Pons Historia, 2007.

Cave, Scott. "Madalena: The Entangled History of One Indigenous Floridian Woman in the Atlantic World." *Americas* 74, no. 2 (April 2017): 171–200.

Clayton, Lawrence A., Vernon James Knight Jr., and Edward C. Moore, eds. *The De Soto Chronicles: The Expedition of Hernando de Soto to North America in 1539–1543*. Tuscaloosa: University of Alabama Press, 1993.

Góngora, Mario. *Studies in the Colonial History of Spanish America*. Cambridge: Cambridge University Press, 1975.

Haring, C. H. *The Spanish Empire in America*. San Diego: Harcourt Brace Jovanovich, 1947.

Herrera y Tordesillas, Antonio de. *Historia general de los hechos de los castellanos en las islas, y Tierra Firme de el mar oceano, Decada VIII, Libro VI*. Madrid: La Oficina Real de Nicolas Rodriguez Franco, 1726.

Lockhart, James. *The Men of Cajamarca: A Social and Biographical Study of the First Conquerors of Peru*. Austin: University of Texas Press, 1972.

———. *Of Things of the Indies*. Stanford: Stanford University Press, 1999.

Mira Caballos, Esteban. *Las Antillas Mayores*. Madrid: Iberoamericana, 2000.

Morales Padrón, Francisco. *Canarias: Crónicas de su Conquista*. Las Palmas: Museo Canario, 1978.

Rumeu de Armas, Antonio. "Cristóbal Colón y Beatriz de Bobadilla en las Ante Vísperas del Descubrimiento." *El Museo Canario* 75–76 (1960): 255–79.

Sauer, Carl Ortwin. *The Early Spanish Main*. Berkeley: University of California Press, 1966.

Solar y Taboada, Antonio del. *El adelantado Hernando de Soto: breves noticias, nuevos documentos para su biografía y relación de los que le acompañaron a la Florida*. Badajoz: Ediciones Arqueros, 1929.

Wheat, David. *Atlantic Africa and the Spanish Caribbean, 1570–1640*. Chapel Hill: Published for the Omohundro Institute of Early American History and Culture, Williamsburg VA, by the University of North Carolina Press, 2016.

Wright, Irene A. *The Early History of Cuba, 1492–1586*. New York: Macmillan, 1916.

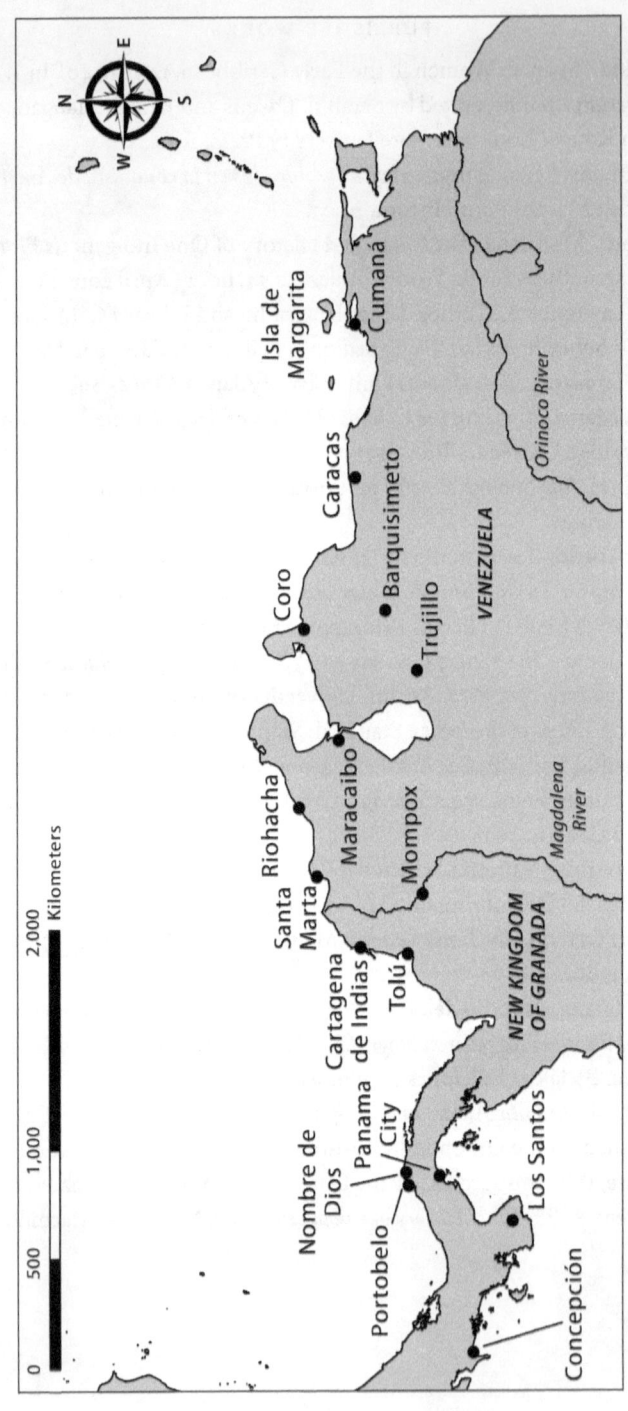

Map 3. The Southern Caribbean: Selected Sites.

6

Between Acceptance and Exclusion

Spanish Responses to Portuguese Immigrants in the Sixteenth-Century Spanish Caribbean

BRIAN HAMM

By the mid-sixteenth century, a growing number of Spanish officials were sounding the alarm about a veritable Portuguese colonization of Spain's holdings in the circum-Caribbean. "In this city and in the towns of this island," one official in Santo Domingo reported, "it is understood that there are more Portuguese than Castilians, and that many of them are permanent residents [*vecinos*]."[1] This specious refrain would be repeated on numerous occasions. Indeed, for men like Admiral Francisco Carreño, the problem extended far beyond Hispaniola: "In all of the towns along the coast of Tierra Firme and on the islands of Santo Domingo [sic], Cuba, and Jamaica, half of the citizens and inhabitants are Portuguese, ... so that it seems like this land is nothing other than the coast of Portugal."[2] Apprehension about the fidelity of this immigrant population fueled this sort of hyperbolic rhetoric. Could the Portuguese be trusted as loyal members of the local community and faithful subjects of the Spanish crown? In one report sent to the Council of the Indies in 1582, the Portuguese were accused of only having "in their soul the things of Portugal, as if in actuality they were established along the Rua Nova in Lisbon."[3] Another official complained that the Portuguese made a practice of obtaining *vecindad* in Castile, then traveling to the Spanish Indies, all the while "holding onto their *naturaleza*, house, family, and wealth in Portugal."[4] As is often the case with immigrant groups, questions of loyalty were frequently raised and not easily answered.

The themes of loyalty and disloyalty are common in the historical literature on the Portuguese in colonial Spanish America. However, they are frequently examined only in reference to the seventeenth century and, in particular, the so-called *complicidades de judíos* that were ostensibly discovered by inquisitors in Lima, Cartagena, and Mexico City during the 1630s and 1640s. These sweeping inquisitorial investigations carried out against the Portuguese concerned not only religious infidelities involving the "Law of Moses" but also certain treasonous political alliances between Spain's enemies and resident Portuguese in Spanish America.[5] Due in large part to the wealth of source material produced by the Inquisition, these "complicities" have long served as the prism through which Portuguese life in the Spanish Indies is interpreted. Time and again, historians have emphasized Spanish contempt for the Portuguese due to Spanish antisemitism and the stereotyped conflation of Portuguese nationality with Jewish ancestry. As the oft-quoted Spanish proverb memorably put it: "A Portuguese was born of a Jew's fart."[6]

The sixteenth-century Caribbean provides an excellent counterpoint to this standard historical image. Comparable fears of Portuguese complicity with Spain's enemies had gained notable circulation during the second half of the century. However, this earlier confluence of geopolitical and religious anxieties had nothing to do with the Law of Moses; instead, what worried many Spaniards was the threat of Portuguese collaboration with French and English corsairs, who continually menaced the coastlines of the Spanish Caribbean. The corsairs frequently relied on Portuguese pilots, renegades, and spies, leading to hostile responses on the part of some Spaniards. Like the better-known complicidades of the seventeenth century, perceptions of treason and heresy were firmly intertwined during this period. Instead of being attacked as Jews, however, these treasonous Portuguese were repeatedly deemed to be co-religionists of the Protestant corsairs. To combat this danger, calls were periodically made for the Portuguese to be expelled from the Indies, but despite numerous instances of corsairs being assisted by Lusitanian renegades, widespread action against the Portuguese never was undertaken.

A primary factor behind these developments was the geopolitical landscape on both sides of the Atlantic, which was profoundly shaped by the rupture of Western Christendom into Catholic and Protestant blocs. All sides understood the conflicts between Catholic Spain and the Protestant corsairs to be rooted, at least in part, in the religious divisions of the era, which explains why Portuguese renegades were often maligned as "*luteranos*."[7] On the whole, however, this shared interpretative framework benefited the Portuguese, since Portugal was an indisputably Catholic kingdom. Even if certain individuals were discovered to have apostatized to Protestantism, this larger paradigm reinforced the conclusion that these treasonous actions were not the collective fault of the Portuguese but rather of individual renegades or, at most, some subgroup of Portuguese (e.g., pilots, contrabandists). In contrast to the seventeenth century, the label "Portuguese" had not yet become synonymous with "Jew."

Indeed, far from being detested pariahs, most Portuguese immigrants proved rather adept at integrating into colonial society and becoming vital contributors to the Spanish imperial project. This certainly did not mean that all Spaniards were pleased to see so many Portuguese in the West Indies, but it did ensure that the majority of Portuguese enjoyed opportunities for social integration and, with some luck, economic ascent as well. Throughout the sixteenth century, Portuguese soldiers and artisans (e.g., carpenters, caulkers, blacksmiths) participated in various expeditions of conquest and "pacification." Additionally, the Spanish crown repeatedly encouraged Portuguese settlement of chronically "underpopulated" areas of the Spanish Caribbean. And even more strikingly, conspicuous numbers of Portuguese served in a variety of military and maritime positions throughout the New World, especially as artillerymen and pilots. These posts allowed them passage to the Indies and enabled them to demonstrate their loyalty to both the crown and the local community, thus smoothing their path toward full integration into local society. Nearly all Portuguese in the sixteenth-century Caribbean, regardless of occupation, were situated between the (legally) foreign and the (culturally) familiar, although thanks to the geopolitics of the period, most Spaniards viewed the latter as far more significant. When this cultural familiarity was joined with individual demonstrations of rootedness and fidelity, Portuguese immigrants to the Spanish Caribbean typically became integrated and often highly valued members of colonial society.

From the earliest years of exploration and settlement, Iberian hegemony in the New World was fiercely challenged by other European nations. Through countless acts of piracy and privateering, France and England forcefully contested the exclusivist claims of the Iberian powers. The Spanish responded to these threats in manifold fashion, including especially the establishment of a fleet system organized to transport American bullion to Seville in a more secure and timely fashion. By the second half of the sixteenth century, however, a disturbing pattern began to emerge. Corsair attacks, assisted by pilots with strong knowledge of the local coastlines, became more injurious to Spanish interests. Given the great numbers of Portuguese who resided in the Spanish Caribbean, it became all the more disconcerting that many of these duplicitous pilots hailed from Portugal.

The 1555 sack of Havana by French corsairs exemplifies this early pattern well. The French employed Pero Bras, a former resident of Havana whom Spanish officials in the captured city decried as a traitor who "sold out this land."[8] Bras was a pilot from the Azores, and his actions during the French occupation of Havana gave great weight to the Spanish claims that he was "more cruel and of more evil counsels than the captain himself."[9] Four years after the sack of Havana, Spain and France signed the Treaty of Cateau-Cambrésis, which officially ended armed hostilities between the two nations, although it allowed for continued belligerence overseas.[10] Despite peace in Europe, violent conflict between the Spanish and the French continued apace throughout the circum-Caribbean. One interesting *relación de las piraterías* from 1571 detailed more than a dozen attacks on Spanish interests since the signing of the 1559 treaty. Each year brought new assaults by corsairs, some of whom were well known, like Jean Bontemps. In more than one instance the Spanish report explicitly indicated that a Portuguese pilot had guided and assisted the French pirates in assaulting Spanish shipping and colonial holdings.[11] The list was hardly exhaustive, as it failed to include other notable French predations, including a 1561 attack on Campeche by three French ships guided by a Portuguese named Borges. Similarly, three years earlier, four French ships attacked Puerto Caballos in Honduras, led by pilots from both Portugal and Vizcaya.[12]

General anxieties about the loyalty of Portuguese pilots took on a much sharper political dimension in the early 1580s with the emergence of Dom António as pretender to the Portuguese throne and ally of the English.[13] Dom António looked to the English for military and naval support, promising significant commercial concessions to English merchants in return. His proposal focused in particular on the Cape Verde Islands and the Azores, two Atlantic archipelagoes that were not only commercially lucrative but also politically supportive of his bid for the throne.[14] These circumstances encouraged the circulation of rumors throughout the 1580s that Dom António was preparing to sail to the New World. Some accounts claimed that he was headed for Brazil.[15] Other reports concerned possible attacks on Spanish America, such as a 1582 *consulta* from the Council of the Indies, claiming that Dom António had left from Terceira Island with 3,500 men, mostly "Portuguese and Frenchmen." Although it was suspected that Madeira and Brazil were the main targets, the Council claimed that "with so many men, [Dom António] could be able to carry out another objective," perhaps an attack on Cartagena. Such an assault would cause "much harm, since there were not enough defenses in the city to resist [Dom António]."[16]

Francis Drake set sail on his famous West Indian voyage in September 1585, although England's queen Elizabeth I prohibited Dom António from joining the expedition. Nevertheless, fears of Dom António remained palpable throughout the Caribbean, and rumors circulated that Drake's voyage was just a prelude to a much larger force being led by Dom António. One witness "heard it said that Don António was coming to these parts and that he would bring a great fleet and that he would raise more than thirty thousand men."[17] The specter of Dom António exercised many Spanish imaginations during this period. As Irene Wright aptly expressed it, "Don António haunted the Spanish Indies in these years—reported to be here, there, and everywhere—as restless and intangible as a ghost."[18] Soon, however, these ghost tales began to fall apart. As the members of the Audiencia of Santo Domingo later testified: "At first it was supposed that the commander of these people was Don António, prior of Crato, but later it was learned that this was not true, that he remains in England at the house of this Captain Francis [Drake], by whose hand so much damage has been inflicted."[19]

Dom António was far from the only Portuguese whom local residents imagined arrived with Drake. One Aragonese seaman, Pedro Sánchez, who had been held captive by the English, reported that Drake's vice admiral was "a Portuguese whom the English called Canbra."[20] Others claimed that Portuguese spies were at work throughout Tierra Firme. For instance, an Indian named Pedro testified before officials in Cartagena that he had been with Drake for twelve years in London and knew the composition of Drake's spy network. One traitor was said to have been housed in Cartagena at the home of a Portuguese pharmacist named González, while two more Portuguese spies, Don Juan and Francisquito, were placed at La Margarita. Unsurprisingly, this Don Juan was said to have been an associate of Dom António. Yet another of Drake's Portuguese agents, Francisco, had left Cartagena for Nombre de Dios, and according to Pedro, he had said that he was going on to Panama.[21]

Although little of Pedro's testimony can be independently verified, it should be noted that there was indeed a Portuguese pharmacist named González who had lived in Cartagena since the early 1570s.[22] Furthermore, both Drake and Dom António did use spies to further their own agendas. Around the same time as Pedro's deposition, testimony was received in Jamaica about an Italian pilot who had served Philip II in Portugal but defected to Dom António and traveled with him to England. Seeking a foothold in the Indies, Dom António sent this pilot to spy out the land around the Orinoco River in order to assess the strength of the Spanish presence in the area. The witness who had spoken with this spy further testified that this man was hoping to come across some Portuguese ship, since he had letters that he wanted to deliver to "a very rich man who was in these parts."[23] The witness suspected that the intended recipient was also Portuguese.

These cases of duplicity, treason, and collusion provoked their fair share of outrage. Juan de Echegoyan, an audiencia judge in Santo Domingo described by Bataillon as "the sworn enemy of the New Christians and the Portuguese," repeatedly urged the king to order that all Portuguese without exception "be denied a license to come to these parts, even if they be married *vecinos* in Spain."²⁴ Sharing Echegoyan's animus against the Portuguese was the aforementioned Admiral Carreño, who volunteered to be the agent tasked with "removing from these Indies and taking the lands of those [Portuguese] who do not have a license from Your Majesty."²⁵ Asking for one-fifth of all of the confiscated property, Carreño confessed that this project would make him "very rich." Nevertheless, he insisted that the king himself would reap the greatest financial benefits, since there would be a "great sum of money" going into the royal coffers, which might otherwise be taken to foreign lands.²⁶

Throughout the sixteenth century, royal *cédulas* were indeed issued against the Portuguese, ordering their expulsion from a certain city or island within the Spanish Caribbean. However, most of these decrees were not as strict as Carreño or Echegoyan desired, since distinctions were routinely made between Portuguese who were well rooted in the land and those who were more recent arrivals.²⁷ As early as 1536 the crown ordered the expulsion of unmarried Portuguese from Tierra Firme but stipulated that those Portuguese who were married and currently living with their wives not only should be allowed to remain in the land but also should be "favored" by the governor and royal officials of the province.²⁸ Another decree from 1608 ordered all Portuguese in Havana to be expelled, except for those who were "established" [*avecindados*] and married in the city for at least ten years.²⁹ Occasionally, however, no such distinctions were made. Such was the case in a 1568 cédula that complained about the "great quantity of Portuguese and gypsies" who posed a "notable danger" to the province of Panama. In light of this threat, the crown ordered that these groups be expelled as soon as possible, and "in no manner and by no means" were any Portuguese or gypsies to remain in the region.³⁰ These expulsion orders were always a challenge for local officials to enforce, since exceptions always abounded. In addition to those Portuguese who were "rooted" in the land, others protested that they had been born in Spain or that they were from the Algarve and thus entitled to the same privileges as Spaniards.³¹ Some Portuguese had useful skills or occupations and received exemptions from local authorities. Still others temporarily "absented themselves," only to return in short order. All in all, as Irene Wright suggests in the case of early seventeenth-century Cuba, when it came to these expulsion orders, governors typically did the bare minimum needed to placate their superiors in Spain, whether that meant expelling small numbers of poorer Portuguese or simply "making a list of those liable for expulsion."[32]

Even if little successful action against the Portuguese resulted, it is striking how rare allegations regarding the "Jewishness" of the Portuguese were in the sixteenth century. Instead, the anti-Portuguese missives sent by Echegoyan and Carreño, as well as the periodic expulsion decrees, typically focused on the economic disadvantages and military threats arising from the presence of Portuguese contrabandists and renegades. In contrast, written criticism of the "Portuguese Nation" during the seventeenth century was frequently imbued with anti-Jewish prejudices and hostility. One famous denunciation written by officials in the *Casa de la Contratación* in 1610 exemplifies this divergence. These officials echoed Echegoyan and Carreño in their apprehension concerning the "very great problems" caused by the Portuguese living in the Spanish Indies—one of the foremost being that "in times of war with England or France or Holland, the pilots who carried these nations to [the Indies] were Portuguese."[33] In addition to this, however, the Jewishness of the Portuguese is presented in sharp and immutable terms: "The Portuguese ... in Cartagena and other parts of the Indies are more numerous than the Castilians, and most are *conversos*,[34] people who *by religion and nature* have so much hatred for Castile."[35] Most anti-Portuguese denunciations of the sixteenth century, by contrast, rarely approached this mixture of xenophobia and flagrant anti-Judaism, although certain vague allusions were made on rare occasions, such as when Echegoyan declared the Portuguese incapable of "leaving their bad roots."[36] Yet this sort of veiled discourse was far less common than the explicit complaints about the economic and political damage committed by the Portuguese. Along these lines, Carreño excoriated the Portuguese for siphoning money away from Castile and assisting pirates in looting Spanish cities in the New World. If the admiral had believed that it would benefit his case, it is hard to imagine his not jumping at the chance to employ religious arguments about the need to defend the Catholic faith against Portuguese Jews, but nothing of the sort was mentioned.

In the mid-sixteenth century, many Spanish officials were cognizant that increasing numbers of New Christians sought to leave Portugal in order to escape the Inquisition and that among them, some likely hoped to practice Judaism with greater freedom elsewhere. In 1569 the Duke of Alba claimed in a letter to Philip II that he had "no doubt that many of them [Portuguese] would like to go thither [England] to live in the law of Moses."[37] Two years earlier, the Spanish ambassador to England, Diego Guzmán de Silva, reported that some Portuguese who joined Peyrot Monluc in sacking Madeira in 1566 were "in union with other Portuguese who live here [England], who are considered by some to be Jews, as they have fled from the Inquisition in Portugal."[38] Yet even here, the contrast with the seventeenth century is instructive. From these testimonies, it was leaving Portugal for England, not being Portuguese per se, that generated these suspicions. Furthermore, those Portuguese who did leave for England in the sixteenth century were not joining communities that openly practiced Judaism. Although some outsiders had their suspicions, the degree of scandal caused by these Portuguese *émigrés* was trivial compared with that of the seventeenth century, when openly practicing Jewish communities existed across northern Europe.

For many sixteenth-century Spaniards, those Portuguese pilots who joined French and English corsairs were not Jews but Protestant heretics ("luteranos"). Reporting about Drake in 1579, one witness declared that "the said Corsair, and all his company, the Portuguese pilot, and negroes were all Lutherans, because ... [they] perform[ed] their Lutheran ceremonies [together]."[39] According to another report from 1588, the pilot of a small number of English corsair ships was "a Lutheran ... and a native of Aveiro."[40] This pilot turned out to be Domingo Díaz, a "Portuguese mulatto" who had served on a "packing-boat which the Marquis of Santa Cruz dispatched in 1586 to Santo Domingo" until he was conscripted by Drake.[41] It is unknown whether he was truly a Protestant or if "Lutheran" here simply indicated that the pilot was a (more or less) willing accomplice of the English, independent of his actual religious persuasion. A more famous luterano from Portugal was Simón Fernández, who was labeled as a "great pilot" and a "Lutheran Portuguese."[42] Trained as a pilot in Seville and married in England, Fernández became an ally of the arch-Protestant "spymaster" Francis Walsingham, whose protection allowed the Portuguese pilot to avoid charges of piracy in England.[43] Throughout the late 1570s and 1580s, Fernández entered into the service of some of the leading English explorers of the era. He was appointed as a pilot to Humphrey Gilbert in 1578 and later served on Ralph Lane's 1585 colonizing expedition to Roanoke Island, as well as on John White's voyage back to the ill-fated settlement two years later.[44]

This intriguing dissimilarity between sixteenth- and seventeenth-century perceptions of Portuguese religious loyalties is reflective of a much more paradigmatic divide. In contrast to the seventeenth century, the operative framework for both Spain and her European enemies during the sixteenth century was the fractured state of Western Christendom. The political and economic battles waged across the Atlantic were understood as manifestations of a larger religious conflict that pitted Catholic Spain against the Protestant corsairs. It was not simply that corsairs like Francis Drake or Jacques de Sores were Protestants but that their piratical incursions were interpreted by all sides as having a marked religious character. For example, according to a consulta from the Council of the Indies, Drake was not only a "corsair" but a "dogmatizer" as well.[45] Of course, the sacrilegious profanations of the English corsairs were legion; yet Drake went further by instructing the maroons of Panama in the "many heresies from the sect of Luther."[46] For his part, Drake viewed his repeated attacks against Spain as efforts to vanquish the chief promoter of the Antichrist on earth. In a letter to Walsingham, Drake declared that his men were prepared "to stand for our gracious Queen and country against Antichrist and his members." The Spanish were, for Drake, "enemies to the truth and upholders of Baal or Dagon's image," and as Nicholas Beasley has noted, "at least rhetorically, Drake seemed to place iconoclasm at the center of his mission in the Caribbean."[47] As part of this undertaking, Drake repeatedly sought to establish religious solidarity with the pilots he had captured. One captured pilot later testified that Drake had "tempted [him] with many promises of silver and gold, to go with him to England and to become a Lutheran, saying that as soon as he would reach his native country, he would confer great mercies upon him."[48]

For both the Spanish and the English, religious antagonism was an integral part of these geopolitical conflicts—a circumstance that greatly benefited the Portuguese, who, despite the apostasy of certain individuals, shared the same Iberian religious culture as their Castilian neighbors. From this perspective, the acts of Portuguese renegades were either the fault of a particular subgroup or of individual traitors. In the multiple accounts of the 1555 sack of Havana, Bras was never condemned for being part of the "Portuguese nation." The pilot's actions were always described as originating in his own malicious intentions, not from his "blood" or his "nation." In other instances, Spanish observers singled out pilots as a particularly untrustworthy group. One such denunciation was leveled by the president of the Council of the Indies, Antonio de Padilla, on the eve of the Union of the Crowns in 1579: "All the pilots who go in these English and French armadas are Portuguese. For this and a hundred thousand other reasons, it would be fitting that Your Majesty should become the King and Sovereign of those countries."[49] Other Spaniards made similar arguments. In the immediate aftermath of Drake's rampage in 1586, one leading vecino of Havana, Alonso Suárez de Toledo, protested that "all these Portuguese pilots have sold out these Indies, and in these ports there are many in whom little confidence is placed."[50] Sweeping condemnations such as those issued by Echegoyan or Carreño were far less common. Because the fight against the corsairs was consistently identified as being, in large part, a battle between Catholics and Protestants, the Portuguese could not collectively be seen as anything other than allies of the Spanish. Even if certain individuals or subgroups proved unfaithful, geopolitical circumstances for most of the sixteenth century still supported the understanding of the Portuguese as a fundamentally Catholic nation.

This view was strongly reinforced by decades of Portuguese participation in Spanish expeditions of exploration and conquest, starting with Columbus's very first voyage to the Americas in 1492, which included an apprentice seaman (*grumete*) from Tavira and three Portuguese mariners.[51] Other well-known expeditions drew Lusitanian participants as well. Hernando Cortés's conquest of Tenochtitlán (1519–21) included fifteen soldiers, a mariner, and a goldsmith from Portugal, while twenty-two Portuguese served in Hernando de Soto's luckless expedition to Florida and the American Southeast (1539–42).[52] As participants in these expeditions, the Portuguese also became embroiled in the factionalism that often emerged in their aftermath. Among the eight Portuguese who served as soldiers in Heredia's 1533 conquest and founding of Cartagena, one of the most important was Héctor de Barros, who, as a reward for his service, was given an *encomienda* consisting of the Indian "pueblos" of Turimaya and Mazaguapo.[53] Remaining firmly loyal to Heredia during the multiple, lengthy investigations of his governorship during the 1530s and 1540s, Barros eventually became a vecino in Mompox, and in 1550 he served as a *regidor* in Tolú.[54] By contrast, Gaspar de Tavira participated in an anti-Heredia rebellion near Mompox in early 1541, and was sentenced to three years of forced servitude on Spain's galleys after the revolt was put down.[55] In many ways indistinguishable from their Spanish counterparts, these Portuguese conquistadors sought profits through a variety of means, including trading in Indian slaves and robbing Cenú graves of their buried gold.[56] Some, like Barros, eventually became *encomenderos*; many others had to settle for far less lucrative livelihoods.

At various times during the sixteenth century, the Spanish crown also encouraged Portuguese to settle in locations such as Hispaniola, which was to receive 150 Portuguese migrants in 1565 because the island was said to be "almost totally depopulated." As was common in these sorts of decrees, a certain percentage of the Portuguese—in this case, one-third—were required to be married and to bring their wives and children with them.[57] It is interesting to note that this cédula also required the new settlers to be farmers (*labradores*). Occupational restrictions of this type were hardly unusual. In 1534, up to thirty farmers (*labradores e gente de trabajo*) from Portugal were invited to settle with their families in Jamaica.[58] At other times, however, no occupational preferences were given, as in 1531, when the crown granted a license to any married Portuguese to move to Cuba, where they would be able to enjoy the rights and privileges of Spanish naturaleza.[59] Given the many long-standing social and cultural ties that linked the Iberian kingdoms together, the Portuguese were an obvious and logical choice for strengthening the Spanish imperial footprint in the Caribbean.

The conquest, pacification, and settlement of the Spanish Caribbean continued throughout the sixteenth century (and beyond) and even late in the century, the Portuguese sometimes played a conspicuous role. Perhaps the most interesting and controversial example was that of Rodrigo Manuel Núñez Lobo, who served as the governor of Nueva Andalucía for two years (1588–90) and sought to expand Spanish settlement of the island of Trinidad. Born of a Portuguese *hidalgo* in Lisbon, Núñez Lobo was a longtime resident of Santo Domingo, where he had amassed a fortune. His bid for the governorship of Nueva Andalucía clearly revealed the divide among Spaniards regarding Portuguese individuals in positions of real economic and political power. As part of his petition, Núñez Lobo gathered testimony from leading citizens in Santo Domingo, including the prior of the Dominican monastery, a cathedral canon, three lawyers from the local *audiencia*, and the general of the galleys stationed in the city. He even managed to gain the support of the *cabildo* in Cumaná, in large part by promising to use his own plentiful resources to spur the settlement's economic growth.[60] Indeed, soon after taking up the post in 1588, Núñez Lobo brought a considerable number of slaves to the province. His prior business connections also attracted Portuguese merchants to the area, contributing to the local economy in multiple ways.[61]

Without question, it was this socioeconomic dimension of Núñez Lobo's governorship that elicited the objections of many. One Spanish official complained that Cumaná had become "a bin of foreigners, traitors, and other delinquents, all of whom are sheltered and provided for by the Governor."[62] Additional complaints came from Pedro de Angulo, the governor of Jamaica, who argued against Núñez Lobo or any other Portuguese serving as governor of Nueva Andalucía, due to the machinations of the French and English to turn the area into a base for piracy.[63] The crown seems to have found merit in these arguments, as Núñez Lobo's tenure as governor was rather quickly cut short due to an investigation into his illicit economic activities. Nevertheless, it is telling that for the crown and many Spanish officials, including a majority of the audiencia judges in Santo Domingo who approved Núñez Lobo's nomination, Portuguese naturaleza was hardly an insurmountable obstacle to high-ranking political or military office.

Throughout both the sixteenth and seventeenth centuries, many Portuguese helped to defend and promote Spanish imperial interests by faithfully serving in sensitive military and maritime positions. A notable example was Blas de Herrera, who served as a captain of artillery in Cartagena during the attack by Drake in 1586. During the English assault, Herrera was reported to have urged the governor to give him more men, in order to move the artillery pieces into the necessary positions. According to one witness, "[Herrera] begged the governor to give him what he needed for the artillery," but the governor, Pedro Fernández del Busto, "would not provide or do anything." Thoroughly incensed, the Portuguese captain "swore to God that he did not know what to do or say in the face of so great remissness."[64] The dedication with which Herrera carried out his duties was seconded by the testimony of the subsequent governor of Cartagena, Pedro de Lodeña, with whom Herrera enjoyed a better working relationship. Declaring that Herrera had served his post with "attentiveness and care," Lodeña even went so far as to suspend the ongoing investigation into Herrera's legal status as a resident foreigner, due to the "fidelity" that the Portuguese captain had demonstrated on numerous occasions.[65]

Although few achieved a rank as high as that of Herrera, it is clear that in Spanish armies and militias across the Atlantic world, Portuguese and other foreigners often filled the position of artilleryman (*artillero*). Although the Spanish crown preferred not to have foreigners serving in such critical military positions, circumstances often dictated otherwise. As was the case for pilots and ordinary sailors, Portuguese artillerymen easily found passage on Spanish ships due to a lack of available Spaniards. The crown became sufficiently concerned about Portuguese artillerymen that it sent a cédula to the Casa de la Contratación in 1575 asking if there were an artilleryman in Seville who could train other Spaniards for the fleets, given the "great problems" that had arisen due to the number of artillerymen who were "foreigners, especially Portuguese."[66] Nonetheless, Portuguese artillerymen continued to serve on Spanish fleets and in Caribbean port cities throughout the rest of the sixteenth and the first half of the seventeenth century.[67] Censuses of foreigners in the Spanish Indies attest to this fact quite clearly. In Cartagena in 1630, for example, it was reported that there were no fewer than three foreign artillerymen serving in the city's *presidio*, two Portuguese and a Sicilian.[68] A fourth foreign artilleryman, a Genoese named Bartolomé de Codar, was investigated in 1620 but does not appear in the 1630 census.[69]

It should not be assumed that this hesitancy on the part of the Spanish crown to employ Portuguese artillerymen was due simply to fears of betrayal, much less questions of crypto-Judaism. Of much greater concern was the potential for maritime or military service to become a conduit for illegal entry and settlement in the New World. Judging from the evidence collected in early seventeenth-century royal investigations, these concerns were entirely justified. Portuguese residents without a license often testified that they arrived in the city through some sort of licit military or maritime service but then fell ill and were forced to remain in the Indies. The story told by one Portuguese artilleryman in Cartagena, Francisco Rodríguez Palma, is typical. He testified that he had been serving as *contramaestre* on a *patache de aviso* in 1619 when he fell ill while docked in Cartagena. He stayed in the city until he recovered, then found employment as an artilleryman in the local presidio. Despite lacking a license to reside in the Indies, Rodríguez Palma established himself as a vecino in Cartagena and married a *criolla* named Maria Fernández.[70] Falling ill in Cartagena was, of course, an all too common experience, but for Portuguese individuals without a license, it also became a highly convenient justification for remaining in the city.[71]

Regardless of their reasons for staying, Portuguese residents, especially in military or medical fields, could quickly transform themselves into respected members of the local community. Some men like Manuel Téllez possessed valuable skills that were in short supply. Téllez was a coppersmith, and many witnesses testified on his behalf in 1611 that he was not only a "valiant" and "honorable man" but also a "very useful and necessary" member of the presidio, because there was no other man of his occupation in the city.[72] Similarly, Andrés González, a Portuguese apothecary, was lauded by witnesses in 1620 as "one of the most useful, necessary, and loyal persons in this land," despite being, in his own words, an "old, sick, and very disabled man."[73] It is quite likely that this was the same González who over three decades previously was accused of harboring one of Drake's Portuguese spies. It appears that the accusations were found to have been baseless, or perhaps there was insufficient evidence of wrongdoing, but González continued to be a valued member of the community. Portuguese immigrants such as Téllez and González were always situated between the familiar and the foreign. Investigated for illegal residence in the early seventeenth century, they nevertheless could demonstrate their deep local roots. By demonstrating their political loyalties (often through militia service), as well as their Catholic piety—González, for instance, was renowned for donating medicine to local convents and monasteries—Portuguese immigrants managed to distance themselves from whatever suspicion might arise from the actions of treasonous renegades.

Yet by the early seventeenth century when González and Téllez were under investigation, the suspicions directed against the Portuguese had taken a much more specific form. The Dutch had become a major Atlantic power, and Spaniards increasingly feared that the Jewish community of Amsterdam was helping to fund Dutch exploits. The conquest of Pernambuco and the establishment of openly Jewish communities in the New World changed the calculus completely. Potential Portuguese betrayal was increasingly viewed as part of a larger Jewish plot to undermine the Spanish Empire. By the late 1630s, events came to a climax when the Inquisition arrested large numbers of Portuguese in Lima and Cartagena on accusations of judaizing. Following these arrests, testimony emerged about a secret group of Portuguese (termed the Cofradía de Holanda) that regularly sent money to the Jews of Amsterdam in order to fund further Dutch conquests in the New World.[74] This ostensible "Jewish" plot has no real parallels for most of the sixteenth century. Only in the 1590s did any reports emerge of Portuguese *judaizantes* in the Spanish Caribbean with connections to northwestern Europe.[75] Similarly it was only in this final decade of the century that Inquisition tribunals in Mexico City and Lima began in earnest to arrest suspected judaizers of Portuguese descent.[76]

For most of the sixteenth century, the dynamics of anti-Portuguese sentiment in the Spanish Caribbean differed greatly from the standard accounts given by historians who have largely focused on the mid-seventeenth century. While suspicions and hostilities against the Portuguese certainly existed, they were rarely based on anti-Jewish prejudices.

Instead, economic and political considerations led some Spaniards to denounce their Portuguese neighbors as treacherous agents of the English or French, and when these fears coalesced with religious hostilities, the Portuguese renegades were castigated as Protestants (luteranos), not as Jews. Nevertheless, because geopolitical conflicts in the sixteenth-century Caribbean were usually interpreted as manifestations of broader religious antagonisms between Protestants and Catholics, the Portuguese generally escaped broad collective censure, since Portugal was as indisputably Catholic as the rest of Iberia.[77] The betrayal of certain individuals, especially Portuguese pilots, was thus understood not as reflecting some inherent "Portuguese" trait but as the result either of individual malice or the general untrustworthiness of pilots as a group.

Since naturaleza was hardly ever the sole grounds for judging a person's loyalty or disloyalty, individual Portuguese found ample opportunity to demonstrate their political and religious fidelity through a wide range of public actions and behavior, including militia service, acts of Catholic piety, and the maintenance of a *casa poblada*. By and large, the Portuguese integrated quite easily into Spanish Caribbean society, marrying and establishing themselves without much difficulty, despite their collective legal status as foreigners to the kingdoms of Castile. Nevertheless, even without this juridical advantage, in the courts of local opinion throughout the circum-Caribbean, most immigrants from Portugal made a persuasive case for their usefulness, their loyalty, and even their *españolidad*.

Notes

ABBREVIATIONS

AGI	Archivo General de Indias	
	-Cttn	Casa de la Contratación
	-IG	Gobierno: Indiferente General
	-Just	Justicia
	-Mexico	Audiencia de Mexico
	-Panama	Audiencia de Panamá
	-Patr	Patronato Real
	-SD	Gobierno: Audiencia de Santo Domingo
	-SF	Gobierno: Audiencia de Santa Fe

1. AGI-IG 740, N.49, fol. 1r.
2. AGI-SF 187, fol. 170r.
3. AGI-IG 740, N.49a, fol. 1r.
4. Quoted in Bataillon, "Santo Domingo 'Era Portugal,'" 115.
5. See Escobar Quevedo, *Inquisición y judaizantes*.
6. Quoted in Boxer, *The Dutch in Brazil*, 101; Liebman, *The Jews in New Spain*, 183; Sachar, *Farewell España*, 170; Friedman, *Jews and the American Slave Trade*, 57; Davis, *In the Image of God*, 68.
7. See Gómez-Centurión Jiménez, "The New Crusade."
8. *Colección de documentos inéditos*, 6:422.
9. *Colección de documentos inéditos*, 6:373.
10. Gould, "Law of Nations," 292.
11. AGI-Patr 267, N.1, R.53.
12. Sarabia Viejo, *Don Luis de Velasco*, 450. See also Wright, "Rescates," 349; Deive, *Tangomangos*, 49–66.
13. McBride, "Elizabethan Foreign Policy in Microcosm."
14. Kelsey, *Sir Francis Drake*, 242; Quinn, "England and the Azores," 205–17.
15. Hume, *Calendar of Letters*, 3: 157.
16. AGI-IG 740, N.99.
17. Wright, *Further English Voyages*, 168.
18. Wright, *Further English Voyages*, xvii.
19. Wright, *Further English Voyages*, 36.
20. Wright, *Further English Voyages*, 167.
21. AGI-SF 37, N.72; Wright, *Further English Voyages*, 226–28.
22. AGI-Esc 589B, pieza 23.
23. AGI-Mexico 22, N.10c, fol. 1v. See also Lorimer, "Ralegh's First Reconnaissance."
24. Quoted in Bataillon, "Santo Domingo 'Era Portugal,'" 115.
25. AGI-SF 187, fol. 170r.
26. AGI-SF 187, fol. 170v.
27. In order to figure out which individuals qualified for any exemptions, Spanish officials periodically conducted censuses of all foreigners living in a given city or region. For discussion of various censuses conducted in the early years of the seventeenth century, see Wheat, *Atlantic Africa*, 110–18.
28. AGI-Panama 235, L.6, fol. 5r.
29. AGI-SD 869, L.5, fols. 151r–151v.
30. AGI-Panama 236, L.10, fols. 113v–114r.
31. See Ventura, *Portugueses no Peru*, 1:66–67; Wheat, *Atlantic Africa*, 105, 116.
32. Wright, "Rescates," 351–53, quotation on p. 352.
33. AGI-Cttn 5171, fol. 181v.

34. Although countless numbers of *conversos* were ordinary Catholics, indistinguishable from their Old Christian neighbors, it is clear that the authors of this letter use "*conversos*" here to mean "Jews," given the emphasis on "religion" and "nature" as distinguishing characteristics.
35. AGI-Cttn 5171, fol. 181v, emphasis added.
36. Quoted in Bataillon, "Santo Domingo 'Era Portugal,'" 115.
37. Hume, *Calendar of Letters*, 2:87.
38. Hume, *Calendar of Letters*, 1:657.
39. Nuttall, *New Light on Drake*, 188.
40. Quinn, *Roanoke Voyages*, 2:783; Wright, *Further English Voyages*, 233–35.
41. Quinn, *Roanoke Voyages*, 2:783. Díaz serves as a helpful reminder that many of those labeled as "Portuguese" were, in fact, persons of African descent. Throughout this period, skilled Afro-Portuguese pilots from Cabo Verde and other African locales found continual employment on both sides of the Atlantic. For more on Afro-Iberians in the Spanish Caribbean, see Wheat, *Atlantic Africa*, especially 118–32.
42. Wright, *Further English Voyages*, 15, 240; Quinn, *Roanoke Voyages*, 2:742.
43. Quinn, *England and the Discovery of America*, 249.
44. Quinn, *Roanoke Voyages*, 1:79, 199–204; 2:515–43.
45. "*Que iban con ellos dogmatizándoles y enseñándoles su falsa y dañada secta y herejías.*" AGI-IG 739, N.271, fol. 1r.
46. AGI-IG 739, N.271, fol. 1r.
47. All quotations taken from Beasley, "Wars of Religion," 161.
48. Nuttall, *New Light on Drake*, 195.
49. Nuttall, *New Light on Drake*, 402.
50. Wright, *Further English Voyages*, 173.
51. Ventura, *Portugueses no descobrimento*, 52–55.
52. Ventura, *Portugueses no descobrimento*, 59–80.
53. Gómez Pérez, *Pedro de Heredia*, 389.
54. Ventura, *Portugueses no descobrimento*, 93–94. For more on Barros, see Goodsell, "Cartagena de Indias," 78–79, 86–88.
55. Gómez Pérez, *Pedro de Heredia*, 194–96.
56. Ventura, *Portugueses no descobrimento*, 94–95.
57. AGI-IG 1966, L.15, fols. 257r–258r.
58. AGI-SD 1121, L.2, fols. 22r–23v.
59. AGI-SD 1121, L.1, fols. 78v–79v.
60. Ojer, *La formación del oriente venezolano*, 1:422–25.
61. Castillo Hidalgo, *Asentamiento español*, 660, 676.
62. Quoted in Norton and Studnicki-Gizbert, "The Multinational Commodification of Tobacco," 261.
63. AGI-Mexico 22, N.10a, fols. 1r–1v.

64. Wright, *Further English Voyages*, 124.
65. AGI-SF 37, N.107, fol. 1v.
66. AGI-IG 1956, L.1, fols. 302v–303r.
67. AGI-IG 1957, L.5, fols. 113r–113v.
68. AGI-SF 56B, N.73a.
69. AGI-Esc 589B, pieza 18. In addition to Portuguese, Italian and German artillerymen were common as well. Wright, "Rescates," 337.
70. AGI-SF 56B, N.73a, fol. 13r.
71. See, for example, the numerous testimonies given in the 1630 census of foreigners in Cartagena, particularly Antonio Jacome (*marinero*), Baltasar Díaz (*grumete*), Domingo Ferrera (*escribano de registro*), Domingo Cardoso (*capitán*), Domingo Antúnez (*soldado*), Fernando de Amaya (*soldado*), Francisco Rodríguez (*marinero*), Geronimo Méndez de la Barbuda (*soldado*), Gonzalo López (*grumete*), Juan de Silva (*marinero*), Juan González de la Cruz (*criado*), Joseph Hernández (*marinero*), Miguel de Chávez (*soldado*), and Manuel de Acosta (*grumete*). AGI-SF 56B, N.73a.
72. AGI-Esc 589B, pieza 35, fols. 78r–81v.
73. AGI-Esc 589B, pieza 23, fols. 6r, 20v.
74. For more on this curious episode, see Hamm, "Between the Foreign and the Familiar," chap. 5.
75. AGI-SD 868, L.3, fols. 154r–154v.
76. In his extensive catalogue of *judaizante* cases in the New World, Ricardo Escobar Quevedo only records three instances of a Portuguese being convicted of judaizing before 1590. In contrast, dozens of Portuguese were put on trial for judaizing in both Lima and Mexico City during the 1590s. Escobar Quevedo, *Inquisición y judaizantes*, appendix 2.
77. When suspicions about the deleterious impact of Jewish blood were raised in the sixteenth century, they were directed at all Iberians, not just the Portuguese. Thus Gonzalo Fernández de Oviedo, writing in the mid-sixteenth century, lamented how "in France, as well as in Germany and Italy, Spaniards are commonly called *marranos* in a vituperative fashion." Indeed, no less of a figure than Erasmus derided Spain as being "strange, sinister, and Jew-ridden." Avalle-Arce, *Las memorias de Gonzalo Fernández de Oviedo*, 1:125; Markish, *Erasmus and the Jews*, 144.

Bibliography

ARCHIVES

Archivo General de Indias (Seville, Spain).

PUBLISHED WORKS

Avalle-Arce, Juan Bautista, ed. *Las memorias de Gonzalo Fernández de Oviedo*. 2 vols. Chapel Hill: University of North Carolina Department of Romance Languages, 1974.

Bataillon, Marcel. "Santo Domingo 'Era Portugal.'" In *Historia y sociedad en el mundo de habla español: Homenaje a José Miranda*, edited by Bernardo García Martínez et al., 113–20. México DF: Colegio de México, 1970.

Beasley, Nicholas M. "Wars of Religion in the Circum-Caribbean: English Iconoclasm in Spanish America, 1570–1702." In *Saints and Their Cults in the Atlantic World*, edited by Margaret Cormack, 150–73. Columbia: University of South Carolina Press, 2007.

Boxer, C. R. *The Dutch in Brazil, 1624–1654*. 1957. Rpt., Hamden CT: Archon Books, 1973.

Castillo Hidalgo, Ricardo Ignacio. *Asentamiento español y articulación interétnica en Cumaná (1560–1620)*. Caracas: Academia Nacional de Historia, 2005.

Colección de documentos inéditos relativos al descubrimiento, conquista y organización de las antiguas posesiones españoles de ultramar (segunda serie). Madrid: Est. Tipográfico "Sucesores de Rivadeneyra," 1891.

Davis, David Brion. *In the Image of God: Religion, Moral Values, and Our Heritage of Slavery*. New Haven: Yale University Press, 2001.

Deive, Carlos Esteban. *Tangomangos: Contrabando y piratería en Santo Domingo, 1522–1606*. Santo Domingo, DR: Fundación Cultural Dominicana, 1996.

Escobar Quevedo, Ricardo. *Inquisición y judaizantes en América española: siglos XVI–XVII*. Bogotá: Universidad del Rosario, 2008.

Friedman, Saul S. *The Jews and the American Slave Trade*. New Brunswick NJ: Transaction, 1998.

Gómez-Centurión Jiménez, C. "The New Crusade: Ideology and Religion in the Anglo-Spanish Conflict." In *England, Spain, and the Gran Armada, 1585–1604*, edited by M. J. Rodríguez-Salcedo and Simon Adams, 264–99. Savage MD: Barnes & Noble Books, 1991.

Gómez Pérez, María del Carmen. *Pedro de Heredia y Cartagena de Indias*. Seville: Escuela de Estudios Hispano-Americanos, 1984.

Goodsell, James Nelson. "Cartagena de Indias: Entrepôt for a New World, 1533–1597." PhD diss., Harvard University, 1966.

Gould, Eliga H. "Law of Nations." In *The Princeton Companion to Atlantic History*, edited by Joseph C. Miller, 291–93. Princeton: Princeton University Press, 2015.

Hamm, Brian. "Between the Foreign and the Familiar: The Portuguese in the Spanish Circum-Caribbean, 1550–1700." PhD diss., University of Florida, 2017.

Hume, Martin A. S. *Calendar of Letters and State Papers Relating to English Affairs Preserved Principally in the Archives of Simancas.* 4 vols. London: Eyre and Spottiswoode, 1892–1899.

Kelsey, Harry. *Sir Francis Drake: The Queen's Pirate.* New Haven: Yale University Press, 1998.

Liebman, Seymour B. *The Jews in New Spain: Faith, Flame, and Inquisition.* Coral Gables: University of Miami Press, 1970.

Lorimer, Joyce. "Ralegh's First Reconnaissance of Guiana? An English Survey of the Orinoco in 1587." *Terrae Incognitae* 9 (1977): 7–21.

Markish, Shimon. *Erasmus and the Jews.* Translated by Anthony Olcott. Chicago: University of Chicago Press, 1986.

McBride, Gordon K. "Elizabethan Foreign Policy in Microcosm: The Portuguese Pretender, 1580–89." *Albion* 5, no. 3 (Autumn 1973): 193–210.

Norton, Marcy, and Daviken Studnicki-Gizbert. "The Multinational Commodification of Tobacco, 1492–1650." In *The Atlantic World and Virginia, 1550–1624*, edited by Peter C. Mancall, 251–73. Chapel Hill: University of North Carolina Press, 2007.

Nuttall, Zelia, ed. *New Light on Drake: A Collection of Documents Relating to His Voyage of Circumnavigation, 1577–1580.* London: Hakluyt Society, 1914.

Ojer, Pablo. *La formación del oriente venezolano*, vol. 1, *Creación de las gobernaciones*. Caracas: Universidad Católica "Andrés Bello," 1966.

Quinn, David B. "England and the Azores, 1581–1582: Three Letters." *Revista da Universidade de Coimbra* 27 (1979): 205–17.

———. *England and the Discovery of America, 1481–1620.* New York: Alfred A. Knopf, 1974.

———, ed. *The Roanoke Voyages, 1584–1590.* 2 vols. London: Hakluyt Society, 1955.

Sachar, Howard M. *Farewell España: The World of the Sephardim Remembered.* New York: Vintage Books, 1994.

Sarabia Viejo, María Justina. *Don Luis de Velasco, virrey de Nueva España, 1550–1564.* Seville: Escuela de Estudios Hispano-Americanos, 1978.

Ventura, Maria da Graça A. Mateus. *Portugueses no descobrimento e conquista da Hispano-América: viagens e expedições (1492–1557).* Lisboa: Edições Colibri, 2000.

———. *Portugueses no Peru ao tempo da união ibérica: mobilidade, cumplicidades e vivências.* 3 vols. Lisboa: Imprensa Nacional-Casa da Moeda, 2005.

Wheat, David. *Atlantic Africa and the Spanish Caribbean, 1570–1640*. Chapel Hill: University of North Carolina Press, 2016.

Wright, Irene A., trans. and ed. *Further English Voyages to Spanish America, 1583–1594. Documents from the Archives of the Indies at Seville illustrating English Voyages to the Caribbean, the Spanish Main, Florida, and Virginia*. London: Hakluyt Society, 1951.

———. "Rescates: With Special Reference to Cuba, 1599–1610." *Hispanic American Historical Review* 3, no. 3 (August 1920): 333–61.

PART 3

Africans and the Spanish Caribbean

Iberian systems of slavery and slave trafficking evolved rapidly in the Caribbean, and by the mid-sixteenth century, Africans and their descendants outnumbered Spanish residents in some Caribbean settlements. Slave labor sustained farms, ranches, and fortifications in addition to mines, plantations, and pearl fisheries. Enslaved Africans also cut timber, paddled canoes, guided mule trains, and provided domestic services. The routes, destinations, volume, and frequency of the transatlantic slave trade evolved throughout the sixteenth century as merchants, mariners, and Caribbean residents adapted to new metropolitan legislation and to changing conditions in various Atlantic arenas. In seaports such as Havana, Africans would encounter free and enslaved people of widely different origins, but even as they responded creatively to their new surroundings, Africans' social ties with one another continued to be informed by their own prior experiences of commerce and geopolitics in western Africa.

7

The Early Slave Trade to Spanish America
Caribbean Pathways, 1530–1580

MARC EAGLE

At the union of the Spanish and Portuguese crowns in 1580, the transatlantic trade in sub-Saharan African slaves had been going on for more than a half century, during which the destinations of slaving vessels to the Americas changed substantially. The evolution of the early slave trade to the Spanish Caribbean between 1530 and 1580 was not only foundational for the later, higher-volume Spanish slave trade but also a reflection of the development of Spain's colonial system in the region.[1] The routes followed by vessels carrying slaves to this region in this time responded to a variety of economic and political factors, as the Spanish crown sought to encourage and control this traffic while slave merchants at various levels worked both with and against royal officials for their own advantage.

Changes in the pathways by which enslaved Africans were brought to the Spanish Caribbean reflected and reinforced structural shifts in Spain's colonial system in the sixteenth century, such as the decline of placer gold mining in the Caribbean islands, the suppression of the Audiencia of Panamá between 1543 and 1564, or the formal organization of the yearly *flotas* (fleets) in the 1560s.[2] The actual patterns of slave imports during this early period were frequently at odds with the crown's aims, necessitating changes in royal policy and a near-constant stream of royal orders to overseas officials tasked with regulating and taxing the arrival of African captives. Between 1530 and 1580 the volume of human traffic and the ways it moved through Caribbean space were affected by the broader Atlantic context, including the demand for both indigenous and African enslaved labor in the Americas, the development of Iberian merchant networks, and conflict in Africa.[3]

Information for the sixteenth century is fragmentary at best. The Trans-Atlantic Slave Trade Database (TSTD) is an invaluable resource for attempting to quantify this traffic, but it reflects the emphasis of generations of historians on later eras, particularly the eighteenth and nineteenth centuries.[4] Most research on the early slave trade to Spanish America has started with 1580, or 1595, when Portuguese merchants held the *asiento de negros* (a monopoly contract to transport slaves), while the dramatic rise in slave imports to Cuba starting in the later eighteenth century has attracted considerable scholarly attention.[5] Because slave arrivals in the Americas were not systematically recorded in metropolitan accounts, sixteenth-century documentation presents a serious challenge to building a reliable portrait of actual ports of embarkation and debarkation.

Records about planned slave ship itineraries, which are especially important for understanding the pre-1580 traffic, summarize the names, *maestres* (cargo masters), and intended destinations of vessels leaving for or returning from the Spanish Indies but generally do not confirm arrivals in American ports or numbers of African captives transported.[6] Both *registros* (cargo registries) made in Spain (usually Seville, but sometimes Cádiz or the Canary Islands) and royal grants of licenses to transport slaves normally use vague wording to describe both provenance zones in Africa and destinations for African captives, so the actual routes of many of these vessels are unclear.[7] Even for voyages with arrival information, treasury records may only note that slaves were landed, or list a handful of captives for whom royal duties were due because of license problems, while failing to provide information about other captives for whom taxes had been paid in Spain.[8] Finally, a substantial number of enslaved Africans arrived on vessels that made *arribadas* (unscheduled or emergency landings) in Spanish ports, often as a cover for contraband slave sales, and these arrivals were rarely compared with departure records by metropolitan authorities. Although historians of the Spanish slave trade in the eighteenth and nineteenth centuries also confront problems of contraband or fragmentary records of voyage itineraries, the pre-1580 period remains significantly understudied by comparison.[9]

Nevertheless there exists a wealth of supplementary records, from legal proceedings about individual voyages to treasury accounts to notarial records from connection points like the Canary Islands, that offer a more complete understanding of the slave trade to Spanish America up to 1580. General trends in the Caribbean, including indigenous population decline and administrative changes, shaped demand for enslaved African labor, and aggregate information on arribadas can help gauge shifts in this demand. Even though we cannot entirely overcome the limitations of the sources, using multiple perspectives offers a productive approach to characterizing this early phase of the slave trade.

Simply labeling the era before 1595 as the "licenses" period obscures much of the evolution in slaving routes up to that time. Instead, the following discussion will proceed by decades in order to describe change over time.[10] Although transatlantic slaving voyages took place in the 1520s, this study begins at 1530 because until then the Spanish crown took a makeshift approach to providing African slave labor for overseas colonies, with many captives departing from Iberia.[11] The first major step to organizing a transatlantic trade came in 1518, when Charles V granted 4,000 licenses to import slaves to the Indies for eight years to the Flemish Laurent de Gouvenot (often "Gorrevod" in Spanish sources). In 1528 a similar but more restricted agreement, called an asiento, gave another 4,000 licenses for four years to Heinrich Ehinger and Hieronymus Sayler, agents of the German Welser family.[12] Many early licenses, however, went unused—Ehinger and Sayler received an extension in 1532 for their remaining ones—and the crown's concessions generated legal battles related to monopoly rights and multiple resales of these licenses.[13] The crown's problematic experience with these arrangements would shape royal policy on the slave trade in subsequent decades. Voyages directly from Africa to the Americas became more common by the late 1520s, while the crown took a more active role in directing how and where to send captives. Yet even in this early period, a variety of sailors, pilots, cargo masters, and large and small merchants across the Atlantic world learned the business of obtaining slaves and developed a mental map of the Spanish Caribbean.

By 1530 treasury accounts and royal letters show that African captives were arriving on a regular basis in Puerto Rico and Hispaniola,[14] but the limited monopoly grants of preceding years proved incapable of meeting demand throughout the region. A royal letter of 1530 noted that almost no captives transported under the 1528 asiento had gone to Cuba, Jamaica, or Tierra Firme (then meaning roughly the region around Panama), despite a need for them.[15] Acting in Charles V's stead, Queen Isabel of Portugal ordered the governor of Puerto Rico to prevent local agents of this contract from receiving or selling further slaves and to send any new arrivals to Cuba until that island had received at least four hundred captives.[16] Although the crown made efforts not to violate license agreements, the broad terms of early grants allowed concessionaires to send enslaved Africans primarily to known, profitable destinations; for this reason, future grants were more restrictive. At the same time, the Welsers' complaint that other merchants transported and sold slaves in violation of their 1528 contract demonstrates that rising demand encouraged a variety of individuals to find quasi-legal or extralegal ways to circumvent royal restrictions on this trade.[17]

During these early decades, sub-Saharan Africans were brought to the Caribbean region primarily for personal service, to provide labor for gold mining and pearl diving, and to participate in conquering and populating territory for Spain.[18] Even later in the century enslaved Africans continued to arrive in small numbers directly from Iberia on vessels that primarily carried goods or passengers by virtue of a royal provision that Spanish emigrants could bring (usually) two slaves as personal servants.[19] Astute merchants used this provision to skirt the monopolistic terms of slave contracts and to concentrate procurement in the hands of specialists. In 1532, when the *Santa Ana* landed twenty captives in Santo Domingo, its maestre presented copies of ten licenses allowing five passengers to take two slaves each.[20] Another ship arrived at Puerto Rico around the same time with twenty-two slaves owned by merchant Juan de Valladolid, by virtue of grants to eleven emigrants.[21] In both cases the captives were seized and sold by treasury officials because they had not been registered with the House of Trade in Seville, but after appeal to the Council of the Indies the proceeds were restored to their owners. Such decisions show that restrictions on the slave trade were, in practice, more flexible than royal orders and the terms of license grants suggested, although this flexibility worked to the advantage of wealthier merchants who could wait for several years to receive their profits.[22]

With the expiration of Ehinger and Sayler's monopoly in 1532, the crown issued a wider variety of slave license grants to both merchants and migrants. One such grant made in 1534, in response to a proposal by Asensio de Villanueva to build a new town in Puerto Rico, demonstrates metropolitan support for using enslaved Africans as settlers. Villanueva called for transporting "25 married Spanish men and 25 married black slave men" to help found the town (named after himself) and also requested that each Spaniard be given the customary right to bring two slaves, so that the town's population would theoretically include one hundred African individuals.[23] The king made many other grants in these years, mostly for small groups of two to ten slaves, plus a few grants for several hundred. As with licenses, the enslaved people themselves were frequently resold, driving the rise of an active financial market for the transport of slaves centered in Seville.[24]

At the end of the 1530s, Puerto Rico and Hispaniola were still the main destinations for slave ships headed to the Caribbean. Of thirty-nine voyages presently known to have sailed during the 1530s, twenty-two landed at Puerto Rico (two continued to Santo Domingo) and ten landed at Santo Domingo (one continued to Jamaica); only two went to Santiago de Cuba.[25] While Upper Guinea and Cabo Verde (with ten voyages) were the main provenance zones for Africans transported to the Caribbean for much of the century, in this decade at least seven voyages departed from São Tomé, which seems to have been particularly important for the Spanish slave trade in these early decades but remained a regular departure point up through 1580.[26] There were also voyages to Nombre de Dios as early as 1531; these increased in subsequent years with the Spanish conquest of the Inca Empire, as the town became a gateway to the Andes.[27] In this early period the region of Panama appears as the focus of both Spanish colonization and slave arrivals; only later in the 1570s would Cartagena de Indias begin to develop into a major slave trading center.[28] Two other voyages went to Cubagua, south of the Venezuelan island of Margarita. Enslaved Africans had been transported to the pearl fisheries there since the 1520s, usually in smaller groups, and this area remained an occasional and minor destination for slave traders throughout the century.[29] Although Veracruz and Cartagena were the two main registered ports for slaves after 1580, there are no confirmed arrivals for the province of New Spain until the mid-1540s, despite the presence of both enslaved and free Africans in the region well before then.[30]

The 1530s also illustrate some of the limits of the sources and problems of trying to analyze only quantifiable data. Caribbean treasury records offer the best information on slave arrivals for this decade, providing a more accurate sense of completed outbound voyages, but these usually cannot be matched with departure information.[31] For later periods most of the available voyage information comes from departure records alone, which describe intended voyages that might not have been completed or that might have deviated from their registered destinations. African provenance zones are less frequently recorded—generally true up through 1580 and beyond—giving an incomplete picture of the origins of people taken to the Spanish Caribbean as slaves. The numbers of captives transported are also in doubt, since treasury entries often did not record this information unless there were import duties owed or in the event of a legal problem.[32] Only a handful of voyages have both detailed information and confirmation from more than one source, as in the case of the vessel arriving in Santo Domingo on June 29, 1530, carrying 231 enslaved Africans under Ehinger and Sayler's licenses.[33]

Royal orders offer a few other clues about slaves transported to Jamaica and Cuba in the 1530s, although currently these cannot be matched with confirmed voyages. Since Jamaica was a possession of the Columbus family, slave arrivals to the island are largely a mystery, but in 1534 local treasurer Pedro de Mazuelo received royal permission to take thirty slaves there to set up a sugar *ingenio* (mill). The grant specified that if he did not use these slaves for the ingenio, he would have to pay normal duties, and if he did not take them to Jamaica, they would be seized for the crown; he was also forbidden to bring Wolofs or other "prohibited" individuals.[34] In this way the Spanish crown attempted to direct captives toward what it considered important industries and to restrict their origins based on the experiences of preceding decades (in this case, uprisings on Hispaniola involving Wolof slaves).[35] A similar grant of fifty slaves the same year for another ingenio in Santiago de Cuba suggests that there was a demand for enslaved Africans in secondary destinations around the Caribbean in the 1530s.[36]

The 1540s showed a significant rise in slave voyages; some seventy-five vessels departed for the Caribbean in these years, compared with sixty-two in the 1550s, fifty-nine in the 1560s, and sixty-three in the 1570s. It also seems that dedicated slaving voyages became increasingly frequent during this time. According to the TSTD, the intended provenance zone for slaves in the 1540s was overwhelmingly Cabo Verde, although this label was often used as shorthand for the entire Upper Guinean region. Only a couple of voyages from São Tomé are listed, though others likely went unrecorded; at the least, it remained connected to the Caribbean during this period. Although the destinations of forty-one of these voyages are currently unknown, those that are recorded show increasing variety as a result of growth and change in Spanish settlements in the greater Caribbean region. The primary disembarkation zone during the 1540s seems to have shifted toward Nombre de Dios, which had twelve recorded slave ship arrivals, while Santo Domingo and Puerto Rico had six each. Since destination information for recorded voyages during the 1540s is so limited, the extent of this change remains uncertain. During this decade, New Spain begins to appear as a port of entry for African captives, likely for new mining and sugar-growing projects.[37] A few voyages also sailed to Cartagena and Honduras. Some of these ships made multiple landings, such as the two that passed through Santo Domingo in 1542 on their way to take slaves to Honduras, suggesting that routes were becoming more complex and slave merchants were finding opportunities to learn about demand and slave prices at intermediate stops in the region.[38] Additionally, treasury accounts from Nombre de Dios record small numbers of captives arriving from Puerto Rico, Hispaniola, and Cuba, indicating a low-volume intra-Caribbean slave trade.[39]

The 1540–41 voyage of the Portuguese crew of the nao *Santa María de las Raíces* offers an example of the complexities of slave routes in this period. The ship left Lisbon for São Tomé, loaded 160 captives, and then departed for Santo Domingo in November 1540. However, it actually arrived in Puerto Rico in January 1541, with approximately 150 surviving slaves. Since it did not have a valid registro, treasury officials there declared these slaves to be royal property, and the Audiencia in Santo Domingo stepped in to claim jurisdiction. They decided that the captives had been brought with valid licenses and should be returned to the maestre.[40] These magistrates were later reprimanded by the king for encouraging a violation of royal trade restrictions, but by then the voyage backers had presumably already profited from the sale of their human cargo.[41] In such ways sympathetic officials encouraged slave imports to specific destinations, providing slave ship crews with an alternative to the laborious process of obtaining approval in Spain.

Two further changes in the 1540s may have had an impact on the routes of slaving vessels. The first was the relocation of the Audiencia of Panamá to Guatemala in 1543, which might have encouraged a slight shift in arrivals of African captives from Nombre de Dios to Honduras or Veracruz. The second was the increasing presence of hostile French ships in Caribbean waters, as the Audiencia of Santo Domingo reported in 1540 and 1545.[42]

The 1550s saw a decline in total voyages from the 1540s, not least because of war with France between 1552 and 1559.[43] This coincided with a drop in voyages to the islands and a corresponding shift toward New Spain and Panama, although officials on Hispaniola claimed that slave traffic there was "blocked" (*estanco*) because of a grant of 23,000 slave licenses to Genoese investors.[44] The major provenance zone for this period continued to be Cabo Verde, where at least eight vessels loaded slaves, compared with two each for Guinea and São Tomé; however, most voyages in the 1550s do not yet have a confirmed embarkation port.[45] In 1564, the Portuguese ambassador in Madrid complained that for the past ten years Spaniards had been illegally obtaining slaves from their territory, suggesting that slave merchants were circumventing both Portuguese restrictions in Africa and Spanish restrictions in the Americas.[46]

Over half of the voyages in this period have a recorded place of arrival, including twelve to either Veracruz or New Spain and nine to Nombre de Dios. Slave voyages to Hispaniola and Puerto Rico (seventeen in all) made use of remote or secondary ports like La Yaguana or Guayama, where supervision was often more lax. Registro information about intended destinations for this period is somewhat at odds with records of overseas arrivals. Out of forty-five voyages for which intended routes are known, twenty-three were bound for New Spain, fourteen for Tierra Firme or Nombre de Dios, three for Honduras, and one each for Santo Domingo, Puerto Plata, and Puerto Rico. While twenty-one of these voyages had confirmed arrivals at their destinations, twenty do not have any matching information to show that they disembarked slaves anywhere. In other cases ships ended up in very different locations, as for two vessels transporting slaves from Africa to Lisbon that ended up across the Atlantic in Santo Domingo. Just the same, the shift in intended destinations of slave voyages during the 1550s suggests that metropolitan conceptions of the need for enslaved labor had begun to change from the 1520s and 1530s, even if Hispaniola and Puerto Rico remained more important disembarkation points than metropolitan departure records indicate.[47]

Although Portuguese crews and merchants had been involved in the slave trade to Spanish America since the beginning, by the 1550s Portuguese domination of most aspects of this trade was evident. In 1556 treasury officials on Hispaniola notified the king that Portuguese slave ships were regularly making arribadas there, since by then the island had a substantial Portuguese population and was a well-known connection point to other Caribbean destinations. Just the same, Portuguese networks were never exclusive, even into the seventeenth century, and royal officials and Spanish merchants on both sides of the Atlantic were essential to the success of most slaving voyages.[48] Likewise, Portuguese financial backers in Lisbon and Seville began to play a more active role in organizing voyages, especially after Manuel Caldeira, a major Portuguese merchant, received a contract for 2,000 slave licenses in 1556.[49] However, Genoese investors continued to trade in African captives after this point, as did Spanish merchants at a variety of levels.[50] Many of them were connected to Caldeira and his agents, and so conceptualizing financial support networks for the Spanish slave trade in terms of national competition obscures the transnational cooperation involved at all stages, from obtaining royal licenses to organizing commercial support to manning the slave vessels themselves.

The Early Slave Trade

Caldeira personifies a truly Atlantic network of contacts; he also jointly held contractual rights from the Portuguese crown to provide slaves in Guinea, Cabo Verde, and São Tomé, and had resident agents in Santo Domingo, Nombre de Dios, and Mexico.[51] While his commercial interests extended beyond the slave trade, he sent African captives to various destinations around the Caribbean, including Honduras, Margarita, and Ocoa, a minor port on Hispaniola southwest of Santo Domingo. For example, in July 1558 three ships—one en route to Puerto Caballos in Honduras—arrived at Santo Domingo with slaves using Caldeira's licenses, as well as some unregistered slaves and goods.[52] The following year the galleon *San Pedro*, financed by Caldeira, anchored at Ocoa and unloaded some goods and slaves before officials in Santo Domingo showed up.[53] Ocoa was used as an occasional supply stop for the Indies fleets by the 1570s, ostensibly because it had a deeper harbor than Santo Domingo, but its main advantage was its lack of official oversight.[54] The voyage of this galleon seems to have been something of an experiment; it had stopped in both Madeira and Cabo Verde, and carried an astonishing 116 crewmembers—most of them actually merchants—and a wide assortment of merchandise, in addition to between 60 and 110 slaves. Even though they ran into easily foreseeable legal troubles in Santo Domingo, Caldeira's entire network gained a great deal of information about local and regional demand.[55]

The increase in slave voyages in the late 1550s and early 1560s coincided with peace with France in 1559. Although it vanished after leaving Cádiz in April 1559, the nao *Sant Julian* planned to take some 360 captives from Cabo Verde to Nombre de Dios, reflecting a growing Andean demand for slave labor.[56] Treasury accounts from Honduras reveal additional intra-Caribbean traffic in enslaved Africans, as well as efforts to find loopholes in royal legislation; a few ships brought some *criollo* slaves from Santo Domingo to Honduras between 1557 and 1559 and presented documents claiming that they did not owe tax because these slaves were "born and raised" on Hispaniola and so counted as local produce (*labranza y crianza*).[57] Meanwhile, as news spread through slave merchant networks of the advantages of Ocoa, more ships began to arrive there. In 1561 and 1562, Cristóbal Rodríguez

Garrucho, a Spaniard, sailed from Tenerife to the "Rivers of Guinea," loading slaves with the assistance of the local Portuguese factor, then crossed to Ocoa (briefly stopping on the south coast of Puerto Rico) instead of returning to Seville as planned.[58] Since one of the voyage organizers lived in Veracruz, the *fiscal* (crown prosecutor) in Santo Domingo accused Garrucho of trying surreptitiously to arrange permission to take these captives to New Spain.

During the 1560s a minimum of fifty-nine voyages set out to take captives to Spanish America, representing only a limited drop from the preceding decade. Roughly half of these voyages have no confirmed embarkation information, but at least twenty-two took slaves in Cabo Verde or Upper Guinea, five in São Tomé, and five in Sierra Leone, also called Magarabomba. The Portuguese had visited Sierra Leone well before then, but several sources strongly suggest an increase in the number of captives taken from that region around this time.[59] These details reflect not only Portuguese activity in Africa but also changes occurring outside the European sphere of involvement, which affected the origins of Africans taken to the Americas as slaves.[60]

Destinations for slave voyages also shifted in the 1560s; although eleven are unspecified, twenty-one went to Veracruz, seven to Nombre de Dios, two to Cartagena (one continuing to Nombre de Dios), twelve to Hispaniola (one each to Nizao and Ocoa), three to different places on Puerto Rico, and two to Margarita. The registered destinations for these voyages were roughly similar, with twenty-four planning to go to New Spain, ten to Tierra Firme, and three to Honduras. However, the formal institution of the flota system in the early part of this decade likely distorted the numbers of slave ships recorded for New Spain, and many may have sold slaves in other ports before sailing to Veracruz and Havana.[61] Generally speaking, by the late 1550s and early 1560s the Caribbean was a more complex commercial arena than it had been in the 1540s, as shown by an increase in voyages that stopped at multiple ports or landed at outlying locations, often to cover up a lack of documentation.

While Cartagena was still an infrequent destination for slaves in this era compared with Nombre de Dios, the rapid sale of the 146 captives carried by the *Santa María de Victoria* after its arrival in 1564 suggests that there was substantial local demand. The ship planned to carry slaves from Upper Guinea to Lisbon, but after leaving Sierra Leone it was driven by storms across the Atlantic all the way to Cartagena. Local officials ordered that the enslaved Africans be sold at public auction; they found no shortage of local purchasers.[62] Although the governor declared the ship and its human cargo to be crown property because the voyage had violated trade restrictions, the Council of the Indies later overturned the decision and returned the proceeds to the voyage backers. Whether or not the ship's emergency was genuine, the successful auction of the slaves aboard encouraged other voyages to Cartagena and nearby secondary destinations like Santa Marta and Riohacha in the following decade. By this point the return of the Audiencia of Panamá to the isthmus in 1564 seems to have been less important than the combination of Andean and coastal demand in shaping slave routes.

During the 1570s, both the volume of the slave trade and the numbers of voyages appear to have been rising, although extant information is even more fragmentary than for previous decades. Some sixty-three individual voyages left records of departures or arrivals in these years (still less than the 1540s), including fifteen arriving in the Caribbean from Cabo Verde or Guinea and three from São Tomé. Registros for some of these voyages offer a contrasting if less reliable picture; while thirty-six of these voyages intended to load captives in Cabo Verde, a handful listed Guinea, or São Tomé, or some combination of the three, and two included Angola as a possible stop. Indeed, slaves from Angola started arriving in significant numbers in the late 1570s following the Portuguese establishment of Luanda in 1575, although it would be several more decades before Angola dominated the traffic to Spanish America.[63] Of the twenty-six voyages with arrival information, fourteen went to Hispaniola, nine landed at Cartagena (one stopped at Riohacha first and another continued to Santa Marta), two to Veracruz, and one to Havana. Again, registro information paints a substantially different picture, with twenty-two ships bound for New Spain, nineteen for Tierra Firme or Cartagena, two for either Tierra Firme or New Spain, three for Puerto Rico, and one each for Havana, Honduras, Santo Domingo, Cabo Verde, and Portugal.

By this point a later phase of the slave trade primarily tied to Cartagena and Veracruz had gotten under way, although comparing arrival records with intended destinations offers a more complex set of pathways. In particular the island of Hispaniola, which hardly appears in registros of this time, continued to be an important stop for slaving vessels, whether to land captives illegally or to load provisions before continuing to a registered destination. Out of fourteen voyages landing there, eight stopped in Ocoa and one each went to Nizao and Puerto Plata; at least one more probably went to La Yaguana.[64] Peninsular and local royal authorities had difficulty tracking legal or illegal arrivals, since overseas treasury accounts were not normally compared against the departure records of the House of Trade. In a few cases resident officials did uncover irregularities, as in 1574 when the *Nuestra Señora de la Luz* arrived at Ocoa with 294 captives and a registro made in the Canary Islands using, according to the captain, slave licenses belonging to the queen's treasurer. However, the audiencia learned from a crewmember that those licenses, which had been transferred several times, already had been used to transport 300 slaves to Cartagena two years earlier. Shortly afterward another ship carrying some 151 African captives under licenses from the same grant landed at Puerto Plata en route to Havana.[65] These voyages offer some idea of the challenges of controlling the transactions involved in moving enslaved sub-Saharan Africans across a vast and increasingly complicated Atlantic space and of the numerous opportunities to evade royal supervision and taxation.

Caribbean slave routes showed other noteworthy shifts by the late 1570s. While treasury accounts for Honduras recorded a handful of slave arrivals in the 1550s and 1560s, none are recorded for the 1570s, when maritime traffic to the region moved eastward from Puerto Caballos to Trujillo.[66] Likewise, Nombre de Dios no longer appears as a significant destination, while Cartagena received ever-greater numbers of African captives. In years to come, royal orders stipulated that these slaves were not to remain in Tierra Firme but should be sent on to the Andes, demonstrating that the crown attempted to channel African slave labor toward mining against persistent and competing coastal demand.

Spanish Jamaica offers a convenient final example of the limits of sixteenth-century sources; since slave arrivals there were not reported, it defies easy characterization for this period.[67] Luis Colón, Columbus's grandson, received two hundred slave licenses in 1536 and 1541, plus four hundred licenses in 1557, so that at least some otherwise unrecorded groups of slaves were likely to have gone to the island.[68] In 1569 the fiscal in Santo Domingo pointed out that Colón's expansive rights offered an excellent opportunity for fraud; according to him, Colón could easily have foreigners bring ten thousand captives per year and charge them only a modest fine to avoid license costs, circumventing royal control over the slave trade.[69] While his claim was intentionally hyperbolic, it suggests that impounding slave cargoes, a standard penalty for illicit arrivals, was also used to obscure fraud and even hints at the possibility that Jamaica acted as a depot for as-yet-unknown slave imports to the Spanish Caribbean.

By the eve of the union of the Spanish and Portuguese crowns in 1580, the outlines of the later slave trade up to 1640 were in place. Portuguese merchant networks dominated much of the trade, although they included many non-Portuguese participants. The origins of enslaved Africans taken to the Caribbean had begun to shift toward the south, although this process would continue into the early seventeenth century. On the other side of the Atlantic, the flota system drove an increasing amount of slave traffic toward the two ports of Cartagena and Veracruz, and this trend would continue beyond 1580.

Well before the Portuguese asiento period began in 1595, the Spanish crown had had decades of experience organizing the delivery of slaves to the Caribbean, including some grants of monopoly rights between 1518 and 1552. The 1580s saw a marked rise in the number of slaving vessels, to about 120 voyages, and the total volume of captives delivered, but this growth happened along lines that were already set. Portuguese traders found new opportunities—for example, Hispaniola experienced a noticeable rise in arribadas, and voyages from the Canaries increased—but 1580 did not bring radical changes in either routes or patterns of both legal and illegal slaving.

Just the same, the slave trade to the Caribbean between 1530 and 1580 differed from the system that followed. Particularly in the early decades, there was more trial and error, negotiation, and competition between the representatives of the crown and those directly involved in transporting slaves to the Americas, as both sides sought to maximize benefits. The routes of slave ships also reflected key changes in the sixteenth-century Caribbean, as early destinations like Nombre de Dios or Puerto Caballos were supplanted by Cartagena and Veracruz towards 1580. While places like Puerto Rico or Margarita continued to see occasional slave ships, the proportion of African captives they received was far smaller than in the first half of the century. Havana, which became a key stop for the yearly fleets in the 1560s, did not become a primary destination for enslaved laborers by the 1580s, but Veracruz rose in importance up to 1580 and beyond, even if it likely received a smaller flow of enslaved Africans than Tierra Firme.[70] Other places had not yet developed to the point of becoming regular destinations for slave ships; Caracas was not founded until 1567, and there are no records of voyages there (or to La Guaira) before 1580. Hispaniola, however, remained an important way station for slave traders. Many of the voyages that came there, whether to Santo Domingo or to outlying ports, were either illicit, emergency, or intermediate arrivals, suggesting that it was a useful place to gather information, both on local conditions for selling slaves and on broader commercial prospects throughout the greater Caribbean. By 1580 Santo Domingo rarely appeared as a destination on registros, but it would show a surprising durability as a haven for vessels claiming distress; it is also likely that slaves continued to be transported from there to secondary destinations.

Despite the limitations of sixteenth-century sources, our understanding of slave routes in this period is improving. The voyages of slave ships to the Spanish Caribbean were linked to other interlocking and overlapping circuits of the transatlantic slave trade, whether between Cabo Verde and Upper Guinea, Angola and Brazil, or Africa and Europe, and these other circuits played a role in the arrival of sub-Saharan Africans to the greater Caribbean area.[71] This early slave trade was also an integral part of broader developments taking place in and beyond the Caribbean basin during the sixteenth century, from Spanish conquests in the Andes to war with France to the organization of the flota system. Slave voyages responded and adapted to these changes, and helped drive the growth, survival, or decline of Spanish population centers within the region.

Notes

ABBREVIATIONS

AGI		Archivo General de Indias
	-Ctdra	Contaduría
	-Cttn	Casa de la Contratación
	-IG	Gobierno: Indiferente General
	-Just	Justicia
	-Panama	Gobierno: Audiencia de Panamá
	-SD	Gobierno: Audiencia de Santo Domingo
AHPLP		Archivo Histórico Provincial Las Palmas
	-PN	Protocolos Notariales

1. I am using *Caribbean* here in a broad sense, to include voyages to New Spain.
2. Muro Romero, *Las Presidencias-Gobernaciones*, 46.
3. Although many parts of Spanish America relied on forced indigenous labor during the sixteenth century, my focus here is on the transport of enslaved sub-Saharan Africans. The pathways followed by the vast majority of indigenous captives during this period were substantially different—and perhaps even more difficult to trace—than the Atlantic routes described in this article, even if these two trades overlapped in many other ways, as discussed by Erin Stone in this volume. For a recent overview, see van Deusen, *Global Indios*, 2.
4. See www.slavevoyages.org.
5. The standard reference for 1595–1640 remains Vila Vilar, *Hispanoamérica y el comercio de esclavos*; compare Mendes, "Foundations of the System," 67–69; and Grandío Moráguez, "African Origins," 182–83.
6. Most of these voyages are listed in Chaunu and Chaunu, *Seville et l'Atlantique*, which draws on AGI-Cttn 2898, a later summary of registered voyages.
7. Pérez García, "Metodología," 829–34.
8. For example, the *Santa Maria de Sale*, which "brought blacks" to Santo Domingo in 1540; AGI-Ctdra 1051, N.1, f. 83r.
9. On contraband, see Murray, "Statistics of the Slave Trade," 132–35, 139–48; and Borucki, Eltis, and Wheat, "Atlantic History and the Slave Trade," 438–39. On vessel itineraries in the late eighteenth and early nineteenth century, see Bassi, "The Space Between."

10. García Fuentes makes a distinction between licenses and asientos, but also offers figures by decade for the sixteenth century in "Licencias para la introducción de esclavos," 5–8.
11. Elbl, "Volume of the Early Atlantic Slave Trade."
12. Pérez García, "Metodología," 831; Fernández Chaves and Pérez García, "Penetración económica portuguesa," 207. See also Ramos Pérez, "El negocio negrero," 71–74; and Spencer Tyce's chapter in this volume.
13. AGI-Just 1169, N.4, R.2 (1530–1533) contains complaints both from and against the Welsers; see also Fernández Chaves and Pérez García, "La élite mercantil," 398.
14. The accounts of Santo Domingo in AGI-Ctdra 1050, N.2 record several arrivals of at least small groups of enslaved Africans in 1529, while royal letters like AGI-SD 2280, L.1, fols. 12r–13r (22 December 1529) reveal that unlicensed captives had been arriving in previous years.
15. AGI-SD 2280, L.1, fols. 46v–47r (10 August 1530).
16. A year later, another cédula instructed the bishop of Cuba to use all income from royal duties for 1531 to purchase slaves to distribute among the inhabitants there, although this does not seem to have brought slave ships to the island; AGI-SD 1121, L.1, fols. 78r–78v (4 April 1531); Cortés López, *Esclavo y colono*, 42–43.
17. AGI-IG 1961, L.2, fols. 69v–71r (16 May 1531).
18. See Warsh, "Enslaved Pearl Divers" and Restall, "Black Conquistadors."
19. Fernández Chaves and Pérez García, "La élite mercantil," 397.
20. These slaves were financed by Ruy Gómez, a merchant of Seville, showing that a financial system for transferring and consolidating slave licenses had begun to develop; AGI-Ctdra 1050, N.2, fol. 445v (3 August 1532); AGI-SD 74, R.1, N.19 (15 July 1532).
21. AGI-SD 2280, L.1, fols. 148r–148v (4 February 1533), 189r–189v (6 January 1534); L.2, fols. 82r–82v (16 December 1535), 143r–143v (18 March 1538).
22. In 1539, the king ordered the audiencia of Santo Domingo to stop reporting on illicit slave voyages from years past, suggesting an emphasis on ensuring new slave arrivals instead. AGI-SD 868, L.1, fols. 158r–159r (8 February 1539).
23. This project was likely not carried out, but was authorized by the king. AGI-SD 2280, L.2, fols. 1v–3r (6 Jan 1634). (Thanks to Ida Altman for sharing her notes on this source.) See also Mira Caballos, *El indio antillano*, 339.
24. Licenses from the 1518 Gouvenot grant were still being purchased as late as 1534; Fernández Chaves and Pérez García, "Penetración económica portuguesa," 207.

25. All figures cited here are from David Wheat and Marc Eagle, unpublished dataset of slave voyages to Spanish America, 1500–1640; once complete it will be made available at www.slavevoyages.org.
26. In 1538, treasury officials in Santo Domingo wrote that many slaves arrived from both Cabo Verde and São Tomé. AGI-SD 74, N.46 (28 October 1538).
27. AGI-Panama 234, L.5, fols. 111r–111v (20 April 1533), 197v–198r (1 March 1535).
28. Cartagena was not founded until the mid-1530s. See Borrego Plá, *Cartagena de Indias*, 3–5.
29. For example, in 1526 Juan de Urrutia was granted permission to bring thirty slaves to Cubagua, while in 1528 a group of slaves were prevented from landing there and sent to Santo Domingo. AGI-IG 420, L.10, fols. 220v–221r (12 Jan 1526); AGI-IG 421, L.12, fols. 277v–278v (24 January 1528). See also Warsh, "Enslaved Pearl Divers," 347.
30. Veracruz was in a different location then, which reduced its usefulness as a port. See J. M. H. Clark's chapter in this volume.
31. The most important for this time are AGI-Ctdra 1050, N.2 and 1073, N. 6.
32. Some entries for Puerto Rico show ships with only one or two slaves, although these may have carried additional captives for whom duties had already been paid. See AGI-Ctdra 1073, N.6.
33. AGI-Ctdra 1050, N.2, fol. 429r (29 June 1530); AGI-Just 973, N.1, R.1, fols. 15v–22v (July 1530).
34. AGI-SD 1121, L.2, fols. 27r–28r (19 July 1534).
35. See Stone, "America's First Slave Revolt," 195–217.
36. AGI-SD 1121, L.2, fols. 6r–7v (6 January 1534).
37. Our dataset currently shows seven voyages to New Spain. Lapeyre lists twice as many ships heading to Nueva España than to Tierra Firme between 1547 and 1555, although these were planned routes only. Lapeyre, "La trata de negros," 338.
38. AGI-Ctdra 1051, N.1, fols. 117r–117v.
39. AGI-Ctdra 1452, fols. 21r, 71r, 75r, 301r.
40. AGI-Just 991, N.1, R.4 (1541). The ship is also called the *Santa María de Ayuda*.
41. The audiencia made at least two such decisions. AGI-SD 868, L.2, fols. 71v–75v (15 April 1541), 116r–118r (16 August 1541).
42. AGI-SD 868, L.2, fols. 71v–75v (15 April 1541), 274v–276r (19 December 1545).
43. Hoffman, *Spanish Crown*, 63–68.
44. AGI-SD 71, L.1, fols. 34r–37v (15 May 1553). This grant, to Hernando de Ochoa, was not an exclusive monopoly; Pérez García, "Metodología," 831.
45. AGI-Ctdra 1051, N.5, fols. 10v, 14v; AGI-SD 74, R.2, N.77 (28 August 1556).
46. AGI-Just 1167, N.4.

47. Gelpí Baíz, *Siglo en blanco*, 136–37. Treasury records offer only limited confirmation of small numbers of African captives arriving in Nombre de Dios and Honduras. See AGI-Ctdra 988, fols. 22r, 22v, 24r, 107r; AGI-Ctdra 1452, fols. 298v, 303r, 308v, 309r.
48. AGI-SD 74, R.2, N.77 (28 Aug 1556). See also Bataillon, "Santo Domingo 'Era Portugal.'"
49. On Caldeira, see Ventura, *Negreiros Portugueses*, 42–50, 75–117.
50. Fernández Chaves and Pérez García, "Penetración económica portuguesa," 216.
51. AGI-Panama 236, L.9, fols. 337v–338v (28 Jun 1561). Caldeira himself traveled extensively in Europe and Africa. Ventura, *Negreiros Portugueses*, 80.
52. A local official testified that this was a common occurrence; AGI-Just 104 (1558), fol. 5768v.
53. AGI-Just 35, N.3; AGI-SD 71, L.2, fols. 144r–145v (26 Apr 1560), 152r–153v (8 Jun 1560).
54. AGI-SD 50, R.12, N.48 (17 Jul 1576).
55. Caldeira's local agents anticipated trouble and offered to pay outstanding duties and cancel additional licenses if necessary. AGI-Just 35, N.3, pza. 1, fols. 3r–4v (6 Jul 1559).
56. AGI-Just 856, N.3; AGI-Just 1156, N.1, R.3.
57. AGI-Ctdra 988, R.1, fols. 24r–25r, 107r.
58. AGI-Just 36, N.2. He was eventually condemned to the loss of his ship, slaves, and goods. See also Green, *Rise of the Trans-Atlantic Slave Trade*, 213–14.
59. AGI-SD 71, L.1, fols. 19r–21v (22 May 1562). The Garrucho voyage described above had also stopped there, while notarial records from the Canaries show slave sales from Magarabomba in 1565. AHPLP-PN 852, fols. 29r–30r, 39r–39v, 53v–55r, 81r–81v, 84v–85r, 132r–132v, 280r–281r, 286v–287r.
60. See Mark, "Towards a Reassessment."
61. In many cases New Spain was only an intended destination. The 1562–63 voyage of Juan de Meçina shows an early example of how the flota influenced slave voyages. He left Cádiz with the flota, departed for Cabo Verde, transported slaves to Cartagena and Nombre de Dios, and then rejoined the flota in Havana for the return journey; AGI-Just 862, N.2.
62. AGI-Just 1120.
63. Wheat, "First Great Waves"; see also his chapter in this volume.
64. See AGI-Ctdra 1052, pza. 6, fols. 33r, 40r. Foreign ships also reportedly traded slaves illicitly in ports like La Yaguana; AGI-SD 50, R.12, N.51 (18 Jul 1576); Andrews, *Spanish Caribbean: Trade and Plunder*, 74–79; Hoffman, *Spanish Crown*, 118–21.
65. AGI-SD 71, L.3, fols. 58r–61v (10 August 1574), 66r–67v (10 August 1574).

66. AGI-Ctdra 988, R.8–16. The 1563–1568 suppression of the audiencia of Guatemala may have played a minor role in this change; Muro Romero, *Las Presidencias-Gobernaciones*, 121.
67. The standard reference remains Morales Padrón, *Jamaica Española*.
68. AGI-IG 422, L.17, fols. 78v–79r (20 Nov 1536); AGI-IG 737, N.50 (24 Mar 1541); AGI-SD 899, L.1, fols. 55r–55v (10 Apr 1557).
69. He also estimated that six hundred slaves had come to Jamaica in recent years; AGI-SD 71, L.2, fols. 483r–486v (8 Jul 1568), 505r–508v (26 Feb 1569).
70. See Mendes, "Foundations of the System," 87.
71. For an excellent example of another of these overlapping circuits, see Gabriel de Avilez Rocha's chapter in this volume.

Bibliography

ARCHIVES

Archivo General de Indias (Seville, Spain).
Archivo Histórico Provincial Las Palmas (Las Palmas de Gran Canaria, Spain).

PUBLISHED WORKS

Andrews, Kenneth R. *The Spanish Caribbean: Trade and Plunder, 1530–1630*. New Haven: Yale University Press, 1978.
Bassi, Ernesto. "The Space Between." *Appendix* 2, no. 4 (October 2014): 132–42.
Bataillon, Marcel. "Santo Domingo 'Era Portugal.'" In *Historia y sociedad en el mundo de habla español: Homenaje a José Miranda*, edited by Bernardo García Martínez et al., 113–20. México DF: Colegio de México, 1970.
Borrego Plá, María del Carmen. *Cartagena de Indias en el siglo XVI*. Seville: Escuela de Estudios Hispano-Americanos, Consejo Superior de Investigaciones Científicas, 1983.
Borucki, Alex, David Eltis, and David Wheat. "Atlantic History and the Slave Trade to Spanish America." *American Historical Review* 120, no. 2 (April 2015): 433–61.
Chaunu, Huguette, and Pierre Chaunu. *Seville et l'Atlantique (1504–1650)*. 8 vols. Paris: S.E.V.P.E.N, 1956.
Cortés López, José Luis. *Esclavo y colono (introducción y sociología de los negroafricanos en la América española del siglo XVI)*. Salamanca: Ediciones Universidad de Salamanca, 2004.
Elbl, Ivana. "The Volume of the Early Atlantic Slave Trade, 1450–1521." *Journal of African History* 38, no. 1 (1997): 31–75.
Fernández Chaves, Manuel F., and Rafael M. Pérez García. "La élite mercantil judeoconversa andaluza y la articulación de la trata negrera hacia

las Indias de Castilla, ca. 1518–1560." *Hispania* 76, no. 253 (May–August 2016): 385–414.

———. "La Penetración económica portuguesa en la Sevilla del siglo XVI." *Espacio, Tiempo y Forma: Serie IV, Historia Moderna*, t. 25 (2012): 199–222.

García Fuentes, Lutgardo. "Licencias para la introducción de esclavos en Indias y envíos desde Sevilla en el siglo XVI." *Jahrbuch für Geschichte von Staat, Wirtschaft und Gesellschaft Lateinamerikas* 19 (1982): 1–46.

Gelpí Baíz, Elsa. *Siglo en blanco: estudio de la economía azucarera en el Puerto Rico del siglo XVI (1540–1612)*. San Juan: Editorial de la Universidad de Puerto Rico, 2000.

Grandío Moráguez, Oscar. "The African Origins of Slaves Arriving in Cuba, 1789–1865." In *Extending the Frontiers: Essays on the New Transatlantic Slave Trade Database*, edited by David Eltis and David Richardson, 176–201. New Haven: Yale University Press, 2008.

Green, Toby. *The Rise of the Trans-Atlantic Slave Trade in Western Africa, 1300–1589*. Cambridge: Cambridge University Press, 2012.

Hoffman, Paul E. *The Spanish Crown and the Defense of the Caribbean, 1535–1585: Precedent, Patrimonialism, and Royal Parsimony*. Baton Rouge: Louisiana State University Press, 1980.

Lapeyre, Henri. "La trata de negros con destino a la América española durante los últimos años del reinado de Carlos V, 1544–1555." *Cuadernos de investigación histórica* 2 (1978): 335–339.

Mark, Peter. "Towards a Reassessment of the Dating and the Geographical Origins of the Luso-African Ivories, Fifteenth to Seventeenth Centuries." *History in Africa* 34 (2007): 189–211.

Mendes, António de Almeida. "The Foundations of the System: A Reassessment of the Slave Trade to the Spanish Americas during the Sixteenth and Seventeenth Centuries." In *Extending the Frontiers: Essays on the New Transatlantic Slave Trade Database*, edited by David Eltis and David Richardson, 63–94. New Haven: Yale University Press, 2008.

Mira Caballos, Esteban. *El indio antillano: repartimiento, encomienda y esclavitud (1492–1542)*. Seville: Muñoz Moya, 1997.

Morales Padrón, Francisco. *Jamaica Española*. Seville: Escuela de Estudios Hispano-Americanos, 1952.

Muro Romero, Fernando. *Las Presidencias-Gobernaciones en Indias (siglo XVI)*. Seville: Escuela de Estudios Hispano-Americanos, 1975.

Murray, D. R. "Statistics of the Slave Trade to Cuba, 1790–1867." *Journal of Latin American Studies* 3, no. 2 (November 1971): 131–49.

Pérez García, Rafael M. "Metodología para el análisis y cuantificación de la trata de esclavos hacia la América española en el siglo XVI." In *Los vestidos de Clío. Métodos y tendencias recientes de la historiografía modernista española (1973–2013)*, edited by Ofelia Rey Castelao and Fernando Suárez Golán, 823–40. Santiago de Compostela: Universidade de Santiago de Compostela, 2015.

Ramos Pérez, Demetrio. "El negocio negrero de los Welser y sus habilidades monopolistas." *Revista de Historia de América* 81 (January–June 1976): 7–81.

Restall, Matthew. "Black Conquistadors: Armed Africans in Early Spanish America." *Americas* 57, no. 2 (October 2000): 171–205.

Stone, Erin. "America's First Slave Revolt: Indians and African Slaves in Española, 1500–1534." *Ethnohistory* 60, no. 2 (Spring 2013): 195–217.

van Deusen, Nancy E. *Global Indios: The Indigenous Struggle for Justice in Sixteenth-Century Spain*. Durham: Duke University Press, 2015.

Ventura, Maria da Graça A. Mateus. *Negreiros Portugueses na Rota das Índias de Castela (1541–1556)*. Lisboa: Edições Colibri, 1999.

Vila Vilar, Enriqueta. *Hispanoamérica y el comercio de esclavos: los asientos portugueses*. Seville: Escuela de Estudios Hispano-Americanos, 1977.

Warsh, Molly A. "Enslaved Pearl Divers in the Sixteenth Century Caribbean." *Slavery & Abolition* 31, no. 3 (September 2010): 345–62.

Wheat, David. "The First Great Waves: African Provenance Zones for the Transatlantic Slave Trade to Cartagena de Indias, 1570–1640." *Journal of African History* 52, no. 1 (2011): 1–22.

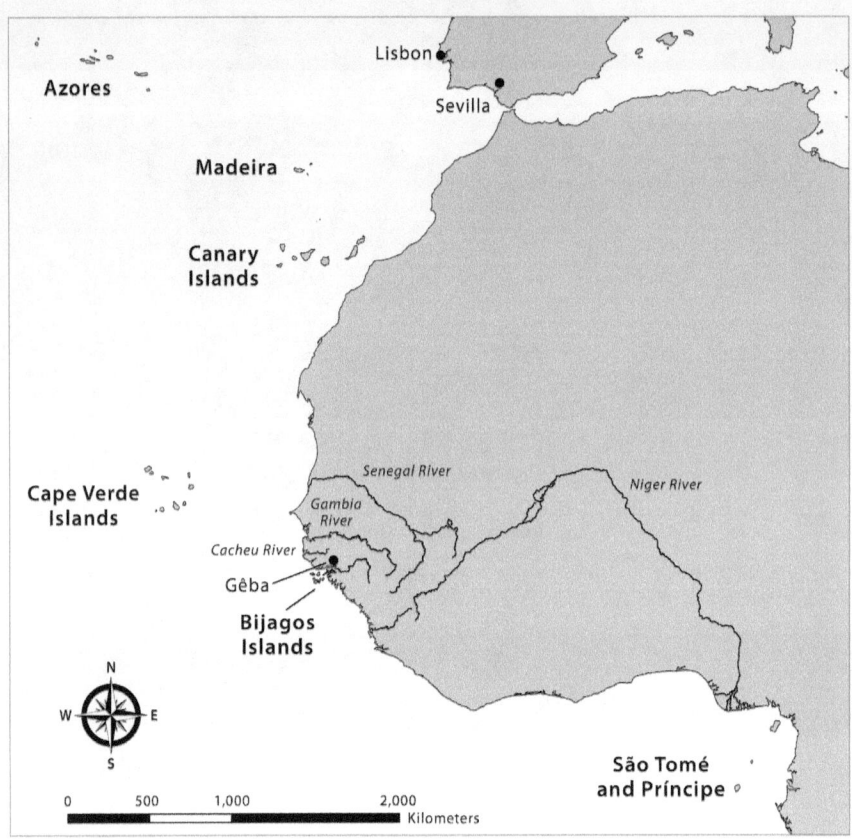

Map 4. West Africa and the Atlantic Islands.

8

Biafadas in Havana

West African Antecedents for Caribbean Social Interactions

DAVID WHEAT

Iberians in the late sixteenth-century Caribbean relied extensively on the labor of enslaved sub-Saharan Africans, but they also understood Africans—particularly those who originated in the "Rivers of Guinea," or coastal Upper Guinea—to be peoples with tangible pasts that neither slavery nor distance could immediately erase. Perhaps the strongest indication of Iberian attentiveness to the Upper Guinean past is that, unlike other African forced migrants, Upper Guineans are regularly identified in early Spanish American sources by "nations" or "lands" that directly correspond to historical and present-day peoples in the modern nations of Senegal, the Gambia, Guinea-Bissau, Guinea-Conakry, and Sierra Leone. Multilingualism was common in Upper Guinean contexts, and markers of identity such as lineage, occupation, and religion may have been just as important as ethnolinguistic designations construed in relation to discrete territorial spaces or ancestral lands.[1] Even though they represent only one of the ways that Upper Guineans likely viewed themselves, the specificity of the ethnonyms recorded in Iberian sources, coupled with recent scholarship on the precolonial Upper Guinea Coast, makes it increasingly possible to view Upper Guineans in colonial Spanish America in light of their own histories.[2]

Today they comprise only a little over 3 percent of the inhabitants of Guinea-Bissau, yet the Biafada or Beafada figure prominently in the history of West Africa's Upper Guinea Coast as merchants, travelers, and go-betweens.[3] European sources for the sixteenth and seventeenth centuries depict them as mariners, hunters, and fishermen who plied rivers and coastal waters in large, seaworthy canoes.[4] Modern historians show the Biafada to have been key agents facilitating regional trade networks, including trade oriented toward the Cape Verde Islands and Portugal; the Biafada may also be viewed as a prime example of the strong political and cultural influence that Mande peoples farther inland exerted on neighboring coastal societies.[5] Alongside other peoples from Upper Guinea, Biafadas were also transported as slaves to Spanish America.[6] While their experiences of enslavement and forced migration were by no means unique, "Biafaras" (Biafadas) were among the numerically best represented Upper Guinean groups to be found in sixteenth-century Spanish American settlements.[7]

Drawing on underutilized parish records, this essay explores patterns of interaction between Biafadas and other inhabitants of Havana during the late 1500s. Rejecting the notion that African cultures were static or fixed in time, historians have shown that diasporic African "nations" were often invented traditions that coalesced around toponyms or pseudoethnic monikers associated with the transatlantic slave trade and subsequently were appropriated, refined, or reconstructed by African migrants themselves.[8] However, social patterning among diasporic African populations in the early Spanish Caribbean was not exclusively a response to local conditions. Analysis of Biafadas' participation in Catholic marriages and baptisms points to the existence of multiethnic social networks that replicated and even reinforced some of the economic and political dynamics that characterized previous cross-cultural exchanges in Upper Guinea.

Like Iberian migrants to Spanish America during the same era, Upper Guineans in late sixteenth-century Havana formed social connections that corresponded to prior alliances and shared regional and ethnolinguistic origins.[9] Enslaved Africans probably had less choice than most of Havana's free residents regarding with whom they would come into contact or work beside, and it is usually unclear when, or if, enslaved people could choose their godparents, godchildren, *compadres*, or sexual partners. Yet notwithstanding that they were uprooted peoples thrust into a new environment, rather than (or in addition to) forging group identities based on shared experiences of dislocation and alienation, Africans' own histories continued to inform the relationships they developed in diasporic settings. Biafadas in late sixteenth-century Havana displayed a strong preference for establishing social ties with one another and with their traditional Upper Guinean trading partners, but almost categorically avoided association with Upper Guinean peoples to whom they formerly had been politically or militarily subjugated.

Biafadas appear in a wide range of early Spanish American sources, typically alongside other Upper Guineans. A roster of captives arriving in Cuba in 1572 on the slave ship *San Pedro* employed no less than seventeen terms to designate their diverse Upper Guinean origins. Among the nearly two hundred captives who had survived the journey from the Cape Verde Islands to Havana, 28 men and 11 women are specifically listed as "Biafara blacks" (*negro[s] viafara[s]*) or as captives "from Biafara country" (*de tierra biafara*); one Biafada woman was accompanied by a small boy.[10] Ostensibly transported to Cuba to construct fortifications and to perform various other labors on behalf of the Spanish crown, some of these captives likely numbered among the royal slaves employed in Havana a decade later. A list of "Your Majesty's blacks" composed in 1583 shows that 116 of the 125 royal slaves laboring under the direction of the town's royal officials bore ethnonyms indicating Upper Guinean origins. Twenty-seven were described as "Biafra" or "Viafra."[11] Biafadas may also be found in contemporary notarial records. Like other Africans and people of African descent in Havana during the 1570s and 1580s, Biafadas appear in slave sales and contracts involving rented slave labor. Enslaved Biafadas are also listed as property or collateral in their owners' last wills and debts.[12]

While the above sources provide insights into Upper Guineans' ethnolinguistic origins, owners, and work routines, Havana's earliest extant parish records—more than 1,200 baptisms spanning the decade from 1590 to 1600, and more than 1,300 marriages from 1584 to 1622—offer an unparalleled glimpse into the port city's social environment, revealing nonelite social ties in greater detail than any other known source.[13] In addition to individuals being baptized, their parents (if known), and owner (if enslaved), each baptismal record typically includes reference to a godmother (*madrina*) and godfather (*padrino*). Marriage records usually list brides and grooms, at least two sponsors (also known as godmother and godfather), and sometimes additional witnesses. Although these formal roles can offer only limited glimpses of social interactions beyond the institution of the church, they nonetheless provide invaluable portrayals of Upper Guineans not only in relation to their owners (as slaves) but also in relation to one another and to other Africans and people of African descent. Nearly one-third of Havana's baptisms (348) and one-tenth of Havana's marriages (135) for this period include at least one person identified by an Upper Guinean ethnonym. As godparents, godchildren, parents, compadres, spouses, or witnesses, Biafadas appear in forty-seven marriages and eighty-nine baptisms that also mention several hundred other Havana residents who are likewise described by name and other characteristics including legal status, occupation, race, and ostensible African origin.

New Social Environments

By the close of the sixteenth century, Havana's population of seven to ten thousand inhabitants was so ethnically diverse that Biafadas would not have been able to limit their social interactions to other peoples from Upper Guinea, even had they so desired.[14] To the contrary, some Biafadas probably sought to establish social ties with Iberians and Afrocreoles whenever possible; parish records give the distinct impression that even as nonelites, individuals belonging to the latter groups generally enjoyed higher status than sub-Saharan Africans of any origin. Sixteen baptisms and two marriages provide information on social relationships between Biafadas and Iberians.[15] In eleven baptisms, Iberian men or women were godparents for children born to Biafada mothers. Enslaved Biafada women served alongside Iberian men as godparents in three additional instances; Iberians were godfathers for newly baptized, enslaved Biafadas in only two cases.[16] Iberians or Spanish Americans were clearly accorded a higher degree of social status in that they were always godparents; Biafadas never served as godparents for children born to Iberian parents. Moreover, although contemporaneous sources suggest that Iberians held Biafada women to have been exceptionally beautiful, and Iberians and Biafadas probably maintained sexual unions that may have featured varying degrees of coercion, no formal marriages between Biafada women and Iberian men are known to have taken place in Havana during the period under study.[17] Biafadas and Iberians participated jointly in only two marriages: Francisco de Texeda served as godfather at a wedding between two free Biafadas in 1612, and Juan Barbosa played the same role for an enslaved Biafada groom and Cassanga bride in 1620.[18]

Biafadas' social ties to Afrocreoles (people of African descent born within Spanish colonial society) appear to have existed about as frequently as those linking Biafadas to Iberians. Afrocreoles, too, probably held higher social status than Biafadas or any other enslaved sub-Saharan Africans in Havana; they served as godparents for Biafadas in seventeen baptisms, but the reverse was never the case, even though all but one of the Afrocreoles mentioned in these baptisms were enslaved. Biafada-Afrocreole interactions, however, were qualitatively different in that of the eighteen Afrocreole godparents who participated in these baptisms, ten were women. Also, whereas Iberian men were much more likely to serve as padrinos for children born to Biafada mothers than for newly baptized Biafada adults, Afrocreoles served as godparents for Biafada mothers' children in four baptisms and for Biafada adults in six.[19] In nine baptisms, Afrocreoles and Biafadas served together as godparents (usually the godfather was Afrocreole and the godmother was Biafada).[20] Afrocreoles and Biafadas participated jointly in only three weddings: women described as "creoles" (*criollas*) served as madrinas at two marriages between enslaved Biafada couples and at a third between a Biafada groom and an Upper Guinean (Brame) bride.[21]

If Biafadas' relationships with other Upper Guineans are excluded, most individuals who interacted with Biafadas in Havana at the close of the sixteenth century, as documented in the parish records, were West Central Africans described as "Angolas." The phenomenon of Upper Guineans serving as godparents (and overseers) for newly arrived forced migrants from Angola around this time was one result of a major surge in the slave trade from Luanda during the 1590s.[22] As measured by godparentage relationships and marital ties, interactions between Biafadas and "Angolas" were comparable to those between Biafadas and Afrocreoles, with the significant difference that Biafadas appear to have nearly always enjoyed higher social standing than the newly arrived "Angolas." Biafadas and "Angolas" appear together in twenty-seven baptisms.

Although only one "Angola" served as godparent for a newly baptized Biafada, Biafadas served as godparents for "Angolas," or for children born to "Angola" mothers, in each of the other twenty-six baptisms.[23] A similar pattern can be discerned in the marriage records. Biafadas and "Angolas" participated jointly in seven marriages. "Angolas" occasionally married Upper Guineans, but none married Biafadas. Instead, in each of these cases, Biafadas are listed as godparents (or, in one instance, as a witness) at weddings featuring "Angola" brides or grooms. Several were free Biafadas described as "libre" or "horra."[24]

Biafada relations with other West Central Africans were often characterized by a greater degree of reciprocity and perhaps fewer differences in their relative social standing. West Central Africans listed in Havana's parish records as "Congo" or "Conga" (or "Manicongo") were comparatively few by the late 1500s, but unlike newly arrived "Angolas," forced migrants from the region of the Kingdom of Kongo had been present in the Caribbean since the first half of the sixteenth century.[25] Thus while two enslaved Biafadas served as godmothers at the baptisms of Manuel Congo and Catalina Congo, an enslaved "Congo" man acted as godfather for Hernando Biafara, who was also enslaved.[26] The marriage records also indicate some degree of parity between Biafadas and "Congos," though again the latter were few in number compared with "Angolas." The free black man Antonio Congo married an enslaved Biafada bride in 1585; an enslaved man named Juan Congo or Juan Morel Congo served as godfather at their wedding and at another slave wedding in which a Biafada woman married a man of unspecified origin. When two Biafadas wed in 1595, Pedro Congo served as their godfather; in this case, all three shared the same owner.[27] In the same fashion, Juan Biafara and María Biafara—described as free (*libre*) and freed (*horra*), respectively—served as godparents at Ysabel Conga's marriage to Pedro Angola and at Antón Congo's marriage to an enslaved woman named María.[28]

Biafada Social Endogamy

Despite their above-mentioned relationships with Iberians, Afrocreoles, and West Central Africans, Biafadas in Havana often displayed a strong tendency toward social endogamy. Between 1585 and 1622, Biafadas participated in forty-seven marriages as brides, grooms, godparents, or witnesses. Among twenty-three Biafada men listed as grooms, ten married Biafada women (one of whom was free); another ten married women ascribed other Upper Guinean ethnonyms. Of their remaining three brides, one was listed as "Terranova," and the other two are described only as "black" or "slave." Biafada-Biafada unions also accounted for more than half of all marriages involving Biafada brides. Among eighteen Biafada brides, ten wed Biafada men (including two free men), and three married Upper Guinean men of other origins. Two Biafada women married West Central Africans described as "Congo" and "Anchico," and the origins of three enslaved grooms who married Biafada women are not specified.[29]

Although enslaved Biafadas' selection of marriage partners likely involved additional factors, common ethnolinguistic origin appears to have been a primary consideration. According to one Spanish observer writing in 1607, Africans in Panama City could typically speak a rudimentary form of Spanish but usually spoke to one another in their own languages.[30] This was not always the case. Based on his experiences in Cartagena de Indias around the same time, the Jesuit missionary Alonso de Sandoval cautioned that Africans' shared or related ethnic origins did not necessarily imply a common language.[31] Yet, as Sandoval noted, Biafadas all spoke the same "more or less elegant" language, despite inhabiting more than seventy "kingdoms and cities" that for the most part did not share the same ruler.[32] The directives of slave owners, and living space or work routines shared with other enslaved persons, may have also influenced Biafadas' choice of spouses. But only four Biafada-Biafada weddings involved enslaved couples who shared the same owners, and two were unions between Biafada royal slaves who lived and labored alongside dozens of other Upper Guinean royal slaves.[33]

Biafadas' roles as godparents at weddings in Havana further indicate a tendency to associate with other Upper Guineans, especially other Biafadas. Fourteen Biafada women served as madrinas at nineteen marriages. The brides and grooms they sponsored included fifteen Biafadas, five Bañuns, two Brames, two Nalus, two "Zapes," one Susu, and one "Mandinga." Eight additional brides and grooms were West Central Africans (five "Angolas," one "Anchico," one "Congo," and one "Embuila"), and the remaining two were unspecified. These Biafada godmothers appeared before the altar with godfathers who, like themselves, were mostly Upper Guineans: three Biafadas, four Brames, one Bañun, and five "Zapes." Three other godfathers were described as "Terranoba," "Angola," and "Anchico," and two were of unspecified African or Afrocreole origin; the remaining godfather was an Iberian man.[34] In short, Biafada women in Havana served as godmothers at weddings in which more than one-third of all brides and grooms were Biafadas, and another third were other Upper Guineans. More than two-thirds of the godfathers attending ceremonies with Biafada madrinas were also Upper Guineans.

Eight Biafada men served as padrinos at eleven weddings in Havana in the late sixteenth and early seventeenth centuries. Although they, too, often sponsored the marriages of Biafadas, unlike their more numerous Biafada madrina counterparts, Biafada godfathers sponsored roughly equal numbers of other Upper Guineans and West Central Africans. The brides and grooms they sponsored included nine Biafadas, one Brame, one Bañun, two Nalus, one "Arará," one "Congo," three "Angolas," and four people of unspecified origin. Six of the eight godmothers who accompanied these Biafada padrinos were Upper Guineans: three Biafadas, one Brame, one Cassanga, and one "Zape" (the others were an "Arará" and an Afrocreole).[35]

Free Upper Guineans probably had relatively greater choice in determining who they would marry and were more likely than enslaved Upper Guineans to serve as godparents. Five grooms and one bride in Havana's marriage register were free Biafadas.[36] In 1596 Hernando Biafara *moreno horro* married Ysabel Biafara, an enslaved woman who would also become free soon afterwards.[37] Two free Biafada men married enslaved "Zape" and Bañun women in 1614, and in 1621 the free man Domingo Viafra wed an enslaved Berbesí woman owned by a free Bañun man.[38] In addition to the free Biafadas who appear in the parish records as spouses, three free Biafada men and two free Biafada women were godparents at nine weddings; one served as *testigo* at a tenth.[39] These appearances as godparents demonstrate free Biafadas' social ties not only with other Biafadas but also with other Upper Guineans and indeed with other Africans. When "Ana Biafara hor[r]a" married "Juan de Herrera Biafara horro" in 1612, their madrina was free woman of color María Biafara. Later that year, María Biafara was also godmother at the marriage of enslaved West Central Africans Pedro Angola and Ysabel Conga.[40] The free man Hernando Biafara (sometimes known as Captain Hernando Biafara) served as padrino at two slave weddings: one between Biafada royal slaves and the other between an Upper Guinean (Nalu) groom and a woman named María Arará.[41]

Table 2. Biafadas as godparents for other Africans in Havana, 1590–1600

BAPTIZED PERSONS	WITH BIAFADA GODMOTHERS	WITH BIAFADA GODFATHERS
BIAFADAS	6	8
BIAFADAS' CHILDREN	4	3
OTHER UPPER GUINEANS		
Bran (Brame)	4	4
Jolofa (Wolof)	1	
OTHER UPPER GUINEANS' CHILDREN		
Brans' children	4	2
Bañons' children	3	2
Nalus' children	1	
WEST CENTRAL AFRICANS		
"Conga" or "Congo"	2	
"Angola"	13	10
Anchico (Ansiku)	1	1
WEST CENTRAL AFRICANS' CHILDREN		
"Angolas'" children	3	3
UNSPECIFIED ORIGIN	2	2
OTHER (UNSPECIFIED)	1	
Totals	45	35

Source: CH-LB/B, fols. 1v, 5r–6r, 18v, 27v, 28v, 33v–34r, 36r, 39v, 42v, 43v, 44v–45r, 50v, 52v–53r, 57v–58v, 60r, 62v–63r, 64r, 69v–69v, 73r, 74v, 78v, 83r, 87v, 91r–92r, 95r, 103v, 104v, 109r, 111r, 115v, 120r–120v, 121v–122r, 123v, 124v, 130v, 142r, 145r, 147v, 152v–153r, 156v–157r.

Baptismal records provide further examples of free Biafadas acting as godparents for other Biafadas and for their children, as well as for other Upper Guineans and Africans of more distant origins. Dominga, daughter of a free woman named Marçela Biafara and an unknown father, was baptized in 1597; her godparents were an enslaved Biafada man and Ysabel Biafara morena horra.[42] Ysabel Biafara also served as madrina at the baptisms of two enslaved Biafada men. In both instances, the padrinos were Biafadas—one of whom was Ysabel's husband, Hernando Biafara.[43] This was only one of six baptisms in which Hernando Biafara was named as padrino. His godchildren included an enslaved Biafada named Domingo, a child born to a Biafada woman, and two children born to other Upper Guinean (Bañun) mothers. He was also godfather for an enslaved "Angola" woman and for a girl born to an enslaved "Angola" mother.[44] Hernando Biafara's status as a free person of color, along with the standing that his Upper Guinean origins provided him in comparison with newly arrived "Angolas," explain his appearance as godfather on multiple occasions. Yet the ethnic distribution of his godchildren resembles that of other Biafada padrinos' godchildren, regardless of whether their godfather was free or enslaved. Biafadas served as padrinos for thirty-five people. Among them, eleven were Biafadas or the children of Biafadas, eight were other Upper Guineans or the children of other Upper Guineans, and fourteen were West Central Africans or children born to "Angola" parents (see Table 8.1).

Upper Guinean Neighbors and Trading Partners

Biafadas' social relations with other Upper Guineans in Havana differed from their interactions with Iberians and Afrocreoles, on the one hand, and with "Angolas," on the other, in that Biafadas' ties to other Upper Guineans were much more likely to have been lateral connections between individuals of similar status. Biafadas played important roles as godparents for the marriages and baptisms of West Central Africans, and when Biafadas' children were baptized, their godfathers were often Iberian men.[45] But as noted above, Biafadas' marriage partners were nearly always Biafadas or other Upper Guineans. Other Upper Guineans described as Bañon (Bañun), Berbesi (Serer), Biocho (Bijago),

Bran (Brame), Casanga (Cassanga), Çoso (Susu), Jolofo (Wolof), Linba (Limba), Nalu, "Çape," or "Mandinga" appear in more than half of all marriages (26 out of 47) in which one or more Biafadas participated as bride, groom, or godparent; in thirteen of these weddings, Biafadas married other Upper Guineans.[46] Individuals ascribed Upper Guinean ethnonyms other than Biafara or a variant of the term also appear in one-third of all baptisms (29 out of 89) featuring Biafada godparents, parents, or godchildren. In eleven of these baptisms, one godparent was a Biafada and the other was an Upper Guinean of different origin.[47] In six baptisms, other Upper Guineans were godparents for newly baptized Biafadas or their children.[48] Biafadas served as godparents for other Upper Guineans or for children born to other Upper Guineans in fifteen baptisms.[49] Havana's sacramental records indicate a degree of reciprocity between Biafadas and other Upper Guineans that is absent from Biafadas' relationships with Iberians, for example, or with "Angolas." However, Biafadas in Havana did not interact with all other Upper Guineans with equal frequency.

The Upper Guineans who appeared most commonly in Havana parish records that mention Biafadas were Brames. Their frequent association with Biafadas in Havana can perhaps most readily be explained by the geographical proximity of their homelands on opposite sides of the Gêba River. Biafada states held political power over Brames in some limited areas, and each group occasionally engaged in small-scale slave raiding at the other's expense, but trade was probably the defining feature of Biafada-Brame interaction in sixteenth-century Upper Guinea.[50] Significantly, Brame lands were positioned at the intersection of two major trade routes that crisscrossed the Upper Guinea coast: the Banyun-Bak network, spreading north from Bañun lands as far as present-day Dakar, and the Biafada-Sapi network, extending south from Biafada territories to "Zape" lands in Sierra Leone. While Bañuns had dominated efforts to link the two trade networks earlier in the sixteenth century, by the late 1500s Brames had appropriated this intermediary role, likely signaling more extensive commercial contact with their Biafada neighbors.[51] Brames appear in 64 weddings and 147 baptisms celebrated in late sixteenth-century Havana, participating jointly with Biafadas in 9 weddings and 15 baptisms.⁵² Two free Brame women, María Bran and Ana Bran, married enslaved Biafada men despite presumably having a wider range of options.⁵³ Royal slave Diego Biafara and a different María Bran maintained a long-term relationship that produced at least two children. At their first son's baptism, María Bran was listed as a royal slave, but at their second son's baptism two years later, she was described as a morena horra.⁵⁴

Biafadas' association with Bañuns in Havana is also fairly notable and can likewise be explained by a prior history of sustained social and economic exchange. In the Cacheu River area, Bañuns had only recently been displaced by Brames as the main intermediaries linking Bañun-Bak and Biafada-Sapi trade routes. Until the late sixteenth century, the customary presence of Bañun merchants in Biafada markets (and vice versa) functioned as the major fulcrum connecting Biafada commercial routes to long-distance trade networks spreading from the Cacheu River northwards. In Havana's parish register, Bañuns appear in twenty-four marriages and thirty-seven baptisms, participating with Biafadas in six marriages and three baptisms. Biafaras and Bañuns wed one another in three marriages, and moreno horro Domingo Viafra wed Dominga Berbesí, a Serer woman owned by the free man Baltasar Bañon. In the remaining marriages, Biafadas were godmothers at slave weddings in which one or both spouses was Bañun.⁵⁵ At three baptisms, enslaved Biafada women served as madrinas for children born to enslaved Bañun mothers, and for two of these children, their godfather was moreno horro Hernando Biafara.⁵⁶

After other Biafadas and Brames, the Upper Guineans with whom Biafadas in Havana were most likely to interact were Nalus and "Zapes," the latter being an umbrella term referring to various peoples who lived south of Biafada lands. The Biafada-Sapi trade network consisted of Biafada merchants traveling south along the Atlantic coast in large canoes, transporting iron, cotton, and gold to Nalu and Zape markets, and returning with captives, kola nuts, malaguetta peppers, and other merchandise.⁵⁷ In Upper Guinea, Biafada-Nalu relations were distinctive in that while the Nalu refused to trade with Iberians, Biafada intermediaries procured captives as well as ivory and mats produced by the Nalu for trade to Iberians.[58] Nalus appear in Havana sacramental records in eleven marriages and twenty-four baptisms; five of these marriages and three of the baptisms also involved Biafadas. Two Biafadas served as godparents at marriages in which the grooms were Nalus. Also, two Biafada men married Nalu women; in one case, the newlyweds shared the same owner but their godparents were a Biafada with a different owner and a Biafada royal slave. In another wedding between a free Biafada groom and an enslaved "Zape" bride, the godparents were free people of color, Francisco Nalo and Ines Vran.[59] As with Brames and Bañuns, the baptismal records further suggest reciprocal Biafada-Nalu social ties. While one enslaved Nalu man was godfather for a newly baptized Biafada woman, an enslaved Biafada was the madrina of a girl born to a Nalu mother who shared the same owner. At the baptism of an "Angola" man, another enslaved Nalu woman served as godmother alongside an enslaved Biafada padrino.[60]

"Zapes," including a handful of individuals described as Linba (Limba) and Çoso (Susu), appear in twenty-five marriages and sixty-four baptisms. They jointly appear with Biafadas in ten marriages and ten baptisms. Again the social relationship was one of general reciprocity. Two Biafada men married "Zape" brides, and two "Zape" men and one Limba woman served as godparents at weddings in which one or both newlyweds were Biafadas. In one royal slave wedding, the bride, groom, and padrino were all "Zapes"; the madrina was Juana Biafara. In five weddings, one godparent was "Zape" and the other was Biafada.[61] In seven baptisms, "Zapes" were godparents for newly baptized Biafadas or for children born to Biafada parents (when Diego Biafara and María Bran's second son, Luis, was baptized in 1595, both of his godparents were "Zapes"). In three additional baptisms, "Zapes" appear alongside Biafadas as godparents for a newly baptized "Angola," for a child born to an "Angola" mother, and for a child born to Brame parents.[62]

Tribute and Warfare

In stark contrast to their association with other Upper Guineans, Biafadas very rarely interacted with "Mandingas" or Biohos (Bijagos) in late sixteenth-century Havana. The virtual absence of Biafada-"Mandinga" social ties is especially striking given Biafadas' extensive prior exposure to Mande culture, including direct contact with the powerful confederation known as Kaabu, located upriver and inland behind a number of coastal Upper Guinean polities. The Biafada town of Gêba, on the Gêba River, was a major crossroads for trade to and from the Upper Gambia River, a commercial circuit that "traversed the core area of the Kaabu Empire," thus linking Mande trade networks to commerce associated with the Biafada-Sapi trade routes farther south. During the period under study, some Biafada states were directly under the rule of Kaabu; for example, Kaabu imposed Mande political leaders in the Biafada state of Degola (subsequently renamed Badour), where Gêba was located. Other Biafada communities maintained their own political authorities, but still paid tribute to Kaabu. This relationship of patronage and subordination, complemented by evidence of Biafadas' participation in slave trafficking, have led some to portray Biafadas (along with Cassangas and Kokolis) as both slave raiders and "agents of Mandinga hegemony."[63]

Surprisingly, although individuals described as "Mandinga" appear in six marriages and fourteen baptisms in Havana's *Libro de Barajas*, there are only two instances of Biafada-"Mandinga" interaction.[64] Both were marriages. In 1589 Martin Biafara married Ysabel Mandinga. Both were enslaved but owned by different people; their padrinos were Brame and Limba royal slaves. Later, in 1593, a Biafada woman served as godmother at a wedding between a free "Mandinga" groom and an enslaved "Angola" bride.[65] Social ties between Biafadas and Cassangas, who were also closely linked to Kaabu, appear to have been minimal as well. Although individuals described as Caçanga or Casanga appear in eleven marriages and eleven baptisms, they are only listed alongside Biafadas in two marriages. The free Upper Guineans Salvador Viafara and Madalena Casanga acted as godparents for an enslaved couple in 1617. In another slave wedding three years later, a Biafada groom married a Cassanga bride.[66] As with "Mandingas," Biafadas' social relations with Cassangas appear to have been limited primarily to interactions between Biafada men and Cassanga women.

Although Jolofos or Jolofas (Wolofs) are relatively scarce in Havana's sacramental records—they appear in only two marriages and fourteen baptisms—their interactions with Biafadas suggest a level of reciprocity comparable to that of Biafadas and Brames, Bañuns, Nalus, or Zapes. In one marriage, Luys Jolofo served as godfather to an enslaved Biafada bride. Meanwhile, Ana Biafara was madrina at a Wolof woman's baptism, and other Biafada women were godmothers for newly baptized West Central Africans whose godfathers were Wolofs.[67] Biafadas' indirect participation in the Banyun-Bak trade network, which stretched north of the Gambia River, could have provided some basis for interaction with Wolofs and other Senegambian peoples in Havana. Also Wolofs—like Biafadas—lived on the fringes of Kaabu and could also often understand the "Mandinga" language, according to Sandoval. Yet Wolofs in late sixteenth-century Havana, it seems, were no more likely to interact with "Mandingas" or Cassangas than were their Biafada contemporaries.[68] That "Mandingas" and Cassangas generally avoided social ties to Biafadas and Wolofs, rather than vice versa, is possible but seems unlikely. Neither Biafadas nor Wolofs had ever forced "Mandingas" or Cassangas to pay tribute, and if the latter groups harbored perceptions of higher status over the former, those perceptions must have been easily surmountable, since neither "Mandingas" nor Cassangas evidently had any qualms about marrying or serving as godparents for other coastal Upper Guinean peoples or for West Central Africans.[69]

Even more than tribute and political pressure exerted by Kaabu, Biafada society was disrupted in the late sixteenth century by slave raids launched by Bijagos, inhabitants of the Bijagos Islands just offshore from Biafada territories.[70] According to Sandoval, Bijagos—"Biojoes or Bijogoes"—departed from their islands in large canoes at night, carrying out raids on mainland villages at dawn. Captives would be taken back to Bijago lands, where Iberian merchants would promptly acquire "innumerable blacks." Although the Bijago raided others as well, Sandoval wrote that their victims were "principally Biafaras, whose kingdoms they have destroyed."[71] Bijagos appear as "Biohos" or "Biochos" in six weddings and twenty-eight baptisms recorded in Havana in the late sixteenth and early seventeenth centuries. While Bijagos are listed as godparents or godchildren for Brames, "Mandingas," "Angolas," "Congos," and even "Mozambiques," the baptisms reveal no trace of social ties with Biafadas. In a single slave wedding in 1608, the enslaved man Gaspar Biocho served as godfather for a groom of unspecified origin and for the bride, Marçela Biafara.[72] As with "Mandingas" and Cassangas, there is little reason to suppose that Bijagos systematically refrained from interaction with Biafadas in Havana. By contrast, a series of Bijago invasions had notoriously and very recently triggered the "social breakdown" of Biafada communities on the Upper Guinea Coast.[73] The near-total absence of Biafada-Bijago ties in Havana during precisely the same era suggests that within the limits imposed by their circumstances, Biafadas selectively reconstructed endogamous and cross-cultural relationships with other diasporic Upper Guineans, avoiding those who had figured prominently as agents of Biafada social upheaval.

If Havana's sacramental records constitute evidence of social ties formalized in (but not limited to) the context of the Catholic Church, then Biafadas in Havana abstained from developing relationships with Bijagos and interacted far less frequently than one might expect with "Mandingas." This pattern may appear surprising given the likelihood that Biafadas, Bijagos, and "Mandingas" would cross the Atlantic as captives on the same vessels and labor side by side, perhaps under shared owners, after arriving in the Americas. The ship that brought forty enslaved Biafadas from the Cape Verde Islands to Havana in 1572 also disembarked fifteen "Mandinga" men and eleven men and women listed as Biho, Bijocho, or Bizogo (Bijago).[74] In 1583 Havana's royal slaves included twenty-seven Biafadas, who worked alongside six Bioho (Bijago) men, a "Mandinga" man, and one "Mandinga" woman.[75] Yet Biafadas almost never married or served as godparents for individuals from either of those groups; they were far more likely to associate with one another and with Brames, Bañuns, Nalus, and "Zapes." In fact, Biafadas in Havana were more likely to develop social ties with Iberians, Afrocreoles, or West Central Africans than with Bijagos or "Mandingas." In other words, Biafadas' subordination to "Mandingas" in Upper Guinea gave way in Havana to new hierarchical social relationships in which Iberians and Afrocreoles acted as godparents for Biafadas, and Biafadas served as godparents for "Angolas."

In addition to shedding new light on Biafadas' experiences at a particular moment in Havana's history, these late sixteenth-century parish records offer a rare glimpse of processes that may have held true for diasporic Africans elsewhere and during other centuries. Previous experiences of warfare and tactical expertise clearly enabled some enslaved Africans to resist oppressive conditions in other diasporic contexts.[76] Yet warfare in Upper Guinea also bore ramifications for everyday social interaction in the colonial Spanish Caribbean. Rather than indiscriminately allying with other Africans, Upper Guineans in sixteenth-century Havana forged social relationships predicated on preexisting political identities and commercial alliances. Shared or mutually intelligible languages and common ritual practices or value systems may have been important factors as well.[77] At the same time, Upper Guineans in Cuba did not immediately cease to distrust their Upper Guinean adversaries; indeed, their recent experience of enslavement may have intensified their distrust. Biafadas in Havana during the late 1500s and early 1600s evidently responded to the memory of violence and captivity at the hands of their Bijago neighbors by avoiding contact with them.[78] Although this social rearticulation and dearticulation of Upper Guinean commercial and political ties in Havana occurred largely at the nonelite level, among slaves and former slaves, it nonetheless provides a closer look at the amalgam of overlapping patterns of social interaction often alluded to as "creolization"—but which, in this case, reflected choices and affinities based on long-term associations and recent developments in Upper Guinea.

Notes

ABBREVIATIONS

AGI   Archivo General de Indias
   -Ctdra   Contaduría
   -SD   Gobierno: Audiencia de Santo Domingo
CH   Sagrada Catedral de La Habana
   -LB/B   Libro de Barajas: Bautismos
   -LB/M   Libro de Barajas: Matrimonios

1. Havik, *Silences*, 47–49, 53–57, 361; Green, *The Rise*, 62–68.
2. Hair, "Ethnolinguistic Continuity"; Bühnen, "Ethnic Origins," 60; Hawthorne, *From Africa to Brazil*, 8–12, 178; Green, *The Rise*, 23; Wheat, *Atlan-*

tic Africa, 20–67. See also O'Toole, "From the Rivers of Guinea"; Graubart, "'So color de una cofradía.'"

3. In keeping with customary usage in African historiography and in early modern Iberian sources, this essay refers to Biafadas or the Biafada. Today Biafadas refer to themselves as Bəjoola (plural) or Ujoola (singular), terms evidently once associated with the Mandinka word *joolaa*, meaning "one who pays." See Wilson, "An Outline Description," 59; Havik, *Silences*, 103–7. In modern Spanish, "Biafara" is usually rendered as "Biáfara," with accent on the second syllable, whereas in English the first and penultimate syllables are accentuated. Quotation marks will be used throughout this chapter to designate African "lands" or "nations" that regularly appear in Iberian sources but cannot be equated with specific African peoples (e.g., "Angolas").

4. See, for example, Almada, *Tratado Breve dos Rios de Guiné*, 93–110.

5. Rodney, *A History*, 26–27, 32, 81, 205, 232; Brooks, *Landlords*, 23, 67, 79–87, 89, 129, 136, 154, 168, 251; Green, *The Rise*, 43–44, 56, 154.

6. Notwithstanding the phonological similarity, no known connection links "Biafaras" to the Bight of Biafra, which was rarely if ever labeled as such during the sixteenth century. Rosters of captives disembarked in the Spanish Caribbean confirm that "Biafaras" arrived alongside other Upper Guineans on voyages sailing from the Upper Guinea Coast or Cape Verde Islands; see, for example, Wheat, *Atlantic Africa*, 32–33.

7. Wheat, *Atlantic Africa*, 43. See also Boyd-Bowman, "Negro Slaves," 140–41; Bowser, *The African Slave*, 40–41.

8. On the construction of "Mahi" identity in eighteenth-century Brazil, for example, see Soares, *People of Faith*.

9. Lockhart, *Spanish Peru*, 15, 18–19, 48–49, 56, 64, 91–92, 102, 113, 126, 174; Altman, *Emigrants and Society*, 210–46; Altman, *Transatlantic Ties*. See also Boyd-Bowman, "Patterns of Spanish Emigration."

10. AGI-Ctdra 1174, N.6, "Relación de los ciento y noventa y un esclavos de su magestad" (3 November 1572), fols. 12v–16r. See also AGI-SD 118, R.2, N.100, Diego Lopez Duran y Juan Bautista de Rojas a S. M. (18 August 1572); Wright, *Historia documentada*, 1:58; de la Fuente, "Introducción," 162; de la Fuente, *Havana*, 102; Wheat, *Atlantic Africa*, 30–34.

11. AGI-Ctdra 1088, N.3, fols. 129r–130v, "Memoria y lista de los negros de su magestad que sirben en la fortaleza" (3 October 1583). See also de la Fuente, *Havana*, 102–3, 151–54; Wheat, *Atlantic Africa*, 64. Gonzalo Aguirre Beltrán argued that "Biafaras" and "Biafras" originated in Upper Guinea and in the Bight of Biafra, respectively; see Aguirre Beltrán, "Tribal Origins," 327–29. However, these terms appear to have been simply alternate

spellings. Royal slaves listed as "Biafras" or "Viafras" in 1583 reappear in baptismal records during the 1590s as "Biafaras."

12. De Rojas, *Índice y extractos*, 1:91–92; 2:83, 213–14, 257–58, 279, 290–91, 357, 373; 3:200, 227, 238–39, 290–91; Archivo Nacional de Cuba, *Protocolos Notariales: Separata del año 1587*, 52–53.
13. CH-LB/B and CH-LB/M. These records may be viewed at the *Slave Societies Digital Archive*, www.vanderbilt.edu/esss/. See also de Rojas, "Algunas datos"; de la Fuente, *Havana*, 8, 38–39, 161–68; Wheat, *Atlantic Africa*, 157–59, 170–80, 237–52, 287–303.
14. For population estimates, see de la Fuente, *Havana*, 107, 121; Wheat, *Atlantic Africa*, 280–81, 287–98.
15. My use of the term *Iberian* here includes Spanish Americans (people of primarily Iberian ancestry born in the Americas). Although individuals who were not ascribed a racial designation or African ethnonym in the parish records are generally assumed to have been Iberian or Spanish American, some were likely people of African origin; see Wheat, *Atlantic Africa*, 175–77, 268.
16. CH-LB/B, fols. 9v–10r, 12v, 22v, 26v, 41v, 63r, 81v–82r, 102r, 132r (godparents to Biafadas' children); 42v, 126r, 157r (godfathers alongside Biafada godmothers); 62r, 146r (godparents to Biafadas).
17. Rodney, *A History*, 202. For the baptism of "María mulata," born to royal slave Beatriz Biafara and unknown father in 1595, see CH-LB/B, fol. 63r. María's padrino was *alférez* (later, captain) Pedro de Portierra.
18. CH-LB/M, fols. 145v, 188r.
19. CH-LB/B, fols. 9v–10r, 18v–19r, 39v–40v, 62v, 91r, 104v, 115v, 120r–120v, 127v, 147v, 156v.
20. CH-LB/B, fols. 18v, 39v, 62v, 104v, 115v, 120r–120v, 147v, 156v.
21. CH-LB/M, fols. 15v, 41v, 45r. "Beatris de Salgado Criolla" (fol. 45r) appears as "Beatriz Criolla negra de Sebastian Salgado" in CH-LB/B, fol. 39v.
22. Wheat, *Atlantic Africa*, 242. See also Heywood and Thornton, *Central Africans*, ix, 39–41.
23. CH-LB/B, fols. 5v–6r, 34r, 45r, 53r, 57v–58r, 62v, 69v, 73r, 78v, 91r–92r, 120r–120v, 123v, 124v, 126r, 142r, 145r, 147v, 150r, 153r, 156v–157r.
24. CH-LB/M, fols. 29v, 36v, 150v, 167r, 172r, 175r, 196v.
25. Some individuals glossed in Iberian sources as "Angolas" were in fact Kikongo speakers or migrants from areas associated with the kingdom of Kongo.
26. CH-LB/B, fols. 62r, 103v, 121v.
27. CH-LB/M, fols. 2v, 8r, 45r. Sharing a common owner also seems to have been a factor in the creation of social ties between Biafadas and "Anchicos" (Ansikus). See CH-LB/B, fol. 122r; CH-LB/M, fol. 63r.

28. CH-LB/M, fols. 150v, 160v. An enslaved Biafada also served as *testigo* at a marriage between West Central Africans in 1618; see fol. 175r.
29. For Biafadas marrying one another, see CH-LB/M, fols. 4v, 28r, 30r, 36r, 41r–41v, 45r, 49v, 51r, 145v. For other brides marrying Biafada grooms, see fols. 8v, 15v, 22r, 29v, 36v, 159r, 160v, 188r, 193v, 195r (Upper Guineans); 171r ("Terranova"); 10r, 16v (unspecified origin). For other grooms marrying Biafada brides, see fols. 30r, 156v, 157v (Upper Guineans); 2v, 63r (West Central Africans); 3v, 8r, 126v (unspecified).
30. Serrano y Sanz, *Relaciones históricas y geográficas*, 162. "En la ciudad no ay indios; los españoles hablan la lengua castellana; los negros entre sí, los de cada tierra la suya; tambien hablan castellano, pero muy mal, si no son los que dellos son criollos."
31. See, for example, Sandoval's discussion of Bañuns in *Un tratado*, 63, 137.
32. Sandoval, *Un tratado*, 107–8.
33. CH-LB/M, fols. 41r, 45r (Biafada spouses with same owners); 30r, 41v (Biafada royal slave couples).
34. CH-LB/M, fols. 4v, 10r, 13r, 21r, 28r, 29v–30r, 31v, 36v, 41v, 49v, 63r, 145v, 150v, 157v, 167v. Royal slave "Francisco piloto" appears as "Francisco piloto Çape" in AGI-Ctdra 1088, N.3, fol. 129v.
35. CH-LB/M, fols. 4v, 28r, 36v, 41v, 94r, 156v, 160v, 172r, 196r–196v.
36. CH-LB/M, fols. 51r, 145v, 159r, 160v, 193v.
37. CH-LB/M, fols. 51r, 63r.
38. CH-LB/M, fols. 159r, 160v, 193v.
39. CH-LB/M, fols. 41v, 63r, 94r, 128r, 145v, 150v, 160v, 172r, 196r–196v.
40. CH-LB/M, fols. 145v, 150v.
41. CH-LB/M, fols. 41v, 196r.
42. CH-LB/B, fol. 111r. For a comparable baptism, see Wheat, *Atlantic Africa*, 240.
43. CH-LB/B, fols. 83r, 87v, 111r.
44. CH-LB/B, fols. 1v, 28r, 57v, 58v, 83r, 120v.
45. For the baptisms of nineteen children born to Biafada mothers, see CH-LB/B, fols. 1v, 3v, 9v–10r, 12v, 22r–22v, 26v, 40v, 41v, 52v, 63r, 81v–82r, 102r, 111r, 115v, 132r. Iberians were padrinos at eleven of these baptisms; see note 15 above.
46. CH-LB/M, fols. 8v, 15v, 22r, 29v–30r, 36v, 156v, 157v, 159r, 160v, 188r, 193v, 195r.
47. CH-LB/B, fols. 6r, 33v–34r, 53r, 60r, 63r, 73r, 74v, 103v, 109r, 124v.
48. CH-LB/B, fols. 3v, 8r, 26v, 27v, 63r, 87r.
49. CH-LB/B, fols. 18v, 27v, 28v, 33v, 36r, 42v, 44v, 58v, 60r, 74v, 104v, 109r, 123v, 130v, 145r.
50. Brooks, *Landlords*, 86; Wheat, *Atlantic Africa*, 42–45.
51. Brooks, *Landlords*, 79–95, 228–29, 237–38.

52. CH-LB/M, fols. 15v, 21r, 22r, 30r, 31v, 41v, 156v, 160v, 195r; CH-LB/B, fols. 18v, 26v, 27v, 33v, 34v, 36r, 44v, 53r, 60r, 66r, 74v, 109r, 123v, 130v, 145r.
53. CH-LB/M, fols. 15v, 195r.
54. CH-LB/B, fols. 34v, 66r.
55. CH-LB/M, fols. 13r, 30r, 31v, 157, 160v, 193v.
56. CH-LB/B, fols. 28v, 58v, 104v.
57. Brooks, *Landlords*, 80–87, 110–11, 251, 260–61.
58. Rodney, *A History*, 105; Brooks, *Landlords*, 267–68, 276; Havik, *Silences*, 118–20.
59. CH-LB/M, fols. 21r, 29v, 36v, 159r, 196r.
60. CH-LB/B, fols. 42v, 73r, 87r.
61. CH-LB/M, fols. 4v, 8v, 10r, 13r, 21r, 22r, 49v, 159r, 193v, 196v.
62. CH-LB/B, fols. 3v, 6r, 8r, 26v, 27v, 33v–34v, 63r, 66r.
63. Rodney, *A History*, 25–27, 81, 104, 111 ("agents"), 146, 232; Brooks, *Landlords*, 84–86, 111, 241 ("traversed"), 247, 265–67. See also Green, *The Rise*, 44–45, 52–57.
64. For discussion of "Mandingas" in association with Kaabu, see Wheat, *Atlantic Africa*, 28, 34–36.
65. CH-LB/M, fols. 22r, 36v.
66. CH-LB/M, fols. 172r, 188r.
67. CH-LB/B, fols. 103v, 109r, 124v; CH-LB/M, fol. 3v.
68. Sandoval, *Un tratado*, 136. For a sole example of Wolof and "Mandinga" interaction, see CH-LB/B, fol. 140v. Neither the baptismal nor marriage records contain examples of social ties between Wolofs and Cassangas.
69. For the married couples Juan Caçanga and Ana Çape, and Francisco Mandinga and Beatriz Angola, see CH-LB/M, fol. 36v; CH-LB/B, fols. 19v, 20v, 54r, 59v, 153v. For "Mandinga" men who married Brames or who appeared alongside Bijago women as godparents for West Central Africans, see CH-LB/M, fols. 129r, 170r; CH-LB/B, fols. 109v, 121r. For Cassangas' social ties to Bañuns, Brames, Nalus, "Mandingas," and "Angolas," see CH-LB/M, fols. 5v, 42v, 45r, 48v, 165r; CH-LB/B, fols. 33r, 69v, 104v, 121v.
70. Bowser, *African Slave*, 40–41; Rodney, *A History*, 103–6; Brooks, *Landlords*, 261–73; Bühnen, "Ethnic Origins," 97, 100–101; Hawthorne, *Planting Rice*, 92, 101–7, 169–70; Havik, *Silences*, 114–18.
71. Sandoval, *Un tratado*, 64, 108, 138, 146–47.
72. CH-LB/M, fol. 126v. The couple's madrina was Ysabel de Quesada, a free woman of color.
73. Brooks, *Landlords*, 268 (quote); Green, *The Rise*, 243.
74. AGI-Ctdra 1174, N.6, "Relación," fols. 12v–16r. For excellent discussion of bonds between former shipmates, see Borucki, *From Shipmates to Soldiers*, 57–83, 218–19.
75. AGI-Ctdra 1088, N.3, fols. 129r–130v, "Memoria."

76. Barcia, *West African Warfare*. See also Thornton, *Africa and Africans*, 280, 292–303; Thornton, *Warfare in Atlantic Africa*, 127–52.
77. Hawthorne, *From Africa to Brazil*, 208–47. By the late 1700s, however, broadly shared Upper Guinean beliefs were increasingly likely to have been influenced by the widespread diffusion of Islam. See da Silva et al., "Transatlantic Muslim Diaspora," 537–40.
78. Similarly, mutual hostility between Bañuns and Cassangas during the sixteenth century may explain their limited interaction in Havana. The parish records suggest that members of each group were far more likely to establish social ties with Brames or "Zapes"—or even with West Central Africans—than with one another.

Bibliography

ARCHIVES

Archivo General de Indias (Seville, Spain).
Sagrada Catedral de La Habana (Havana, Cuba).

PUBLISHED WORKS

Aguirre Beltrán, Gonzalo. "Tribal Origins of Slaves in Mexico, III: San Thome." *Journal of Negro History* 31, no. 3 (July 1946): 317–52.

Almada, André Álvares d'. *Tratado breve dos Rios de Guiné do Cabo Verde* [circa 1594]. Transcription, introduction, and notes by António Brásio. Lisboa: Editorial L.I.A.M., 1964.

Altman, Ida. *Emigrants and Society. Extremadura and Spanish America in the Sixteenth Century*. Berkeley: University of California Press, 1989.

———. *Transatlantic Ties in the Spanish Empire: Brihuega, Spain and Puebla, Mexico, 1560–1620*. Stanford: Stanford University Press, 2000.

Archivo Nacional de Cuba. *Protocolos Notariales: Separata del año 1587*. Havana: Academia de Ciencias de Cuba, 1984.

Barcia, Manuel. *West African Warfare in Bahia and Cuba: Soldier Slaves in the Atlantic World, 1807–1844*. Oxford: Oxford University Press, 2014.

Borucki, Alex. *From Shipmates to Soldiers: Emerging Black Identities in the Río de la Plata*. Albuquerque: University of New Mexico Press, 2015.

Bowser, Frederick P. *The African Slave in Colonial Peru, 1524–1650*. Stanford: Stanford University Press, 1974.

Boyd-Bowman, Peter. "Negro Slaves in Early Colonial Mexico." *The Americas* 26, no. 2 (October 1969): 134–51.

———. "Patterns of Spanish Emigration to the Indies until 1600." *Hispanic American Historical Review* 56, no. 4 (November 1976): 580–604.

Brooks, George E. *Landlords and Strangers: Ecology, Society, and Trade in Western Africa, 1000–1630*. Boulder: Westview Press, 1993.

Bühnen, Stephan. "Ethnic Origins of Peruvian Slaves (1548–1650): Figures for Upper Guinea." *Paideuma* 39 (1993): 57–110.

da Silva, Daniel B. Domingues, David Eltis, Nafees Khan, Philip Misevich, and Olatunji Ojo. "The Transatlantic Muslim Diaspora to Latin America in the Nineteenth Century." *Colonial Latin American Review* 26, no. 4 (2017): 528–45.

de la Fuente, Alejandro. "Introducción al estudio de la trata en Cuba: Siglos XVI y XVII." *Santiago* 61 (1986): 155–208.

de la Fuente, Alejandro, with the collaboration of César García del Pino and Bernardo Iglesias Delgado. *Havana and the Atlantic in the Sixteenth Century*. Chapel Hill: University of North Carolina Press, 2008.

de Rojas, María Teresa. "Algunos datos sobre los negros esclavos y horros en la Habana del siglo XVI." In *Miscelánea de estudios dedicados a Fernando Ortiz*, II: 1275–87. Havana: Sociedad Económica de Amigos del País, 1956.

———, ed. *Índice y Extractos del Archivo de Protocolos de la Habana, 1578–1588*. Havana: [s.n.], 1947–1950; Ediciones C. R., 1957. 3 vols.

Graubart, Karen B. "'So color de una cofradía': Catholic Confraternities and the Development of Afro-Peruvian Ethnicities in Early Colonial Peru." *Slavery and Abolition* 33, no. 1 (March 2012): 43–64.

Green, Toby. *The Rise of the Trans-Atlantic Slave Trade in Western Africa, 1300–1589*. Cambridge: Cambridge University Press, 2012.

Hair, P. E. H. "Ethnolinguistic Continuity on the Guinea Coast." *Journal of African History* 8, no. 2 (1967): 247–68.

Havik, Philip J. *Silences and Soundbites: The Gendered Dynamics of Trade and Brokerage in the Pre-Colonial Guinea Bissau Region*. Münster: Lit Verlag, 2004.

Hawthorne, Walter. *From Africa to Brazil: Culture, Identity, and an Atlantic Slave Trade, 1600–1830*. Cambridge: Cambridge University Press, 2010.

Hawthorne, Walter. *Planting Rice and Harvesting Slaves: Transformations along the Guinea-Bissau Coast, 1400–1900*. Portsmouth: Heinemann, 2003.

Heywood, Linda M., and John K. Thornton. *Central Africans, Atlantic Creoles, and the Foundation of the Americas, 1585–1660*. New York: Cambridge University Press, 2007.

Lockhart, James. *Spanish Peru, 1532–1560: A Social History*, 2nd ed. Madison: University of Wisconsin Press, 1994.

O'Toole, Rachel Sarah. "From the Rivers of Guinea to the Valleys of Peru: Becoming a *Bran* Diaspora within Spanish Slavery." *Social Text* 25, no. 3 (Fall 2007): 19–36.

Rodney, Walter. *A History of the Upper Guinea Coast, 1545–1800*. New York: Monthly Review Press, 1970.

Sandoval, Alonso de. *Un tratado sobre la esclavitud*, introduction and transcription by Enriqueta Vila Vilar. Madrid: Alianza Editorial, 1987.

Serrano y Sanz, Manuel, ed. *Relaciones históricas y geográficas de América central*. Madrid: V. Suárez, 1908.

Slave Societies Digital Archive, www.vanderbilt.edu/esss/ (accessed March 1, 2018).

Soares, Mariza de Carvalho. *People of Faith: Slavery and African Catholics in Eighteenth-Century Rio de Janeiro*. Translated by Jerry D. Metz. Durham: Duke University Press, 2011.

Thornton, John K. *Africa and Africans in the Making of the Atlantic World, 1400–1800*, 2nd ed. New York: Cambridge University Press, 1998.

———. *Warfare in Atlantic Africa, 1500–1800*. New York: Routledge, 1999.

Wheat, David. *Atlantic Africa and the Spanish Caribbean, 1570–1640*. Chapel Hill: University of North Carolina Press, 2016.

Wilson, W. A. A. "An Outline Description of Biafada." *Journal of West African Languages* 23, no. 2 (1993): 59–90.

Wright, Irene A. *Historia documentada de San Cristóbal de la Habana en el siglo XVI*. 2 vols. Havana: Siglo XX, 1927.

PART 4

Environment and Health

Although Europeans often found the Caribbean to be uncomfortably hot, unhealthy, and characterized by extreme environmental hazards such as hurricanes, they and the Africans they brought to the region unintentionally introduced new dangers in the form of diseases to which the native populations had no immunities. Although the first known epidemic occurred in 1518–19, both before and after that date all groups—Europeans, Africans, Indians—suffered from a variety of illnesses and high mortality. Environmental conditions along with administrative and economic considerations affected choices regarding the sites of new towns. Port towns could be especially prone to climate and health problems because of their coastal locations and the large numbers of people who arrived from many points of origin. Over time Spaniards responded to these challenges by devising new means of meeting public health needs.

9

Environment and the Politics of Relocation in the Caribbean Port of Veracruz, 1519–1599

J. M. H. CLARK

On July 10, 1519, Hernando Cortés and his associates wrote a letter to the Spanish crown announcing their establishment, two months earlier, of a new settlement called La Villa Rica de la Vera Cruz on a sandy strip of beach opposite the island San Juan de Ulúa. In their petition and subsequent letters, Cortés and his companions made a self-conscious effort to separate Mesoamerica from previous Spanish discoveries in the Caribbean. Referring to Mexico as "this country of the rich land of Veracruz," the *villa*'s first magistrates described how an Aztec embassy bearing "precious jewels of gold" greeted the Spaniards on the coast. Judging by this offering, Cortés "declared that this land was good, and . . . he believed it to be very rich." Drawing a contrast with indigenous communities in the Caribbean, they described the people they met as "well clothed" and the towns they visited in Yucatán, Tabasco, and Veracruz's near interior as "well laid out" with stone and clay houses, courtyards, and multistory buildings. Above all, the Aztec embassy's diplomacy and display of wealth during the exchange on the Ulúacan coast persuaded the Spaniards to "establish and populate a town . . . so that Your Majesty may have lordship in this land."[1]

Later, after Cortés and his allies had captured the Aztec capital of Tenochtitlan in central Mexico, he described how he had settled on a name for his conquest, saying that since Mexico "resembled Spain in its fertility and size and its cool airs . . . it seemed that the most suitable name to call this land was New Spain of the Ocean Sea."[2] Equating the greatness of Mexico with that of Spain, Cortés built on the justification for conquest and settlement that he laid out in Veracruz. If Columbus had found a "New World" in the Caribbean, then Cortés boasted to have found a "New Spain" within it, a land that he described as prosperous, temperate, and civilized. In so doing, he portrayed Veracruz as the gateway to a new land, where the world of the Caribbean ended and the intricate human web of mainland empire began.[3]

The division of the Caribbean and the mainland into separate worlds has persisted in historical discourse, as scholars have followed Cortés's lead in identifying Veracruz as "a dividing point from the prior activities of Spaniards in the New World."[4] Yet this perspective overlooks the degree to which the Spanish settlement at Veracruz followed a pattern that had been established earlier in the Caribbean. In establishing Veracruz Cortés and his compatriots followed a rhetorical formula that aggrandized their achievements and emphasized the suitability of their discovery for settlement. Such declarations usually were intended to elicit royal patronage or, in Cortés's case, to justify his refusal to obey his superiors in Cuba at the outset of the expedition.[5]

After its foundation, other similarities between Veracruz and earlier Spanish settlements in the Caribbean became apparent as well. The Spanish settlement at Veracruz was subject to many of the same environmental phenomena that sometimes shaped Spanish perceptions of other Caribbean locales, including depopulation, hurricanes, and disease. The prevalence of environmental and spatial considerations in administrative exchanges and early descriptions of Veracruz suggests that Spanish migrants understood the Caribbean's coastal and island settlements as parts of a single regionally coherent unit.

As was true for other early Spanish Caribbean port towns the interplay between local environmental needs and large-scale political and economic goals shaped the development of the city of Veracruz. Much like Havana, Santo Domingo, and San Juan, the site of Veracruz also shifted, with the town relocating three times in the sixteenth century: in 1519, 1526, and 1595–99. The early iterations of Veracruz were not intended to be permanent or to produce stable urban environments. Rather, they were meant to serve the needs of mainland conquest or maritime commerce, leaving the city's residents to contend with the environmental externalities that accompanied relocation. Like some other Caribbean ports, Veracruz was subject to environmental conditions that European writers and later historians would use to malign the city: extreme heat and humidity, exposure to hurricanes, limited resource endowment, and a deadly disease climate.

Within months of its founding on the mainland coast opposite the island of San Juan de Ulúa, the city's *cabildo* moved more than fifty miles to the north to the outskirts of a Totonac city called Quiahuiztlan. There Veracruz served as a staging ground for Cortés's march inland to the Aztec capital of Mexico-Tenochtitlan. In 1526 Veracruz moved thirty miles south, most of the distance back to the Ulúacan coast, to the mouth of the Antigua River.[6] At La Antigua (as the area came to be known), the city was closer and more accessible to its port, which had remained at San Juan de Ulúa, while also gaining estuary access to the hinterland. Its final relocation came more than seventy years later, following a prolonged dispute over the city's location that pitted Veracruz's cabildo against imperial officials and mercantile elites in Seville, Mexico City, and Puebla de los Ángeles. This disagreement culminated with the construction of a road that connected Mexico City to the Ulúacan coast directly, bypassing Antigua Veracruz. When the road was completed in the 1590s, Veracruz's residents began relocating in large numbers to the Ulúacan coast until a viceregal decree officially moved the city in 1599, renaming it "la Nueva Ciudad de la Veracruz."[7]

These relocations entailed different environmental challenges and reflected the peripatetic and contested nature of the early colonial project.[8] The political and economic motives that underlay each move evoke the shifting and competing priorities of metropolitan officials and colonial elites. At its founding in 1519 Veracruz was intended to serve the Cortés expedition's immediate goals of military and political conquest of the Mexican interior. By the end of the sixteenth century its ideal imperial role was to facilitate the viceroyalty's Atlantic maritime commerce and strategic defense against Spain's European enemies. While the needs of empire had changed throughout the century, large-scale political and economic concerns remained a constant force in the determination of the city's physical location, eventually overriding local elites' concerns about climate and disease.

Foundation and Relocation in the Conquest Era, 1518–1526

The first Spaniards to land on the shore facing San Juan de Ulúa arrived with the expedition of Juan de Grijalva in June 1518. They spent one week exploring the coast, resulting in two of the earliest written assessments of its environment: one by the chronicler Pedro Mártir de Anglería—who never was in the Indies and based his accounts on reports that he received—and the other by expedition member Bernal Díaz del Castillo.[9] Both accounts drew a contrast between the deficiency of the land and the superiority of the port. Recalling his first impressions of San Juan de Ulúa, Díaz described how he and his companions "built huts atop the highest crests of sand to escape the mosquitoes, of which there were many, and with our boats we made a thorough sounding of the port, finding that the island provides good shelter against the northern gales and has a good harbor."[10]

The harbor included four coral islands of considerable size: San Juan de Ulúa, Sacrificios, Pájaros, and Verde. San Juan de Ulúa was the largest, at about one league square, which may have been why the Spaniards chose to dock there and later developed it to house the city's port facilities and its primary fortress. Ulúa was favored over the mainland as a port for three reasons: its harbor depth of thirteen meters; the lee of the island that provided ships shelter from the northern gales; and the shoals and reefs that made navigation to the mainland difficult for large vessels.

The shoreline directly across from San Juan de Ulúa was primarily sandy marshland. Within a short distance of the shore there were several hundred small lakes, but the water filling them was brackish and undrinkable. There was also a river, which the Spanish called Tenoya, at the southern extent of the harbor. The river was always too shallow for boats larger than canoes to enter, and some years the riverbed dried completely during winter months. Further to the south (about 12 km, or approximately two leagues) there was another river, called the Jamapa. Unlike the water of the Tenoya, which was often stagnant and filled with sediment, the Jamapa had what one seventeenth-century writer claimed was "the best water that there is in all the world."[11] For this reason, there were multiple attempts to divert the Jamapa to the Ulúacan coast during the colonial period.[12] In addition to the lack of potable water, the coast was more or less an arid plain, bare of all vegetation except a small amount of brushwood. Its soil was too sandy for routine planting or large crops, although it could sustain small-scale gardening. Likewise, the coast had no pastureland for livestock, but the higher lands of the near interior sported dozens of cattle ranches from the middle of the sixteenth century onward.[13]

Early reports indicated no substantial indigenous presence in the immediate area. The island of Sacrificios had two small temples dedicated to the Aztec god of hurricanes, Tezcatlipoca, but otherwise was uninhabited. On the mainland the Spaniards made contact with traders from "neighboring regions" in the interior but reported no settlements on the coast. A *real cédula* issued in 1532 indicated that the indigenous inhabitants from as far away as Oaxaca may have used the Ulúacan coast to collect wild "vines and other plants," but reported no other systematic resource extraction.[14] A "Descripción de la Tierra," also written in 1532, specifically noted that the Ulúacan coast had no indigenous population prior to the Spaniards' arrival. Although the original document has been lost, according to Peter Gerhard a contemporary description of it suggested that the coast was notorious among indigenous people for its mosquito infestations and poor climate.[15]

The absence of large towns on the Ulúacan coast may have been one of the reasons that the Spaniards selected the site as the location of their first mainland settlement.[16] Although Grijalva failed to establish an outpost in 1518, his expedition produced a wealth of information on the physical and human geography of the coast that influenced Cortés's choice to return to Ulúa a year later. Grijalva's encounter with local traders also gave indigenous groups forewarning of Cortés's expedition. By the time Cortés landed in April 1519, word of the Spanish intrusion had reached the Aztec capital of Tenochtitlan. Moctezuma II dispatched a coterie from the town of Cotaxtla—ten leagues into the interior—to meet the foreign landing party and invite them to the capital. With the arrival of the Aztec embassy the Ulúacan coast became something of a neutral zone. By docking their ships at San Juan de Ulúa, Cortés and his men could work with the Aztecs while the two sides kept a cautious distance from one another.

The Cortés expedition described the coastal environment in terms that were identical to those of Grijalva the year before. The sixteenth-century chronicler Antonio de Herrera wrote that "the land was hot [*calurosa*], discomforting, and filled with mosquitoes [*çancudos*], the worst of which attacked and fatigued the men."[17] Despite the drawbacks, the lack of nearby enemies and the material support of the Aztec embassy made the coast a safe harbor for the Spaniards on the mainland. By the second week of May 1519 the decision had been made to establish a settlement.

The first iteration of Veracruz was the shortest lived. Around the time that the expedition founded Veracruz, Cortés declined an invitation to return with the Aztec embassy to Tenochtitlan, and Moctezuma's emissaries decamped. Cortés and his men then had to provision themselves, no easy task in the barren, sandy marshland of the Ulúacan coast. Soon the Spaniards found themselves "lacking in supplies, with their stores of cassava bread [*Caçabi*] diminished and molding."[18] Consequently, Spanish priorities shifted from gaining a toehold on the mainland to obtaining local sources of food and water and a staging ground for further incursions into the interior.

They found both in the Totonac village of Quiahuiztlan. About thirteen leagues (75 km) north of Ulúa, the outskirts of Quiahuiztlan became Veracruz's second home in August 1519. Sources differ on whether the Spanish approached the Totonacs or whether the Totonacs, sensing a potential ally, approached the Spanish. In either case, the act of relocation is indicative of the logistical limitations of the Ulúacan coast for the Spanish newcomers. Cortés's plan to make a foray into the interior necessitated provisions and access to the hinterland, neither of which was available at Ulúa. Tellingly, it was only after arriving in Quiahuiztlan that Cortés famously gave the order to scuttle the ships that had brought the Spaniards to Mesoamerica, a symbolic acknowledgment that "Veracruz" no longer faced seaward but instead to the interior. From Quiahuiztlan the expedition soon advanced further inland to the larger Totonac town of Cempoala, and from there to Tlaxcala, eventually reaching Tenochtitlan on November 8, 1519. Within two years Cortés and his indigenous allies had seized control of Tenochtitlan and large swaths of land from the Gulf coast to the valley of Mexico. The Spanish conquerors then began the process of reorganizing Mesoamerica's political and commercial landscape in the territories that they controlled. Veracruz had moved to Quiahuiztlan for the prerogative of mainland conquest, but emerging commercial systems continued to rely on San Juan de Ulúa as the functional port of call.

Although later chroniclers praised Cortés for finding a "superior" port in Quiahuiztlan, there is little evidence that oceangoing vessels routinely docked there. Instead, arriving ships docked at Ulúa, where passengers and goods were off-loaded and ferried up the coast to Veracruz, which the Spaniards had begun calling "Medellín" by the mid-1520s.[19] Returning ferries brought goods for export to the Caribbean and across the Atlantic. While the settlement at Quiahuiztlan had been expedient in the early phase of conquest, it was not long before Spanish officials began to identify the location's weaknesses. First, the coastal ferrying process proved inefficient and costly. The process was slow in good weather, and rough weather sometimes resulted in the loss or damage of merchandise. Second, the indigenous population of Quiahuiztlan declined rapidly after the conquest, as it did elsewhere in Mesoamerica, eliminating one of the principal advantages of keeping the Spanish settlement nearby. Third, the conquest had altered overland paths into the hinterland, as Spaniards eschewed old overland routes in search of faster routes that would connect the coast to new centers of wealth and production in the interior.

These limitations proved enough to prompt Spanish administrators to move the city for the second time in 1526. The new location, at the nexus of the Antigua (Huitzilapan) and San Juan (Actopan) Rivers, addressed each of these concerns. "Antigua Veracruz," as it would come to be known, was more than ten leagues (approximately 61 km) south of Quiahuiztlan and therefore only three leagues north of San Juan de Ulúa, cutting ferry time significantly. It was also only four leagues (approximately 22 km) south of the indigenous city of Cempoala, a much larger population center than Quiahuiztlan. Finally, the Antigua and San Juan Rivers were larger than the Tenoya River on the Ulúacan coast and provided estuary access to the interior more than half of the way to Xalapa.

The Ulúacan coast was chosen at the outset of conquest not as the ideal site of a new settlement but rather as a port of refuge. The city's founders sought a more advantageous site almost immediately, moving the city to Quiahuiztlan, where they would stage their conquest. When Quiahuiztlan proved too distant from San Juan de Ulúa, the city moved a second time. In relocating to La Antigua instead of directly to Ulúa, however, they made a conscious choice to maintain a separation from the port itself.

Although the city remained at La Antigua for the next seventy years, it was only a few decades before mercantile elites and imperial officials in Seville, Mexico City, and Puebla de los Ángeles began calling for it to be moved closer to the port. The city's cabildo resisted the admonitions of the imperial center for much of the sixteenth century, citing the unhealthiness of the Ulúacan coast and advocating instead for the city to be moved further into the interior. The section that follows examines this dispute, demonstrating how the economic motives of the empire began to outweigh the concerns of Veracruz's leading residents, just as the motives of conquest had dictated the terms of the city's foundation.

Metropolitan Priorities and Local Preferences 1526–1600

On Friday evening, September 2, 1552, residents of the city of Veracruz began to notice "very great winds" arriving in the city from the north and from "other points of the compass, blowing in such a way that it was understood to be a hurricane." The next morning Bartolomé Romero, one of the city's priests, woke early as usual to give mass but was prevented from leaving his quarters due to the "water that fell from the heavens and the wind that accompanied it." Trees began to split and fall and houses soon followed, beginning with those built of wood and thatch. Eventually even houses made of stone began to falter. The city's *alcaldes* mounted horses and raced through the streets, warning residents to take shelter in a "strong house" that could sustain the wind. Other residents, "men and women, and children and slaves," evacuated to the hills of the interior.[20]

Soon the San Juan and Antigua Rivers began to rise, flooding streets and houses. Residents with canoes and small boats braved the storm in an attempt to rescue people trapped by the flood. One of these responders, Juan Romero, was later honored for his bravery. Not honored—and not mentioned by name in later testimony—were the two black men who accompanied him in his rescue efforts.[21] Over the next several days, as news of the cyclone circulated inland, two residents of the interior, Alonso Núñez and Alonso de Buiza, were given commissions to commandeer supplies from nearby stores and warehouses to aid refugees who were left "very sick and weak."[22]

In the weeks that followed, rescue efforts gave way to assessments of the damage. Wind had destroyed a number of buildings, including those of tabby concrete, adobe, and even stone. Buildings that were not demolished in the storm were flooded, including several warehouses and bodegas. Textiles, wine, olive oil, and vinegar worth thousands of pesos were damaged or destroyed. Cases of silver, gold, and other precious commodities had been swept out to sea. At the port of San Juan de Ulúa, dozens of small coastal and regional trading vessels—described as "carabelas de Tabasco"—were demolished. Five transatlantic ships sank and four others sustained extensive damage. Four of the island's dockyards were swept to sea, taking four or five dockworkers with them. Many sailors and dockworkers took refuge on the island, but dozens of others drowned when their entire shelter was swept to sea. Only a few of their bodies were recovered.[23]

In the aftermath, Veracruz's *alcalde mayor*, García de Escalante Alvarado, traveled the coastal highlands and the near interior on horseback, surveying possible locations to which the city could be moved in order to prevent future disasters. On May 12, 1553, Escalante formally petitioned the crown and the viceroy to move the city, recommending an area called the Hato de Doña María. According to Andrew Sluyter, the *hato* (cattle ranch) that Escalante suggested was owned by a woman named María del Rincón who held several titles to land dispersed throughout the plain and highlands of Veracruz's interior. She also held three *encomiendas* inherited from three deceased husbands and an *estancia* that she ran independently.[24] According to Escalante, the Hato de Doña María was northwest of Antigua Veracruz and inland from the coast "one league more towards Mexico."[25]

In his petition Escalante cited a number of benefits of relocating the city to the interior. Hato de Doña María was on higher ground than the coast, so it would not flood as easily. It was on a plain, with good pastures for raising livestock, and the ground underneath was limestone that would make for stouter foundation than the sands of the coast. He also claimed that the water was cleaner and, above all, that the new location would offer "healthier" airs than the coast. Antigua Veracruz, Escalante averred, was "sickly" and suffered from oppressive humidity and a brackish river that flooded in rainy seasons, turning the entire city into a marshy breeding ground for mosquitoes.[26]

Escalante was hardly the first Spanish official to address the crown on the topic of Veracruz's health. One of the earliest assessments came from New Spain's first bishop, fray Juan de Zumárraga. Arriving in the city in 1528, Zumárraga petitioned both the Spanish crown and Pope Clement VII for support to build two hospitals: one on the island of San Juan de Ulúa (the Hospital Real de San Juan de Ulúa) to treat gravely ill passengers and sailors arriving from Spain or from other locales, and one at Antigua Veracruz (the Hospital de San Martín).[27] In a 1533 letter to the pope the Spanish crown supplemented Zumárraga's request, saying that a hospital at San Juan de Ulúa would allow the "good reception" of the ill.[28]

Rather than ascribing the apparently high rate of illness in Veracruz to long voyages and close quarters aboard crowded ships, early modern officials often cited the general climate of the Ulúacan coast. A real cédula responding to Zumárraga's request suggested that "many who disembark [in San Juan de Ulúa] fall ill due to the great indisposition and extremity of that land."[29] Implicit in the cédula's reasoning is the notion that illness was linked not to the rigors of a long journey but rather to a fixed physical space that was perceived as being inherently unhealthy.

In the decades after receiving royal approval and papal support for the building of two hospitals on the coast, administrative discourse in Veracruz continued to address the city's public health. Some of this discourse focused on the smallpox epidemics that ravaged indigenous populations in surrounding areas. In 1539 the city passed an ordinance banning the disposal of indigenous corpses in its rivers, declaring that "those [*indios*] who were Christians" should be buried in the Catholic cemetery, while those who were not should be buried elsewhere. The penalty for those who did dispose of an indigenous corpse in the river, regardless of religion, was to be a fine of fifteen *pesos de oro*.[30]

Yet Veracruz itself was uncommon among early Spanish settlements in New Spain for its relatively small indigenous population. The earliest census of the city, a 1571 *relación geográfica*, explicitly noted that the pueblo contained neither indigenous nor *mestizo* residents among a population of "more than 200 vecinos" and "more than 600 black slaves," plus a few free blacks and a few *mulatos*. Among the total population there were more or less 500 Christians."[31] The diminished presence of Amerindians in the greater Veracruz region again elicited comment from city officials in 1580. In a *relación geográfica* physician Alonso Hernández Diosdado expressed concern over the "very remarkable decline of the indios of this region," which he claimed "could not be explained but by the bad temperance and inclemency of this land in general, and the miserable plague of mosquitoes that it has." Like some earlier Spanish writers, Hernández tied the threat of the "total ruin and extermination" of the indigenous population not to external factors but to what he saw as the intrinsic febricity of the coastal lowlands.[32]

While it is clear that illness and public health were central concerns of sixteenth-century officials—both locally and in the viceregal and metropolitan centers—there was no consensus either on the severity of the problem or what should be done about it. Writing in the aftermath of a devastating hurricane, Escalante had used the city's reputed ill health in an attempt to provoke a move to a different location. Five years before the 1552 hurricane, Escalante's predecessor as alcalde mayor, Alonso de Herrera, wrote that Veracruz was "an unhealthy city but the key to New Spain nonetheless." Seeking royal patronage, he characterized Veracruz's residents as "loyal vassals" who provided essential security to New Spain and its supply routes in the Caribbean, guarding the port against foreign corsairs and maroons alike, in spite of the city's pestilential environment.[33]

Unlike Escalante, who represented Veracruz's climate as a debilitating weakness, Herrera drew on perceptions of the city's ill health in an attempt to demonstrate that its residents were essential to the functioning of empire. As we shall see, the Spanish crown and New Spain's viceroys would later use this same reasoning, which in 1547 was intended to elicit royal support, against Veracruz's own *cabildo*, as tangible evidence of the danger inherent in further removing the city from its port.

Official anxiety that Antigua Veracruz was located too far from San Juan de Ulúa to service the port's needs effectively is evident, if inchoate, as early as the 1533 *cédula* requesting papal support for a hospital. San Juan de Ulúa needed a hospital of its own, the crown reasoned, because "the closest population is that of the city of Veracruz, which is five leagues [away]," suggesting Antigua Veracruz was too far away to play an active role in the public health of the port. Luis de Velasco the Elder's appointment as viceroy in 1550 seems to have allayed these concerns. Initially Velasco appeared to support a movement among local civil and church authorities to relocate the city to an area that was "healthier, richer, and more secure."[34]

Following the 1552 hurricane, however, Velasco reversed his position. While local officials requested a move into the interior, Velasco was more alarmed by the storm's impact on shipping than on the city. Because the city and port were separated by more than a dozen miles, relief had to be funneled to not one but two disaster zones. Moreover, the storm had damaged the port's facilities, which would require money and manpower to rebuild. To support this effort, Velasco approved an additional 1 percent tax on shipping to fund the purchase of "fifteen or twenty black slaves" to work on the repairs and aid in the unloading of ships. Responding to the request to move Veracruz to the interior, Velasco expressed concern that moving the city at such a trying time could hinder the recovery effort and make the port more vulnerable to foreign attack. Writing three years after the hurricane and just one month before the French pirate Jacques de Sores's famed sack of Havana, Velasco cited reports of increasingly daring attacks on Caribbean ports as a key strategic reason for keeping the city close.[35] If Veracruz moved further into the interior, it would not be able to reinforce its battered and vulnerable port. At no point in his report to the crown discussing the repairs did he mention public health.

In the second half of the sixteenth century, metropolitan discourse on the city's location began to focus more on the efficiency of shipping and the port's vulnerability to attack than on public health. Subsequent viceroys followed Velasco's example by using their authority over the port's defenses to put pressure on the city's cabildo. This was evident after San Juan de Ulúa was attacked by corsairs in September 1568, when five English vessels under the command of John Hawkins engaged in a naval battle with ships of the Spanish fleet.[36] Although the Spanish ships scored a decisive victory, the new viceroy Martín Enríquez wrote an urgent missive to the crown requesting financing to construct two bulwarks on the mainland, at the northern and southern extents of the Ulúacan harbor.[37]

Enríquez's appeal came two years after construction began on a fortress on the island.[38] The same year, the previous viceroy, Gastón de Peralta, granted a concession (*merced*) to a man named Juan González de Buitrón to construct a private residence on a plot (*solar*) on the mainland across from the island and a license to open a tavern (*venta*) to serve the overflow population of soldiers, sailors, laborers, and incoming migrants during the period of construction on the island.[39] The grant to Buitrón was the first of fifty that viceroys would hand out to settlers on the Ulúacan coast between 1566 and 1599, sponsoring the establishment of inns, shops, and farms. These mercedes, all of which were handed out before the city was officially moved to the Ulúacan coast, represent more than 90 percent of all such grants made for the Ulúa-Veracruz area during the entire colonial period.[40]

In effect, New Spain's viceroys used their power over defense to drive a redistribution of population, commerce, and infrastructure to the Ulúacan coast. While this redistribution may not have been the primary goal of defense spending, the flow of settlers to the Ulúacan coast set an important precedent. The establishment of a baseline population and infrastructure on the mainland coast fueled the growth of an ever-larger service economy. As more sailors and travelers made use of the inns and shops on the mainland, the focus of the service economy shifted from La Antigua to the Ulúacan coast.

As a service economy was forming across from San Juan de Ulúa, merchants in Puebla, Mexico City, and Seville grew agitated about the slow pace of trade. Delays resulting from the transshipment of goods between Ulúa and La Antigua could take as long as two weeks. Once goods arrived in La Antigua, the pace of trade did not speed up, as the Antigua River frequently proved too shallow to support riverine transport. In some places the river was so shallow that riverboats were forced to transfer their cargo to teams of muleteers and proceed unladen until the water was deep enough to transfer the cargo back.[41] The river's shallowness and the lack of a good road meant that some cargo could take as long as two years to arrive in Mexico City from the time it arrived in Ulúa.[42]

Responding to these delays, in 1572 a group of ship owners, captains, and pilots based in Seville and Triana lobbied the crown to move the city closer to the port. They claimed that trade would be better off if cargo entered the mainland at Ulúa rather than being ferried from the port to Antigua Veracruz.[43] Meanwhile, a separate group of merchants in Puebla petitioned viceroy Martín Enríquez to supply funding for the building of a new dockyard (*atarazana*) at San Juan de Ulúa, which he approved.

The growing sentiment in Seville, Puebla, and Mexico City to relocate the city was not received well in Antigua Veracruz. In August 1575 the city council sent a letter to the Spanish crown stating unequivocally the dangers of moving the city:

> This city has written to Your Majesty to tell of the general and universal damage that will be done to Your Majesty's treasury and to the merchants and vecinos of this city and this kingdom if the viceroy is indeed successful in his attempt to have ships unload their goods in the mainland of the port of San Juan de Ulúa. There will be no sailor who will not die of work and sun, nor could he leave the city by foot, for that land is greatly unpopulated and the terrain is rough, its rivers dangerous, and its swamps and marshes large and deep. Nor is there wood nor grass nor anything that is good for the sustenance of life. The site is beaten with great northern gales and the wind is very bad in such a way that moves the sand dunes, creating mountains of sand that shift from one place to another, so that one year the city is blind and the next it is open for the mosquitoes that make this land uninhabitable.[44]

Not only did the cabildo object to the moving of the city. They also lambasted the "remarkable" underhandedness and "prejudice" of the Poblano elites who had persuaded the viceroy to undermine the city of Veracruz, causing "irreparable damage ... to our royal service and the general good of the Republic."[45]

Alongside protestations about the dubious actions of Poblano merchants and the viceroy, the cabildo made several requests for concessions that would allow them to improve the city at La Antigua, including funds for a new roof for the cathedral, a prison "for the large quantity of *galeotes* (convicts or galley slaves) and other prisoners who arrive with the fleets," a new cabildo building, and convents to house itinerant clergy.[46] These requests often met with no response, a fact that the cabildo complained about in subsequent letters. But if Antigua Veracruz's requests for more public buildings and infrastructure went unanswered, those of the burgeoning settlement on the Ulúacan coast did not.

In the 1590s the Ulúacan coast underwent rapid development, drawing hundreds of migrants from the settlement at La Antigua. Beginning in 1594 new residences, shops, and guesthouses were joined by a series of convents and hospitals granted to various religious orders—first to the Jesuits and later to the Franciscans, Carmelites, and Augustinians.[47] In 1595 New Spain's viceroy also approved the construction of the city's first *portales*, though it is unclear when that project was completed, since it is not mentioned in subsequent reports or urban plans. Since no city had yet been established on the site, these grants referred to the area as the *"ventas de Buitrón,"* after the original shopkeeper who had established himself there. Although Veracruz officially remained at the Antigua River, it was evident that metropolitan and mercantile interests had succeeded in turning San Juan de Ulúa into the magnetic force around which the coastal population would gather.

Metropolitan subversion wore away the resistance of Veracruz's residents. The construction of two roads from central Mexico to San Juan de Ulúa—one through Xalapa, the other through Córdoba—bypassed Antigua Veracruz, cutting it out of the commercial circuit entirely. In 1590 the port's chief accountant, Antonio Cotrina, wrote the first of two letters to the Council of the Indies requesting the city's formal relocation. Both letters referred to the opening of the new roads. Writing from San Juan de Ulúa in June 1590, Cotrina explained that "the new road . . . is further [from the Antigua Veracruz] than the old road by twenty-four leagues (by Xalapa), thirty-five leagues by the Sierra Caliente [Córdoba]."[48] By the time Viceroy Gaspar de Zúñiga Acevedo issued an order to relocate the city to the Ulúacan coast in 1599, rechristening it the "Nueva Ciudad de Veracruz," it was the culmination of a process that metropolitan authorities in Puebla, Mexico City, and Seville had orchestrated for at least three decades.

Conclusion

Veracruz's many early movements reveal not only the truism that the city's geography responded to the dictates of colonial priorities but also that shifting priorities reflected the negotiation of what kind of city Veracruz would be. In its initial foundation on the Ulúacan coast, it was a city facing seaward, a terminus for a group of conquerors arriving by ship from Cuba. When the city moved to Quiahuiztlan, its mission shifted to providing land-based infrastructure to facilitate Spanish incursions into the interior. Following the success of those incursions, the city moved southward, first to La Antigua, where estuary access to the hinterland and proximity to San Juan de Ulúa complemented both the city's landward and seaward uses. Finally, as it became clear that the city's central purpose was as a hub of maritime traffic, it returned to its original location on a strip of land that was once considered too barren and mosquito-infested to inhabit.

These movements underscore the many similarities between Veracruz and other Caribbean ports.[49] Much as scholars once depicted island ports such as Havana as "weigh stations" or "nodes" on commercial trunk lines, Veracruz has often been described as a conduit that linked the vast interior of New Spain to the sea.[50] More recent scholarship on Havana has shown that early Spanish Caribbean populations participated more extensively in intercolonial and insular trade than previously imagined.[51] In similar fashion Veracruz's sixteenth-century relocations demonstrate the seaport's position as a locus for multiple, and often competing, agendas. The sea remained central in official thinking about the city even as its residents sought to move farther inland. Veracruz's return to the shores facing San Juan de Ulúa in 1599 was in essence a sign that its leading vecinos had been forced to acknowledge that the city's primary purpose was its maritime functions.

As common as epidemic disease was in the early modern Atlantic world, Veracruz's lack of a large indigenous population enabled European observers to portray the port's struggles with illness as an atypical phenomenon resulting from a poor physical location. This view was evident in the 1530s, when Veracruz was called the "tomb of the Spaniards," and it may have contributed to the city's adoption of Saint Sebastian—known as a protector against the plague in late medieval Europe—as its chief patron in the seventeenth century. Veracruz also acquired the nickname "ciudad de los muertos" among sailors in the transatlantic fleet.[52] Finally, arriving travelers regularly noted the incongruity of the port's wealth of trade and the city's penurious built environment, earning it yet another dubious moniker as the "ciudad de tablas."

In the seventeenth century, especially after the first yellow fever outbreaks in the 1640s, European and creole writers frequently linked Veracruz's reputation with its social and cultural milieu, especially its large African population. But this trend was apparent already in 1585, when a Franciscan priest named Antonio de Ciudad Real described Veracruz as "a very hot and sick land, a land where the mosquitoes reign, and even the *negros*, because of all the people they are the greatest in number."[53] In the eyes of many European observers, Veracruz was a city whose humoral temperance—its airs and waters—often differed from that of the Mexican interior. Because of this, its natural world was more compatible with black bodies than it was with European or Amerindian ones. As the rhetorical coupling of blackness and disease became more common, early modern European writers increasingly understood Veracruz as a region distinct from the interior of New Spain, rather than the beginning of the mainland empire as described by Cortés in 1519.

Notes

ABBREVIATIONS

AGI   Archivo General de Indias
         -IG   Gobierno: Indiferente General

	-Mexico	Gobierno: Audiencia de México
	-MP	Mapas y Planos
	-Patr	Patronato Real
AGN		Archivo General de la Nación
	-Jes	Jesuitas
	-Merc	Mercedes
AHCV		Archivo Histórico de la Ciudad

1. Cortés, *Cartas*, 105–58. See also Schwaller and Nader, *First Letter*, 13–15, 63–106.
2. Cortés, *Cartas*, 132.
3. Rabasa, *Inventing America*, 98–100.
4. Schwaller and Nader, *First Letter*, 1.
5. For Cortés in particular, the pursuit of royal patronage was hastened by the need to justify his defiance of Cuban governor Diego Velázquez, who had revoked his authorization of the expedition before it began.
6. To avoid confusion when discussing Veracruz's relocations, I use the term *Ulúacan coast* to refer to the coastline directly across from the island of San Juan de Ulúa where the city ultimately settled. The Ulúacan coast covered just under 10 km of coastline from the Punta de Mocambo in the south to the Vergara River in the north and terminated inland at the sand dunes that eventually formed the western border of Nueva Veracruz, a total area just under 50 km square.
7. Lerdo de Tejada, *Apuntes Históricos*, 250.
8. For extensive discussion of this topic, see García de León, *Tierra adentro, mar en fuera*, 83–126. See also Ruiz Gordillo, "Fundaciones urbanas."
9. See Mártir de Anglería, *Décadas*, 1:405–10, 415–16, 419–23, and 2:440; Díaz del Castillo, *Historia*, 67–73.
10. Díaz del Castillo, *Historia*, 67.
11. de la Mota y Escobar, *Memoriales*, 47.
12. AHCV Caja 1, vol. 1, 1652, fols. 403r–422v.
13. See Sluyter, *Black Ranching Frontiers*, 19–60 and "Ecological Origins," 161–77.
14. AGI-Mexico 1088, L.2 (25 April 1532), fols. 76v–77r.
15. Gerhard, *Guide*, 362.
16. See Ruiz Gordillo, "Fundaciones urbanas"; Herrera, *Historia General*, 4th década, 236.
17. Herrera, *Historia General*, 225–26.
18. Herrera, *Historia General*, 225–28.
19. AGI-Patr 20, N.5, R.21 (1527).
20. AGI-Patr 181, R.25 (27 September 1552); AGI-Mexico 351, N.5, fols. 51r–66r (27 September 1552). See also Paso y Troncoso, *Epistolario*, 6:181–206; Schwartz, *Sea of Storms*, 1–5.

21. Paso y Troncoso, *Epistolario*, 6:183 and 6:189.
22. García Acosta et al., *Desastres agrícolas*, 109–10.
23. Paso y Troncoso, *Epistolario*, 7:36–39.
24. Sluyter, *Colonialism and Landscape*, 90–91.
25. Paso y Troncoso, *Epistolario*, 7:36–39.
26. Paso y Troncoso, *Epistolario*, 7:36–39. Following Galenic theory, sixteenth-century Iberians commonly believed that the body produced four humors (black bile, yellow bile, phlegm, and blood), the particular balance of which dictated a person's health, character, and physical traits like skin color. A person's humoral balance could change depending on a number of internal and external conditions, including spatial factors like climate, air, and food, which were among the considerations that went into founding and planning new settlements in the Americas.
27. Rodríguez-Sala and Ramírez, *Los cirujanos*, 102–4.
28. AGI-IG 422, L.16 (1533), fols. 25r–26v. See also Pablo F. Gómez's chapter in this volume.
29. AGI-IG 1962, L.6, fols. 50v–51r. As quoted in Rodríguez-Sala and Ramírez, *Los cirujanos*, 104. See also AGI-MP Bulas Breves 20 (20 February 1534).
30. AGI-Mexico 350 (3 July 1539), fols. 1r–10v.
31. AGI-IG 1529, N.5 (11 March 1571), fol. 4v.
32. Acuña, *Relaciones geográficas*, 2:301–36. See also Pardo-Tomás, "'Antiguamente vivían,'" 41–66.
33. AGI-Mexico 350, N.2 (15 June 1547) fols. 11r–13v.
34. Sarabia Viejo, *Don Luis de Velasco*, 450–52.
35. AGI-Mexico 19, N.17 (3 June 1555). See also Lane, *Pillaging the Empire*, 13–22.
36. Arróniz, *La Batalla naval*.
37. AGI-Mexico 19, N.39 (1568).
38. See Calderón Quijano, *Historia de las fortificaciones*, 12–15.
39. AGN-Merc vol. 9 (1567), fol. 97r.
40. AGN-Merc vol. 10–24 (1577–1599).
41. AGI-IG 1529, N.5 (11 March 1571), fol. 6v.
42. AGI-Mexico 350 (24 December 1595), fols. 268r–272v.
43. AGI-Patr 259, R.41 (1572).
44. AGI-Mexico 350 (17 August 1575), fols. 96r–97v.
45. AGI-Mexico 350 (13 February 1576), fols. 98r–171v.
46. AGI-Mexico 350 (3 May 1583), fols. 177r–178v.
47. AGN-Merc vol. 18 (1594), fol. 303v; vol. 21 (1598), fol. 316v; vol. 20 (1595), fol. 40r; vol. 22 (1597), fols. 130v, 160v; (1598), fol. 216v.
48. Paso y Troncoso, *Epistolario* (1590), 13:252–53.
49. See Altman, "Key to the Indies."

50. See Moore, *Forty Miles*, 25–26.
51. See de la Fuente, *Havana and the Atlantic*, 11–50.
52. Musset, *Ciudades nómadas*, 67; AGI-MP Bulas Breves 20 (20 Feb 1534).
53. Ciudad Real, *Tratado Curioso*, 116–18. For further examples in the seventeenth century, see de la Mota y Escobar, *Memoriales*, 50–53; Gage, *A New Survey*, 48–53; AHCV caja 1, 1 (1620), fols. 34r–35r; AGN-Jes I-26, exp. 1 (1632), fols. 2r–3v; Gemelli Careri, *Giro*, 138–42.

Bibliography

ARCHIVES

Archivo General de Indias (Seville, Spain).
Archivo General de la Nación (Mexico City, Mexico).
Archivo Histórico de la Ciudad (Veracruz, Mexico).

PUBLISHED WORKS

Acuña, René, ed. *Relaciones geográficas del siglo XVI: Tlaxcala*. 2 vols. México DF: Universidad Nacional Autónoma de México, Instituto de Investigaciones Antropológicas, 1985.

Altman, Ida. "Key to the Indies: Port Towns in the Spanish Caribbean: 1493–1550." *The Americas* 74, no. 1 (January 2017): 5–26.

Arróniz, Othón. *La batalla naval de San Juan de Ulúa*. Xalapa: Universidad Veracruzana, 1982.

Calderón Quijano, José Antonio. *Historia de las fortificaciones en Nueva España*, 2nd ed. Madrid: Gobierno del Estado de Veracruz, Consejo Superior de Investigaciones Científicas, Escuela de Estudios Hispanoamericanos, 1984.

Ciudad Real, Antonio de. *Tratado Curioso y Docto de las Grandezas de La Nueva España*, 2nd ed. Edited by Josefina García Quintana and Victor M. Castillo Farreras. Mexico City: Universidad Nacional Autónoma de México, Instituto de Investigaciones Histórica, 1976.

Cortés, Hernán. *Cartas de Relación*. Edited by Ángel Delgado Gómez. Madrid: Editorial Castalia, 1993.

de la Fuente, Alejandro, with the collaboration of César García del Pino and Bernardo Iglesias Delgado. *Havana and the Atlantic in the Sixteenth Century*. Chapel Hill: University of North Carolina Press, 2008.

de la Mota y Escobar, Alonso. *Memoriales del obispo de Tlaxcala: un recorrido por el centro de México a principios del siglo XVII*. Edited by Alba González Jácome. Mexico City: Secretaría de Educación Pública, 1987.

Díaz del Castillo, Bernal. *Historia de la conquista de la Nueva España*. Edited by Joaquín Ramírez Cabañas. Mexico City: Editorial Porrúa, 1976.

Gage, Thomas. *A New Survey of the West Indies.* London: M. Clark for J. Nicholson and T. Newborough, 1699.

García Acosta, Virginia, Juan Manuel Pérez Zevallos, and América Molina del Villar, eds. *Desastres agrícolas en México: catálogo histórico.* México DF: Centro de Investigaciones y Estudios Superiores en Antropología Social, Fondo de Cultura Económica, 2003.

García de León, Antonio. *Tierra adentro, mar en fuera. El puerto de Veracruz y su litoral a Sotavento, 1519–1821.* México, D. F.: Fondo de Cultura Económica; Xalapa: Gobierno del Estado de Veracruz, Universidad Veracruzana, 2011.

Gemelli Careri, Giovanni Francesco. *Giro del Mondo del dottor d. Gio. Francesco Gemelli Careri. Parte Sesta contenente le cose più ragguardevoli vedute nella nuova Spagna.* Vol. 6. Naples: Stamperia di Giuseppe Roselli, 1708.

Gerhard, Peter. *A Guide to the Historical Geography of New Spain.* Cambridge: Cambridge University Press, 1972.

Herrera y Tordesillas, Antonio de. *Historia general de los hechos de los castellanos en las islas i tierra firme del Mar océano.* 4th Década. Edited by Andrés González de Barcía Carballido y Zúñiga. Madrid: Imprenta Real de Nicolás Rodríguez Franco, 1730.

Lane, Kris E. *Pillaging the Empire: Global Piracy on the High Seas, 1500–1750.* New York: Routledge, 2015.

Lerdo de Tejada, Miguel M. *Apuntes históricos de la heróica ciudad de Veracruz,* 2 tomos. México DF: Impresos Ignacio Cumplido, 1850–1857.

Mártir de Anglería, Pedro. *Décadas del Nuevo Mundo.* 2 vols. México DF: Secretaría de Educación Pública, 1945.

Moore, Rachel A. *Forty Miles from the Sea: Xalapa, the Public Sphere, and the Atlantic World in Nineteenth-Century Mexico.* Tucson: University of Arizona Press, 2011.

Musset, Alain. *Ciudades nómadas del nuevo mundo.* México DF: Fondo de Cultura Económica, 2012.

Pardo-Tomás, José. "'Antiguamente vivían más sanos que ahora': Explanations of Native Mortality in the *Relaciones Geográficas de Indias.*" In *Medical Cultures of the Early Modern Spanish Empire,* edited by John Slater, Maríaluz López-Terrada, and José Pardo-Tomás, 41–66. Burlington VT: Ashgate, 2014.

Paso y Troncoso, Francisco del, ed. *Epistolario de Nueva España.* 16 vols. México DF: Antigua librería Robredo, de J. Porrúa e hijos, 1939–1942.

Rabasa, José. *Inventing America: Spanish Historiography and the Formation of Eurocentrism.* Norman and London: University of Oklahoma Press, 1993.

Rodríguez-Sala, María Luisa, and Verónica Ramírez. *Los cirujanos de hospitales de la Nueva España (siglos XVI y XVII): miembros de un estamento profesional o de una comunidad científica?* Mexico City: Universidad Nacional

Autónoma de México, Instituto de Investigaciones Sociales; Academia Mexicana de Cirugía; Secretaría de Salud; Patronato del Hospital de Jesús, 2005.

Ruiz Gordillo, J. Omar. "Fundaciones urbanas en México: La Veracruz en el siglo XVI." *Altepetl. Revista Geografía Histórica—Social y Estudios Regionales* 5–6 (2012). https://www.uv.mx/altepetl/No7/anteriores/alt02/arts/funcaiones%20urbanas.pdf (accessed July 21, 2017).

Sarabia Viejo, María Justina. *Don Luis de Velasco, virrey de Nueva España, 1550–1564*. Seville: Escuela de Estudios Hispano-Americanos, 1978.

Schwaller, John F., and Helen Nader. *The First Letter from New Spain: The Lost Petition of Cortés and His Company, June 20, 1519*. Austin: University of Texas Press, 2014.

Schwartz, Stuart B. *Sea of Storms: A History of Hurricanes in the Greater Caribbean from Columbus to Katrina*. Princeton: Princeton University Press, 2015.

Sluyter, Andrew. *Black Ranching Frontiers: African Cattle Herders of the Atlantic World, 1500–1900*. New Haven: Yale University Press, 2012.

———. *Colonialism and Landscape: Postcolonial Theory and Applications*. New York: Rowan and Littlefield, 2002.

———. "The Ecological Origins and Consequences of Cattle Ranching in Sixteenth-Century New Spain." *Geographical Review* 86, no. 2 (April 1996): 161–77.

10

Hospitals and Public Health in the Sixteenth-Century Spanish Caribbean

PABLO F. GÓMEZ

Epidemic diseases together with the unprecedented Atlantic exchange of biota occurring during the sixteenth century are central to the history of the New World. Fevers, poxes, and buboes modeled Spanish colonial enterprise in the Americas as much as political alliances, commercial interests, and military campaigns did. Nowhere was the effect of disease more pronounced and decisive than in the Caribbean. Pestilences of all varieties, aided by forced-labor policies imposed by Spanish colonists, the displacement of Amerindian communities, and food shortages resulting from Spanish imperial designs, overwhelmed Amerindian bodies, societies, and destroyed their life-worlds. The forced enslavement of millions of Africans and their arrival in the Americas was largely spurred, if not uniquely caused, by the lack of manpower to propel the American sinews of early modern capitalism in the wake of the demographic collapse of Amerindian societies.

Surprisingly, considering its centrality in the history of the sixteenth-century Caribbean, little has been written about how the Spanish crown first responded to epidemic diseases and Caribbean population crises during the sixteenth century.[1] This essay, focusing on the history of hospitals and quarantines, describes how governmental authorities both in Spain and in the New World responded to the challenges posed by diseases and the high morbidity and mortality that prevailed in the sixteenth-century Caribbean. Royal officials in the Caribbean initially deployed public health policies that first developed in the Iberian peninsula in the midst of legal reforms affecting poor relief and the management of pestilences. Spaniards' experiences in the Caribbean, however, forced them to depart from Old World strategies and policies within decades of the establishment of their first settlements in the region.

There are two distinct periods in this history. The first, a stage of contact that began when Europeans arrived in the Caribbean during the 1490s, was characterized by mostly local and disorganized responses to epidemic diseases and Native American morbidity and mortality. A second period, starting after the implementation of the fleet system and the intensification of the transatlantic slave trade during the late sixteenth century, was defined by an expansion of the region's sanitary infrastructure mainly directed toward providing health care for European and African immigrants and a growing American-born population. This was particularly true in cities that functioned as crucial nodes for the *Carrera de Indias*, including Cartagena de Indias, Veracruz, and Havana. The political, military, and societal consequences of the overwhelming presence of disease in Caribbean locales made Spanish imperial actors think in novel ways about matters of public health (a relatively new concept for early modern Europeans) and the management of colonial bodies. Spanish officials increasingly saw these bodies not as unique (an essential concept of contemporary notions about corporeality in Europe) but as part of larger groups that they identified by their place in a new reality of disease susceptibility within imperial political and social imaginaries.

The history of Caribbean hospitals reflects Spaniards' innovative strategies for dealing with the same public health issues that fueled the appearance of the modern hospital in Europe centuries later. Early Caribbean hospitals were very different institutions from the "houses of science" familiar to twenty-first-century readers. Caribbean hospitals, nevertheless, were indicators of the range of meanings, changing relationships, transgression of old models, and the new possibilities for social functioning that emerged in the region during the sixteenth century.

The New Public Health of the Sixteenth Century

Ideas about the functioning of human bodies obviously determine how people experience disease and how people and governments think illness can be managed. Even if the terms used for them are recognizable today, diseases such as leprosy, *apostemas*, dropsy, *tabardillo*, *vómito negro*, or smallpox had very different meanings for early modern Atlantic people.[2] Ideas about the balance between the individual body and the natural and spiritual worlds dominated notions about the etiology of disease for early modern Europeans.[3] Apart from epidemic outbreaks, health was not a central concern for governments.[4] Miasmas and, in the aftermath of the fourteenth-century epidemic of bubonic plague, "seeds of disease"—rather than microbes—caused pestilences.[5] In addition, for most early modern people, God—or Gods—were ultimately responsible for determining the physical fate of communities during plague outbreaks.[6]

Repeated epidemics of bubonic plague and the changing relationship between the state and the bodies of individuals spurred by these epidemics initially shaped Spanish imperial designs in relation to public health in the Americas. The idea of kings as providers of health for the realm and as actual physical healers was a foundational part of the relationship between political power and public health in medieval and early modern Europe.[7] Pestilences and mortality as such were seen as a disruption of equilibrium within the physical body of the realm that spoke ill of the abilities of rulers to govern. Public health was thus already a central preoccupation for Spanish monarchs during the late fifteenth and early sixteenth centuries.[8]

Repeated visitations of *pestilencias*, a term that referred not only to outbreaks of bubonic plague but also to influenza, typhus, and other respiratory and gastrointestinal ailments, made New World epidemics a central preoccupation for Spanish rulers. In addition, the crown faced a challenging situation because of the increasing number of dispossessed people arriving in its burgeoning but inadequately planned and structured cities in the Americas.[9] To address these challenges in the Caribbean, the crown initially adopted Old World models that depended heavily on local charitable efforts and civic sponsorship and administration of public health facilities.[10]

Caribbean Lands: Pestilences and Quarantines

A number of Caribbean ports quickly gained fame for their insalubrious nature. Europeans' life expectancy in some Caribbean locales may have been severely limited, with as many as 45 percent of them not surviving their first year in the Americas.[11] Not surprisingly, royal functionaries sent to the Caribbean frequently asked for transfers to other locales in the Indies or to return to Spain.[12] Disease clearly influenced European thinking about the region, even if some places in the hinterlands of Caribbean cities were considered to be relatively healthy.

The Council of the Indies and the House of Trade in Seville functioned not only as recipients and cataloguers of worrying news related to health matters coming from the Caribbean. They were also the architects of the mostly haphazard and reactive policies that initially characterized the crown's response to public health issues in the region. Information about health matters, cures, and pestilences such as the ones compiled in the second half of the sixteenth century in the *Instrucción y memoria de las relaciones de Indias*, are examples of the much larger flow of correspondence, reports, and petitions related to demographics and public health that arrived in Spain from Caribbean locales. More conspicuously, the *relaciones* underscore the urgent role within the overextended Spanish colonial project of the physical body of the inhabitants of the New World and the challenge that circumstances there posed.[13] The Caribbean was at the forefront of these concerns.

The Caribbean increasingly functioned as a place of transit for throngs of people, including seamen, poor immigrants, slaves, and military personnel, among others, who relied on public health provisioning for their health care. The region also became a site of recurrent armed conflict and imperial contestation where disease played an enormous role in the ability of military expeditions to overtake or retain newly acquired and strategically crucial sites. More important, unlike any other locale in the Americas, the Caribbean was directly linked to the Atlantic circulation of biota, including germs and pestilences, and as such it functioned as an early site for the containment of epidemic diseases arriving in the New World.

Some of these issues are evident in a December 1535 decree that Queen Juana sent to Tierra Firme. In it the queen ordered the founding and provisioning of a hospital in the city of Nombre de Dios, "because [Nombre de Dios] is a very busy port with many poor and sick people."[14] Some months later, on April 30, 1536, the queen wrote in similar terms, saying that she "had been informed by the governor of Tierra Firme," Fernando Jiménez, "that because of news of the riches of Peru," many people had traveled to the city of Panama "and continued to do so." And "because the city is sick," many people suffered from illnesses. In addition, "as there was not a licensed physician or medicine with which to cure [the immigrants], they die."[15] As in Tierra Firme, the demand for health services increasingly overwhelmed the ability of Caribbean cities to cope with it throughout the sixteenth century.

Writing decades later, Alonso de Coronado y Ulloa sent a letter in 1612 from Portobelo to the Council of the Indies. Like Juana's, Coronado y Ulloa's letter represents a sentiment common to the places where the Indies fleet made a stop in the Caribbean. He wrote that "because of all the people that arrive in times of fleets and armadas, dead paupers are found in the streets due to the lack of a place to host them."[16] These were not isolated events. Reports from Cartagena detail how the city's hospital, the largest in the Caribbean, was in some cases not able to cope with all the sick people who arrived in the fleet; royal officials had to adapt fleet ships to accommodate some of the diseased arriving in the city. The accountant of the armada, Juan de Alvarado, for example, resorted in 1610 to transferring some of the ill from the hospital to the galleon *San Martín*, anchored in the city's port. According to Lorenzo Bernal, the pilot of another galleon named the *Santiago*, there were so many sick people that not even the thirty that were transferred to the *San Martín* were enough to ameliorate the situation; less critical patients were also sent to smaller ships (*pataches*) anchored in the bay.[17] The arrival of boatloads of sick people, most of them poor seamen, passengers, and slaves in need of public health support, required new ideas about the crown's involvement in the provision of these spaces.

If Europeans thought differently about disease, this did not mean that they were not keenly aware of the relationship between epidemic illness and the arrival of sick people and vessels from different Atlantic locales. This is evident in measures that the Spanish crown enacted early in its colonial project. In 1507, for example, the crown ordered a temporary halt to travel to Hispaniola because of the fear that a *pestilencia* that was raging in the Atlantic would spread to the island. This prohibition applied to everybody, even those "who go [to Hispaniola] to work."[18] This measure undoubtedly was informed by Europeans' experiences with repeated episodes of bubonic plague since the fourteenth century when quarantines were first imposed.[19] By 1536 the crown had put in place similar measures restricting the transit of ships coming from Atlantic islands like Cape Verde to the Indies because "many people [had] died of a pestilence" in Cape Verde and Upper Guinea.[20] The order stipulated that no ship coming from Spain, specifically from San Lúcar de Barrameda, could stop in these Atlantic locales on their way to the Indies. Penalties for not following the regulation included barring the unloading of goods carried by suspect boats and, if the ships arrived in a Caribbean port, sequestering all the goods, including slaves, after an appropriate quarantine. Ordinances specifying these provisions were regularly sent to Santo Domingo and other Caribbean cities.[21]

These prohibitions also affected ships departing from Spain. On April 7, 1581, Diego Gasca de Salazar, the president of the Casa de la Contratación, wrote to the Council of the Indies about the measures he thought were necessary to avoid the spread to the New World of a pestilence that was rampant in Spain at the time. In the letter Gasca de Salazar emphasized "the care and diligence that a matter of such importance requires" and insisted that it was necessary to make sure that "the clothes being shipped" in the fleet "were clean and procured in places and sites not suspected" of being affected by the plague. "No sick person with this illness, being as contagious as it is," should be allowed on any ship going to the Indies, he declared, independent of whether the person was "a soldier or seaman."[22] The crown quickly acted to prohibit the circulation and shipping to the Indies of "clothes that might have been contaminated with pestilence" as well as people suspected of having been in contact with pestilence in Europe.[23]

The reception of measures restricting trade in ports around the Atlantic was mixed at best and in some cases downright violent, not a surprise as they threatened the livelihood of these trade-dependent communities. For example, in 1600 the crown prohibited ships going to the Indies from anchoring in Puerto Real in Cádiz Bay. Pedro del Castillo, "official judge of Cádiz," recognizing that Puerto Real was badly affected by "the disease of the plague," ordered an armored ship to guard the bay and stop the passage of people and things "from [Puerto Real's harbor] to ships belonging to the fleet of New Spain." Puerto Real denizens responded by sending another warship to break through the blockade that del Castillo had put in place. In answer to the defiant attitude of Puerto Real's people, the Council of the Indies sent a communiqué on April 10, 1600, "to all the official judges" of the Indies and officers of the fleets sailing between the New World and Spain ordering them to avoid any interaction with any ship that had stopped in Puerto Real or had received merchandise coming from that city or from any other "pestilent place." The blockade, the Council said, was necessary in order to "stop the great inconveniences that could result" from even the smallest contact with people and goods from Puerto Real.[24]

Containment measures put in force throughout the sixteenth and seventeenth centuries in the Atlantic remained as precedents for how to deal with epidemics in the following centuries—even if they were largely improvisational at the time.[25] Examples of regulations of this type appear, for instance, in eighteenth-century compilations of royal orders for governing the Indies. These measures were resisted and only partially followed in Spain and the Caribbean, and it is hard to gauge how successful they were in containing specific outbreaks of disease.[26] It seems unlikely that such orders would have been strictly followed given the prevalent smuggling that characterized trade in the Caribbean.

Even the Spanish crown became increasingly aware of the necessity of adapting to particular circumstances in times of pestilence. In 1536 the Council of the Indies issued a series of measures prohibiting ships from "getting close [to] or visit[ing]" places with known plague outbreaks in Atlantic islands like Cape Verde and in Upper Guinea. Yet the Council also gave permission to merchants Pedro de Cifuentes, Valian de la Forte, Juan Alfaro, and Hernando de Jerez y Juan Núñez to bring merchandise—including two hundred slaves from Upper Guinea in the case of Jerez and Nuñez—to Hispaniola "in spite of the prohibition of doing so because of pestilence."[27] The "balanced" method that the crown adopted to manage public health underscores how changing economic and political interests and the need to accommodate the needs of Atlantic communities frequently trumped Spanish rulers' fears regarding the enforcement of quarantines.[28] This early, evolving, and inchoate approach to public health provided the basis for the development of the networks of hospitals that appeared in the sixteenth-century Caribbean.

Hospitals in the Caribbean

Caribbean hospitals were built soon after the establishment of the first settlements in the region. Fray Nicolas de Ovando founded the first hospital in the Americas in Santo Domingo, Hispaniola, on November 29, 1503. The hospital was initially named Espíritu Santo and later known as San Sebastián.[29] The crown clearly understood the need to develop a network of hospitals to accommodate the new circumstances of the Caribbean, especially in strategic places. There is, for example, evidence of the existence of hospitals in Cartagena de Indias and Santiago de Cuba by 1533. On September 13, the Council of the Indies sent an order to Cuba mandating that a percentage of the alms should be spent on the hospital in Santiago de Cuba.[30] The Council of the Indies also ordered the establishment of a hospital in Nombre de Dios in 1535. The city of Panama already had a hospital in place by 1535, and in January 1537 Charles V wrote to the governor of Tierra Firme informing him that he had ordered the House of Trade to send "stonemasonry masters" to "finish constructing" the hospital.[31] In 1540 the city council of Santo Domingo donated parcels of land in the town of Azua in Hispaniola for the construction of a hospital and a religious college.[32] Similarly on October 1, 1554, the crown sent a communication to officials in Puerto Rico ordering them to accommodate one Salgado Correa "in the hospital" located in San Juan.[33] Also in 1565 Pedro Núñez, the administrator of the hospital in Veracruz, asked for an additional "1,000 gold pesos" to sustain the "sick poor" in the city.[34] The hospital San Juan de Dios in Portobelo was already in place by 1603,[35] and we have records of the existence of a hospital in the town of Puerto Plata in Hispaniola for the same year.[36] As in Puerto Plata, there were other smaller hospitals founded in Caribbean cities such as the hospital of San Andrés in Santo Domingo which, established in the 1560s, was in reality a small house for the care of indigent women that by 1593 hosted no more than three or four patients at a time.[37]

Demand for hospitals in the Caribbean grew in the sixteenth century. Pedro Núñez, the administrator of the hospital in Veracruz, wrote in 1565 to the crown saying that it was the most crowded hospital in New Spain, "being the place where the fleet arrives."[38] Similar reports came from Cartagena, which by the beginning of the seventeenth century had the largest and busiest hospital in the Caribbean. Cartagena's San Sebastián, after all, was the main hospital in a port that was the first place of arrival for many of the ships crossing the Atlantic to the Americas and a destination for sick people coming from the northern New Kingdom of Granada, Venezuela, and the southern Caribbean islands. During the second half of the sixteenth century, Cartagena also had a hospital called the Espíritu Santo located in the Getsemaní neighborhood. During the early seventeenth century, San Sebastián hospital was located within the walled city itself and remained at a site two blocks from the cathedral for the rest of the seventeenth century.[39] By 1577 the bishop of Cartagena was asking for increased resources for the hospital and a chaplain to serve it. He wrote that in 1576 alone more than four hundred men from the Indies fleet were cured at the hospital in addition to all the poor from the city and its hinterlands that came to it. The bishop also said that there were no hospitals in the nearby towns of Tolú, María, and Mompóx, and that "all the sick people in these places" were "cured in the hospital in Cartagena."[40]

Lazarettos—places of exile or seclusion for people with infectious diseases, especially leprosy—slowly appeared during the sixteenth century in the Caribbean. In Santo Domingo there is news of the establishment of the first one on the American continent in 1520.[41] Already in 1598 there are records attesting to the existence of the San Lázaro Hospital in Cartagena.[42] And in 1626 the Spanish crown designated funds for the establishment of a larger lazaretto in that city.[43] In Cuba, on the other hand, *vecinos* fought hard not to have a lazaretto in the island because of fears of contagion, and they continued sending all lepers to New Spain. The first official lazaretto in Havana does not appear until late in the seventeenth century.[44] New ideas about contagion also strongly influenced where hospitals would be located. Philip II decreed in 1573 that during the planning of new cities (particularly those in the New World), "the hospitals ... for people sick from contagious diseases" should be established in "high places" so that "harmful winds, passing through the hospitals," did not "hurt the people in the new towns."[45] Furthermore, Philip IV ordered in 1627 that lepers admitted to Cartagena's lazaretto must carry all of their belongings with them to the hospital to avoid the dissemination of the disease.[46]

Many of these hospitals were initially no more than a collection of houses, and petitions for the reform and provisioning of more appropriate buildings were legion throughout the sixteenth century when most of these institutions were remodeled and grew in size and capacity. Initially the crown left hospitals to be managed by civic organizations such as religious brotherhoods or by city councils. The situation in Santo Domingo's hospital exemplifies the process. By 1577 the hospital had four separate infirmaries: one for curing people sick from "calentures," another for those ill of "buboes," a third for people being treated for "wounds and sores," and the fourth one for women. Sick people who did not have resources were buried at the hospital. The hospital generally treated fifty to eighty patients at a time and was overseen by a *mayordomo* (administrator), who was named by the city council in consultation with the *cofradía* of Nuestra Señora de la Concepción. As in other Caribbean places, the hospital took care of poor people in the city as well as those arriving in fleets and armadas. The administrator said in 1577 that a physician visited the hospital every day to make rounds of the sick. The hospital also had surgeons, nurses, and "some black slaves who clean the clothes, prepare food, and clean the sick people and the buildings of the hospital."[47]

In the Caribbean, medical practitioners of all origins practiced openly. By the early seventeenth century, health practitioners of African descent, who had created their own experientially based methods for dealing with disease, were the most frequently consulted; they were powerful dealers in matters of health in the region.[48] Amerindians also figure as health care providers in Caribbean hospitals during the sixteenth century. In 1577 Cartagena's bishop wrote to the crown asking for resources to maintain "the Indian slave women and men nurses" who served in the hospital.⁴⁹ Back in Santo Domingo, the administrator of the hospital wrote to the crown in the same year that the hospital in that city had "some black slaves that clean the clothes, prepare food, and clean the sick people and the buildings of the hospital."⁵⁰ When it was handed over to the order of San Juan de Dios around 1621, the inventory of the hospital in Portobelo included six black slaves.⁵¹ Similarly, when royal officials inventoried the San Sebastián hospital in Panama, there were seventeen black slaves, including several African *bozales*.⁵²

In charge of seemingly menial labor in the hospital, such as cleaning the building and patients and cooking, black slaves were also increasingly training at the hospital as bona fide health providers. In a prominent example, Diego López, a *mulato* from Cartagena de Indias, entered the San Sebastián hospital as a young slave. In subsequent years, López trained to be a surgeon, gained manumission in the 1610s, and later practiced as a surgeon in the hospital until his death sometime in the mid-seventeenth century. Black surgeons became a staple of Caribbean hospitals. Some of them worked as practitioners even while they were still slaves. This was in addition to dozens of health specialists of African descent who were, paradoxically, condemned because of their healing practices to serve their sentences in hospitals in Cartagena by the Inquisition—a royal institution, one should not forget.⁵³

Administration of Hospitals

In the early modern Caribbean, caring for the indigent and sick fell within a contested realm that involved competition among a number of political, social, and professional groups. In line with tradition in the Old World, the Spanish crown first gave licenses to city councils and religious sodalities to found and administer hospitals in the region. Throughout most of the sixteenth century, the hospital in Santo Domingo was under the charge of the Nuestra Señora de la Concepción brotherhood.⁵⁴ The financing of sixteenth-century Caribbean hospitals depended heavily on alms, on funds that the crown specifically allocated for hospitals, and on diverse taxes and fees that the crown dedicated to their maintenance. In addition to alms, among the funds that the crown made available to hospitals were *penas de cámara* (fines for a number of specific categories of crimes) and *derechos de anclaje* (anchorage rights).[55] In 1565, for example, Pedro Núñez, the administrator of the hospital in Veracruz, asked for "1,000 gold pesos" to maintain the sick poor of the city.[56] Similarly, in 1606 the Council of the Indies designated 2,000 ducats per year for the hospital in Portobelo.[57]

Records from Cartagena from 1575 to 1578 show the payments that Indies fleets and armadas made to hospitals in the region for treating and feeding their crews. In one report Gaspar Hernández, the administrator of the hospital in Cartagena, wrote that sick people from one of the fleets spent a combined total of 403 days in the hospital.[58] The hospital would charge the fleet a per diem rate for each sick person. In 1610 the fleet paid four *reales* per day for each seaman treated at the hospital in Cartagena.[59]

These fees were precious resources, and city councils often refused to follow strictly the dictates of people who left donations to the hospitals.[60] In some cases wills included the meager possessions of seamen from all over the Atlantic like Juan Genovés, a Genoese sailor who died in the hospital at Panama City.[61] But available resources could be more significant and inevitably harder to access for the beneficiaries. This was especially true in places like Cartagena and Havana where the wealthy left large endowments to "pious institutions." The prior and friars of the Santo Domingo convent in Cartagena wrote to the Casa de la Contratación 1595 that "a number of dead people" had left the monastery and the hospital in Cartagena 1,300 ducats. This money had not been disbursed by the royal treasury in the city, in spite of repeated petitions on the part of the religious brothers and the hospital.[62] The Council of the Indies answered in February 1598, ordering royal officials to provide the money to the hospital.[63] In 1577 and 1581 Cartagena's bishop wrote to the Council asking that the administration of the hospital in the city be returned to him "as was the case when it was founded." The bishop argued that the city council and governor of Cartagena had been embezzling the resources that Cartageneros had left for the hospital."[64] The bishop, however, was not successful, and the administration of the hospital passed directly from the council to that of the order of San Juan de Dios at the beginning of the seventeenth century.[65]

The crown, however, constantly negotiated with local authorities in its overextended realm. On April 29, 1596, the Council of the Indies ordered that the estate of one Catalina de Cabrera, initially intended to found a "school of grammar" in the city for the training of the sons and daughters of elite Cartageneros, instead should be devoted to the maintenance of the city's hospital. Because of all the expenses it incurred, the city council argued, the hospital was always in debt. Furthermore, they said, the money that would be given to the school would be wasted because "people from [Cartagena] were not very devoted to letters."[66] Funding for hospitals also included the celebration of special festivities that provided opportunities to collect donations. The allotment for the hospital in Cartagena in the 1570s, for instance, was supplemented by specially designated Jubilee days that promised the remission of sins for denizens who donated alms to the hospital and visited the sick.[67]

Notwithstanding these funds, cities and hospital administrators constantly squabbled over money and refused to obey royal ordinances.[68] On April 3, 1605, the crown sent an order to the governor of Cuba asking him to coordinate the relocation of Havana's hospital "because the place where it was located was unhealthy." The Council of the Indies also ordered the governor to refrain from involving himself in the management of the hospital, which by then was ostensibly already in the hands of the San Juan de Dios order. The crown reprimanded the governor for attempting to manage the finances of the hospital and name its chaplain.[69] Similarly, in 1611 the Council of the Indies had to intervene in the management of the hospital of the city of Santo Domingo in Hispaniola, ordering governor Diego Gómez de Sandoval and the archbishop of the city to return the chaplaincy of the hospital to one Rodrigo Velásquez.[70] Rather than being the exception, conflicts over the administration of hospitals between religious and secular authorities were the norm, particularly in the case of large hospitals with greater resources.

Even if Caribbean communities chronically complained about the lack of funds and institutions to take care of the poor and ill in their cities, they were also well aware of the significant resources and political importance that such places commanded in the local social and political economy. City councils frequently wrote to the Council of the Indies asking for an increase in the funds assigned for the maintenance of the hospitals. In Cartagena, calls for a larger hospital, more appropriate to the influx of sick people from all over the Caribbean, were common.

Pedro Meléndez, one of the crown's officials in the city of Portobelo, wrote in 1612 about the chronic lack of funds for the hospital, which at the time was still administered by the city council.[71] This lack of financial support was especially acute in places that had seen a downturn in their fortunes over the course of the sixteenth century. By 1586, for example, the *cofrades* in charge of the Hospital of San Sebastián in Santo Domingo were worried because "with the attack of the Lutheran English," the hospital had been badly damaged.[72] Santo Domingo resorted to asking the crown to instruct the Casa de la Contratación to send "clothes and medicines" from Seville for the four infirmaries that the San Sebastián hospital still maintained in 1596. The response was a onetime donation of 500 ducats in February 1602.[73] Charitable work connected with public health efforts could serve as a means of gaining social standing in a highly visible way. Ideas about public health were closely linked with early modern notions about political health. Similarly, charitable work in hospitals or during pestilences was also closely linked to notions of Christian duty.

Colonial functionaries in Portobelo demanded in 1608 that the crown fund a second hospital in the city.[74] In the opinion of royal officials in the Caribbean, hospitals were much more than just places of poor relief and were directly linked to the ability of the city to defend itself. Officials in Portobelo emphasized that "one of the greatest needs" of military garrisons, such as the one the Spaniards maintained in the city, "was that they lacked hospitals to serve soldiers and artillerymen."[75] On July 2, 1612, Coronado y Ulloa sent a communication to the council confirming the receipt of three *cédulas reales*. In one of them the king approved the establishment of a second hospital in Portobelo, San Felipe.[76] The crown also invested significant resources in hospital infrastructure. Records from Cartagena from around 1612 detail that the crown spent 225,000 maravedís in the erection of the new San Sebastián hospital in the city.[77] The continuous demand for new hospitals and their poor administration motivated the Spanish crown to move away from traditional approaches to overseeing public health efforts and to exercise tighter control over the region's network of hospitals by the end of the sixteenth century.

Reform

By the turn of the seventeenth century, the crown pursued a new approach to enforcing the consolidation of public health provisioning and poor relief in the region. The crown had realized by then that the maintenance of a healthy realm in the Caribbean demanded changes in a number of long-standing assumptions about the individualistic nature of health and the responsibilities that political and social actors had in its maintenance. The new models of public health that the crown designed were delivered through long-standing religious institutions that glued together the social body of the Spanish colonial realm. This development took place in the Caribbean earlier than in other places in the Americas. Starting in the first decades of the century, the Spanish crown gave direct control of the largest hospitals in the region to the most efficient and experienced hospital administrators it could find: the brothers of San Juan de Dios.

In 1628 Fray Juan Pobre, prior of the hospital and convent of San Sebastian in the city of Panama and a member of the San Juan de Dios order, wrote to Madrid asking for the confirmation of the order's authority over the houses where the hospital in Panama was located and which local authorities wanted to repossess. He said that the brothers of San Juan de Dios had been in charge of the hospital for seven years by then. Before the order's arrival, the hospital was in the hands of an administrator who witnesses said was named by either the bishop or the local city council but in either case was derelict in performing his functions. The hospital's buildings, according to Father Pobre, were in bad shape by the time the San Juan de Dios brothers took charge.[78] He said that since 1621 more than 1,200 *enfermos de cama* (bedridden patients) had been treated there every year. Father Pobre emphasized that the brothers of San Juan de Dios had maintained the buildings housing the old hospital and added some more "without abandoning" their healing activities.

The crown had already given licenses on August 1, 1602, to Brothers Bruno de Avila and Cristobal Muñoz and eleven other priests to cross the Atlantic to take charge of Caribbean hospitals. Four of these priests were bound for Havana, four for Cartagena, and four for Portobelo.[79] Transferring the management of other Caribbean hospitals took some time. In the city of Panama, control over the hospital was also given to the San Juan de Dios order in July 1620.[80] As with hospitals in Havana, Cartagena, and Panama, the royal hospital in Portobelo, San Sebastián, was officially handed over to the order in 1629. As in the other cases, the crown said that it had done so "because [the hospital] suffers from the same inconveniences and damages" that resulted from the poor administration of these institutions by city councils across the region.[81]

These changes were not accepted without resistance. In letter after letter Caribbean city councils complained about the hospitals' transfer to the San Juan de Dios order. In Portobelo the city council argued that under its administration the San Sebastián hospital already fulfilled the needs of attending the "poor, the incurable, seamen, military personnel [and] vagabonds."[82] As late as 1670 the council in Cartagena was still fighting the crown for the patronage of the San Sebastián hospital after attempting to take it away from the San Juan de Dios order.[83] By granting the administration of hospitals to the order of San Juan de Dios, the Spanish crown not only reasserted the necessity of uniform health care provisioning throughout the Caribbean but also linked it to centralized policies. No longer viewing hospitals merely as places for charity, or for the enactment of medieval ideas about social standing, public health had become a matter of imperial design.

The Hospital as an Index

The scattered references to sixteenth-century Caribbean hospitals in the existing literature are deceptive. They portray hospitals as places of last resort—dirty, damp, and ineffective. In them the aspirations and models of Atlantic histories do not appear to be reflected. Hospitals seem unchanging in their inability to offer "real" cures or are portrayed as the last bastions of desperate and ineffective prayer. Early hospitals in the Caribbean appear as anachronistic, if harrowing, reminders of the portentous difficulties of early modern life and of the inability of people to deal with corporeal realities. As this chapter has shown, however, hospitals were also contested spaces of social standing and sites of change for reimagining the relationship between the state and its subjects' bodies.

A study of the history of early Caribbean health provisioning sheds light on dynamics at the center of an increasingly globalized world and the conflicting and paradoxical ways by which such projects developed. Most of the existing work on public health analyzes the history of these institutions during the eighteenth and nineteenth centuries, when more visible attempts at bureaucratic reform and recognizable biomedical discourses flowed through the region. The sixteenth century, however, provides at least an equally rich example of the innovative and transformative ways in which early modern Europeans reimagined the physical, social, and spiritual composition of their realm and the not always "modern" fashion in which they dealt with these challenges.[84]

Caribbean hospitals function as an index of Spanish colonial efforts. They reflect the fluid societies and changing notions about the relationship between the state and public health emerging in a multicultural region where most people came from poor socioeconomic backgrounds. Hospitals brought together practitioners of a multiplicity of origins that included outcasts of the medical establishment in Europe. Furthermore, these spaces functioned as a place of transit and a space of reception for much of the biota being exchanged in the Atlantic, including its plagues. Caribbean hospitals in all of their fluidity are representative of the promises of the New World, its immense dangers, and the gargantuan transformations in the ideation of bodies and public health that took place in the region.

Notes

ABBREVIATIONS

AGI	Archivo General de Indias
-Ctdra	Contaduría
-Cttn	Casa de la Contratación
-Esc	Escribanía de Cámara de Justicia
-IG	Gobierno: Indiferente General
-Just	Justicia
-Panama	Gobierno: Audiencia de Panamá
-Patr	Patronato Real

	-SD	Gobierno: Audiencia de Santo Domingo
	-SF	Gobierno: Audiencia de Santa Fe
AHN		Archivo Histórico Nacional de España
		-Códices Colecciones: Códices y Cartularios
ARCV		Archivo de la Real Chancillería de Valladolid
	-CP	Cédulas y Pragmáticas
RAHE		Real Academia de Historia de España
	-CSC	Colección Salazar y Castro

1. Some scholars have considered the history of hospitals and medical practices through the lens of missionary work, religious charity, Christianization, or heroic medical history, mostly in New Spain and the Andes. See, for instance, Ramos, "Indian Hospitals"; Muriel, *Hospitales*. Other works consider the history of colonial Spanish American hospitals through modernist lenses, most notably in the eighteenth century with the advent of the Bourbon reforms. See Barbier and deForest Craig, "Lepers"; van Deusen, "The 'Alienated' Body"; Warren, *Medicine and Politics in Colonial Peru*.
2. Gómez, *Experiential Caribbean*, chaps. 2 and 4.
3. Siraisi, *Medieval and Early Renaissance Medicine*, chaps. 1 and 2.
4. For a basic overview, see Nutton, *Ancient Medicine*, 298–316.
5. Among many others, see McNeill, *Plagues and Peoples*, 208–42.
6. Siraisi, *Medieval and Early Renaissance Medicine*, chaps. 3 and 4.
7. Elliot, *Imperial Spain*, 139.
8. Clouse, *Medicine*, 150–51.
9. This development reflected similar dynamics of disorganized urban growth in Iberian cities. See Bowers, *Plague*, 2.
10. Bowers, *Plague*, 2–5; see also Carmona García, *El sistema*.
11. We do not have reliable data for most of the sixteenth century. These estimates are extrapolated from late seventeenth- and eighteenth-century statistics, mostly from the British Caribbean. See Miller, *Way of Death*, 440; Klepp, "Seasoning and Society," 473–506. See also J. M. H. Clark's chapter in this volume.
12. See, for example, AGI-Panama 45, exp. 36.
13. Pardo-Tomás, "Antiguamente," 42, 48–65; AHN-Códices, L.744, "Peste."
14. AGI-Panama 234, L.5, fols. 231v–232r.
15. AGI-Panama 235, L.6, fols. 25v–26r.
16. AGI-Panama 47, exp. 60.
17. AGI-Esc 572B, fols. 4r–6r.
18. AGI-IG 1961, fols. 4r–5r.
19. McNeill, *Plagues and Peoples*, 161–207.

20. AGI-IG 422, L.17, fols. 32v–33v.
21. ARCV-CP Caja 1, 10 (1530-9-24); ARCV-CP Caja 4, 32 (1566-4-10), 35 (1566-4-30), 38 (1566-8-5), 45 (1567-1-24); ARCV-CP Caja 5, 12.
22. AGI-IG 1956, L.3, fol. 129v.
23. AGI-IG 441, L.29, fol. 155v; AGI-IG 1956, L.3, fols. 129v–130v.
24. AGI-IG 1957, L.5, fol.155v.
25. See, for instance, the 1678 reference to measures based on ideas about "*como se ha hecho en el pasado*" (as it has been done in the past) in AGI-IG 441, L.29, fol. 155v.
26. See examples of quarantine in outbreaks of bubonic plague in Bowers, *Plague*, 12–13; Clouse, *Medicine*, 144–45.
27. AGI-IG 422, L.17, fols. 32v–33v (Cifuentes), 63v–64r (de la Forte), 67v–68r (Alfaro), 39v–40v (Jerez and Núñez).
28. During the 1530s, for instance, the crown issued 9,500 slave licenses that were not necessarily used by slave traders. The selling of the licenses, however, shows that the crown's need for hard cash and for laborers was more important than the enactment of strict trading restrictions. García Fuentes, "Licencias."
29. AGI-SD 13, N.29, fol. 3r; AGI-SD 14, N.36; AGI-Patr 173, N.1, R.8, N.3, fol. 1r.
30. AGI-SD 1121, L.1, fols. 161v–162r.
31. AGI-Panama 235, L.6, fols. 83v–84r.
32. AGI-Patr 278, N.2, R.7.
33. AGI-IG 1965, L.12, fols. 223v–224v.
34. AGI-Just 1013, N.4.
35. AGI-Panama 271.
36. AGI-SD 868, L.4, fol. 80v.
37. AGI-SD 870, L.8, fols. 14v–15v.
38. AGI-Just 1013, N.4.
39. RAHE-CSC 34, Carpeta 2, fol. 77v.
40. AGI-SF 228, N.11a.
41. Barbier and deForest Craig, "Lepers," 385.
42. AGI-SF, 666.
43. AHN-Códices, L.744, "Peste."
44. Gómez, *Experiential Caribbean*, chap. 2.
45. Barbier and deForest Craig, "Lepers," 387.
46. AHN-Códices, L.744, "Peste."
47. AGI-SD 13, N.29, fols. 3v–14v.
48. Gómez, *Experiential Caribbean*, chaps. 1–2.
49. AGI-SF 228, N.11a.
50. AGI-SD 13, N.29, fols. 14r–14v.
51. RAHE-CSC 35, Carpeta 1, N.1., fol. 8r.

52. RAHE-CSC 34, Carpeta 4, N.1., fols. 4r–4v.
53. Gómez, *Experiential Caribbean*, chap. 2.
54. AGI-SD 13, N.29, fols. 1r–3v.
55. AGI-SF 666; AGI-SD 418, "Instancia del doctor D. Francisco Tenesa confirmación de merced de un pedazo de tierra" (1713); AGI-SF 240, "Carta del fraile Francisco López, hermano mayor del hospital de San Sebastián" (16 May 1603); AGI-SF 97, N.24, fols. 268–71; AGI-Panama 104, fols. 418–41; AGI-SF 98, N.12, fols. 33–39; AGI-SF 100, N.37, fols. 576–86; AGI-SF 232, N.54; AGI-SF 38, R.2, N.72; Mena Serra and Cobelo, *Historia de la medicina*, 127.
56. AGI-Just 1013, N.4.
57. AGI-Panama 1, N.214.
58. AGI-Ctdra 496, Pieza 16.
59. AGI-Esc 572B, fol. 99r.
60. Clouse, *Medicine*, 145; Bowers, "Balancing Individual and Communal Needs"; MacKay, *Limits*, 3.
61. AGI-Cttn 498B, N.5, R.2, fol. 1v.
62. AGI-SF 1, N.123.
63. AGI-SF 1, N.181.
64. AGI-SF 228, N.11 and N.14.
65. AGI-SF 228, N.57.
66. AGI-SF 1, N.153.
67. AGI-SF 228, N.11a.
68. See, for instance, AGI-SD 176, N.11A, fols. 117–26.
69. AGI-SD 869, L.5, fol. 5r.
70. AGI-SD 869, L.6, fols. 123v–124r.
71. AGI-Panama 46, exp. 51.
72. AGI-SD 14, N.36.
73. See, among others, AGI-SD 971, "Hospitales" (1596–1794).
74. AGI-Panama 46, exp. 4.
75. AGI-Panama 47, exp. 65.
76. AGI-Panama 47, exp. 60.
77. AGI-Ctdra 1388, fols. 403r–404v.
78. AGI-Panama 64A, N.8.
79. AGI-SD 154, N.20., fols. 297r–309r.
80. RAHE-CSC 34, Carpeta 4, N.1.
81. RAHE-CSC 35, Carpeta 1, N.1, fol. 2r.
82. RAHE-CSC 34, Carpeta 2, fol. 38v.
83. AGI-SF 64, N.3.
84. Michel Foucault's classic work on the subject is *The Birth of the Clinic*. Foucault's premises have been the object of intense criticism over the past decade.

Bibliography

ARCHIVES

Archivo de la Real Chancillería de Valladolid (Valladolid, Spain).
Archivo General de Indias (Seville, Spain).
Archivo Histórico Nacional de España (Madrid, Spain).
Real Academia de Historia de España (Madrid, Spain).

PUBLISHED WORKS

Alchon, Suzanne Austin. *A Pest in the Land: New World Epidemics in a Global Perspective*. Albuquerque: University of New Mexico Press, 2003.
Barbier, Jacques A., and Lynda deForest Craig. "Lepers and Hospitals in the Spanish Empire: An Aspect of Bourbon Reform in Health Care." *Ibero-Amerikanisches Archiv* 11, no. 4 (1985): 383–406.
Barry, Jonathan, and Colin Jones, eds. *Medicine and Charity before the Welfare State*. London: Routledge, 1994.
Bowers, Kristy W. "Balancing Individual and Communal Needs: Plague and Public Health in Early Modern Seville." *Bulletin of the History of Medicine* 81, no. 2 (2007): 335–58.
———. *Plague and Public Health in Early Modern Seville*. Rochester: University of Rochester Press, 2013.
Carmona García, Juan Ignacio. *El sistema de hospitalidad pública en la Sevilla del antiguo régimen*. Sevilla: Diputación Provincial de Sevilla, 1979.
Clouse, Michele L. *Medicine, Government, and Public Health in Philip II's Spain: Shared Interests, Competing Authorities*. Burlington: Ashgate, 2011.
Cook, Noble David. *Born to Die: Disease and New World Conquest, 1492–1650*. Cambridge: Cambridge University Press, 1998.
Crosby, Alfred W. *The Columbian Exchange: Biological and Cultural Consequences of 1492*. Westport: Greenwood Press, 1972.
Elliott, John H. *Imperial Spain, 1469–1716*. New York: New American Library, 1977.
Foucault, Michel. *The Birth of the Clinic: An Archaeology of Medical Perception*. New York: Vintage Books, 1994.
García Fuentes, Lutgardo. "Licencias para la introducción de esclavos en Indias y envíos desde Sevilla en el siglo XVI." *Jahrbuch für Geschichte von Staat, Wirtschaft und Gesellschaft Lateinamerikas* 19 (1982): 1–46.
Gómez, Pablo F. *The Experiential Caribbean: Creating Knowledge and Healing in the Early Modern Atlantic*. Chapel Hill: University of North Carolina Press, 2017.
Kiple, Kenneth F. *The Caribbean Slave: A Biological History*. Cambridge: Cambridge University Press, 2002.

Kiple, Kenneth F., and Brian T. Higgins. "Yellow Fever and the Africanization of the Caribbean." In *Disease and Demography in the Americas*, edited by John W. Verano and Douglas H. Ubelaker, 237–48. Washington DC: Smithsonian Institution Press, 1992.

Klepp, Susan E. "Seasoning and Society: Racial Differences in Mortality in Eighteenth-Century Philadelphia." *William and Mary Quarterly* 51, no. 3 (1994): 473–506.

MacKay, Ruth. *The Limits of Royal Authority: Resistance and Obedience in Seventeenth-Century Castile*. Cambridge: Cambridge University Press, 1999.

McNeil, J. R. *Mosquito Empires: Ecology and War in the Greater Caribbean, 1620–1914*. Cambridge: Cambridge University Press, 2010.

McNeill, William. *Plagues and People*. New York: Anchor Books, 1997.

Mena Serra, César A., and Armando F. Cobelo. *Historia de la medicina en Cuba*. Miami: Ediciones Universales, 1992.

Miller, Joseph C. *Way of Death: Merchant Capitalism and the Angolan Slave Trade, 1730–1830*. Madison: University of Wisconsin Press, 1988.

Muriel, Josefina. *Hospitales de la Nueva España*. Vol. 1, *Fundaciones del Siglo XVI*. Mexico DF: Instituto de Historia, 1956.

Nutton, Vivian. *Ancient Medicine*. New York: Routledge, 2012.

Pardo-Tomás, José. "'Antiguamente vivían más sanos que ahora': Explanations of Native Mortality in the *Relaciones Geográficas de Indias*." In *Medical Cultures of the Early Modern Spanish Empire*, edited by John Slater, Maríaluz López-Terrada, and José Pardo-tomás, 41–66. Burlington VT: Ashgate, 2014.

Ramos, Gabriela. "Indian Hospitals and Government in Colonial Andes." *Medical History* 57, no. 2 (2013): 186–205.

Siraisi, Nancy G. *Medieval and Early Renaissance Medicine*. Chicago: University of Chicago Press, 1990.

van Deusen, Nancy E. "The 'Alienated' Body: Slaves and *Castas* in the Hospital de San Bartolomé in Lima, 1680 to 1700." *Americas* 56, no. 1 (July 1999): 1–30.

Warren, Adam. *Medicine and Politics in Colonial Peru: Population Growth and the Bourbon Reforms*. Pittsburgh: University of Pittsburgh Press, 2010.

PART 5

International Commercial Networks

International and trans-imperial merchant networks played powerful roles in the establishment and development of Spain's Caribbean settlements during the sixteenth century. Commercial agents of many nationalities resided in Seville, and some merchant houses had representatives posted in the Caribbean. Rather than consistently attempting to maintain direct control over all aspects of overseas trade and colonial administration, the Spanish crown often sought contractors to temporarily oversee specific economic sectors in exchange for trade monopolies, the right to appoint factors in certain ports, and in some cases broader administrative responsibilities. Financiers and merchants who were not subjects of the crown of Castile but were from lands allied to or associated with the Habsburg monarchy were frequently successful in their bids for such contracts. At the same time, sea routes linking the Caribbean to Iberia overlapped with broader vectors of international commerce, even facilitating trans-imperial connections that could bypass mechanisms for Spanish crown control and taxation.

11

The Hispano-German Caribbean

South German Merchants and the Realities of European Consolidation, 1500–1540

SPENCER TYCE

The dramatic exploits of successful Spanish explorers and conquistadors such as Cortés and Pizarro belie the truth of the early colonial period in Latin America. Rather than successful campaigns against established indigenous societies that led to economic and political prosperity, much of the early history of Latin America and the Caribbean is about failure, loss, and misunderstandings. The concept of a unified "Spanish" conquest itself is misleading, as a great many explorers, soldiers of fortune, priests, businessmen, and other participants were from different areas of Europe.

One area that became heavily involved in the Spanish enterprise in the Indies lay within the Holy Roman Empire in modern-day Germany. Several merchant companies from the city of Augsburg and nearby Ulm played a significant role in the development of Spanish imperial power in the Caribbean. Although not as famous as their Italian counterparts, the Medici, the Fugger and Welser families were in many ways just as politically and economically powerful. The Fuggers, with commercial branch offices and factory warehouses throughout Europe, gained solid control over central European gold, silver, and copper mining. The Welsers directed their own branches and commercial agents but depended on the trade of textiles, spices, and consumer commodities. Both firms lent money. In nearly every major city and port on the continent, south German agents provided ready cash to members of the nobility, royalty, and even the Catholic Church. Business was about taking risks and expanding to new locations and customers.

When the Welser Company obtained a contract to pacify and settle Venezuela in 1528, this appeared to be a logical step in the trajectory of a solid European business. The Welsers were major economic actors in the early modern world, and they hoped to provide support to European settlers in the Caribbean while earning new revenues. That did not happen. They struggled to make a profit, and what might have been a successful trading hub in the southern waters of the Caribbean devolved into a poorly organized pursuit of gold and indigenous slaves.

To say that Venezuela was a German colony would be inaccurate. Venezuela was not a colony of Germans, but one of Iberians administered by south Germans with strong Iberian and continental ties. These ties included the Catholic Church as well as established trade networks that spanned all of Western and Central Europe. European settlement and expansion in the Americas relied on a synergetic system of individuals and institutions that regularly crossed state and ethnic borders. Welser Venezuela exploited those networks, but international efforts could not overcome highly localized obstacles and problems.

South German Merchants

German merchants populated Iberia's port cities many years before the reign of Charles V.[1] Among foreign merchants in Lisbon during the first few years of the sixteenth century, German merchants were second in numbers only to Italians. Commercial agents in the Augsburg-Ulm corridor took notice of Vasco de Gama's 1497 voyage to the east coast of Africa and ports in India. By 1504 German firms such as the Fuggers and Welsers and others had set up offices in Portugal to exploit goods arriving from Africa and Asia. Portuguese access to Central European metals helped ensure commercial success in India. South German merchants, especially the Fuggers, quickly became the leading suppliers of copper and silver to the subcontinent with the Portuguese as the primary distributor.

The 1505 voyage of Francisco de Almeida, which cemented Portuguese dominance in the Indian Ocean, required significant financial backing to fund a fleet of nearly two dozen vessels. The Germans were major contributors, with the Fuggers, Welsers, and other merchant houses paying for at least three ships.[2] Antón Welser managed several small offices that brought precious metals to the Iberian ports, setting the stage for his family's business future. Using a network of contacts acquired through his business dealings as well as those of his son-in-law, Welser invested in the 1506 fleet of Tristão de Cunha, whose occupation of the African and Indian coasts helped Portugal dominate trade in the Red Sea. Because of their reputation for supporting royal enterprises and the state economy, the Portuguese crown gave the Germans full trading privileges and the civil rights of Portuguese subjects, including access to goods from India. With these new goods and privileges, the Welsers and Fuggers sought to expand their enterprises beyond Portugal, especially to the new overseas realms of Castile and Aragon.[3]

While the Fuggers dominated mining, the Welsers focused on commercial goods such as textiles, medicinal products, and spices. This kept the two major south German firms from engaging in destructive trade wars, but they remained competitors in Europe. Both families operated offices out of Italy, Iberia, and Antwerp, the port city that supplanted Lisbon and Venice as the premier trading center during the first two decades of the 1500s. Easy access to English, French, and German trade, in addition to the ease with which Iberian and eastern European traders could reach the area, attracted the attention of the Fuggers and other merchants from the Augsburg-Ulm corridor.[4]

Charles V's grandfather, Emperor Maximilian I of the Holy Roman Empire, had difficulties with tax collection.[5] For years he was unable to implement a system that would guarantee the financial support of his military campaigns in the Italian states and against French encroachment on his territory. To remedy this problem, Maximilian conducted regular transactions with the south German merchant firms, owing the merchants 4 million ducados at the time of his death in 1519.[6] This financial relationship continued during and after the election of Charles as the Holy Roman emperor. He hoped to use his political alliances rather than money to cement victory against other rulers who sought the throne. One of his rivals, Francis I of France, was quick to use bribes to attempt to sway the election. Welser agent Heinrich Ehinger represented the firm in the Spanish court and guaranteed Charles a loan of 156,000 ducados. The Welsers could not challenge the treasury of the French, but they could help offset some of Charles's financial burdens, thereby strengthening their economic interests should he win. The Fuggers offered a larger sum to Charles but only after it seemed certain that Francis would not prevail in the election.[7]

Charles continued to borrow money from the Germans after his election as emperor. Until the end of his reign in 1556 he was in constant need of financial support to fund his military campaigns across Christian and Ottoman Europe. Fugger and Welser agents routinely met with Charles or his representatives to discuss new loans and payments of old debts. Often the Spanish crown would pay its debts in the form of papal indulgences, the royal fifth from the Americas (*quinto*), or income earned from the landed estates of Spain's orders of knights, the Maestrazgos.[8] As the Spanish sovereign, he borrowed 3.7 million ducados from 1520 to 1530 with more than 40 percent coming directly from the Germans. The Welser firm was a regular source of income throughout Charles's reign, carrying out forty-one official transactions with the king between 1520 and 1556 for a total of 4 million ducados.[9] The Welsers also sought business opportunities beyond Europe. The firm could not supplant the Fuggers as the dominant merchant firm in Antwerp, but they could get a jump on the rest of Europe if they expanded beyond Iberia. For them the Atlantic and the Caribbean, especially the areas under Spanish control, represented untapped markets that would need to be outfitted with textiles and domestic goods.

Opening the Caribbean to the Germans

The south German merchants could not simply establish a commercial house and appoint an agent in the Indies on their own. They needed help from experienced businessmen who understood how to negotiate Spanish economic and political systems. One such individual was Jakob Cromberger, a German who ran a successful print shop in Seville and later in Portugal. He regularly worked with Portuguese, Flemish, German, and Genovese merchants and was the first to print books concerning the exploration of the Americas, the letters of Hernando Cortés, and the catechism translated for the indigenous peoples of Michoacán.[10] Welser agents approached him through the efforts of Cromberger's son-in-law, Lazarus Nüremberg. Trained in managing the trade in metals and minerals for the Hirschvogel firm operating in Lisbon, Nüremberg opened up a commercial house in Seville where he met Cromberger and married his daughter.[11] Nüremberg became an attractive partner for various south German firms, including the Welser Company and the Fuggers. Through these contacts, he was able to offer goods to the New World, including weapons.[12] With his connections to the south German merchant elite, Nüremberg was able to recruit investors to projects that interested him. This is what allowed him to make contact with Ambrosius Alfinger, the first Welser governor of Venezuela. Investing more than 600 ducados in the 1526 South American voyage of Sebastian Cabot, Nüremberg convinced other merchants, like Alfinger, to follow suit. While the voyage did not yield any serious returns for the investors, his professional relationships with the merchants only improved. During this time, Nüremberg set up a commercial house in Santo Domingo for the Welser Company.

Through Nüremberg and his father-in-law, the Welser Company managed to convince Charles V to grant them access to the Americas equal to that of Iberians.[13] The first south Germans who made their way to the commercial house set up by Nüremberg, Alfinger, and Jorge Ehinger (brother of Heinrich Ehinger) crossed the Atlantic in 1526 with licenses to carry weapons and trade freely. Other German merchants would soon follow.[14] The first major client of the Welsers' Santo Domingo branch was Rodrigo de Bastidas, who led an expedition into Santa Marta in 1527. After his death, other conquistadors and settlers on the Caribbean coast of South America began to vie for access to the territory. The Welser commercial house was well suited to meet their needs. Trade was steady, with the Welser agents selling wine, weapons, tools, and other goods in the Caribbean while shipping back cases of sugar, gold, pearls, and other commodities to Seville and Antwerp.[15]

South German Contracts

On March 27, 1528, Heinrich Ehinger and Gerónimo Sailer agreed to the provisions of a contract set before them in Madrid by the Spanish crown to settle and exploit the territory of Venezuela. In 1528 the authors and signatories of the contract clearly had little understanding of the interior geography of South America or of its indigenous populations, nor had they developed a strategy concerning what to do with Venezuela.[16] The contract appears to be overly advantageous to the Welser Company, giving them tax benefits and providing decent salaries to administrative officials. The crown, however, made no concessions, nor did it provide any special privileges to the Welser Company that it did not extend to other individuals or groups seeking rights to conquer and settle the lands of the Americas. More important, the Spanish crown offered up as little of its own money as possible. The entire occupation and settlement of Venezuela was a high-risk gamble with unknown potential.[17]

The contract outlined the physical territory that the Welsers could claim. Beginning with the easternmost boundary of the province of Santa Marta at Cabo de la Vela and the western boundary of the Gulf of Venezuela, the territory extended east to Maracapana near Cumaná. With the northern boundary being the Caribbean, the contract specified that the area south of their east-west boundary was to be a part of their province until it reached the Pacific Ocean. Naturally, the Welser Company never explored the entirety of the territory outlined in the contract. The crown demanded the construction of two settlements populated with at least three hundred men within two years of Welser officials entering Venezuela. These settlements could be constructed anywhere and in any way Ehinger and Sailer saw fit. Finally, the merchants were ordered to build three forts. All of these demands were to be funded entirely by the Germans.[18]

Many clauses of the contract revealed that the conquest and settlement of Venezuela was primarily an economic enterprise. The crown required that the merchants pay for the passage of German-speaking master miners to the Indies. The crown allowed the merchants to assign the miners to any of the major islands in the Caribbean, Venezuela, or New Spain. The contract suggested that the miners direct the labor of four thousand slaves that the Welsers were allowed to transport to the Caribbean. The miners could seek out gold, silver, or any other mineral, and their treatment would be similar to that of master miners working in Iberia.[19]

Other sections of the contract ordered an annual salary for a governor (533 ducados), a captain-general (266 ducados), and the commanders of the forts the Welsers would have to build (200 ducados). Whoever held the title of *adelantado* could enjoy ten leagues of hereditary land and a share of 4 percent of all the profits earned in the province, with the caveat that *alcabalas* and *almojarifazgos* (sales taxes and tariffs) were not included in the 4 percent share because these were not profits earned from the land itself. The contract granted an almojarifazgo exemption to the adelantado as long as the goods brought in from outside Venezuela were not traded or sold.[20]

Later sections of the Welser contract dealt almost exclusively with the rights of the vecinos. At first the settlers of the province would only pay a tax of one-tenth of the total profits for gold mined in Venezuela for a number of years. The first wave of settlers would receive the status of vecino of one of the towns, two *caballerias* (tracts of rural land that varied in size), and two *solares* (housing lots). The contract also granted vecinos the right to enslave any indigenous peoples who refused to acknowledge European authority. The settlers were likewise permitted to acquire slaves directly from indigenous slave merchants, as long as multiple officials were present to witness the exchange and certify that the individuals in question could be legitimately held as slaves. The contract did not concede the right to hold or issue encomienda grants.[21]

Before the crown would consent to the terms of the contract, however, Ehinger and Sailer had to agree to support another conquest and pacification project to the west of Venezuela in the province of Santa Marta. In 1526 rebellious Europeans mortally wounded the governor of Santa Marta, Rodrigo de Bastidas. Following his death, both Europeans and indigenous peoples contributed to growing disorder. The Spanish crown contracted García de Lerma to restore order and complete the conquest and pacification of Santa Marta. To assist in this project Ehinger and Sailer agreed to equip and transport at least four ships loaded with two hundred men and necessary provisions. The crown, of course, required that the two merchants pay for this project on their own.[22]

The Welser Company was not the only south German merchant group to have access to American lands. The Fuggers had long been friends of Charles V and the Holy Roman Empire, contributing more money and political support to the young sovereign than the Welsers ever had. It is unclear why the Welser Company received a conquest contract before the Fuggers, but it may have been a matter of convenience. Company representatives in Santo Domingo enjoyed a strong relationship with other merchants and the local population whereas the Fuggers did not have a permanent presence in the Caribbean. In 1531 the Fugger agent in Spain, Veit Hörl, settled a contract with the Spanish crown. Under this agreement, Charles granted the firm territory from the pueblo of Chincha (on the coast of southern Peru), south to the Straits of Magellan and as far east as Portuguese Brazil.[23]

The Fugger contract is much longer and more specific than the Welser contract, outlining the operations for settlement and conquest over a period of several years with multiple armadas of ships to transport men and supplies. The contract offered the same tax exemptions for settlers and men in leadership positions but over longer periods of time. A Fugger-funded vessel was lost off the coast of South America while scouting the territory that same year. With no report from the vessel or guarantee of profits, the Fuggers did not follow up on their contract. With Pizarro's victories over Inca imperial forces only months away, perhaps the Fuggers avoided a costly legal and physical battle over the area.[24]

In order to make Venezuela into an economically productive territory, the Welsers needed to transport a labor force, professionals to oversee work, and large settler populations. Mining for precious metals required master miners, as outlined in the royal contract, settlers to support mining and exploratory operations, and laborers. The miners were trained professionals, having worked in the dynamic silver, copper, and tin mines of Central Europe. By 1528 the Welsers had access to a labor force, one that they had been arranging for some time.

African Slavery and the Welsers

The regular goods and commodities supplied by the Welsers in Europe were certainly profitable, but a new market was opening in the Caribbean: physical labor. As mentioned in Marc Eagle's chapter, the first large-scale commercial enterprise to bring slaves from Africa to the Americas took the form of a royal license or asiento awarded by the Spanish crown to Laurent de Gorrevod in 1518. Gorrevod and his Genovese subcontractors agreed to transport four thousand African slaves to the Caribbean;

the contract was renewed five years later to last until 1528. Although the Genovese benefitted from this early trade, they soon left the business to others willing to operate in such a risky enterprise. While Caribbean vecinos argued for the Portuguese to bring slaves to the Caribbean, the Spanish crown had another group in mind: the German merchants.[25]

The Welser Company did not have any significant experience in the African slave trade in the 1520s. Ehinger and Sailer, the Welsers' principal agents during this time, regularly bought individual slave licenses and sold them to merchants in Spain. In 1526 Francisco de los Cobos, personal secretary to the king, sold his license for two hundred slaves given to him by Charles V to the Welsers, who in turn sold it to other merchants.[26] There was little economic risk in this endeavor, as the Welsers did not have to arrange for transportation of the slaves, and demand for slave labor in the Caribbean was high. A license to carry large numbers of slaves was another matter entirely. In early 1528, before completion of the Venezuela contract, the Spanish crown agreed to a different arrangement with the Welser agents. They were to supply four thousand slaves to the New World. In this new contract, the crown permitted the Welser Company to distribute the slaves over a period of four years with a maximum sale price of 55 ducados for each slave. In total, the crown stood to gain 40,000 ducados from taxes and the Welser firm's initial payment for the contract. The Welser Company's potential profit of more than 200,000 ducados must have been attractive.[27]

The Welsers found a commercial contact with access to enslaved Africans through the Portuguese at São Tomé. The realities of the slave trade, however, proved more difficult than they anticipated. The first shipment of captives suffered heavy losses, and the vecinos of Santo Domingo complained that the quality of Welser slaves was lacking.[28] Subsequent shipments did not restore confidence in Caribbean consumers. In the summer of 1530, a ship arrived in Santo Domingo with a sizeable shipment of healthy female slaves and a less impressive number of males, most of them unfit to work. In addition to the physical conditions of Welser-supplied slaves, Caribbean consumers complained of credit problems with the company. While lesser merchants and traders could offer lines of credit to individuals purchasing slaves, the Welser Company often refused. The cabildo of Santo Domingo forwarded a request to the crown to void the Welser slave contract on the grounds that it was detrimental to the development of the island. The crown did not respond.[29]

By the early 1530s the Welsers stopped participating in the African slave trade altogether, although in Santo Domingo they continued to sell indigenous slaves brought from the mainland. Still in demand by Caribbean settlers, indigenous slaves may have been more profitable for the Welsers because they were easier to acquire and transport. From 1529 to 1538, the only date range available, the Welsers reported and paid quintos for 1,005 indigenous slaves, netting 8,800 ducados in the process.[30]

Master Miners and the Caribbean

For many years scholars routinely labeled the experienced laborers brought from Central Europe to the Indies as "German miners" or more specifically as silver miners from the Tyrol region in modern Austria.[31] In fact, many of the miners were not from that region, nor did they all specialize in silver ore extraction. Furthermore, it is unclear how many miners went to the New World, because statistical data, legal documents, and personal recollections do not always agree.[32] The most difficult question, however, is where the miners went once they arrived in the Indies. The 1528 contract does not specify where the Welsers were to place the master miners, only that they should be brought to the New World. Welser interests extended beyond Venezuela, however, as the company participated in mining and other economies of both the Caribbean and New Spain.[33]

The most reliable data suggest that company agents brought fifty-three miners to the Indies, mostly men with experience in extracting silver, gold, and copper. All came from the Holy Roman Empire, but a majority originated in the Erzegebirge region near the Ore Mountains in eastern Germany. The area was known for silver, but it developed as a mining area based on its tin deposits in the 1400s.[34] Curiously, that area was almost entirely under the influence of Fugger commercial agents, the Welsers' biggest competitor.

In July 1528 fourteen men from the mining hub of Joachimsthal met a Welser agent at Leipzig. He agreed to pay the miners a small weekly allowance including medical expenses if the miners reached Antwerp. Some men brought their families, and the company promised to pay them for their time and work as well. The wife of Sisto Enderlein of Pöttmes, for example, accompanied her miner husband and was compensated for cooking and washing the clothes for the other men in the group. From Antwerp, the Welsers arranged transport to Seville where they would meet Gerónimo Sailer, one of the architects of the Venezuela contract. Sailer agreed to cover the costs of transporting miners and their families to the New World where they would keep 16 percent of all extracted ore for themselves. To sweeten the deal further, Sailer also guaranteed to send any miner who wished to leave after one year to Seville or Antwerp at the company's expense. The Welser agent in Seville made similar arrangements with other mining parties that arrived in port over the next few years. Perhaps as many as eighty miners from German-speaking areas of Europe went to the Indies under these kinds of contracts.[35]

The Welsers transported the miners to Santo Domingo, but records beyond that are sparse. Few miners returned to Europe, and colonial sources rarely mention them. After their arrival in Hispaniola the mining contingent probably moved around the Caribbean to areas that needed mining expertise. Mining operations already under way on the island of Hispaniola no doubt convinced several miners to remain there. Others probably moved to newly discovered and conquered areas, seeking out riches on the frontiers of European power in Mexico and elsewhere.[36] They found neither the riches nor the glory to which they aspired. An unknown number returned to Europe before their year officially ended because of the hardships they faced in the Americas. The chief concern appears to have been the climate, which they had not anticipated. Titus Neukomm, a native of Lindau, wrote in 1535 that "it is a very hot country and for us [Germans] . . . very unhealthy."[37] Indeed, even the bishop of Venezuela, writing long after the miners arrived in the Americas, commented that the climate was too difficult for the Germans to survive.[38]

Among those who returned, many complained that Welser Company mismanagement worsened their experience. In a series of lawsuits filed in Leipzig and Dresden in the 1530s, some surviving miners argued that the Welsers did not pay them and worked them nearly to death. Out of their numbers, they argued, only eleven returned to Europe, eighteen died in the Americas, and the fates of the remaining master miners were unknown. The lawsuits did not mention the fates of the slaves who worked for them.[39] The only known master miner who survived the Welser period and remained in the Americas was one Urban Belem, a native of the Erzgebirge region. In a 1549 deposition Belem testified that twenty-five miners arrived with him in Venezuela, but most had died or gone to New Granada and never returned. The weather, he explained, was a factor that made it very difficult for Germans to live and work in Venezuela.[40]

The Welser Company took a considerable gamble in getting German miners to leave their homes and begin excavations in America. The weather and mineral makeup of the coast of Venezuela was not conducive to mining. Had ore been excavated in Venezuela as it was in the Caribbean in the early years or later in larger quantities in New Spain and Peru, things might have been different. Venezuela was not a mining colony, but every effort was made to make it so during the early years of Welser occupation. Some miners returned home, but a great many died or disappeared from the historical record. A few, perhaps the same percentage as those who would have struck it rich mining in the Erzgebirge, managed to survive and live in this challenging New World. The enslaved Africans had it far worse. Their voyage to America was not voluntary, and they did not have the option to return to their homes.

A German Province?

In addition to bringing in miners and maintaining business connections in the Caribbean and Europe, the Welser Company needed to introduce settlers. The company was in a position to gather soldiers of fortune, skilled laborers, and farmers from Iberia and other parts of Europe where the Welser name had positive connotations. With the addition of settlers, men and women who would not only contribute to the exploitation of the province but also the replication of European political and social culture, the Welsers brought legitimacy to their experiment in the New World. The Spanish House of Trade only recorded individuals and families that legally sailed from Seville or nearby secondary port cities.

More important, there are significant periods that are unaccounted for, notably 1530 to 1533. The period from 1534 to 1540 appears to have the most accurate passenger rolls and arrivals in the Indies, especially a 1534 armada to Welser Venezuela.[41]

Legally, 246 people arrived in Venezuela in 1534. Three women figured officially among the group, but the catalogue does not always list the wives or children of all of the men who arrived in the New World. The voyage also brought four friars, three of them from the Trinitarian Order. The majority of the new arrivals had no declared occupations or professions, but among the group was a tailor, a choir singer, a silversmith, and a crossbowman (*ballestero*). Most were from Castile, Andalucía, and León. The typical European who went to the Americas originated in a geographic corridor that stretched from the arid, southern lands of the Mediterranean coast north to the Duero River basin. In Venezuela this regional makeup was no different, as Table 11.1 demonstrates. Other Spanish speakers, mostly those from the northern and eastern regions, made up a smaller percentage of the total population of colonists. This group also included non-Iberians, but not in such numbers that would make visitors to Welser Venezuela think they were in a radically distinct German-speaking colony.

Table 3. Regional origins of selected conquest and settlement campaigns

REGION OF ORIGIN	VENEZUELA	PERU	NEW GRANADA
	COLONISTS IN 1534	PIZARRO'S 1532 ENTRADA	BOGOTÁ'S 1537–39 FOUNDING
Andalucía	48	34	49
Aragon	8	2	4
Asturias	5	-	1
Baleares	-	-	1
Basque Country	11	8	7
Canary Islands	-	-	2
Catalonia	4	-	-
Extremadura	16	36	18

REGION OF ORIGIN	VENEZUELA COLONISTS IN 1534	PERU PIZARRO'S 1532 ENTRADA	NEW GRANADA BOGOTÁ'S 1537–39 FOUNDING
Flanders	4	-	-
France	3	-	3
Galicia	7	-	-
Germany	-	-	2
Greece	-	2	-
Italy	2	-	1
León	35	15	17
Murcia	-	-	3
Navarre	3	2	-
Netherlands	-	-	2
New Castile	29	15	20
Old Castile	58	17	25
Portugal	-	-	10
Valencia	2	-	2
Total persons (known origin)	235	131	167
Unknown origin	11	37	-
Total persons	246	168	167

Sources: AGI-Cttn 5536, "Pasajeros a Indias," L.1 and L.2; Avellaneda Navas, *Conquerors*, 59; Lockhart, *Men of Cajamarca*, 28. Numbers under "Bogotá" are the combined totals for three entradas led by Quesada, Federmann, and Belalcázar.

The Welser Company invested in miners and merchants to assist in their development of the province of Venezuela and also in transporting colonists. Like other enterprises in South America during this time, they attracted settlers mainly from the "Conquest Corridor" of central and western Spain. Many of the men who came hoping to find cities of silver and gold and to achieve success like Cortés in Mexico were greatly disappointed. Some stayed in Venezuela or New Granada, but life in the New World proved incredibly hard.

Entradas and Raids

The German merchants quickly established a governing structure in Venezuela after Charles V finalized the contract. The first governor and captain-general was one of the Welsers' longtime Caribbean agents, Ambrosius Alfinger. Setting off to find a possible waterway that connected the Gulf of Maracaibo with the Pacific Ocean, Alfinger and 160 men left their main settlement at Coro virtually abandoned in the autumn of 1529. After several months of searching, they realized that the gulf was actually the mouth of a large lake and that the only way of readily extracting profit from the region was to enslave and export its inhabitants.[42] Alfinger's lieutenant, Nicolas Federmann, organized his own entrada the next year. Without authority from Alfinger, Federmann charted the physical and human landscape of the eastern sections of Welser territory. Like Alfinger, Federmann returned without significant riches but with plenty of indigenous slaves. Alfinger returned to the Maracaibo area and proceeded south along the Andes foothills to seek larger indigenous populations, but he only found death from poisoned arrows in 1533.[43]

The new governor of Venezuela, Jorge Espira, set off to follow the course of Alfinger's second entrada in 1535. Espira, like Alfinger, was a capable commercial agent but no explorer. Espira and his men sought out rich and powerful indigenous cities but mainly encountered small, wary indigenous nations that confirmed the existence of great cities while directing the Europeans deeper into the interior. Espira returned to Coro in 1539 and died there unexpectedly in 1540.[44]

Federmann, banished by Alfinger after going rogue, returned to Venezuela and Coro in 1534. Unable to stay in the settlement and bored with the minutiae of colonial policy and organization, he led another illegal entrada in 1537. Federmann marched his men west into the northern Andean mountains, hoping to find something besides the small settlements and increasingly hostile indigenous groups that lived west of the Maracaibo region. In the spring of 1538 Federmann encountered a group of Europeans trying to organize their own settlement in a town they called Santa Fe de Bogotá. Federmann and his men helped build the town and briefly enjoyed the pleasant climate and economic potential, but Federmann left Bogotá in 1539 for Europe. He planned to make an appeal to the Spanish crown for control over Bogotá, but the Welser firm blocked his efforts. He died in Spain in 1542.[45]

The last major entrada out of Venezuela was that of Philip von Hutten, a wealthy German who survived Espira's entrada. Pressured by the bishop of Venezuela to seek out whatever resources he could find in the spring of 1541, von Hutten commanded a force of more than 300 along Espira's old route looking for anything of value. While later accounts specifically mention that El Dorado was his main goal, von Hutten was looking for the same things that every conquest-era explorer sought: valuable metals and minerals, populated cities, and fertile soil. Depending on the geographic location and period of the conquest, El Dorado was a gold-ornamented chieftain, a city of riches, or some other physical manifestation of wealth in gold. There is little evidence to suggest that the company actively sought this form of treasure, although they did seek gold on their multiple entradas. The Welser occupation, however, coincided with a moment when three separate versions of the legend placed western Venezuela as the location of the fortune.[46] This led many to seek gold and glory in the interior, no matter the cost. In a 1540 letter to his brother, von Hutten wrote that the search for gold in Venezuela might lead to conflicts not only with the indigenous populations but also with fellow Europeans who were seeking it for themselves. His entrada was a disaster, and Spanish usurpers murdered him south of Coro in 1546.[47]

Von Hutten was never appointed governor of Venezuela, but he was the last south German official to hold power in the province. By 1540 the region could barely support the few hundred men and slaves who struggled just to maintain a simple camp to which entradas could return. After the death of von Hutten, the few remaining settlers reorganized in towns under new leadership, hoping their own entradas might prove successful.

Heavy Investments and Few Returns

Without successful entradas, settlers were less likely to opt for Venezuela as a colonial destination. The company, particularly with the efforts of Espira and von Hutten after 1538, continued to find recruits in Santo Domingo for expeditions into the interior of Venezuela. Perhaps the El

Dorado legend was more pervasive in the minds of sixteenth-century conquistadors than scholars have realized. Another attraction was the reputation of the Welser Company, still recognized as a significant financial power in both the New World and Europe.

Welser entradas must have been preferable to farming or some other occupation in the Caribbean. Unlike Peru, New Granada, or New Spain, Welser Venezuela did not have access to encomienda grants. Work had to be performed by the Europeans or their slaves. Paying for the labor needed to keep Coro and the rest of the Venezuela province solvent required more gold and silver. Entradas were undertaken to find those things.

The success of an entrada was based on what Europeans discovered or acquired from the interior. In the late 1530s it became clear that gold and silver were not going to be easily found. A waterway that might have connected Coro to the riches of Peru did not exist either. After 1538 the company could only claim true political and financial control of Venezuela for another eight years. After the death of von Hutten, the company made only token attempts to continue the development of the province. They abandoned their claim and nullified the contract by 1556. The problems of Venezuela were neither political nor social, although the last decade of Welser involvement in the province certainly appeared so in later lawsuits and testimonies. In multiple depositions given after the death of von Hutten, Iberian settlers and conquistadors railed against Welser leadership for not being Spanish and for harboring Protestant views.[48]

The risks and investments taken by the company in the early part of the century were almost always successful or they laid the groundwork for expanding personal and commercial networks. Unable to fully replicate this model in the Americas, the administrators of Welser Venezuela did what they could to maintain the settlement. Colonists drifted in and out of the province, hoping to find the same riches and wealth that the Welsers sought so desperately. Without direction and regular oversight, Welser officials repeated the same ineffective efforts because they lacked the training or direction to do otherwise. The reality was that the company had expanded too quickly, over great distances, without maintaining the levels of command and control that made them a major economic power in the first place.

Notes

ABBREVIATIONS

AGI	Archivo General de Indias (Seville, Spain)
-Cttn	Casa de la Contratación
-IG	Gobierno: Indiferente General
-Just	Justicia
-Panama	Gobierno: Audiencia de Panamá
-Patr	Patronato Real
-SD	Gobierno: Audiencia de Santo Domingo

1. While Spanish speakers used the word *Alemanes* to describe German-speaking peoples in the sixteenth century, there is no evidence that they used the term to mean a state or nation of Germans. German conquistadors and merchants described themselves by using the word *Cristianos* in documents to signify that they were unified with other Europeans during the conquest era. This chapter will use the term *Germans* to mean German speakers, understanding that the term is imprecise.
2. Häberlein, *The Fuggers*, 50–52.
3. Grosshaupt, "Commercial Relations," 359–70, 376–78.
4. Häberlein, *The Fuggers*, 52–54.
5. In many of the documents, Charles is referred to as Charles I, Charles V, or simply *el rey*. This chapter uses Charles V for simplicity.
6. Brady, "The Rise of Merchant Empires," 144–46. For clarity and consistency, this chapter uses the ducat (*ducado*) as the primary unit of currency, even though the *Casa de Contratación* in Seville used the *maravedí* as the currency of record. The conversion is one ducat for every 375 maravedís.
7. Ehrenberg, *Capital and Finance*, 75–76; Strieder, *Jacob Fugger*, 100.
8. Häberlein, *The Fuggers*, 77–79.
9. Carande, *Carlos V y sus banqueros*, 386–415, 426–27; Tracy, *Emperor Charles V, Impresario of War*, 101.
10. AGI-IG 1962, L.6, fol. 128r, "Tasación y venta de libro a indios de Michoacán" (22 September 1528); AGI-IG 1962, L.5, fols. 108r–108v, "Orden de impressión de libro" (2 March 1537).
11. Johnson, *German Discovery*, 97.
12. AGI-IG 421, L.11, fols. 11r–11v (4 June 1526).
13. AGI-IG 421, L.11, fols. 140v–141r. The license does not name the agents, but Alfinger might have been one of them as he appears on a list of persons traveling to the New World in 1526.
14. Otte, *Von Bankiers*, 119–21; Friede, *Los Welser*, 91.

15. Otte, *Von Bankiers*, 123–25. Nüremberg remained in Seville, managing his commercial operation from one location. His trade network would soon span four continents.
16. Despite some coastal settlements on the mainland, most conquistadors and royal officials were ignorant of the true size of the continent. Some maps produced during the period showed South America as a series of islands. Welser-led entradas contributed to European geographical education.
17. AGI-Patr 27, R.3 (1526), fols. 1r–17v; AGI-Patr 27, R.7 (27 March 1528), fols. 1r–6v; AGI-Panama 234, L.3, fols. 84r–88r.
18. AGI-Patr 27, R.3, fols. 2r–3r.
19. AGI-Patr 27, R.3, fol. 3r.
20. AGI-Patr 27, R.3, fols. 3r–5r. During the early colonial period, an adelantado was a royal administrative official in a frontier area. While their duties varied according to time and place, adelantados usually led or organized conquest expeditions called entradas.
21. AGI-Patr 27, R.3, fols. 5v–6v. The lack of encomiendas in Venezuela may have been the result of Bartolomé de Las Casas lobbying the Spanish crown. To have men from the heart of Protestant Europe settle in the territory that he attempted to establish as an indigenous colony free of slavery and encomiendas only a decade earlier must have been troublesome. While other New World territories could have encomiendas, the institution was forbidden in Venezuela in these years.
22. AGI-Patr 27, R.3, fols. 2r–2v.
23. AGI-Patr 28, R.52 (1531), fol. 1r.
24. AGI-Patr 28, R.52, fols. 1v–3r; Häberlein, *The Fuggers*, 80.
25. AGI-IG 419, L.7, fols. 78r–78v (18 August 1518); Otte, *Von Bankiers*, 129–31. See also chapter 7 of this volume.
26. Thomas, *Slave Trade*, 100–101.
27. AGI-IG 421, L.12 (12 Feb 1528), fols. 296r–297r; Otte, *Von Bankiers*, 133.
28. Thomas, *The Golden Empire*, 151.
29. Otte, *Von Bankiers*, 135–38. For a detailed account of the company's slave trading problems in the 1530s, see Otte's chapter, "Die Welser in Santo Domingo."
30. AGI-Patr 193, R.25 (1538), fol. 1v. For additional information on the indigenous slave trade in the Caribbean, see Erin Stone's chapter in this collection.
31. Oviedo y Baños, *Conquest and Settlement*, 15; Moses, *Spanish Dependencies*, 60; Haring, *Trade and Navigation*, 99; Arciniegas, *Germans in the Conquest*, 66–67.
32. Friede, "Mineros Alemanes," 101.
33. Haring, *Spanish Empire*, 262; Wagner, "Early Silver Mining," 58–59.
34. AGI-Just 992, N.4, pza. 2 (1548), fols. 7r–7v; Paul, *Mining Lore*, 57–58.
35. Friede, "Mineros Alemanes," 100–101; Koch, "Sächsische Bergleute," 113–14. Friede's claim of eighty miners is not supported by firm documentation.

Koch claims fifty-five miners came via the Welser Company, using court records made in Leipzig by some of the miners who returned from the Americas. Available AGI documents list fifty-three miners.

36. Oviedo y Baños, *Conquest and Settlement*, 15; Brown, *A History of Mining*, 5–14, 30; Elliot, *Empires*, 20–21.
37. Friede, "Carta de 1535," 409. "Que aquí todos soportamos una tierra muy caliente y para nuestra nación, como ya antes te había escrito desde Santo Domingo, muy malsana" (author's English translation).
38. Friede, "Mineros Alemanes," 102.
39. Friede, "Mineros Alemanes," 102–4; Koch, *Sächsische Bergleute*, 117–18.
40. AGI-Just 992, N.3, R.1 (13 July 1549), fol. 105v.
41. Friede, "Catálogo de Pasajeros," 333–38.
42. AGI-Just 990, N.2, 12a (30 June 1530), fols. 1r–31v; Simmer, *Gold und Sklaven*, 110–15.
43. AGI-SD 206, r.1, n.4 (6 October 1533), fols. 33v–37r.
44. Von Hutten, *Das Gold*, 110–25.
45. Friede, *Los Welser*, 298–309. For an engaging study of Federmann's entrada and the men who accompanied him, see Avellaneda Navas, *Los compañeros de Féderman*.
46. Friede, "Geographical Ideas," 151–54. Friede notes that one version of El Dorado, as understood by Alfinger, relates to a group of wealthy Indian nations such as the Chibcha and Muisca west of Coro. A second version identified several indigenous groups living near the Meta River as being unusually rich. These groups, Friede points out, traded with the Muisca. Finally, a legend born in Santo Domingo claimed that immense wealth could be found south of the Caribbean islands between Peru and Rio de la Plata. Avellaneda Navas, *Conquerors*, 20; Thomas, *The Golden Empire*, 167, 249, 379, 409. See also Von Hagen, *The Golden Man*; Hemming, *Search for El Dorado*; Ramos Pérez, *El mito de El Dorado*.
47. Von Hutten, *Das Gold*, 138–39; Friede, *Los Welser*, 397–400.
48. AGI-Just 65, "Residencia por el licenciado Juan Pérez de Tolosa" (1545).

Bibliography

ARCHIVES

Archivo General de Indias (Seville, Spain).

PUBLISHED WORKS

Arciniegas, Germán. *Germans in the Conquest of America: A Sixteenth-Century Venture*. Translated by Angel Flores. New York: Macmillan, 1943.

Avellaneda Navas, José Ignacio. *Los compañeros de Féderman: Cofundadores de Santa Fé de Bogotá.* Bogotá: Academia de Historia de Bogotá, 1990.

———. *The Conquerors of the New Kingdom of Granada.* Albuquerque: University of New Mexico Press, 1995.

Brady, Thomas A., Jr. "The Rise of the Merchant Empires, 1400–1700: A European Counterpoint." In *The Political Economy of Merchant Empires: State Power and World Trade, 1350–1750*, edited by James D. Tracy, 117–60. Cambridge: Cambridge University Press, 1991.

Brown, Kendall W. *A History of Mining in Latin America: From the Colonial Era to the Present.* Albuquerque: University of New Mexico Press, 2012.

Carande, Ramón. *Carlos V y sus banqueros.* Barcelona: Editorial Critica, 2000.

Ehrenberg, Richard. *Capital and Finance in the Age of the Renaissance.* Translated by H. M. Lucas. New York: Harcourt, Brace, 1928.

Elliott, John H. *Empires of the Atlantic World.* New Haven: Yale University Press, 2006.

Friede, Juan. "Carta de 1535." In *Descubrimiento y Conquista de Venezuela*, edited by Joaquín Gabaldón Márquez, 409. Caracas: Academia Nacional de la Historia, 1988.

———. "The Catálogo de Pasajeros and Spanish Emigration to America to 1550." *Hispanic American Historical Review* 31, no. 2 (May 1951): 333–48.

———. "Geographical Ideas and the Conquest of Venezuela." *Americas* 16, no. 2 (October 1959): 145–59.

———. "La introducción de mineros alemanes en America por la compañia Welser de Augsburgo." *Revista de Historia de América* 51 (June 1961): 99–104.

———. *Los Welser en la conquista de Venezuela.* Caracas: Ediciones EDIME, 1961.

Grosshaupt, Walter. "Commercial Relations between Portugal and the Merchants of Augsburg and Nuremberg." In *La Decouverte, Le Portugal et L'Europe*, edited by Jean Aubin, 359–70. Paris: Foundation Calouste Gulbenkian, 1990.

Guitar, Lynne A. "Boiling It Down: Slavery on the First Commercial Sugarcane Ingenios in the Americas (Hispaniola, 1530–45)." In *Slaves, Subjects, and Subversives: Blacks in Colonial Latin America*, edited by Jane G. Landers and Barry M. Robinson, 39–82. Albuquerque: University of New Mexico Press, 2006.

Häberlein, Mark. *The Fuggers of Augsburg: Pursuing Wealth and Honor in Renaissance Germany.* Charlottesville: University of Virginia Press, 2012.

Haring, C. H. *The Spanish Empire in America.* New York: Oxford University Press, 1947.

———. *Trade and Navigation between Spain and the Indies in the Time of the Hapsburgs.* Gloucester: P. Smith, 1964.

Hemming, John. *The Search for El Dorado*. London: Michael Joseph, 1978.
Hutten, Philipp von. *Das Gold der Neuen Welt: die Papiere des Welser-Konquistadors und Generalkapitäns von Venezuela*, edited by Eberhard Schmitt and Friedrich Karl von Hutten. Hildburghausen: Verlag Frankenschwelle, 1996.
Johnson, Christine R. *The German Discovery of the World*. Charlottesville: University of Virginia Press, 2009.
Koch, Herbert. "Sächsische Bergleute in Venezuela anno 1559." *Südamerika* 2, no. 6 (September/October 1955): 112–18.
Lockhart, James. *The Men of Cajamarca: A Social and Biographical Study of the First Conquerors of Peru*. Austin: University of Texas Press, 1972.
Mellafe, Rolando. *Negro Slavery in Latin America*. Berkeley: University of California Press, 1975.
Moses, Bernard. *The Spanish Dependencies in South America*. New York: Harper, 1914.
Otte, Enrique. *Von Bankiers und Kaufleuten, Räten, Reedern und Piraten, Hintermännern und Strohmännern*. Stuttgart: Franz Steiner Verlag, 2004.
Oviedo y Baños, José. *The Conquest and Settlement of Venezuela*. Translated by Jeannette Johnson Varner. Berkeley: University of California Press, 1987.
Paul, Wolfgang. *Mining Lore*. Portland: Morris Printing, 1970.
Ramos Pérez, Demetrio. *El mito de El Dorado*. Madrid: Ediciones Istmo, 1988.
Simmer, Götz. *Gold und Sklaven: die Provinz Venezuela während der Welser-Verwaltung (1528–1556)*. Berlin: Wissenschaft und Technik, 2000.
Strieder, Jacob. *Jacob Fugger the Rich*. Translated by Mildred L. Hartsough. New York: Archon Books, 1966.
Thomas, Hugh. *The Golden Empire: Spain, Charles V, and the Creation of America*. New York: Random House, 2010.
———. *The Slave Trade: The Story of the Atlantic Slave Trade, 1440–1870*. New York: Simon & Schuster, 1999.
Tracy, James D. *Emperor Charles V, Impresario of War: Campaign Strategy, International Finance, and Domestic Politics*. New York: Cambridge University Press, 2002.
Von Hagen, Victor W. *The Golden Man: A Quest for El Dorado*. London: Book Club Associates, 1974.
Wagner, Henry R. "Early Silver Mining in New Spain." *Revista de Historia de América* 14 (June 1942): 49–71.

12

The Azorean Connection

Trajectories of Slaving, Piracy, and Trade in the Early Atlantic

GABRIEL DE AVILEZ ROCHA

In the age of sail, vessels making transatlantic treks out of the Spanish Caribbean tended to follow the winds and currents of the Gulf Stream that brought them east to the Azores, a Portuguese archipelago of nine islands some 1,600 kilometers off the Iberian coast.[1] While Atlantic historians have long noted the important position of the Azores as sites of convergence for global maritime trade routes in the early modern era, the unique ways in which the Caribbean became linked to the archipelago over the sixteenth century have received little sustained scrutiny to date.[2] Foregrounding how the great majority of people and goods leaving the Caribbean passed at least temporarily through the Azores allows us to better ascertain how the tangible aftershocks of the contact era in the Americas filtered eastward across maritime space.[3] An Azorean connection, it becomes clear, decisively influenced and extended the Caribbean's reach across the Atlantic.

In the decades following 1492, the pattern of arrivals to the Americas from Europe and Africa, together with departures from the Caribbean to the Azores and beyond, created a core Atlantic circuit.[4] As early as Christopher Columbus's first Caribbean voyage, mariners, merchants, and officials viewed a stop in the Azores ahead of the final leg of their eastbound voyages as desirable and in many cases necessary, much as they understood stops in the Canaries and Cape Verde on westward trips as matters of course. While a range of interactions brought the Caribbean into continuing contact with the Azores over the long sixteenth century, this chapter focuses on maritime ventures that ensued from Iberian-led campaigns of reconnaissance, trade, plunder, and human trafficking. It traces how from the earliest decades of the sixteenth century many of the voluntary itinerants who plied the northern edges of the Sargasso Sea due east—be they French corsairs, Spanish merchants, or Portuguese crown agents—used the Azores as an Atlantic base for rerouting commodities of Caribbean provenance, as well as persons in bondage, in directions that did not always include the customs houses of Seville and Lisbon. Forced migrants, including Amerindians transported by slavers out of the Greater Caribbean in the early sixteenth century, experienced Azorean stopovers as periods of potential reorientation in their prolonged trajectories of dispossession.

By the sixteenth century's closing decades, eastbound voyages no longer brought native Caribbean or South American captives to the Azores in the same numbers or with the same frequency as they had in previous decades. The archipelago still fulfilled many of its long-standing functions in the Atlantic circuit but in a new context determined to a large extent by rival European imperial projects. While scholars have fruitfully examined how French, English, and other northern Europeans infiltrated the Spanish Caribbean in the hope of establishing more permanent territorial and economic footholds in the late sixteenth and early seventeenth centuries, much less attention has been given to contemporaneous and linked developments in the Azores in the 1580s and 1590s that helped inaugurate a new phase of the Caribbean's enduring connection to the archipelago and other corners of the Atlantic world.

Early Connections: The Provisioning Loophole

On the morning of February 19, 1493, three inhabitants of the Azorean island of Santa Maria sold fresh bread and chickens to crew members aboard the *Niña*, a recently arrived Spanish vessel.[5] The vendors likely learned that the caravel had left from Palos the previous summer as part of a crown-supported fleet under the command of Christopher Columbus.[6] Only a few months earlier, the crew had made initial contact with the native inhabitants of the Caribbean basin. Now on its journey back to Iberia, the *Niña* carried Columbus himself, several dozen Spanish mariners, and at least ten Taíno individuals, most if not all of whom were likely taken under coercion from various islands during the course of the expedition.[7]

At the time of the Columbian voyage, the Azores had been actively settled by a diverse population of Europeans and Atlantic Africans for more than sixty years.[8] Fifteenth-century Azoreans lived from extensive agro-pastoral production and trade with Europe, North Africa, and other Atlantic archipelagos.[9] As subjects of the Portuguese crown, islanders such as the bread and poultry vendors on Santa Maria continued to foster trade relations between the archipelago and Euro-African sea lanes in the early sixteenth century at the same time that they began to traffic in people and goods hailing from the Caribbean.

In the wake of Columbus's voyage, mariners departing the Caribbean regularly sought an Azorean connection on their eastward treks. What quickly became a standard trajectory invited scrutiny by Spanish and Portuguese officials, who rightly perceived that the islands presented a plethora of opportunities for contraband trade in the spoils of the Indies. On the surface Iberian mariners and merchants with backing from the crown and private investors seemed to flout the interests of their financiers when steering their vessels to the Azores, many of their ships loaded with Amerindian captives and the material returns of plundering ventures. One royal license drafted in 1500 for an expedition led by Alonso Vélez de Mendoza stipulated that upon departing from the Caribbean, the ships would sail directly to Seville in order to pay the requisite taxes to the crown, including a 25 percent levy on all Amerindians "who in these kingdoms [of Spain] are known and reputed as slaves."[10] Before casting off from Andalusia, Vélez was reminded to avoid making landfall on any of the Portuguese king's possessions, a category under which the Azores clearly fell.[11]

But Vélez's instructions, like those for his contemporaries and successors, also stipulated that it was sometimes necessary to "salvage the ship, its persons, and the merchandise" in foreign domains.[12] In such circumstances, the official directive stated that ships stopping in lands claimed by other sovereigns were restricted to trading for necessary victuals, maintaining the majority of the crew onboard, and leaving within a day or two at most.[13] In practice, however, such expectations were perceived as eminently flexible. Mariners testifying before Casa de la Contratación officials in 1514 spoke openly of stopping in Cape Verde, a Portuguese possession, on outbound voyages.[14] Similar norms applied to the Azores. One summer in the 1510s, for instance, Castilian royal officers asked their Portuguese counterparts to send support for a fleet of five Spanish vessels that had momentarily docked in Angra, the principal harbor on the Azorean island of Terceira, while "coming from the Antilles with gold."[15] The mariners and merchants pausing in the Azores could dutifully await reinforcements but may also have welcomed opportunities to circumvent or ignore official directives that were themselves malleable.

In the case of Vélez's expedition of 1500–1501, the fleet first stopped in the Canaries and Cape Verde Islands before crossing over to the South American coast, turning south at the Cape of Santo Agostinho away from the Caribbean, contrary to original plans. The mariners disembarked on Tupinambá lands somewhere between present-day Pernambuco and Bahia. In the clashes that ensued, Vélez's crew took at least four people captive, including two children, a twenty-year-old woman, and a twenty-five-year-old man who were subsequently sold into bondage in Seville.[16] As suggested by the trajectory of Columbus's first voyage and as becomes clearer with evidence from later crossings, we can entertain the possibility that Vélez's expedition stopped in the Azores on its eastbound trek, perhaps selling Tupinambá captives on the archipelago before returning to Iberia.[17]

Certainly the Atlantic thoroughfares linking the Caribbean and the Azores drew increasing maritime traffic in the decades after Vélez's voyage. Forced migrants experienced the Azorean connection in the midst of facing the physical and socioemotional struggles of exile. Meanwhile Azorean merchants looking to trade their way into profits from ventures to the Americas had entirely different avenues of action at their disposal that ranged from licit to illicit trade. For most, however, arriving on the archipelago offered the possibility for a radical reorientation of their voyages, whether or not they had a hand in deciding what this change of direction would be.

Alonso del Algava, who sailed to the Caribbean in 1521 aboard the *Madalena*, found the Azores to be a particularly mercurial threshold. The *Madalena* enjoyed the backing of 130 investors from Andalusia, Extremadura, and Genoa when it left Seville. Spending only weeks in

Puerto Rico and Santo Domingo, Algava and the merchants who traveled on the *Madalena* lost no time gathering large quantities of sugar, leather, gold, and pearls. They left Santo Domingo for Andalusia in early 1522.[18] Before arriving in Iberia, however, Algava and his crew dropped anchor outside of Angra on the Azorean island of Terceira.

Their arrival in the Azores came at a moment when Angra was coming into its own as a major entrepôt for Caribbean voyages.[19] On Terceira Algava and other passengers on the *Madalena* found ample opportunity to acquire victuals. They engaged in other dealings as well. Three local businessmen—Sebastião Rodrigues, Francisco Rodrigues, and Simão Dias—obtained spots on the vessel despite standing crown directives that ships returning from the Caribbean not take on any additional passengers. But such formalities were conveniently ignored when Azorean merchants had considerable funds at their disposal. Their main objective in boarding the *Madalena*, in the words of a witness, was to pursue "matters of business" both onboard and in Seville.[20]

Events quickly diverted the *Madalena* from its intended course. After departing from Terceira, Algava's ship was approached by a corsair fleet captained by the Norman privateer Jean Fain.[21] Algava, the Azorean merchants, and others aboard soon found Fain's crew storming their vessel amid artillery fire. In the melee, several crewmembers of the *Madalena* perished, as Fain's men seized the Andalusian ship and its Caribbean cargo.[22] Soon after the privateers captured the *Madalena*, however, they came upon a Portuguese royal armada deployed to patrol the waters between the Azores and Iberia. After a skirmish, the Portuguese apprehended Fain's crew and vessels and brought them to Lisbon alongside the surviving passengers of the *Madalena*. While Fain awaited trial before the crown as a corsair, officials in Lisbon held the ship and its cargo. It would not be long before Charles V's advisers entreated Portuguese officials to relinquish the cargo.[23]

An avalanche of lawsuits soon brought Andalusian and Genoese investors to Lisbon to sue the incarcerated French mariners and their sponsors for losses and damages. Other lawsuits in Seville would pit the expedition's financiers against one another for the remainder of the cargo, with accusations flying that much of the better quality merchandise had been sold off to the highest bidder while in Lisbon. Several years later the Azorean merchants who joined the venture in Angra filed a suit before Castilian authorities for what they claimed to be their portion of the returns as well.[24] The ranks of the expedition's stakeholders swelled and shifted in ways that were profoundly marked by its passage from the Caribbean to the Azores. As we will see, similar circumstances affected a great number of slaving and contraband voyages that sailed east across the Atlantic in the mid-sixteenth century.

Slaving and Smuggling along the Caribbean-Azores Route

Ethnohistorians of the Caribbean and Mesoamerica in recent decades have productively reframed the European invasions of the Americas as an episodic series of incursions intended to cement alliances, establish tributary relations, and acquire captives, provisions, and valuables for their participants.[25] As noted in the previous chapter, sixteenth-century Iberians called such undertakings *entradas* (entries), and these more often than not relied on substantial native backing and grappled with the complex landscapes of indigenous geopolitics. In 1536 the Spanish nobleman Alonso de Lugo led one such entrada into the lands of the Tairona people (today part of eastern Colombia).[26] After the conclusion of a slaving and plunder campaign that meandered across a region known to the Iberians as the Sierra Nevada, Lugo and a small retinue of accomplices left the colonial enclave of Santa Marta on a caravel carrying several captives and the bulk of the expedition's plunder, including a significant quantity of precious metals taken from Native American burial sites.[27]

Lugo's first stop was the port of Santiago, Cuba, where he found an ally in the colonial official Gonzalo de Guzmán. Four years before Lugo's arrival, Guzmán had been temporarily stripped of his office following a slew of accusations by his many professed foes. A year prior to Lugo's arrival, however, Guzmán had been reinstated as the island's lieutenant governor.[28] From his prominent position, and using family connections in the crown's minting operations, Guzmán handed Lugo licenses allowing him to leave the Caribbean without having to travel to Seville.[29] Instead Lugo would head to Tenerife Island in the Canaries, but not without first paying a visit to Terceira Island in the Azores.[30]

During their time on Terceira, Lugo and his companions spent a portion of the appropriated gold to purchase a new caravel. A witness later testified that Lugo and his companions sold at least two or three Taironas—their identities opaque in the records—into slavery in the Azores.[31] To be sure, the Taironas brought by Lugo were not the only people sold into bondage in the Azores. Using parish and notarial records, Azorean historians have noted the proportionally small but not insignificant population of enslaved people on Terceira island in the sixteenth century.[32] Uncovering that a high percentage of Angra's merchants claimed to own more slaves, on average, than other slaveholders on the island, Maria Hermínia Morais Mesquita hypothesizes that a significant market in the resale of captives may have existed in Angra specifically and the Azores more generally.[33] Lugo's sale of the Taironas—hitherto unrecognized in scholarship on this expedition—provides us with a case in point.

Whether the Tairona people sold as slaves in Angra stayed in the Azores is more difficult to ascertain. While some individuals forcibly brought to the archipelago were likely taken elsewhere by other itinerant slave traders, many remained on the islands, where their children were born into slavery. This was the case with an African-descended woman by the name of Isabel, identified in Azorean sacramental records as a "Black slave" (*escrava preta*) living in the western Terceira parish of Santa Bárbara in the mid-sixteenth century.[34] It is unclear how long Isabel lived in the Azores before 1553, when she gave birth on Terceira to a son baptized António. An adult by the 1570s, António gained manumission, purchased a series of agricultural plots where he grew wheat, and made a home on leased property in the town of his birth. For half a decade prior to his death in 1584, he shared the dwelling with a childhood acquaintance who owed him several years' worth of back rent.[35]

António's testament demonstrates that although the Azores' demographic balance differed from those of sixteenth-century Spanish Caribbean settlements that had large African and African-descended majorities, the Azores nevertheless constituted Atlantic locales in which the varied expressions of slavery and manumission were central to the lives of people in and out of bondage and the communities of which they were a part. His experience and that of his mother, along with those of other enslaved or freed inhabitants of the Azores, highlight how slaving ventures touching on the archipelago potentially interfaced with wider social horizons of slavery and manumission, whether or not they brought captives from the Caribbean who would remain in the Portuguese islands.

Conforming to standard practice noted by scholars studying other early modern Atlantic thoroughfares through the Canaries and Cape Verde Islands, slaving ventures pausing on the Azores routinely engaged in contraband and licit trade in the course of the same voyage.[36] Crown officials apprised of prevailing commercial patterns accordingly grouped the Azores in the same category as other major Atlantic hubs of slave trafficking for purposes of fiscal oversight.[37] An arrangement between the Portuguese crown and tax collectors in the Azores, Cape Verde, and São Tomé in the 1520s and 1530s included references to revenues specifically from "slaves sold in the Azores," showing that slave merchants at that time did not necessarily operate clandestinely when they came to the Azores.[38] Portuguese crown officials frequently received notice that this was the case. Writing to a royal audience in the mid-sixteenth century, the prominent Angra-based merchant Sebastião Muniz observed that Azoreans often sought to exchange "slaves and woad and leather and sugar and other merchandise on this land" with visiting traders.[39] Muniz and many of his contemporaries likely noted that the volume and provenance of Amerindian captives brought to the islands changed according to the directions and repercussions of Spanish entradas in the Greater Caribbean and the general state of affairs of the Iberian colonial presence in the Americas.

Together with evidence that slave trading in the Azores was oriented toward both local markets and broader Atlantic networks, the testimony affirming that Lugo sold Taironas in the Azores appears well founded. Details of the lives of Isabel and Antonio, meanwhile, afford a glimpse of how later sixteenth-century Azorean society included individuals who experienced diverse conditions of bondage and sometimes manumission.[40] Equally important, the Lugo expedition and its context illustrate that slaving and contraband played out in the Azores in ways that were synchronous with the rhythms of Iberian colonization efforts in the circum-Caribbean during the first half of the sixteenth century.

The presence of enslaved and free people of color in the Azores, in combination with the frequency with which Azorean towns served as ports of call for ships making the voyage between the Caribbean and Iberia, places the arrival of Amerindian captives to slave markets in Portugal and Andalusia in a new light. In 1530, for instance, several vessels brought captives to Lisbon who were sold as "slaves from the Antilles." Tax rolls show that Iberian slavers and buyers in Portugal haggled over the prices of sixteen Amerindians sold into bondage between February and August.[41] Given the standard trajectories of transatlantic voyages departing from the Caribbean, it is not unlikely that at least some of these enslaved children, adolescents, and adults came to Portugal by way of the Azores. It also may have been the case that additional captives taken from the Caribbean were sold in Azorean slave markets such as Angra along the way. Later in the century the pace of eastbound slaving voyages from the Caribbean appears to have slackened, as the role of the Azores shifted in a changing Atlantic geopolitical order.

Itineraries of Maritime Banditry in the Later Sixteenth Century

At midcentury, pilots like Nicolás Álvarez admitted matter-of-factly to Santo Domingo authorities that ships departing the Caribbean on an eastward path "all touch on the islands of the Azores."[42] Iberian mariners likewise treated the routes taken by ships through the nine-island archipelago as a navigational commonplace.[43] These maritime traffic patterns were not lost on privateers, corsairs, and merchant mariners hailing from northern Europe. Much to the contrary, French and English sailors active between the Caribbean and the Azores in the late sixteenth century took advantage of long-standing connections between Spanish America and the Portuguese islands. Yet they also played a part in a broader shift in the function of the Caribbean within the newly consolidating Ibero-American colonial order and in the Atlantic writ large. Signaling a new era in the Azorean connection, the pace of voyages that brought Amerindian captives from the Caribbean to Europe after the 1550s likely decreased significantly, as mariners, merchants, and elites from northern Europe searched for new trading and plunder opportunities in Atlantic circuits.[44]

Fearful of corsair attacks, the Iberian crowns had organized regular convoys to await ships returning from the Caribbean in the Azores since the days of Algava. In a royal edict of 1522 the Castilian crown pushed for resources against "the French and any other corsairs" with designs on Iberian vessels.[45] Beginning in 1527, the Portuguese crown appointed a special official known as the *provedor das armadas*, based in Angra, to supply armada fleets patrolling Azorean waters, citing similar reasons.[46] A letter written by Angra's city officials to the Portuguese crown in 1553 illuminates the continued habitual presence of French corsairs in the Azores in the mid-sixteenth century:

> On September 20th, a French *armada* arrived in these islands, according to a man who informed us that he was taken by the French near Santa Maria Island in a small boat that they found off the coast. He escaped off of São Jorge Island while on a small vessel [*pataxa*] that the French had sent to find provisions. We know that they came with six large vessels and three small *pataxas*, with much artillery and many soldiers, and that they were searching for . . . ships from Peru, and they went towards Corvo Island where the Castilian *armada* was also heading. We presume that their paths crossed there.[47]

Just as northern European "interlopers" became familiar with locations in the Caribbean where they could conduct trade and diplomacy with Caribs and maroon communities, mariners from France were no strangers to the range of avenues for commerce and plunder that could be found in the Azores. Forced to haggle for victuals on São Jorge Island, the Portuguese informant signaled that French seafarers may have periodically attacked ships near the Azores and settlements on the archipelago, but they also sought basic goods and knew where to look for them. Sometimes the aims of plunder and provisioning were met together. In one instance in the 1570s, French mariners negotiated with residents of Santa Maria for fifty cows, twenty pigs, and thirty sheep in exchange for a pledge to refrain from burning the island's main port town.[48]

Tracking changes in how northern Europeans exploited the Azorean connection in the late sixteenth-century Atlantic shows that the increasing porosity of Iberian claims to exclusivity in the Caribbean, well studied by historians, was accompanied by a shift in the role played by the Portuguese archipelago as a pivot between the Americas and the Atlantic. Maritime enterprises continued to hew to the Caribbean-Azores route in the century's closing decades, but fledgling English and French schemes for colonial occupations in the Caribbean and other parts of the Americas at that time also aspired to establish a more permanent presence in the Azores.

A new set of geopolitical considerations overlaid on enduring maritime patterns thus factored into the plans of mariners aboard the *Tercelette*, a vessel that left the Norman port town of Le Havre in 1582 with the backing of a wealthy monseigneur from Bruges and a license from the French king. With Louis Marchant as its captain, the *Tercelette* brought textiles, shoes, and other merchandise to trade in the Caribbean.[49] Its voyage coincided with a popular insurrection on Terceira Island, where residents had rebuffed several attempts by the Spanish to conquer the Azorean hub of trade following Philip II's rise to the Portuguese throne.[50] Sensing an opportunity to challenge Spain in Atlantic trade, French crown allies actively abetted the resistance on Terceira, with an entire French fleet deployed to the Azores in 1582—and talk from the English of Francis Drake joining—in the same months that the *Tercelette* embarked on its Caribbean voyage.[51]

According to several witnesses, the Normans' first Caribbean destination was Trinidad, where they engaged in sustained trade with unidentified Native Americans for several months beginning in late June. By August the mariners and merchants aboard the French ship had headed to an area notoriously frequented by corsairs, maroons, and smugglers: the northern coast of Hispaniola. There they encountered a group of northern European smugglers, including an individual whom they called Captain Richard, who reported having recently arrived in the Caribbean on a ship laden with slaves from "Guinea." Richard's crew had lost their vessel to a Spanish patrol and were now left to fend for themselves on Hispaniola.[52] Promptly, Richard and some of his crewmembers joined the *Tercelette* and located the Spanish ships that had first attacked them, taking back their original vessel along with remaining cargo that included upwards of 1,500 leather hides and a significant quantity of ivory.[53] Making haste, the newly constituted fleet headed for France. Before reaching Europe, however, they followed the same route that had been plied by innumerable transatlantic expeditions before them, riding the potent oceanic current that would bring them to the Azores.

Nearing Terceira, Richard's ship, which at that point had a sizeable contingent of crew members from the *Tercelette*, was taken into custody by the Portuguese and French vessels supporting the insurrection against Philip II. Subjecting the crew to interrogations, Azorean notaries and French officials jointly inspected the ship's cargo in December 1582 and signed off on the affidavits together. At a moment when Terceira's uprising had been dealt a substantial blow with losses to the Spanish at the battle of Vila Franca, as well as in a storm in October that had crippled the Franco-Azorean fleet, news of even a minor success against the Spanish in the Caribbean would have been welcomed—as, no doubt, would a shipment of leather.

In the same years, English privateers including John Hawkins, Francis Drake, and the Earl of Cumberland periodically assaulted and invaded Azorean towns or intercepted ships in the vicinity of the archipelago, often in the course of expeditions to the Caribbean.[54] For Elizabethan privateers at war with Spain, stopping in the Azores remained a possibility when contemplating an eastward transatlantic journey. Following an unsuccessful attack on Salvador da Bahia in 1587, English privateers considered their options: should they head to the Caribbean or the Azores or should they cut their losses and return to London? One mariner opined that he "would rather goe derectlie for the Ilandes of Assurres then for the Ilandes of the Indyes," adding that "many good things might happen unto us" on the Portuguese archipelago, where the crew could "spend some time lockinge for purchace."[55] The English mariner's perception of the Azores as an arena for potentially profitable exchanges was not altogether of a different order than Lugo's assessment nearly half a century before, but rising northern European interest in Atlantic commerce and colonization had changed the geopolitical context significantly.

Advisers to Philip II in the 1580s had cause to identify the Caribbean and the Azores under the same strategic rubric: one confidante called for "the greatest care" to be taken "with the islands of Havana and the Azores, especially São Miguel and Terceira, because the English intend, if they can, to land and seize one of those three . . . to impede the Indies trade."[56] With the center of economic gravity in Spanish America shifting to Peru and Mexico, the Caribbean's increasingly critical role as a hub for the transshipment of goods from elsewhere in the Americas aligned the region even more, from the perspective of many Iberian officials, merchants, and mariners, with the Azores. For their northern European rivals, intercepting vessels passing through the Azores continued to be an attractive option, but if designs for acquiring territory in the Caribbean could be entertained, so could schemes to seize the Azores from Spain outright, perhaps even with the support of remaining pockets of resistance against Philip II.

Clashes among French, English, and Iberian actors were also accompanied by more habitual vectors of trade between northern Europe and the Azores.[57] French, English, and Dutch merchants continued to find favorable trading partners in the Azores even after the Spanish conquest of Terceira, despite occasionally drawing suspicion from crown officials.[58] In the late 1590s, for instance, crown administrators in Lisbon commissioned an investigation into "English merchants conducting business under the guise of being Scottish" in São Miguel Island. In a report filed in August 1598, a Portuguese official in Ponta Delgada noted that "there is no one in all of this island who wants to be against them [the English] because they are everyday merchants in this port."[59] The strategies of these English traders indicate that northern Europeans did not always plunder their way into profiting from the Caribbean-Azores trading route. The content of their trade reflected the material offshoots of local island production as well as more recent Iberian colonization efforts in the Americas. The chances that they encountered slave traffickers such as Lugo bringing captives from the Greater Caribbean to the Azores were likely slimmer than they would have been earlier in the century.

Conclusion

This chapter has outlined the contours of an under-scrutinized set of links between the Caribbean and the Azores over the sixteenth century. Heeding the human and material connections that brought the two regions together through patterns of trade (both licit and contraband), slaving, and piracy gives us a new vantage point on the early Atlantic. For one, it shows that the repercussions of European invasions in the contact period, which scholarship continues to nuance in productive ways for Caribbean and American contexts, can be aligned with other Atlantic sites such as the Azores. From this perspective, the impact of the European colonization of the Caribbean on the broader Atlantic world cannot be dissociated from the circuitous and contested ways in which captives, plunder, and wealth coursed through sea lanes and shaped the maritime and island spaces through which they moved.

For the coerced and voluntary migrants who followed eastward winds and currents out of the Caribbean, motives of necessity and profit made the Azores a critical juncture where their voyages could take unexpected directions. Historians' views of the contact-era Caribbean remain incomplete if they fail to take into account the relationship between dispossession and extraction in the Americas and the routes taken by people and goods across Atlantic space in directions that changed over time and often did not heed Iberian metropolitan interests. Recovering early Spanish Caribbean history's Azorean connection brings into focus a vision of pervasive interpenetrations between northern European and Iberian colonization efforts at a much earlier moment—with the late sixteenth century a culmination of earlier patterns—and with much greater geographic scope than is generally assumed.

Notes

ABBREVIATIONS

AGI		Archivo General de Indias (Seville, Spain)
	-Ctdra	Contaduría
	-Cttn	Casa de la Contratación
	-Guatemala	Gobierno: Audiencia de Guatemala
	-IG	Gobierno: Indiferente General
	-Just	Justicia
	-Patr	Patronato Real
	-SD	Gobierno: Audiencia de Santo Domingo
	-SF	Gobierno: Audiencia de Santa Fe

ANTT   Arquivo Nacional da Torre do Tombo (Lisbon, Portugal)
    -ADA   Arquivo D. António
    -NA   Núcleo Antigo
    -CC   Corpo Cronológico
BA   Biblioteca da Ajuda (Lisbon, Portugal)
BL   British Library (London, United Kingdom)
BPARAH   Biblioteca Pública e Arquivo Regional de Angra do Heroísmo (Angra do Heroísmo, Terceira Island, Portugal)
    -VII   Secção VII
    -AAAH   Auditoria Administrativa de Angra do Heroísmo
    -RP   Registos Paroquiais

1. The distance between the easternmost Azorean island of Santa Maria and Lisbon is 1,300 kilometers; Flores, the westernmost island of the archipelago, and Lisbon are separated by 1,900 kilometers. Meanwhile, 5,000 kilometers separate Havana and the Azores. Spatial measurements must be taken with a grain of salt, however, given that voyage duration was a function of prevailing wind patterns, oceanic currents, weather events, vessel conditions, and piloting decisions.
2. Mauro, *Le Portugal et l'Atlantique*, 21–27, 105–6; Chaunu, *Séville et l'Amérique*, 64–68, 70, 222–28; Godinho, *Os Descobrimentos*, 1:415–19 and 2:75–76; Matos, "Os Açores e a Carreira das Índias"; Lorenzo Sanz, *Comercio de España*, 2:127–29; Duncan, *Atlantic Islands*, 13–17, 120–21; João Marinho dos Santos, *Os Açores*, 400–406.
3. The Atlantic history paradigm has been criticized for privileging perspectives from "the caravels and galleons [that] sail[ed] west to the Americas." Bushnell, "Indigenous America," 191. Tracing eastward Atlantic trajectories offers one approach to begin to address this common and important line of critique.
4. Critical to reconstructing the spatial contours of an emergent Atlantic circuit is the work of paleoclimatologists and oceanographers who have outlined the range of climactic and hydrological patterns characterizing the North and South Atlantic Ocean systems during the Little Ice Age (1450–1700). See, e.g., Salgueiro et al., "North Atlantic Storminess."
5. Varela, *Cristóbal Colón*, 129.
6. Their cordial reception in the Azores would soon turn into a confrontation with local officials. See Catz, *Christopher Columbus and the Portuguese*, 37–48.
7. Soon upon landing in the Bahamas, Columbus noted in his journal that he intended to take a number of Native inhabitants to Spain. Varela, *Cristóbal Colón*, 31. For a careful analysis of the extant evidence for the numbers of

Taíno captives brought by Columbus's crew to Spain in 1493, see Cook, "¿Una primera epidemia?" 57–59.

8. The oldest extant document pertaining to the settlement of the Azores dates to the 1430s. *Monumenta Henricina*, 6:334. For a richly sourced treatment of the settlement era, see Gregório, *Terra e fortuna*.
9. Continental Portugal and Portuguese military garrisons in North Africa continued to receive shipments of wheat from the Azores in the early sixteenth century. See, e.g., ANTT-NA 714, fol. 2v.
10. AGI-Cttn 5873, N.1. Published with accompanying document in Ramos Pérez, *Audacia*, 431–39. Initial designs targeting the Caribbean were scrapped ahead of their departure in late 1500. For background on the Vélez expedition and contemporaneous ventures, see Ramos Pérez, *Audacia*, 109–30.
11. See licenses for Rodrigo de Bastidas (1500), Alonso de Ojeda (1501), and Vicente Yáñez Pinzón (1501) in Ramos Pérez, *Audacia*, 440–53.
12. AGI-Cttn 5873, N.1, fol. 2v.
13. Marinho dos Santos, *Os Açores*, 406–15.
14. AGI-Patr 12, N.2, R.23, fols. 60v, 62v, 66v. See also a 1512 petition by residents of Santiago Island (Cape Verde) referencing frequent arrivals of ships from Portugal, Castile, and the Atlantic islands. Brásio, ed., *Monumenta Missionaria Africana*, 2:54.
15. *Archivo dos Açores*, 3:27–28, 5:126.
16. Andalusian notarial records identify these individuals as natives of "Topia," and depositions by participants confirm that the ship hewed to the coast of Brazil, suggesting that the geographic marker recorded by Spanish scribes referred to "Tupi," the umbrella ethnonym for a variety of Native polities across northern and eastern South America. Vigneras, "Three Brothers Guerra," 627–34. Upon returning, Luis Guerra and Pero Ramirez, merchant participants in the Vélez expedition, resisted paying crown taxes on the slave sales in Seville. AGI-IG 418, L.1, fol. 114.
17. Vélez returned to Spain in the summer of 1501, during a time of year when wind patterns were most conducive to bringing sailing vessels from the Caribbean to the Azores. Marinho dos Santos, *Os Açores*, 359; Lorenzo Sanz, *Comercio de España*, 2:278–79; Vigneras, "Three Brothers Guerra," 630. For his role in the expedition, Vélez was awarded a grant to found a settlement on Hispaniola, where he died prior to 1512. AGI-IG 418, L.1, fols. 78r–79v.
18. AGI-Just 697, R.4, pza. 1, fol. 7r; AGI-Just 696, R.1, N.1, pza. 2. It is unclear whether the *Madalena* carried captives at any point in this voyage.
19. The town earned the designation of a *cidade* (city) from the court of João III in 1534. BPARAH-VII, L.1, fols. 5r–5v.
20. AGI-Just 697, N.4, pza. 1, fol. 10v: "*para cosas de mercadurías.*"

21. Fain expected substantial support from the Dieppois merchant Jean Ango and other prominent political figures in Rouen and the court of François I. Guénin, *Ango et ses Pilotes*, 67.
22. AGI-Just 696, R.1, N.1, pza. 2, fol. 3r.
23. AGI-IG 420, L.9, fols. 26v–28r.
24. AGI-Just 697, N.4. The latter lawsuit reveals that the ship stopped in the Azores and Terceira specifically. In other litigation, witnesses described the *Madalena*'s route from the Caribbean to Iberia without mentioning the Azores.
25. For an overview, see Restall, "New Conquest History."
26. The expedition's initial *capitulación* as well as alternative proposals from late 1534 are published in English translation in Francis, ed., *Invading Colombia*, 19–33.
27. For background on the Lugo expedition and its repercussions for the establishment of New Granada, see Avellaneda Navas, *La expedición de Alonso Luis de Lugo*.
28. Marrero, *Cuba*, 1:156–57, 234–39. On Guzmán see also Ida Altman's chapter in this volume.
29. In exchange, Lugo deposited a number of gold statuettes pillaged from Tairona burial sites in the Santiago mint where they were melted, forged into bars, and subjected to local taxes. It is also likely that Lugo and his companions exchanged a portion of their plunder for silver in Cuba. AGI-Just 693, fol. 15v.
30. AGI-Just 693, fols. 18v–29r. Guzmán appears to have known of Lugo's full itinerary, as corroborated by a December 1536 letter from treasurer Lope Hurtado in Santiago mentioning that Guzmán threatened a pilot with physical harm should he refuse to transport Lugo to the Azores (*le echaria de cabeça en el cepo*). *Colección de documentos ineditos . . . de la isla de Cuba*, 413–18. See also Marrero, *Cuba*, 2:17.
31. Another Tairona captive, known to the Spanish as Francisco, also passed through the Azores at that time, but continued on with Lugo and was ultimately sold to Diego Borges, a merchant in Tenerife. AGI-Just 693, fols. 45r, 107v–108v.
32. Gregório, "Escravos da Ilha Terceira."
33. Mesquita, "Escravos em Angra."
34. Azorean sacramental records lack ethnonyms or other identifying markers for people of color other than "black" or other phenotypical descriptors, providing a marked contrast with contemporary practices in Cuba as detailed by David Wheat in this volume.
35. BPARAH-AAAH, mç. 181, doc. 26. In his will, Rodrigues is identified as a black man who had previously "belonged" to Rodrigo Eanes (*Antonjo Roiz precto que foy de Rodrigueanes*). Parish records from Sete Ribeiras, on

Terceira Island, show an Antonio Preto born in June 1553 to "Isabel, black slave" (*Preta escrava*). Antonio's tenant in arrears in the 1580s, Diogo Balieiro (born 1551, also in Sete Ribeiras), was married to a servant of Amador Peres, whose widow, Madalena Peres, offered a bed in her home to the ailing Antonio when he had his will drafted. BPARAH-RP: Santa Bárbara, Baptismos, L.1, fols. 89r, 104r; Santa Bárbara, Casamentos, L.1, fol. 16v (img_0035). Digitized parish records for the Azores dating back to the sixteenth century are accessible at http://www.culturacores.azores.gov.pt/ig/registos/.

36. For treatments of the persistent synergy between the legal and contraband channels of the slave trade between Atlantic Africa and the Caribbean during this period, see Wheat, *Atlantic Africa*, 78, 109–12; Green, *The Rise*, 191–92, 208–30; and Marc Eagle's chapter in this volume.

37. Though the major archipelagos ringing the core Atlantic circuit formed part of different regional dynamics, they also fulfilled similar functions for east- and westbound transatlantic fleets in acting as waystations for merchant mariners who perhaps had other destinations in mind, but in the meantime were open to doing business. In this respect, it is less useful to typologically separate the Azores, Madeira, and the Canaries from Cape Verde and São Tomé, as suggested by scholars of the early modern Atlantic islands. See Vieira, *Portugal y las islas del Atlántico*, 100.

38. *Archivo dos Açores*, 5:142–44. A surviving account book held by royal customs officials from São Miguel for approximately three years between the late 1520s and early 1530s reveals a total of at least twenty slave sales involving tax payments to royal officials. *Archivo dos Açores*, 4:97–103. Native Brazilians sold as captives in the Azores in the mid- to late sixteenth century were exempt from taxes. Marinho dos Santos, *Os Açores*, 2:591.

39. *Archivo dos Açores*, 5:136–37.

40. For further evidence of slavery as experienced and resisted by Native peoples of the Canaries on the island of São Miguel in the 1510s, see ANTT-Gavetas 20, mç. 2, N.46.

41. ANTT-NA 548, fols. 5v, 36r–37r.

42. AGI-Just 103A, fol. 3333v. I am grateful to David Wheat for finding and sharing this source. Another merchant in the same years echoed this sentiment before Spanish authorities by stating that "passengers and Spaniards returning from Peru [*peruleros*] often remain in the Azores with a lot of money." Lorenzo Sanz, *Comercio de España*, 127.

43. The trajectory involved passing between the islands of Corvo and Flores toward the "*islas de abajo*" group—São Jorge, Graciosa, Pico, Faial, and Terceira. Marinho dos Santos, *Os Açores*, 450–51.

44. As is well known, the destructive array of conflicts following the Iberian invasions of the Caribbean in the early sixteenth century played an important role, alongside epidemics from diseases introduced by Europeans, in the demographic collapse of the Taíno and other Native populations of the Greater Caribbean. Amerindian captives would therefore have been more likely to be taken in entradas in the Greater Caribbean in the decades following 1492. Later in the sixteenth century, Iberians and other Europeans organized entradas that often also included slave raiding in other parts of the continent, but from these locations Amerindian captives were less likely to be transported to the Caribbean and once more to the Azores.
45. AGI-IG 420, L.8, fols. 327r–328v.
46. For a further treatment of Iberian protection fleets in the early sixteenth century, see Rocha, "Plunder and Profit." For background on the Canto family and its influential role in the provedoria das armadas, see Gregório, *Pero Anes do Canto*.
47. *Archivo dos Açores*, 5:368–69.
48. Marinho dos Santos, *Os Açores*, 302.
49. ANTT-ADA, mç. 1, doc. 96, fol. 2r.
50. For a near-contemporary written account, see de Herrera y Tordesillas, *Cinco libros*.
51. The most thorough treatment of the resistance on Terceira and its aftermath remains de Meneses, *Os Açores e o Domínio Filipino*.
52. It is unclear from witness testimonials whether or not the African captives were present on Hispaniola. Compare the testimonials from Robert, a ship officer on *La Tercelette*, who said that Richard was "bringing with him *negros* whom he had taken on the coast of Guinea" (*trazemdo comsiguo negros q tinha tomado na costa de guiné*) and Pedro Larón, a soldier, who noted that Richard "brought many *negros* whom he had sold" but also that of these captives, one African woman presently remained aboard (*trazia muytos negros q tinha vendido das qe hua neste navio em q hora vem*). ANTT-ADA, N.96, fols. 2v, 6r.
53. ANTT-ADA, N.96, fol. 4r.
54. See, for instance, "The Voyage of the Right Honorable George Erle of Cumberland to the Azores," in Hakluyt, *The Principal Navigations*.
55. BL, Landsdowne, vol. 100, N.3, fol. 45r.
56. Hume, *Calendar of Letters and State Papers*, 3:653 and 4:538–39. For references to English attacks on the Azores during this period, see Andrews, *Elizabethan Privateering*, 68, 72.
57. This dynamic, which merits further research in English and French archives, should qualify standard views that the British Empire "lacked the 'stepping-stones' into the Atlantic provided to the Portuguese and Spaniards" by the Atlantic islands. Black, *The British Seaborne Empire*, 25.

58. See, for instance, a letter from a merchant from Ponta Delgada named Gaspar Dias to Francis Walsingham in 1587 expressing hopes that the Spanish crown would confirm a "grant for English men to trade with us, as they have done heretofore." Lomas, *Calendar of State Papers, Foreign Series, Elizabeth* (1586–88), 21:1, 227.
59. BA 44-XIV-10, fols. 174r–175v, 211r. See also a 1592 case involving English merchants selling grains to residents of São Miguel: BA 44-XIV-6, fol. 269v.

Bibliography

ARCHIVES

Archivo General de Indias (Seville, Spain).
Arquivo Nacional da Torre do Tombo (Lisbon, Portugal).
Biblioteca da Ajuda (Lisbon, Portugal).
Biblioteca Pública e Arquivo Regional de Angra do Heroísmo (Angra do Heroísmo, Terceira Island, Portugal).
British Library (London, United Kingdom).

PUBLISHED WORKS

Andrews, Kenneth R. *Elizabethan Privateering: English Privateering during the Spanish War, 1585–1603*. New York: Cambridge University Press, 1964.
———. *The Spanish Caribbean: Trade and Plunder, 1530–1630*. New Haven: Yale University Press, 1978.
Avellaneda Navas, José Ignacio. *La expedición de Alonso Luis de Lugo al Nuevo Reino de Granada*. Bogotá: Banco de la República, 1994.
Black, Jeremy. *The British Seaborne Empire*. New Haven: Yale University Press, 2004.
Brásio, António, ed. *Monumenta Missionaria Africana: África ocidental*. 2nd ser., 2:1500–1569. Lisboa: Agência-Geral do Ultramar, 1963.
Bushnell, Amy Turner. "Indigenous America and the Limits of the Atlantic World, 1493–1825." In *Atlantic History: A Critical Reappraisal*, edited by Jack P. Greene and Philip D. Morgan, 191–222. New York: Oxford University Press, 2009.
Catz, Rebecca. *Christopher Columbus and the Portuguese, 1476–1498*. Westport CT: Greenwood Press, 1993.
Chaunu, Pierre. *Séville et l'Amérique: XVIe–XVIIe siècle*. Paris: Flammarion, 1977.
Cook, Noble David. "¿Una primera epidemia americana de viruela en 1493?" *Revista de Indias* 63, no. 227 (2003): 49–64.
de Matos, Artur Teodoro. "Os Açores e a Carreira das Índias no Século XVI." In *Estudos de História de Portugal: Homenagem a A. H. de Oliveira Marques*, 2:93–110. Lisboa: Editorial Estampa, 1983.

de Meneses, Avelino de Freitas. *Os Açores e o domínio filipino: 1580–1590*. 2 vols. Angra do Heroísmo: Instituto Histórico da Ilha Terceira, 1987.

Dias Dinis, António Joaquim, ed. *Monumenta Henricina*, vol. 6, *1437–1439*. Coimbra: Comissão Executiva das Comemorações do V Centenário da Morte do Infante D. Henrique, 1964.

do Canto, Ernesto, and Francisco Afonso Chaves, eds. *Archivo dos Açores*. 14 vols. Ponta Delgada: Tip. do Archivo dos Açores, 1878–1904.

Duncan, T. Bentley. *Atlantic Islands: Madeira, the Azores, and the Cape Verdes in Seventeenth-Century Commerce and Navigation*. Chicago: University of Chicago Press, 1972.

Ferreira, Ana Maria. *Problemas marítimos entre Portugal e França na primeira metade do século XVI*. Lisboa: Patrimonia, 1995.

Francis, J. Michael. *Invading Colombia: Spanish Accounts of the Gonzalo Jiménez de Quesada Expedition of Conquest*. University Park: Pennsylvania State University Press, 2007.

Godinho, Vitorino Magalhães. *Os Descobrimentos e a economia mundial*. 2 vols. Lisboa: Editora Arcádia, 1963.

Green, Toby. *The Rise of the Trans-Atlantic Slave Trade in Western Africa, 1300–1589*. Cambridge: Cambridge University Press, 2012.

Gregório, Rute Dias. "Escravos da Ilha Terceira na Primeira Metade do Século XVI." In *O reino, as ilhas e o mar oceano: estudos em homenagem a Artur Teodoro de Matos*, edited by Avelino de Freitas de Meneses and João Paulo Oliveira e Costa, 2:443–59. Ponta Delgada: Universidade dos Açores; Lisboa: Universidade Nova de Lisboa, 2007.

———. *Pero Anes do Canto: Um homem e um patrimônio (1473–1556)*. Ponta Delgada: Instituto Cultural de Ponta Delgada, 2001.

———. *Terra e fortuna: os primórdios da humanização da ilha Terceira (1450?–1550)*. Ponta Delgada: Centro de História de Além-Mar, 2007.

Guénin, Eugène. *Ango et ses Pilotes, d'après des documents inédits, tirés des archives de France, de Portugal et d'Espagne*. Paris: Imprimerie nationale, 1901.

Herrera y Tordesillas, Antonio de. *Cinco libros de la historia de Portugal, y conquista de las islas de los Açores, en los años de 1582 y 1583*. Madrid, 1591.

Hume, Martin A. S. *Calendar of Letters and State Papers Relating to English Affairs Preserved Principally in the Archives of Simancas*. 4 vols. London: Eyre and Spottiswoode, 1892–1899.

Lomas, Sophie Crawford, ed. *Calendar of State Papers, Foreign Series of the Reign of Elizabeth*, 21:1 (June 1586–June 1588). London, 1927.

Lorenzo Sanz, Eufemio. *Comercio de España con América en la época de Felipe II*. 2 vols. Valladolid: Diputación Provincial, 1979–1980.

Marinho dos Santos, João. *Os Açores nos Séculos XV e XVI*. 2 vols. Ponta Delgada: Universidade dos Açores, 1989.
Marrero, Leví. *Cuba: Economía y sociedad*. 15 vols. Madrid: Playor, 1974–1992.
Mauro, Frédéric. *Le Portugal et l'Atlantique au XVIIe Siècle (1570–1670): Étude économique*. Paris: École Pratique des Haute Études, 1960.
Mesquita, Maria Hermínia Morais. "Escravos em Angra no século XVII: Uma abordagem a partir dos registos paroquiais." *Arquipélago: História*, 2a série, 9 (2005): 209–30.
Quinn, David B. *England and the Discovery of America, 1481–1620*. New York: Alfred A. Knopf, 1974.
Ramos Pérez, Demetrio. *Audacia, negocios y política en los viajes españoles de descubrimiento y rescate*. Valladolid: Casa-Museo de Colón, Seminario Americanista de la Universidad, 1981.
Real Academia de Historia. *Colección de documentos inéditos relativos al descubrimiento, conquista y organización de las antiguas posesiones españolas de ultramar: De la isla de Cuba*. 2a serie, vol. 4. Madrid: Sucesores de Rivadeneyra, 1888.
Restall, Matthew. "The New Conquest History." *History Compass* 10, no. 2 (2012): 151–60.
Rocha, Gabriel de Avilez. "Plunder and Profit in the Name of Protection: Royal Iberian Armadas in the Early Atlantic." In *Protection and Empire in World History*, eds. Bain Attwood, Lauren Benton, and Adam Clulow, 72–90. New York: Cambridge University Press, 2017.
Salgueiro, E., et al. "North Atlantic Storminess and Atlantic Meridional Overturning Circulation during the Last Millennium: Reconciling Contradictory Proxy Records of NAO Variability." *Global and Planetary Change* 84–85 (March 2012): 48–55.
Varela, Consuelo, ed. *Cristóbal Colón: Textos y documentos completos: relaciones de viajes, cartas y memoriales*. Madrid: Alianza, 1982.
Vieira, Alberto. *Portugal y las islas del Atlántico*. Madrid: Editorial MAPFRE, 1992.
Vigneras, Louis-André. "The Three Brothers Guerra of Triana and Their Five Voyages to the New World, 1498–1504." *Hispanic American Historical Review* 52, no. 4 (November 1972): 621–41.
Wheat, David. *Atlantic Africa and the Spanish Caribbean, 1570–1640*. Chapel Hill: University of North Carolina Press, 2016.
Wright, Edward. "The voyage of the right honorable George Erle of Cumberland to the Azores, &c., written by the excellent mathematician and engineer master Edward Wright." In Richard Hakluyt, *The Principal Navigations*, 2:2, 154–66. London, 1599.

Glossary

adelantado	leader granted military and political power to explore, conquer, and govern a territory
alcabala	sales tax
alcalde ordinario	magistrate of the first instance
alcalde mayor	district administrator or district governor
alguacil	constable (alguacil mayor = chief constable)
almojarifazgo	duty on imports or exports
areito	ceremonial song-dance
armada	fleet or squadron
arribada	unscheduled or emergency naval landing
artillero	artilleryman, gunner
asiento	monopoly contract (e.g., for trafficking slaves or providing supplies)
atarazana	dockyard
audiencia	high court
ballestero	crossbowman
behique	shaman or ritual specialist
bodega	wine cellar, warehouse
boticario	pharmacist
caballería	tract of rural land
calderero	brazier, tinker
cabildo	municipal council
cacica	female indigenous chief
cacique	indigenous chief
cacicazgo	chiefdom
Carrera de Indias	"The Indies run." Maritime trajectories formalized in the 1560s that linked ports in southwestern Spain to ports in the Caribbean. One fleet sailed to San Juan de Ulúa in New Spain; another sailed to Cartagena and Nombre de Dios (or Portobelo). Both fleets usually stopped in Havana on the eastbound voyage back to Iberia, sometimes wintering there.
casa poblada	large, wealthy household

Casa de la Contratación	House of Trade
cédula	decree, ordinance
cemí	religious icon made of stone, wood, or cotton that served as intermediary between humans and the divine
cofradía	lay religious confraternity
comendador	commander in a military order
compadre	coparent; godfather of one's child (comadre = godmother of one's child)
compañero	partner
compañía	commercial partnership
complicidad	complicity or plot
comunidad	commune
consulta	report
contador	royal accountant
contramaestre	boatswain, overseer
conuco	cultivated field
converso	Christian of Jewish origin or antecedents
criado(a)	retainer, servant
criollo(a)	creole, native of a particular place
curador(a)	guardian of minor children
encomendero	holder of a grant of indigenous labor
encomienda	official name for grants of indigenous labor
entrada	expedition
escribano	notary, scribe
factor	representative or agent
fiscal	crown prosecutor
flota	fleet
grumete	apprentice seaman
guatiao	ritual name exchange
guerra	war
hato	ranch or grazing lands for livestock, usually cattle
horro(a)	freed, formerly enslaved
indios amigos	friendly or allied Indians
información	deposition
ingenio	sugar mill
judaizante	Jewish convert to Christianity accused of practicing Judaism
judío	Jew

juez de residencia	official appointed to conduct investigation of an officeholder
licenciado	holder of a postgraduate degree
madrina	godmother
maestre	shipmaster or cargo master
maravedí	smallest unit of account for currency
mayordomo	steward, manager
merced	favor, concession
montón	mound in which yucca and aje were planted
morisco(a)	person of Muslim origin or descent
mulato(a)	person of mixed European or African and Indian descent
nao	ship
naboría	permanent servant
naturaleza	place of origin
padrino	godfather
paje	page
patache	small dispatch ship
pestilencia	disease outbreak
picota	pillory
pieza	unit of sale (e.g., for the sale of slaves)
pleito	suit, litigation, legal dispute
poder	power of attorney
portales	arcade around a plaza
procurador	representative of a town
quinto	royal tax on gold; the royal fifth
relación	account
recogedor	person responsible for recapturing escaped slaves or encomienda workers
regidor	town councilman
registro	ship registry
repartimiento	grant of indigenous labor
rescate	trade or barter (including slave trafficking) that took place beyond the purview of Iberian officials; contraband. Also, rescue or ransom.
residencia	judicial review of an officeholder
solar	house lot
teniente de justicia	lieutenant justice of the peace
teniente de gobernador	lieutenant governor

vara	staff of office
vecindad	citizenship
vecino	head of household, citizen, neighbor
venta	inn or tavern
villa	town

Contributors

Ida Altman (PhD, Johns Hopkins University, 1982) is professor emerita of history at the University of Florida. She has published books and articles on early Mexico, the Caribbean, and the Spanish Empire, including *Emigrants and Society: Extremadura and Spanish America in the Sixteenth Century* (1989), *The War for Mexico's West: Spaniards and Indians in New Galicia, 1524–1550* (2010), "The Revolt of Enriquillo and the Historiography of Early Spanish America," *Americas* 63, no. 4 (2007), and "Marriage, Family, and Ethnicity in the Early Spanish Caribbean," *William and Mary Quarterly* 72, no. 2 (2013).

Joseph M. H. Clark (PhD, Johns Hopkins University, 2016) is assistant professor of history at the University of Kentucky. His research focuses on the relationship between Mexico and the Caribbean during the colonial period and on slavery and the African diaspora in the Atlantic world. He recently completed his dissertation, "Veracruz and the Caribbean in the Seventeenth Century."

Marc Eagle (PhD, Tulane University, 2005) is associate professor of history and codirector of Latin American studies at Western Kentucky University. His current research interests are the intersection of administration and society in seventeenth-century Spanish Hispaniola and the slave trade to Spanish America to 1640. He has recently published articles in *Slavery & Abolition*, on contraband slave trading in the 1630s, and in *Colonial Latin American Review*, on initiatives for reform in Hispaniola in the late seventeenth century. His research has been supported by the Fulbright Program and the American Council of Learned Societies.

Cacey Farnsworth received his bachelor of arts in 2010 from Brigham Young University, where he focused on early modern Portuguese history. A graduate student at the University of Florida since 2013, he received his master's degree in 2015. His interests include the early Spanish Caribbean, Iberian migration, Portuguese expansion, colonial Brazil, and urban history. His dissertation addresses Lisbon's role in the seventeenth-century Atlantic world. He was awarded a Fulbright fellowship for research in Lisbon in 2018–19.

Pablo F. Gómez (PhD, Vanderbilt University, 2010) is assistant professor in the Department of Medical History and the Department of History at the University of Wisconsin, Madison. His work examines the history of health and corporeality in the early modern Atlantic world. His essays have appeared in the *Social History of Medicine*, *Small Axe*, and edited collections. His book, *The Experiential Caribbean: Creating Knowledge and Healing in the Early Modern Atlantic* (2017), was awarded the *Journal of Africana Religion*'s Albert J. Raboteau Prize.

Brian Hamm (PhD, University of Florida, 2017) taught as adjunct professor of history at the University of Central Florida in 2017–18 and is currently a postdoctoral fellow at the Frankel Institute for Advanced Judaic Studies at the University of Michigan. His dissertation examined Spanish-Portuguese relations in the sixteenth- and seventeenth-century Caribbean, focusing on Cartagena de Indias. His article "Constructing and Contesting Portuguese Difference in the Spanish Circum-Caribbean, 1500–1650" was recently published in *Anais de História de Além-Mar*.

Shannon Lalor is a doctoral candidate in history at the University of Florida. Her dissertation, "Women, Power, and the Expansion of Empire: The Bobadilla Women of Early Modern Spain, 1450–1550," examines women's roles in the transfer of Spanish society to the early colonial Americas and in its transmutation in the sixteenth-century Caribbean. She won the University of Florida History Department's Linda K. Vance Award in Women's History. Her research in Spain was supported by a travel grant from the University of Florida's Graduate School.

Lauren MacDonald (PhD, Johns Hopkins University, 2018). Her doctoral dissertation, "The Regular Clergy and Reformation in the Early Spanish Caribbean, 1493–1580," examines the role of the Church's regular clergy in the Spanish colonization of the Caribbean. She has received support for her research from the Jacob K. Javits Fellowship Program, the Fulbright U.S. Student Program, and the John Carter Brown Library.

Gabriel de Avilez Rocha (PhD, New York University, 2016) is assistant professor of history at Drexel University. A specialist in the social, legal, and environmental history of the early Atlantic world, his manuscript "Empire from the Commons: Political Ecologies of Colonialism in the Early Atlantic" examines how popular struggles over shared property and collective resources contributed to the formation of the Portuguese and Spanish Atlantic empires over the long sixteenth century. His research has received support from the Social Science Research Council, the Fulbright Commission, the Mellon Foundation, and the Huntington Library.

Erin Woodruff Stone (PhD, Vanderbilt University, 2014) is assistant professor of Latin American history at the University of West Florida. She is currently working on her book manuscript entitled "Captives of Conquest: How Indigenous Slavery Shaped the Spanish Atlantic, 1490–1570." In her work she focuses on the rise and consequences of indigenous slavery. She is also the author of "America's First Slave Revolt: Indians and African Slaves in Española, 1500–1534," published in *Ethnohistory* (Spring 2013) and "Slave Raiders vs. Friars: Tierra Firme, 1513–1522," published in *The Americas* (Spring 2017).

Spencer Tyce (PhD, Ohio State University, 2015) completed a dissertation on the economic and political strategies of German conquistadors in the sixteenth-century Caribbean and Venezuela. He has presented papers on issues concerning ethnohistory, Caribbean Indian slavery, and legal and Church history. Currently, he is working on the roles non-Iberian actors played in the Caribbean and mainland frontiers in the first few decades of the Conquest. He is assistant professor of history at Fairmont State University in West Virginia.

David Wheat (PhD, Vanderbilt University, 2009) is associate professor of history at Michigan State University. His book *Atlantic Africa and the Spanish Caribbean, 1570–1640* (2016) was awarded the American Historical Association's Rawley Prize, the Lapidus Center's Harriet Tubman Prize, and the Omohundro Institute's Jamestown Prize. His essays on the early Spanish Caribbean have appeared in *Slavery & Abolition*, *Journal of Early Modern History*, *Journal of African History*, and several edited collections.

Index

adelantados, 71, 95, 241, 253n20
Africans, xix–xx, 74, 163–79, 205, 212, 259, 263; enslaved, xvi, xix, 18, 26, 37–38, 47, 50, 61–62, 69, 72, 76, 88n18, 98, 100, 109n18, 139, 140, 141–42, 143, 144–45, 147, 148–49, 150, 151, 152, 153, 154n3, 155n14, 157n47, 163, 164, 165–66, 167, 168, 169, 170, 171, 172, 174, 175, 176, 177, 178, 179, 211, 221, 242, 246, 275n52; free, xix, 144, 167, 168, 169, 170–72, 174, 175, 176; as settlers, 143. *See also* Ararás; Mozambiques; slaves, royal; slave trade, transatlantic; Terranova; Upper Guineans; West Central Africans
Afrocreoles, 148, 166, 167, 168, 170, 172, 178, 181n21, 182n30
Afro-Portuguese, 131n41
agriculture, xvi, 9, 15, 27, 37, 40n6, 100, 193, 197, 201, 246, 251, 263. *See also conucos*
Agüeybana I, 27–31
Agüeybana II, 31, 33–34, 39
alcaldes mayores: in Cubagua, 56; in Puerto Rico, 31, 36; in Veracruz, 197, 199
alcaldes ordinarios in Cuba, 74–75, 81, 90n33, 98
Alfinger, Antonio de (Ambrosius), 55, 57–58, 239, 249, 252n13, 254n46
Algarve, 119
Algava, Alonso del, 260–61, 266

alliances, Spanish-indigenous, 40n2, 194, 262; in Cuba, 77; in Hispaniola, 10; in Puerto Rico, 25, 26, 27, 28, 29–30, 33–34, 39, 43n77; in Venezuela, 57, 60
Almagro, Diego de, 94
Amerindians. *See* Indians
Amsterdam, 128
Andalucía (Andalusia), 247, 259, 260, 261
Andean region, xiii, xx, 143, 148, 150, 151, 153, 228n1, 249. *See also* Peru
Angola, 150, 153, 167. *See also* West Central Africa
Angola, Pedro, 168, 171
Angra (Terceira), 260, 261–63, 264, 265, 266
Antigua (Huitzilapan) River, 191, 195, 196, 202
Antigua Veracruz, 191, 195–96, 197–98, 200, 201–4
Antwerp, 237, 238, 239, 245
apothecaries, Portuguese, 118, 127
Aragon, 21n48, 118, 237
Ararás, 170, 171
Archive of the Indies, xiv, xv
areitos, xx, 5, 9, 13, 16, 17–18, 20n7
arribadas, 140–41, 147, 150, 152, 153
asientos: for conquest of La Florida and Bimini, 36; for conquest of Puerto Rico, 27, 30–32; for conquest of Venezuela, 235, 239–42; for transatlantic slave trade, 140, 141–42, 147–48, 155n10, 242–44

287

Asunción (Cuba). *See* Baracoa
Atlantic world, xiii, xv, xx, 62, 139, 141, 151, 211, 214, 222, 227, 258, 270; disease and plagues in, 205, 211, 214–16, 227; history of, xxi; military in, 126
audiencias: of Guatemala, 146, 158n66; of New Spain, 51; of Panamá, 139, 146, 150; of Santo Domingo, xx, 59, 78–79, 81–84, 88n22, 89n29, 90n32, 102, 104, 117–18, 125, 146, 151, 155n22, 156n41
Augsburg, 235, 236, 237
Augustinians, 203
Ávila, Bruno de, 225–26
Ávila, Pedrárias de, 92–94, 106, 108n4
Azores, 116–17, 257–75. *See also* Angra; Corvo, Island of; Ponta Delgada; Santa Maria, Island of; São Jorge, Island of; São Miguel, Island of; Terceira
Aztecs, 50, 189, 191, 193–94
Azua (Hispaniola), 49, 218

Bahamas, 49–50, 271n7
Balboa, Vasco Núñez de, 106
ballesteros, 247
ball games (indigenous), 17, 41n18
baptisms, 3, 8, 11, 29, 164, 165–68, 171, 172–75, 176–77, 181n17, 182n42, 182n45, 263, 273n35
Baracoa (Cuba), 100, 101
Bastidas, Rodrigo de, 239, 241, 272n11
behiques (shamans), 6, 14
Belize, xvii
Berbesí, Dominga, 170, 174
Biafara, Ana, *horra*, 170–71
Biafara, Diego, 174, 175
Biafara, Hernando, *horro*, 170, 171, 172, 174
Biafara, María, 168, 171

Biafara, Ysabel, 170, 172
Bijagos Islands, 177
Biminí, 36
Biocho, Gaspar, 177–78
Bobadilla, doña Isabel de, 91–99, 104–7, 109n25
Bobadilla, doña Leonor de, 98
Bobadilla, fray Francisco de, 96, 98–99
Bobadilla family, 92, 93, 94, 97, 105, 106
Bogotá, xv, 249–50
Bran, María (parter of Diego Biafara), 174–75
Brazil, 62, 65n74, 117, 153, 180n8, 242, 272n16. *See also* Cape of Santo Agostinho; Pernambuco; Salvador da Bahia
British, xix, xx, 275n57. *See also* English
British West Indies, xvii, 228n11
burials, 198–99, 220; of icons, 9
burial sites (indigenous), desecration of, 124, 262, 273n29

Cabeza de Vaca, Álvar Núñez, 72
cabildos, 80, 221–23, 226; in Cartagena de Indias, 222, 223, 226; in Cuba, 74–75, 80, 81, 82, 102, 104; in Cumaná, 125; in Panama City, 225; in Portobelo, 224, 226; in Santo Domingo, 218, 220, 244; in Veracruz, 191, 196, 200–203
Cabo de la Vela, 240
Cabo Verde, 117, 131n41, 143, 145, 146, 148, 149, 150, 153, 156n26, 157n61, 164, 165, 178, 180n6, 216, 217, 257, 259–60, 264, 272n14, 274n37
Cáceres (Extremadura), 72
Cacheu River, 174
cacicas, 17; in Puerto Rico, 30, 37

288 Index

cacicazgos, 29; in Puerto Rico, 29, 33, 41n17

caciques, in Cuba, 72, 76, 88n17; in Hispaniola, 17, 99; in New Spain, 51–52; in Puerto Rico, 27, 28, 29, 30, 31, 32, 33, 36, 37, 38, 41n17; in Venezuela, 56

Cádiz, 140, 148, 157n61, 216–17

Caldeira, Manuel, 147–48, 157n51, 157n55

Camagüey (Cuba), 78

Canary Islands, 98, 140, 141, 151, 152, 157n59, 257, 260, 262, 264, 274n37, 274n40. *See also* Tenerife (Canary Islands)

canoes, 34, 35, 163, 174, 177, 192, 196

Caparra (Puerto Rico), 28–30, 33, 36–38

Cape of Santo Agostinho (Brazil), 260

Cape Verde Islands. *See* Cabo Verde

Captain Richard, 267–68, 275n52

Caquetíos, 57

Caracas, 153

Caribs, 28–29, 32, 34, 35–37, 38, 39, 40n15, 42n60, 48–49, 55, 57, 62, 65n72, 266

Carmelites, 203

Carreño, Admiral Francisco, 113, 119–20, 123

Carrera de Indias. See Indies fleet system

Cartagena de Indias, xv, xvii, 35, 108n2, 114, 117, 118, 120, 124, 126–28, 132n71, 143, 144, 145, 149–50, 151, 152, 153, 156n28, 157n61, 169, 212, 215, 218, 219–20, 221, 222, 223–24, 225–26

Casa de la Contratación, 37, 102, 120, 126, 142, 151, 214, 216, 218, 222, 224, 246, 252n6, 258, 259

casa poblada, 88n20, 129

cassava bread, 194

Castile, 6–7, 9, 10, 14, 15, 74, 80, 113, 120, 129, 237, 247, 272n14

Castilla del Oro, 94

Castro, Hernando de, 100–105, 110n39

Catholic Monarchs (Fernando and Isabel), 4, 7, 213. *See also* Fernando, don (King)

cattle, 51, 54, 93, 193, 197, 266. *See also* livestock

cédulas, xx, 97, 101, 103, 109n18, 110n31, 119, 124, 126, 155n16, 193, 198, 200, 224

cemís, 4, 6, 19

Cempoala, 194, 195

Central America, 92, 94–96, 105. *See also audiencias*; Honduras; Nicaragua; Panama

Cerón, Juan, 31, 33, 36

Chanca, Dr., 28

Charles V, 60, 71, 141, 142, 218, 236, 237–38, 239, 241–42, 243, 249, 252n5, 261

Chichimecas, 51

children, 52, 78, 91, 98, 99, 100, 101, 102, 103, 196, 247, 260, 263, 265; of Africans in Cuba, 165, 166, 167, 168, 172, 173, 174, 175, 181n16, 182n45; Christian education of, 11, 18; mestizo, 72–73, 80, 85

Christianity, 6, 8–9, 10, 11, 13, 18, 19; indigenous views of, 10, 13–14, 19

Christianization, xvi, xvii, xxi, 1, 3, 6, 7, 8, 14, 42n51, 101, 228n1; indigenous resistance to, in Hispaniola, 9, 10, 13, 18

Church, Roman Catholic, 1, 4, 178, 235, 236; organization of, 7

Cisneros, Cardinal Francisco Jiménez de, 14–16, 61, 65n66

Index 289

clergy, 4, 6–7; regular, xvi, 7, 13, 19, 203; secular, 7, 79, 89n24. *See also* Dominicans; Franciscans; Hieronymites; Mercedarians; San Juan de Dios, order of; Trinitarians

Cofradía de Holanda, 128

Cofradía of Nuestra Señora de la Concepción, 220

Colombia, 48, 57, 262. *See also* New Kingdom of Granada

Colón, don Diego, 25, 30–33, 35, 36, 38

Colón, don Luis, 152

Columbus, Bartolomé, 9

Columbus, Christopher, 3, 4, 5, 6, 7, 8, 9, 10, 16, 17, 28, 92, 123, 152, 257, 258, 259, 260, 271n7; privileges of, 30; second voyage of, 15, 27, 29, 48

Columbus family, 30, 144. *See also* Colón, don Diego; Colón, don Luis; Columbus, Bartolomé

compadres, 164, 166

complicidades, 114

comunidades: in Castile, 74, 87n12; in Cuba, 74–76, 80–81

Concepción de la Vega (Hispaniola), 12, 49

Conga, Ysabel, 168, 171

contraband. *See* trade, illicit

Contreras, Rodrigo de, 94, 105, 108n8, 109n17

conucos, 27, 36, 40n6

conversion. *See* Christianization

conversos, 120, 131n34. *See also* New Christians

Córdoba (Mexico), 203, 204

Coro, 56–57, 249, 250, 251, 254n46

Coronado y Ulloa, Alonso de, 215, 224

corsairs, 109n18, 109n27, 114–16, 121–23, 199, 201, 258, 261, 265–66, 267

Cortés, Hernando, 50, 54, 72, 74, 93, 123, 189–90, 191, 193–95, 205, 206n5, 235, 238, 248

Corvo, Island of (Azores), 266, 274n43

Cotrina, Antonio, 203–4

cotton, 6, 174

Council of the Indies, 102, 113, 117, 122, 123, 142, 150, 203, 214, 215, 216, 217, 218, 222, 223

creolization, 179

criollas or *criollos* (creoles), 18, 100, 127, 148, 167, 181n21, 181n15, 182n30, 205, 212. *See also* Afrocreoles

Cromberger, Jakob, 238–39

crown, French, 267. *See also* François I

crown, Portuguese, 139, 148, 237, 258–59, 264, 266

crown, Spanish, xv, 32, 48–50, 55–57, 61, 63n11, 65n72, 69, 79, 80, 89n30, 91–93, 100, 102, 104–6, 108n8, 113, 115, 119, 124–27, 139, 141–44, 151–52, 165, 198–200, 211, 213–17, 218–21, 223–26, 229n28, 233, 238–41, 242–44, 259, 261–62, 266, 276n58. *See also* Catholic Monarchs; Charles V; Fernando, don; Philip II

crypto-Judaism, 127

Cuba, xvii, xix, 6, 21n48, 40n2, 48, 50, 52, 54, 55, 71–72, 80–81, 83–85, 86n2, 86n4, 87n13, 88n18, 89n25, 91, 93, 95–107, 110n48, 113, 119–20, 124, 140, 142, 143, 144, 145, 155n16, 165, 179, 190, 204, 206n5, 218, 219, 223, 262, 273n29, 273n34; conquest of, 13, 14, 73–74, 77; in 1520s, 74–90; punishment of Indians in, 78–79. *See also* Bobadilla, doña Isabel de; Guzmán, doña Guiomar de; Havana, San Cristóbal de la; Santiago de Cuba; Trinidad (Cuba)

Cubagua, xvii, xix, 47–48, 55–56, 59–60, 143, 156n29
Cumaná, 56, 125, 240
Cumanagoto, 59–60
Curaçao, xvii

Darién (Panama), 92, 108n4
death, 3, 5, 12, 18, 28, 42n46, 51, 57, 73, 85, 88n14, 89n29, 91, 92, 93, 94, 96, 100, 101, 103, 110nn30–31, 187, 202, 221, 222, 250–51, 263, 272n17; from disease, 211–13, 215–16; of German miners, 245–46; of Hatuey, 13–14; of indigenous slaves, 47, 50, 52, 58; violent, 6, 74, 77, 78, 86n2, 87n7, 241, 249, 250–51. *See also* demography: indigenous population loss
demography, xvi, xix, 5, 10, 36, 61, 69, 115, 124, 143, 145, 166, 190, 199, 201, 214, 250, 259, 263; and indigenous population loss, 15, 18, 41n23, 60, 77, 84–85, 89n25, 108n6, 195, 198, 199, 211, 275n44
disease, xvi, 5, 18, 38, 41n23, 47, 61, 187, 190–91, 205, 211–17, 220, 224, 275n44. *See also* epidemiology
dockyards, 202
doctors. *See* health practitioners
Dom António, 117–18, 267
Dominicans, 7, 8, 11–16, 125
Drake, Francis, 117–18, 121–23, 126, 128, 267–68
Duele, Juan de, 8, 13
Duques de Feria, 73, 87n5
Dutch, xvi, 120, 128, 269
Dutch Antilles, xvii

Echegoyan, Juan de, 118–20, 123
education, 223, 253; of indigenous boys, 11

Ehinger, Heinrich, 141, 143–44, 237, 239–41, 243
Ehinger, Jorge, 239
El Dorado, 59, 250–51, 254n46
encomenderos, 48, 60, 75, 76, 89n25, 93, 99, 100, 124
encomiendas, 14–16, 80, 87n13, 93, 97, 105, 108nn5–6, 241, 251, 253n21; in Cartagena de Indias, 124; in Cuba, 74, 76–77, 100, 106; in Hispaniola, 10, 99–100; in Mexico, 54, 72, 87n7; in Nicaragua, 94, 97; in Panama, 96; in Puerto Rico, 37
England, 118, 121
English, 123, 124, 129, 258; attacks by, 126, 201, 224, 275n56; in Caribbean, xvi, 267; corsairs, 114, 121–22, 268; merchants, 117, 269; sailors, 265; spies, 118, 122; trade with, 237, 276nn58–59
Enmanagoia, 59
Enríquez, Martín, 201, 202
Enriquillo, 11
entradas, 51–52, 54, 56–60, 249–51, 253n16, 253n20, 254n45, 262, 264, 275n44
environment: Caribbean, xvi, xix, 14, 187, 190; of Venezuela, 245; of Veracruz, 190–94, 198–99
epidemiology, xix; and illness, 12, 51, 97, 127, 187, 197–99, 205, 214–16, 218–24; and leprosy, 212, 219–20; and plague, 205, 213, 216–17, 227, 229n26; and smallpox, 15, 198, 213; and yellow fever, 205
Escalante Alvarado, García de, 197–99
Española. *See* Hispaniola
Espira, Jorge, 58, 249–50
evangelization. *See* Christianization
Extremadura, 72, 90n35, 260

Index   291

Fain, Jean, 261, 273n21
Féderman (or Federmann), Nicolás (or Nicolas), 56–58, 249–50, 254n45
Fernández de Oviedo, Gonzalo, xiv, 27–28, 33, 34, 87n5, 106, 132n77
Fernando, don (King), 25, 30–32, 35–38, 42n60
fiscal (crown prosecutor), 149, 152
Flemings, 141, 238, 267. *See also* Antwerp
Florida, xvii, 71–72, 81, 86n2, 91, 95–98, 124
fortifications, 7, 10, 37, 137, 165, 192, 201, 240
France, 120, 123n77, 146, 148, 153, 268
Franciscans, 7, 8, 11, 12, 13, 14, 15, 16, 203, 205
François I, 237–38, 273n21
fraud. *See* trade, illicit
French, 129; attacks by, 117; corsairs, 109n18, 114, 116, 122, 125, 200, 258; in Caribbean, xvi, 99, 267; merchants, 269, 273n21; Normans, 261, 267; sailors, 261, 265, 266; ships, 268; trade, 237
French Antilles, xvii, xix
Fugger family, 235–39, 241–42, 244

galleys, 124–25, 203
Gambia River, 176, 177
Gêba (town), 176
Gêba River, 173, 176
Genoese, 127, 146–47, 222, 238, 242–43, 261
geophagia, 89n23
Germans, 48, 55–57, 60, 64n39, 132n69, 132n77, 141, 235–41, 243, 244–47, 249–51; definition of term, 252n1; involvement of, in indigenous slave trade, 55–60; involvement of, in transatlantic slave trade, 141–42, 155n13, 242–44. *See also* Alfinger, Antonio de; Ehinger, Heinrich; Ehinger, Jorge; Fugger family; Sayler, Hieronymus; Welser family
Getsemaní, neighborhood of, 219. *See also* Cartagena de Indias
Gilbert, Humphrey, 122
goats, 54
godparents, 164–78, 181nn16–17, 182n45, 183n69, 183n72
gold, 12, 13, 48, 49–50, 55, 69, 122–24, 139, 142, 174, 189, 197, 235, 239–40, 244, 248, 250, 260–61, 263, 273n29; in Cuba, 50, 76, 80, 96; in Hispaniola, 16, 47, 99; in Puerto Rico, 25, 27–28, 30, 31–32, 38, 40n4, 41nn22–23; in Venezuela, 55, 57–58, 236, 241, 251. *See also* burial sites (indigenous), desecration of; mining: gold
Gómez de Sandoval, Diego, 223
González de Buitrón, Juan, 201, 203
Gorrevod, Laurent de, 141, 155n24, 242–43
Granada (Spain), 7, 17
Greater Antilles, xvii, 9, 25, 39
Grijalva, Juan de, 72, 75, 88n17, 192–94
Guánica (Puerto Rico), 31
Guanina, 33
Guarionex (indigenous leader in Hispaniola), 3–4, 7–10, 18
Guarionex (indigenous leader in Puerto Rico), 33
Guatemala, 51, 146
guatiao, 27–28, 40n8
Guatícabanú, 3, 4, 5, 7, 10
Guayama (Puerto Rico), 146–47
Guianas, xvii

Guinea, 146, 148, 150, 267, 275n52. *See also* Upper Guinea
Gulf of Mexico, xvii, 194
Gutiérrez Calderón, Hernando, 81–84
Guzmán, doña Guiomar de, 91–93, 100–107, 110n39, 110n44, 110n48
Guzmán, Gonzalo de, 71, 80–85, 86n2, 88n17, 89n29, 107, 262, 273n30
Guzmán, Nuño de, 51–55
Guzmán, Pedro de Paz de, 91, 103
Guzmán, Pero Núñez de, 91, 93, 99–100, 107
gypsies. *See* Roma people

hatos, 197
Hatuey, 13–14
Havana, San Cristóbal de la, 74, 81, 190, 204, 212, 222, 268–69, 271n1; Africans in, 137, 164, 168–70, 174–79, 184n78; baptisms in, 171–73; *flota* in, 157n61; French attack on, 116, 123, 200; hospitals in, 219, 223, 225–26; Isabel de Bobadilla in, 97–98, 105; parish records of, 165–66; Portuguese in, 119; slave voyages to, 149–51, 153
Hawkins, John, 201, 268
health practitioners: of African descent, 220–21; Amerindian, 220; enslaved hospital workers, 220–21; nurses, 220; physicians, 199, 215, 220; surgeons, 220, 221
Hieronymites (Order of St. Jerome), 3, 7, 14–17, 61, 65n66
Higüey, 27, 40n4
Hirschvogel firm, 238–39
Hispaniola, xvii, xx, 26, 30, 31, 35, 42n60, 48, 50, 51, 52, 55, 65n66, 69, 82, 84; African slaves in, 61, 88n18, 93, 99, 100, 113, 141, 143, 215–16, 245, 267, 272n17, 275n52; *audiencia* in, 78, 146; *caciques* in, 41n17; economy of, 36; hospitals in, 128, 223; Indians of, xix; indigenous slaves in, 49–50, 56, 58, 61–62, 63n11; pacification of, 27–28, 40n2; Portuguese in, 124; slave voyages to, 146–48, 150–53, 217; religion in, 3–19; Wolof revolt in, 145. *See also* Higüey; La Yaguana; Nizao; Ocoa; San Juan de la Maguana; Santo Domingo
Holy Roman Empire, 235, 237, 241, 244
Honduras, 48, 51, 145–47, 148, 149, 150–51, 157n47
horses, 51, 54, 71, 75, 86n2, 93, 196, 197
hospitals, 211–12, 218–27, 228n1; in Cartagena de Indias, 215, 218–24, 226; in Cuba, 218, 222–23, 226; in Hispaniola, 218, 220–21, 223–24; in New Spain, 198, 200, 203, 218–19, 222; in Panama, 214, 218, 221–22, 224–26; in Puerto Rico, 218. *See also* health practitioners
House of Trade. *See* Casa de la Contratación
hurricanes, 14, 187, 190–91; in Puerto Rico, 37; in Veracruz, 193, 196, 199–200

immigrants, 69, 212, 214–15; Portuguese, 113, 115, 124, 128–29
Inca Empire, 57, 95, 143, 242
Indians, xx, 5, 17–18, 35–36, 211; in or near Cartagena, 118, 124, 220; in Cuba, 6, 13, 71, 74, 76–81, 83, 85, 86n2, 89nn24–25, 91, 97, 101–2, 109n18; enslaved, xvi, 32, 35, 47–62, 65n65, 69, 72, 76–77, 87n13, 88n4, 94, 99, 103, 124, 258–59, 264–65, 275n44; in Hispaniola, 3–20, 27,

Indians (*continued*)
99–100; in Puerto Rico, 17, 25, 28, 31–32, 34, 36–39, 42n51; in Santa Cruz (St. Croix), 42n60; in Trinidad (island), 267; in Venezuela, 254n46; near Veracruz, 199. *See also* alliances, Spanish-indigenous; Caribs; Taínos; Tairona; Totonacs; Tupinambá

Indies fleet system (*Carrera de Indias*), 116, 126, 139, 148, 149, 152, 153–54, 157n61, 201, 203, 205, 212, 215–17, 219–20, 222, 274n37

indigenous peoples. *See* Indians

ingenios. *See* sugar: estates and *ingenios*

Inquisition, Spanish, xv, 11, 14, 114, 121, 128, 221

interpreters, 12, 27, 28

Isabel (enslaved woman in Terceira), 263

Isabel (queen of Portugal), 142

Islam, 5, 7–8, 12–13, 17, 184n77

Italians, 118, 127, 132n69, 235, 236, 237

ivory, 174–75, 267–68

Jamaica, xvii, 13, 58, 64n51, 113, 118, 124, 125, 142, 143, 144, 152, 158n69

Jamapa River, 192–93

Jews, 114–15, 120–21, 128–29, 131n34, 132n77

Juana, Queen, 214–15

just war, 1, 48–49, 51, 54, 55, 59

Kaabu, 175–77, 183n64

Kongo, Kingdom of, 168, 181n25

labor: in the Caribbean, xxi, 1, 47, 137, 141–42, 147–48, 151, 154n3, 163, 211; in Cuba, 14, 74, 77–78, 85, 87n13, 99, 165, 169, 178, 229n28; in *encomiendas*, 10, 93; in Hispaniola, 5, 12–13, 18; in hospitals, 221; in mines, 240, 244–46; in Puerto Rico, 25, 31–32, 36, 38–39, 41n23; in Venezuela, 242–43, 251. *See also* Africans: enslaved; Indians: enslaved

La Guaira, 153

La Margarita, xvii, 118, 143, 148, 149, 153

languages: African, 169, 179; Amerindian, 26; Biafada, 169; German, 240, 245, 247, 252n1; Kikongo, 181n25; Macorix, 7; Mandinga, 177; Spanish, 169, 247, 252n1. *See also* interpreters

Las Casas, Bartolomé de, xiv, 12, 13–15, 253n21

Laws of Burgos, 11, 17–18, 38, 43n72

La Yaguana, 146–47, 151, 157n64

lazarettos, 219–20

leather, 261, 264, 267–68

Leipzig, 244–45, 253n35

Lesser Antilles, xvii, xix, 25, 29, 36, 38, 48–49

Lima, xv, 114, 128, 132n76

Lisbon, 113, 125, 145, 147, 150, 236, 237, 238–39, 258, 261–62, 265, 269, 271n1

livestock, 50, 51, 54, 74, 93, 100, 193, 198. *See also* cattle; horses; mules; pigs; sheep

London, 118, 268

Luanda, 150, 167

Lucayos Indians, 49

Lucayos Islands. *See* Bahamas

Lugo, Alonso de, 262–64, 268–69, 273

Lutherans, 121–22, 224. *See also* Protestants

Mabo, 28

Madalena (ship), 260–61, 272n18

Madeira, 117, 121, 148, 274n37

Madrid, 146, 225, 239

Magarabomba. *See* Sierra Leone
malaguetta peppers, 174
Maracaibo (town), 58, 249
Maracaibo, Lake, 56, 249
Maracapana, 59, 240
María (Cartagena de Indias province), town of, 219
maroons, 50, 109n18, 122, 199, 266–67
marriages, 17, 36, 80, 87n7, 93, 95, 103, 165–78, 182nn28–29
Martyr, Peter (Pedro Mártir), xiv, 192
master miners, 240, 242, 244–46
mayordomos (stewards), 52, 95–96, 98, 106; as hospital administrators, 220
medicines, 128, 215, 224, 237
Mercedarians, 13, 21n45
merchants, xx, 47, 49, 61, 137, 141, 142–43, 145, 146, 147–48, 155n20, 177, 201–2, 217, 233, 238, 242–43, 257–61, 264–65, 273n31, 274n42; Azorean, 260–64, 276n58; Dutch, 269; English, 117, 269, 276n59; French, 267, 269, 273n21; German, 235–43, 248–49, 252n1; Native American, 241; Portuguese, xix, 125, 140, 147, 152, 238; Upper Guinean, 163, 174
Mesoamerica, xiii, xx, 189, 194–95, 262
mestizos, 42n51, 72, 80, 85, 101, 199
Meta, 58, 59, 254n46
Mexico, xvi, 8, 26, 40n2, 47, 50–55, 63n11, 72–75, 85, 87n10, 89n24, 144, 145, 146–50, 154n1, 156n37, 157n61, 189–205, 217, 219, 228n1, 240, 244–46, 248, 251, 269. *See also* Veracruz; Yucatán
Mexico City, xv, 26, 50, 51, 54, 75, 114, 128, 132n76, 191, 196, 201–2, 204. *See also* Tenochtitlan
migration, xx–xxi, 69, 143, 164, 180n9, 201. *See also* immigrants; passengers; slave trade, transatlantic

mining, xvi, 86n4, 91, 100, 137, 145, 151, 237, 240–42, 244–46; copper, 235–26, 242, 244; gold, 1, 27, 32, 36, 38, 41n23, 47, 49–50, 76, 80, 99, 139, 142, 235, 241, 244; silver, 235–26, 242, 244; tin, 242, 244
Mompóx, 124, 219
Mona, isla de, 27
monasteries, 7, 12, 103, 125, 128, 222
Montesinos, fray Antonio de, 12, 14
moriscas/moriscos, 17, 99. *See also* Islam
mosquitos, 14, 192–94, 198–99, 204–5
mothers, 3, 9, 18, 28, 93–94, 101, 103, 106, 166–68, 172, 174–75, 182n45, 263–64
Mozambiques, 177
Muiscas, 58
mules, 54, 137, 202
Muslims. *See* Islam

naborías, 10, 12, 13, 74, 76
Narváez, Pánfilo de, 72
Native Americans. *See* Indians
networks, patronage, xx, 91–93, 97–98, 104–7; social, 18, 164–66, 170, 174–75, 178–79. *See also* hospitals; merchants; slave trade, transatlantic; spies; trade networks
Neveri, 60
New Christians, 118, 121. *See also* conversos
New Kingdom of Granada, 57–58, 64n39, 219, 246, 248, 251, 273n27. *See also* Bogotá; Cartagena de Indias; Colombia; Santa Marta
New Laws, 60–61, 65n72
New Spain. *See* Mexico
Nicaragua, 48, 51, 94, 97, 105–6, 108n8
Niña (caravel), 258
Nizao (Hispaniola), 149, 151

Index   295

Nombre de Dios, xvii, 118, 143, 145–49, 151, 153, 157n47, 157n61, 214, 218
North Africa, 13, 259, 272n9
Nueva Andalucía, 125
Nueva Cádiz (Cubagua), 55, 59
Nueva Galicia, 55
Nuevo Reino de Granada. *See* New Kingdom of Granada
Núñez, Pedro, 218–19, 222
Núñez Lobo, Rodrigo Manuel, 125
Nüremberg, Lazarus, 238–39, 253n15

Ocoa (Hispaniola), 148, 149, 151
Ortal, Gerónimo, 58–60
Ortiz, Licenciado Bartolomé, 97–98
Ottoman Empire, 12, 79, 238
Ovando, frey Nicolás de, 10, 27, 40n5, 218
overseers, 86n2, 91, 102, 105, 167, 242

Pacabueyes, 58
Pacific Ocean, 240, 249
Palos, 258
Panama, xvii, 48, 92–97, 105–6, 108n4, 118–19, 112, 142, 146. See also *audiencias*: of Panamá; Nombre de Dios; Panama City; Portobelo
Panama City, 109n17, 118, 169, 215, 218, 221–22, 225–26
Pané, Ramón, 3–10, 13, 15, 17
Pánuco, 51–55
Parada, Andrés de, 82–83, 89n31
Paria, 58–60
passengers, 142, 195, 198, 215, 247, 261, 271n42
Paz, Pedro de, 91, 93, 99–103, 107, 110n31, 110n44
Pearl Islands, 55, 59. See also Cubagua; La Margarita
pearls, 239, 261; fisheries for, 2, 47–49, 143–44; divers for, 48–49, 142

Pedrárias. *See* Ávila, Pedrárias de
Peñalosa, María de, 94, 97, 105
penas de cámara, 221–22
Pernambuco, 128, 260
Peru, xvi, 48, 86n4, 93–95, 97, 215, 242, 246, 251, 254n46, 266, 269, 274n42. *See also* Andean region
pestilencias (pestilences). *See* disease
Philip II, 118, 121, 220, 267–69
physicians. *See* health practitioners
piezas, indigenous slaves referred to as, 60
pigs, 54, 266
pilots, 114–18, 120–23, 126, 129, 131n41, 141, 202, 215, 265, 273n30
Pinzón, Vicente Yáñez, 27, 30, 272n11
Pizarro, Francisco, 93–95, 235, 242
Pizarro, Gonzalo, revolt of, 87n4
Ponce de León, Hernán, 94–97
Ponce de León, Juan, 26, 27, 28, 30, 32, 38, 40n5, 42n60, 93, 99, 106
Ponce de León, Juan González, 26, 28, 33, 38, 40n1
Ponta Delgada (São Miguel Island, Azores), 269, 276n58
Porcallo de Figueroa, Vasco: biography of, 72–73, 85–86; in Cuban politics, 81–85; estate of, 77, 83; as *teniente de justicia*, 74–81
Portobelo, xvii, 215, 218, 221, 222, 224, 226
Portuguese: in African slave trade, 145–47, 149–50, 243; and Azores, 259–61, 264, 266, 269, 272n9, 275n57; in Caribbean, 69, 113–15, 118–20, 123–27, 129, 132n71; in Indian Ocean, 236–37; in indigenous slave trade, 65n74; and Inquisition, 121, 128, 132n76; merchants, xix, 140, 152, 238; pilots, 116–17, 121–22; revolt against Philip II, 268. *See also* Afro-Portuguese

privateers, 116, 261, 265, 268
Protestants, 114–15, 121–23, 129, 251, 253n21. *See also* Lutherans
poverty, 8, 120, 211, 214–15, 218–20, 222–27
public health, xvi, xix, 187, 198–201, 211–18, 224–27
Puebla de los Ángeles, 191, 196, 201–4
Puerto Caballos (Honduras), 116, 148, 151, 153
Puerto del Príncipe (Cuba), 71
Puerto Plata (Hispaniola), 49, 147, 151, 218
Puerto Real (Cádiz Bay), 216–17
Puerto Rico, xvii, 17–18, 25–32, 36–39, 41n17, 42n60, 48, 52, 56, 60, 93, 141–43, 145–47, 149–50, 153, 156n32, 218, 261; Africans as settlers in, 143; conquest of, 26, 99; indigenous revolt in, 25–43, 48–49

quarantines, 211, 215–18, 229n26
Quiahuiztlan, 191, 194–96, 204
quinto, 50, 55, 102, 238

ranches, 137, 193, 197. *See also* livestock
recogedores, 50
religion, 4, 13–14, 19, 114–15, 120–23, 129, 163; indigenous, 1, 4, 6, 14, 17–19. *See also* clergy; Christianity; Christianization; Islam; Jews; Lutherans; Protestants
religious orders. *See* clergy: regular; Augustinians; Carmelites; Dominicans; Franciscans; Hieronymites; Mercedarians; San Juan de Dios, order of; Trinitarians
Repartimiento of 1514 (Hispaniola), 12, 99–100, 109n28

repartimientos, 10, 41n23, 87n13, 108n5, 109n28; in Hispaniola, 99–100; in Puerto Rico, 31–32, 38; in Venezuela, 60. See also *encomiendas*
rescate, 49, 51–52, 55
revolt, Sancti Spíritus (Cuba), 74–76
revolts, African: in Hispaniola, 144–45; in Puerto Rico, 26, 37–38
revolts, indigenous: in Cuba, 71, 76–78, 86n2, 86n4, 88n21; in Hispaniola, 5; in Mexico, 87n10; in Puerto Rico, 17–18, 25–43, 48–49, 63n7; in Venezuela, 57
Riohacha, xvii, 150
Rivers of Guinea. *See* Upper Guinea
Rodrigues, António, 263, 273n35
Rodríguez de Córdoba, Juan, 74, 87n12
Rodríguez Garrucho, Cristóbal, 148–49
Rojas, Juan de, 97–98
Rojas, Manuel de, 54, 77, 83, 85, 86n4, 88n16, 89n25, 89n29, 89n30, 90n32
Roma people, 119
Romero, Pedro, 16–17

Saavedra, Lope de, 52, 54
sailors, 118, 123, 126, 132n71, 137, 141, 163, 197–98, 201–2, 205, 214–16, 222, 226, 257–61, 265–69, 274n37. *See also* slave trade, transatlantic: shipmasters and crews
Saint Croix, 40n15
Saint-Domingue, xvi
salt deposits, 94
Salvador da Bahia, 260, 268
Salvaleón (de Higüey). *See* Higüey
Sánchez del Corral, Alonso, 77, 81–83
Sancti Spíritus (Cuba), 71; *comunidad* in, 74–77, 80–83
Sandoval, Alonso de, 169, 177, 182n31

San Germán, 36, 38
San Juan, 31, 35–36, 99, 190. *See also* Puerto Rico
San Juan de Dios, order of, 218, 221–23, 225–26
San Juan de la Maguana (Hispaniola), 99–100, 109n28
San Juan de los Remedios (Cuba), 77
San Juan de Ulúa, 189–206
Santa Cruz (St. Croix), 29, 35, 40n15, 42n60
Santa Lucía, 35
Santa Maria, Island of (Azores), 258–59, 266, 271n1
Santa María de Victoria (ship), 149–50
Santa Marta, xvii, 57, 63n11, 150, 239–41, 262
Santiago, Island of (Cape Verde Islands), 272n14. *See also* Cabo Verde
Santiago de Cuba, 74–76, 80–83, 86n2, 88n17, 89n31, 100, 104–5, 143, 145, 218, 262, 273nn29–30; cabildo of, 102
Santiago del Daguao, 38
Santiago de León de los Caballeros (Nicaragua), 94
Santisteban (Pánuco), 51–53; indigenous slaves taken from, 53
Santo Domingo, 12, 28, 52, 121, 190, 216, 239, 245, 250, 254n46, 261; enslaved African arrivals in, 142–45, 147–50, 153, 154n8, 155n14, 155n22, 156n29; hospitals in, 218–21, 223–24; merchants in, 243–44; officials in, 76, 79, 81, 113, 152, 156n26, 265; Portuguese in, 125; sale of indigenous slaves in, 58
Santo Domingo, fray Bernardo, 16, 81
San Vicente (Saint Vincent), 35

São Jorge, Island of (Azores), 266, 274n43
São Miguel, Island of (Azores), 269, 274n38, 274n40, 276n59
São Tomé, Island of, 143, 145–46, 148, 149–50, 156n26, 243, 264, 274n37
Sarmiento, fray Diego, 71, 77
Sauer, Carl O., xiv
Sayler, Hieronymus (Gerónimo Sailer), 141, 143–44, 239–41, 243, 245
Sedeño, Antonio, 58–60
Seville, 73, 91, 100–103, 107, 116, 121, 126, 140, 142–43, 147, 149, 155n20, 191, 196, 201–2, 204, 214, 224, 233, 238–39, 245, 246, 252n6, 253n15, 258–62, 272n16
sheep, 54, 266
Sierra Leone, 149–50, 163, 173
silver, 96, 98, 122, 197, 235–36, 240, 242, 244, 247–48, 251, 273n29
slave merchants, 49, 61–62, 139–40, 142–43, 145–48, 152, 155n20, 177, 217, 241, 243, 248, 258–59, 264
slave owners, 77, 88, 99, 142, 165–66, 168, 169–70, 174–76, 178, 181n27, 182n33
slaves. *See* Africans: enslaved; Indians: enslaved; slaves, royal
slaves, royal, 165, 169, 171, 174, 175, 176, 178, 180n11, 181n17, 182nn33–34
slave trade, from Caribbean to Azores, 260, 262–65. *See also* Indians: enslaved; slave trade, indigenous
slave trade, indigenous, xix, 18, 34, 47–65, 253n30; ports of disembarkation, 52, 56, 58–60. *See also* Indians: enslaved; *rescate*
slave trade, intra-Caribbean, 145, 148. *See also* slave trade, indigenous

trade, from Caribbean to Azores;
slave trade, transatlantic
trade networks, xiii, xvi, xxi, 139, 147–48, 152, 163–64, 173–74, 176–77, 233, 236–37, 251, 253n15, 264
Trans-Atlantic Slave Trade Database, 140
Treaty of Cateau-Cambrésis, 116
Trinidad (Cuba), 71, 74, 76–79, 81, 83, 88n17, 88n21, 89n24, 90n33
Trinidad (island), xvii, 35, 57, 59, 125, 267
Trinitarians, 247
Trujillo (Honduras), 151
Tupinambá, 260, 272n16

Ulm, 235–37
Union of the Crowns, 123, 139, 152
Upper Guinea: internal trade routes, 165, 173–77; plague in, 216–17; slave trade from, 143–50, 153, 163–64, 180n6, 217. See also Kaabu; Upper Guineans
Upper Guineans, 163–79; Bañuns (Bañones), 169–70, 172–75, 177–78, 182n31, 183n69, 184n78; Biafadas, 163–82; Bijagos (Biochos), 172, 175, 177–79, 183n69; Brames (Branes), 167, 169–70, 172–78, 183n69, 184n78; Cassangas, 167, 170, 173, 176–78, 183nn68–69, 184n78; Kokolis, 176; Limbas, 173, 175–76; "Mandingas," 169, 173, 175–78, 183n64, 183nn68–69; Nalus, 169–71, 173–75, 177–78, 183n69; Serer (Berbesí), 170, 172, 174; Susus, 169, 173, 175; Wolofs (Jolofas, Jolofos), 144–45, 173, 176–77, 183n68; "Zapes" (Çapes), 169–70, 173–75, 177–78, 182n34, 183n69, 184n78. See also Upper Guinea

Vázquez de Ayllón, Lucas, 49–50
Velasco, Luis de, the elder, 200–201
Velásquez, Sancho, 38, 43n72
Velázquez, Diego de, 13, 72, 74, 81, 85, 93, 100
Venezuela, xvii, 55–60, 64n39, 143, 219, 235–36, 239–51, 253n21
Veracruz, xvii, xix, 144, 146, 149–53, 156n30, 189–205, 206n6, 212, 218–19, 222. See also Antigua Veracruz
Viafra, Domingo, 170, 174
viceroys of the Indies, 25, 30–38; in Mexico, 191, 197–204
Vieques, 29
Villota, Sebastián del Hoyo, 103–4
Virgin Islands, 29. See also Santa Cruz (St. Croix)
von Hutten, Philip, 250–51

Walsingham, Francis, 122, 276n58
Welser, Antón, 236–37
Welser family, 58, 141–42, 155n13, 235–51, 253n16, 253n35
West Africa, xiii, 137, 163, 177. See alsoArarás; Terranova; Upper Guinea; Upper Guineans
West Central Africa, xiii, 150, 153, 167–72, 177–78, 182nn28–29, 183n69, 184n78. See also Kongo, Kingdom of; West Central Africans
West Central Africans, 150, 168–72, 177–78, 182nn28–29, 183n69, 184n78; Anchicos (Ansikus), 169–70, 181n27; "Angolas," 167–73, 175–78, 180n3, 181n25, 183n69;

slave trade, transatlantic, xix, 18, 47, 65n69, 80, 137, 139–58, 164–65, 167, 212, 242–44, 274n36; administrative aspects of, 140–46, 151–52, 155n10, 155n24, 156n29, 156n44, 242; factors, 142, 147–49, 157n55, 243; ports of disembarkation, 139–58; shipmasters and crews, 140–41, 145–48, 151, 267. *See also* Africans; *arribadas*; *asientos*; passengers; pilots; slave merchants

smuggling. *See* trade, illicit

soldiers, 56, 59–60, 123–24, 132n71, 201, 216, 224, 235, 246, 266, 275n52

Sores, Jacques de, 122, 200

Soto, Hernando de, 71–73, 81, 86n2, 91–99, 105; expedition of, 109n25, 124

Sotomayor, Alonso de, 72, 84, 90n33

Sotomayor, don Cristóbal de, 30–33, 42n46

South America, 55, 95, 96, 239, 242, 248, 253n16, 258, 260, 272n16. *See also* Andean region; Brazil; Colombia; Guianas; New Kingdom of Granada; Peru; Venezuela

Spanish Caribbean, archaeological work on, xv; as a region, xiv, xvii, xx; historiography of, xiv–xv, 26, 34

Spanish Empire, xvi, 47, 48, 61–62, 92–93, 100, 107, 124, 128, 190, 196, 199, 205

spices, 235, 237

spies, 114, 118, 122, 128

Suárez de Figueroa, Gómez, 72, 87n5

sugar, xix, 15, 61, 80, 145, 239, 261, 264; estates and *ingenios* (mills), 1, 15, 48–49, 61, 144–45

Suriname, xvii

Tabasco, 189, 197

Taínos, 18, 40n15, 48, 258, 271n7, 275n44. *See also* Indians

Tairona, 262–64, 273n31

Távora, 31, 36

taxes, 49–50, 55, 58, 102, 139–40, 148, 151, 200, 221, 233, 237, 240–43, 259, 264–65, 272n16, 273n29, 274n38; *alcabalas*, 241; *almojarifazgos*, 241; *derechos de anclaje*, 222; *diezmo*, 63n11. See also *quinto*

Tenerife (Canary Islands), 148–49, 262, 273n31. *See also* Canary Islands

Tenochtitlan, 50–51, 123, 189, 191, 193–94

Tenoya River, 192, 195

Terceira, 117, 260–64, 267–69, 273n24, 273n35, 274n43, 275n51. *See also* Angra (Terceira)

Tercelette (ship), 267–68, 275n52

Terranova (in West Africa), 169–70, 182n29

textiles, 197, 235, 237–38, 267

Tierra Firme, 35, 55, 57, 59, 61, 93, 113, 118–19, 142, 147, 149–51, 153, 156n37, 214–15, 218

Tisin, Juan, 8, 13

Tolú, 124, 219

Totonacs, 191, 194

trade, illicit, 49, 115, 120, 125, 140, 152–53, 154n9, 155n22, 157n64, 217, 259–60, 262, 264, 267–68, 270, 274n36

trade, regional, xix, 29, 47, 50–51, 56, 59, 197, 204. *See also* slave trade, indigenous; slave trade, intra-Caribbean

trade, transatlantic, xvi, xix, 47, 191, 204–5, 239, 259, 267. *See also* Indies fleet system; merchants; slave

Index   299

"Congos," 168–71, 177; Embuilas, 169. *See also* West Central Africa
Windward Islands, 29, 40n15
wine, 17, 197, 239
women, 76, 219–20, 247; African, 15, 165–78, 183n69; Afrocreole, 167; indigenous, 3–5, 8–9, 11, 16, 18, 28, 29–30, 33, 48, 52, 72–73, 99, 101, 220; Spanish, xvi, 69, 91–93, 105, 107, 166, 219. *See also* Bobadilla, doña Isabel de; *cacicas*; Guzmán, doña Guiomar de; *moriscas/moriscos*
Wright, Irene A, xiv, xxin2

Xalapa, 195, 203–4

Yucatán, xvii, 48, 189

Zuazo, Licenciado Alonso de, 53, 61
Zumárraga, fray Juan de, 51, 53–54, 198

www.ingramcontent.com/pod-product-compliance
Lightning Source LLC
Chambersburg PA
CBHW021344300426
44114CB00012B/1077